D0534776

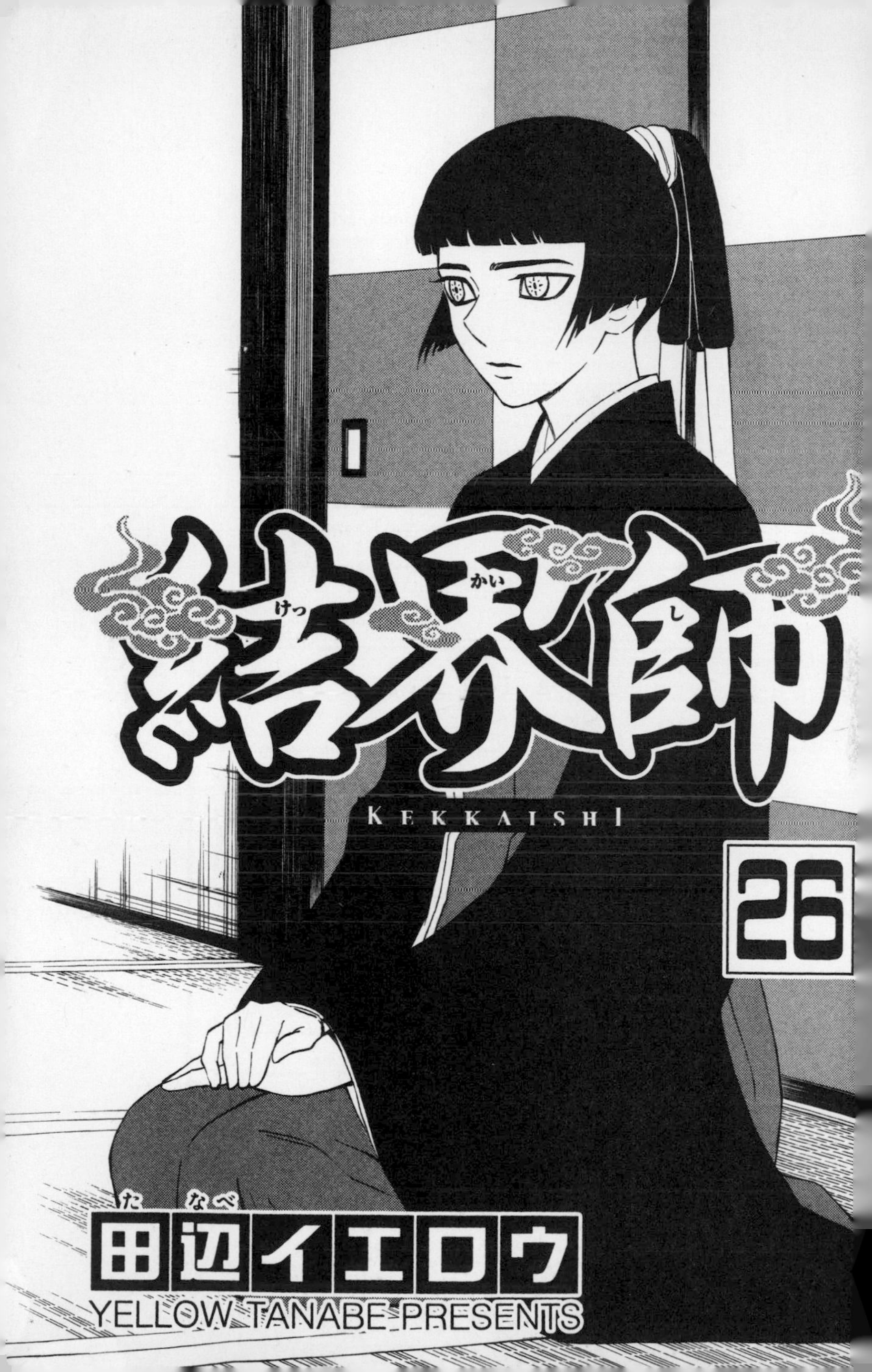

結界師
けっかいし
KEKKAISHI
26
たなべ
田辺イエロウ
YELLOW TANABE PRESENTS

THe StOry THUS Far

Yoshimori Sumimura and Tokine Yukimura have an ancestral duty to protect the Karasumori Forest from supernatural beings called ayakashi. People with their gift for terminating *ayakashi* are called *kekkaishi*, or "barrier masters."

Yoshimori is desperately trying to learn the kekkai discipline of emptying his mind. Meanwhile, his older brother Masamori travels to the stronghold of his archrival Ichiro Ogi (a monstrous amalgamation of several Ogi brothers!) to apprehend him. But before Masamori arrives, the youngest Ogi brother and heir apparent murders his older siblings!

Next, Okuni, Masamori's ally on the Council of Twelve, is found dead. Who is responsible? And does someone have designs on the Shadow Organization itself?!

Now Saki, the prophet of doom, reappears at Karasumori...

KEKKAISHI   VOL. 26
TABLE OF CONTENTS

CHAPTER 246: CRUEL FUTURE

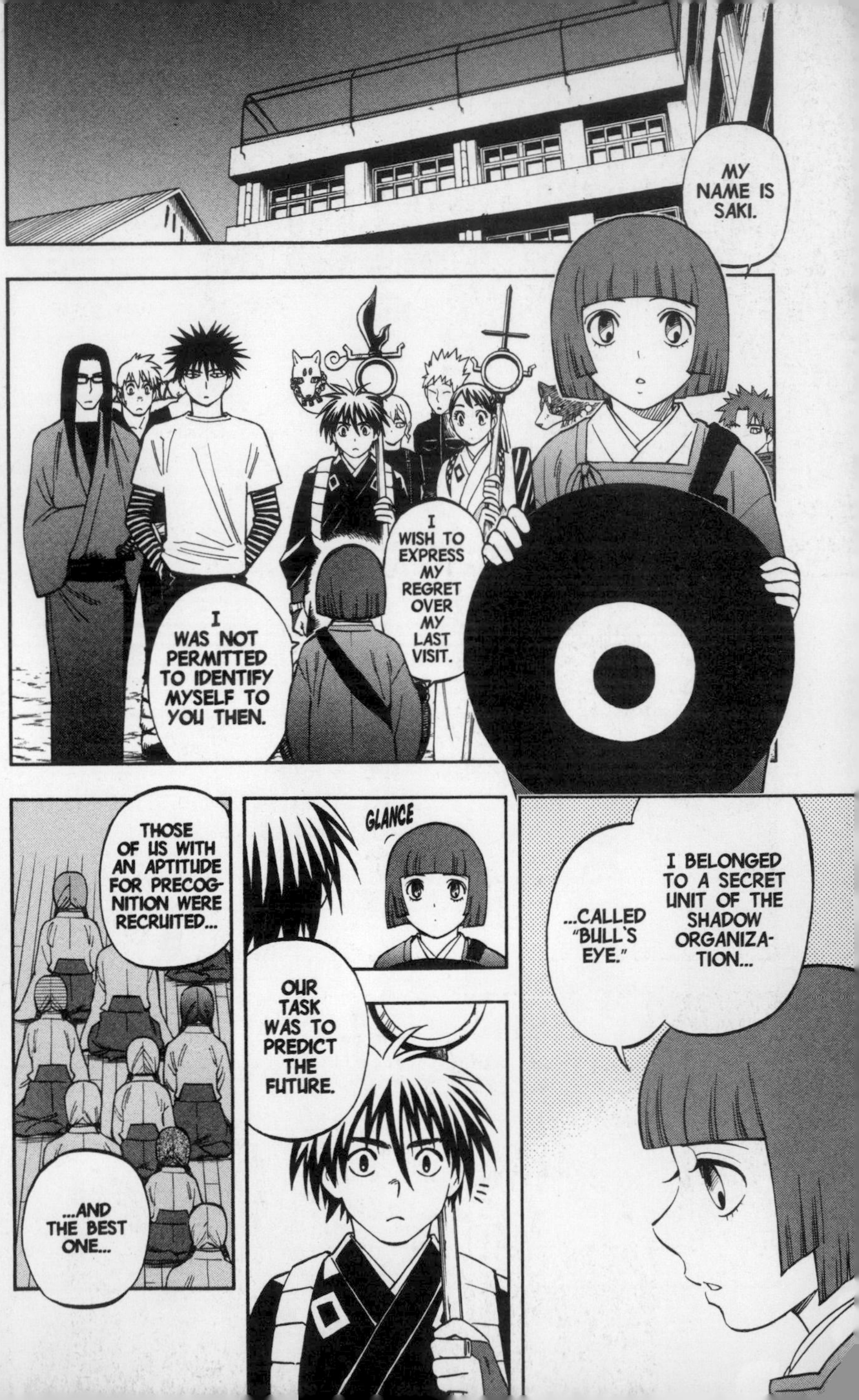
MY NAME IS SAKI.
I WISH TO EXPRESS MY REGRET OVER MY LAST VISIT.
I WAS NOT PERMITTED TO IDENTIFY MYSELF TO YOU THEN.
I BELONGED TO A SECRET UNIT OF THE SHADOW ORGANIZA-TION...
...CALLED "BULL'S EYE."
GLANCE
OUR TASK WAS TO PREDICT THE FUTURE.
THOSE OF US WITH AN APTITUDE FOR PRECOG-NITION WERE RECRUITED...
...AND THE BEST ONE...

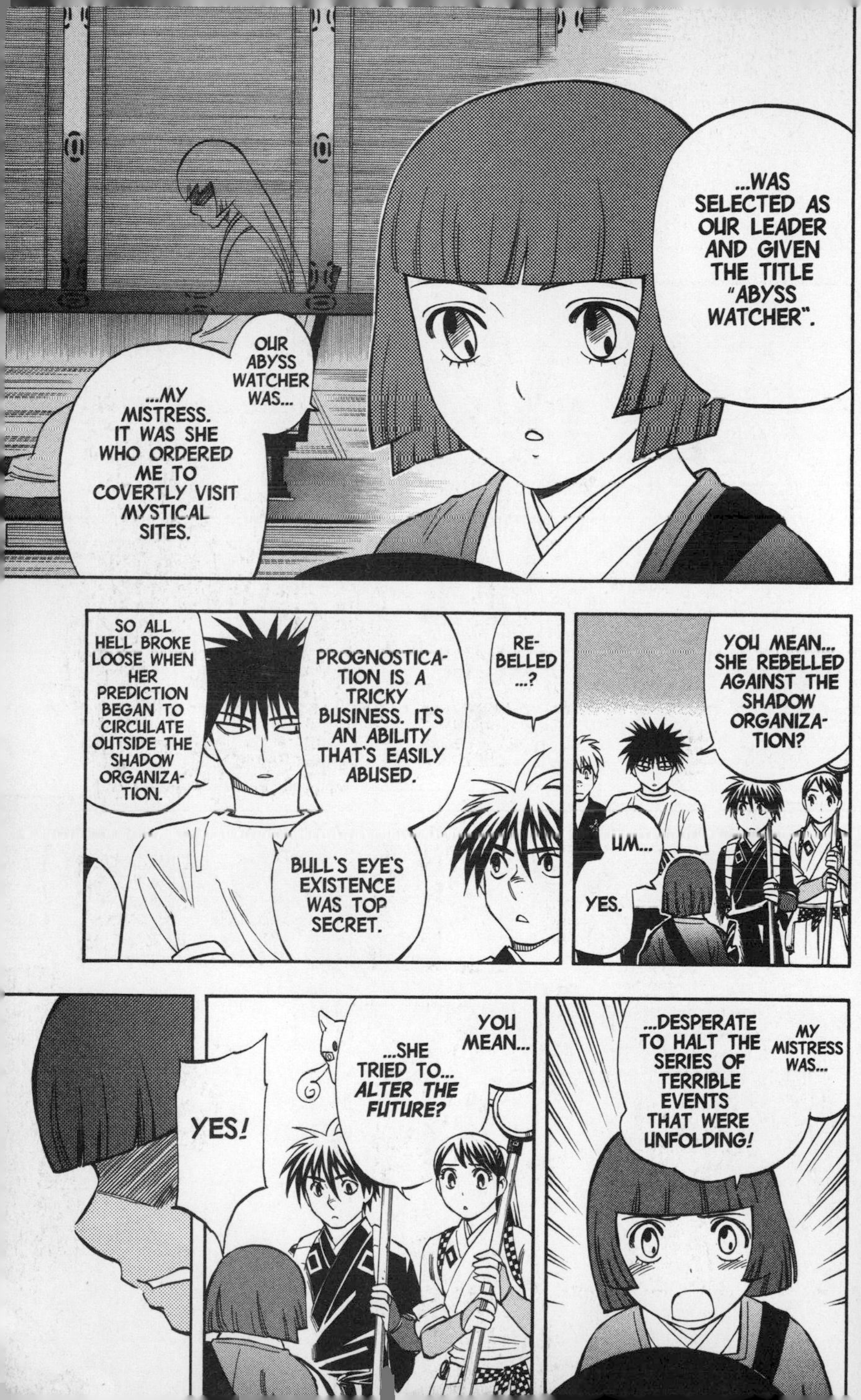
...WAS SELECTED AS OUR LEADER AND GIVEN THE TITLE "ABYSS WATCHER".
OUR ABYSS WATCHER WAS...
...MY MISTRESS. IT WAS SHE WHO ORDERED ME TO COVERTLY VISIT MYSTICAL SITES.
YOU MEAN... SHE REBELLED AGAINST THE SHADOW ORGANIZATION?
UM...
YES.
RE-BELLED ...?
PROGNOSTICATION IS A TRICKY BUSINESS. IT'S AN ABILITY THAT'S EASILY ABUSED.
BULL'S EYE'S EXISTENCE WAS TOP SECRET.
SO ALL HELL BROKE LOOSE WHEN HER PREDICTION BEGAN TO CIRCULATE OUTSIDE THE SHADOW ORGANIZATION.
MY MISTRESS WAS...
...DESPERATE TO HALT THE SERIES OF TERRIBLE EVENTS THAT WERE UNFOLDING!
YOU MEAN...
...SHE TRIED TO... *ALTER THE FUTURE?*
YES!

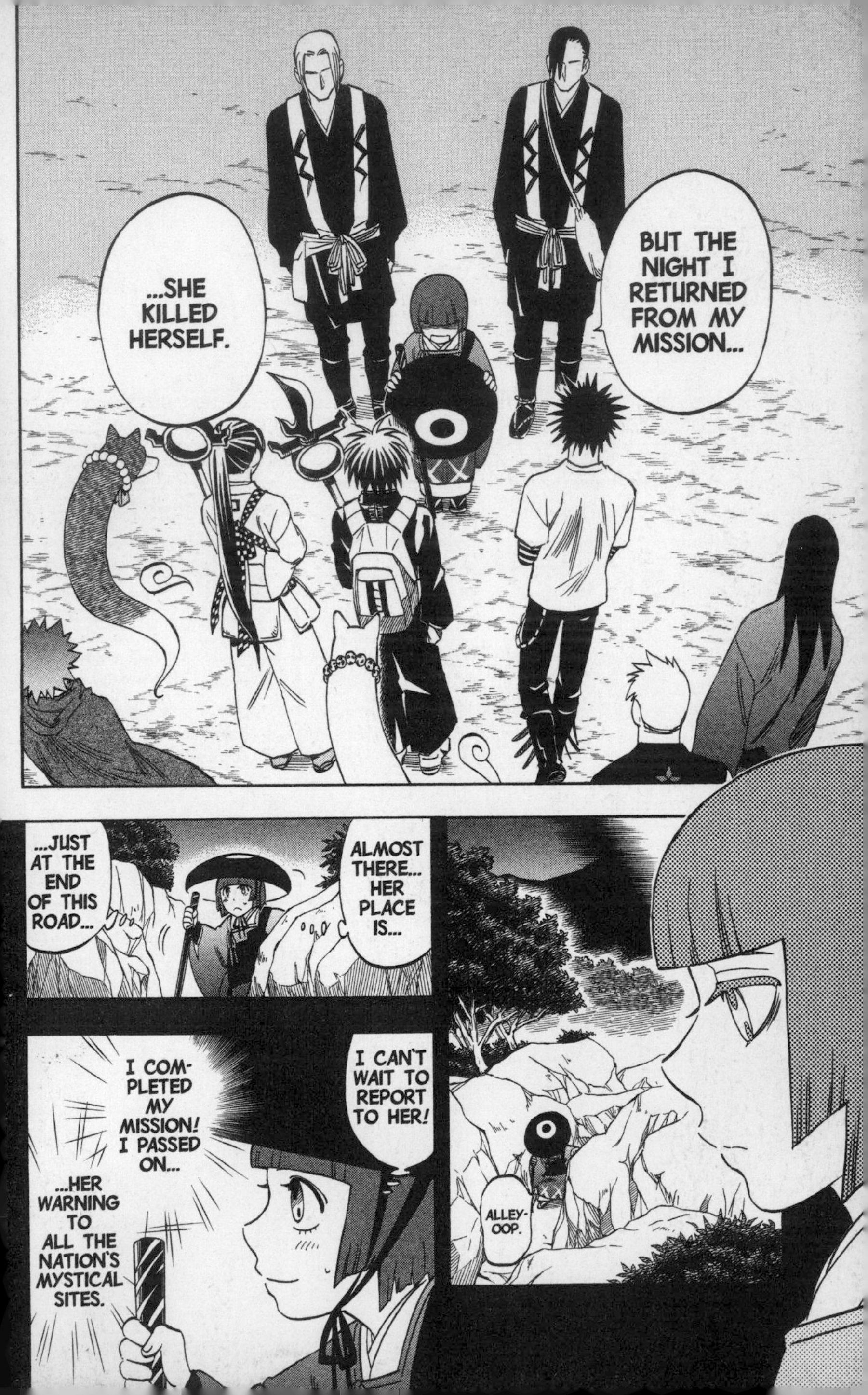
BUT THE NIGHT I RETURNED FROM MY MISSION...
...SHE KILLED HERSELF.
ALLEY-OOP.
ALMOST THERE... HER PLACE IS...
...JUST AT THE END OF THIS ROAD...
I CAN'T WAIT TO REPORT TO HER!
I COM-PLETED MY MISSION! I PASSED ON...
...HER WARNING TO ALL THE NATION'S MYSTICAL SITES.

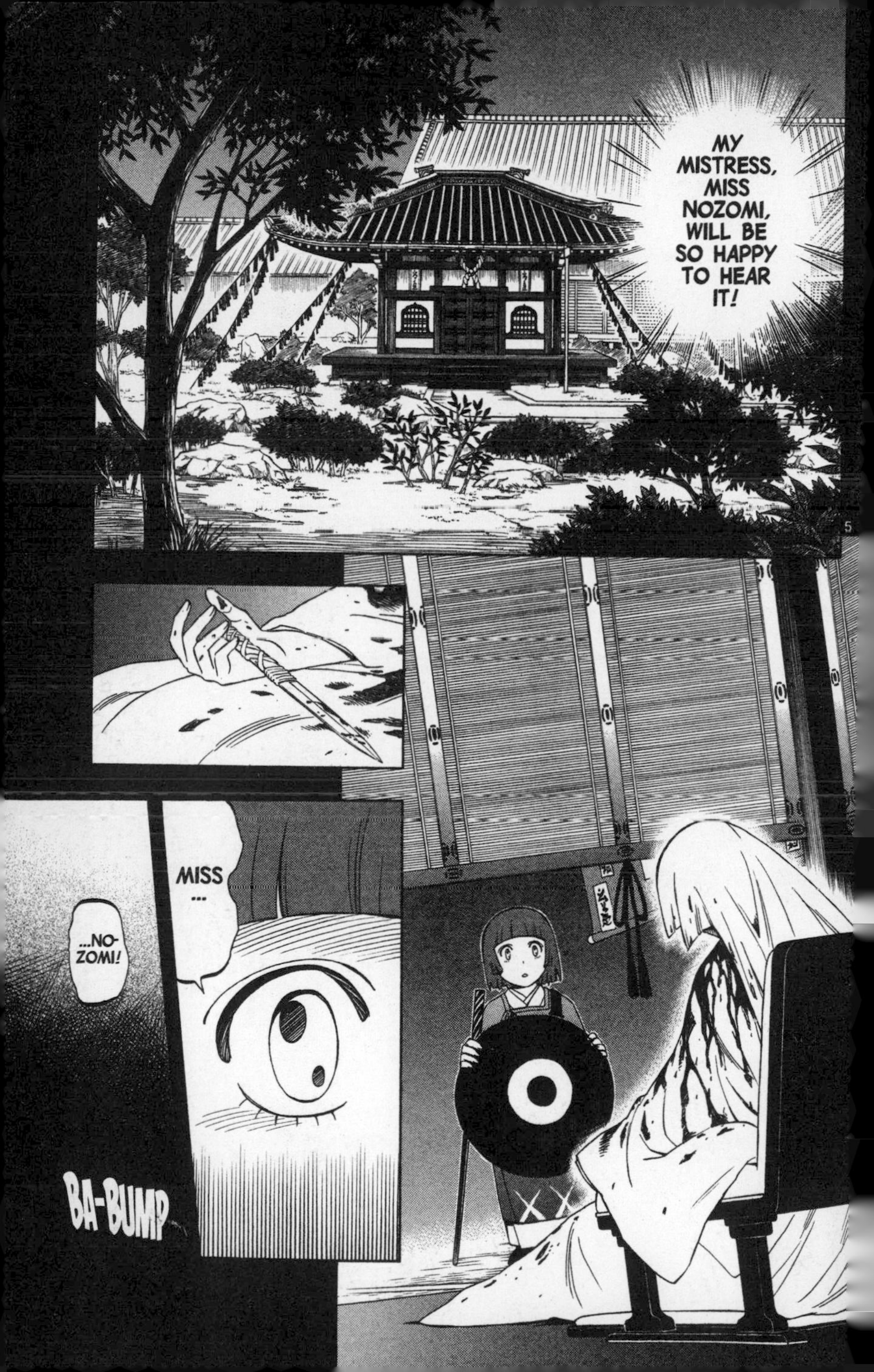
MY MISTRESS, MISS NOZOMI, WILL BE SO HAPPY TO HEAR IT!
MISS ...
...NO-ZOMI!
BA-BUMP

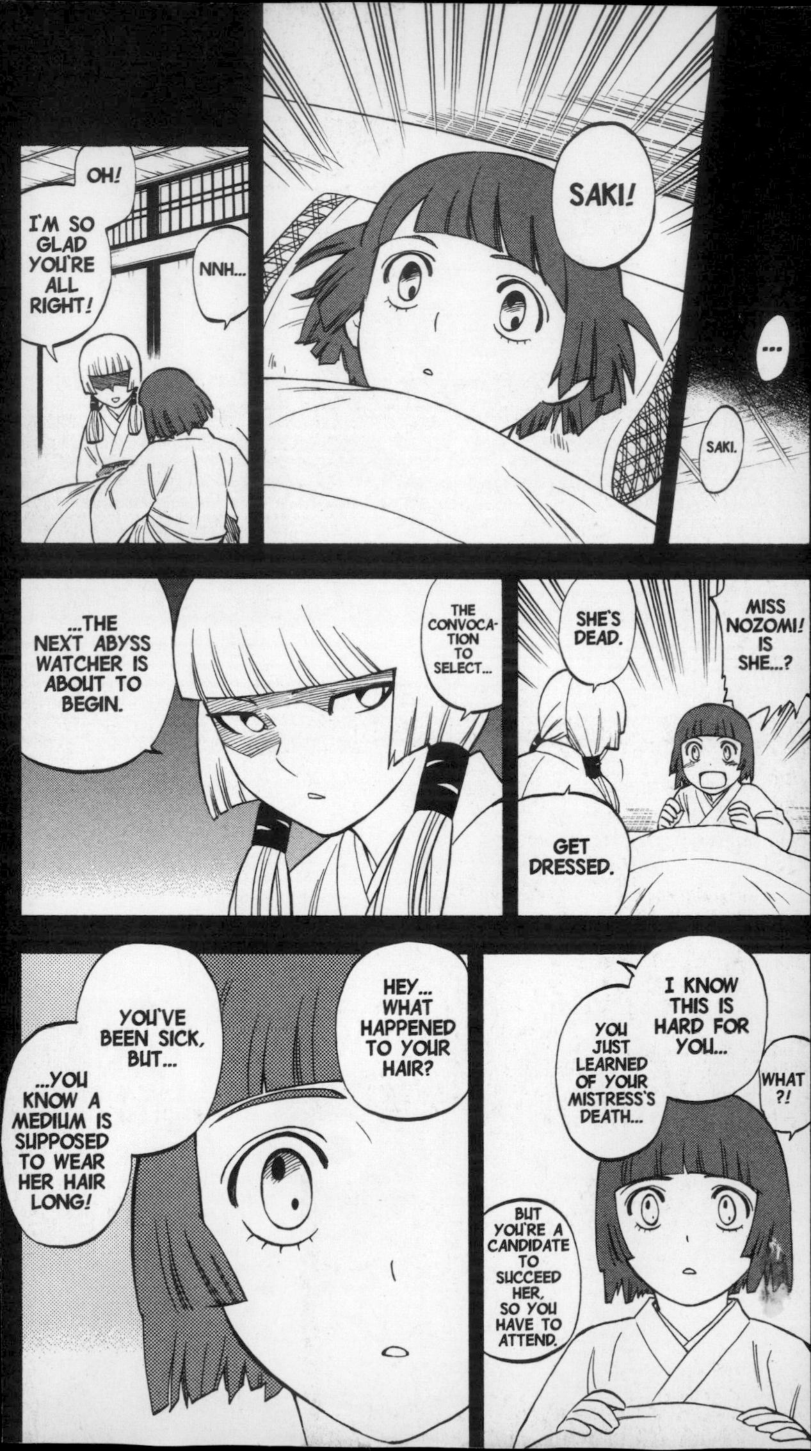
...
SAKI.
SAKI!
NNH...
OH!
I'M SO GLAD YOU'RE ALL RIGHT!
MISS NOZOMI! IS SHE...?
SHE'S DEAD.
GET DRESSED.
THE CONVOCATION TO SELECT...
...THE NEXT ABYSS WATCHER IS ABOUT TO BEGIN.
WHAT ?!
I KNOW THIS IS HARD FOR YOU...
YOU JUST LEARNED OF YOUR MISTRESS'S DEATH...
BUT YOU'RE A CANDIDATE TO SUCCEED HER, SO YOU HAVE TO ATTEND.
HEY... WHAT HAPPENED TO YOUR HAIR?
YOU'VE BEEN SICK, BUT...
...YOU KNOW A MEDIUM IS SUPPOSED TO WEAR HER HAIR LONG!

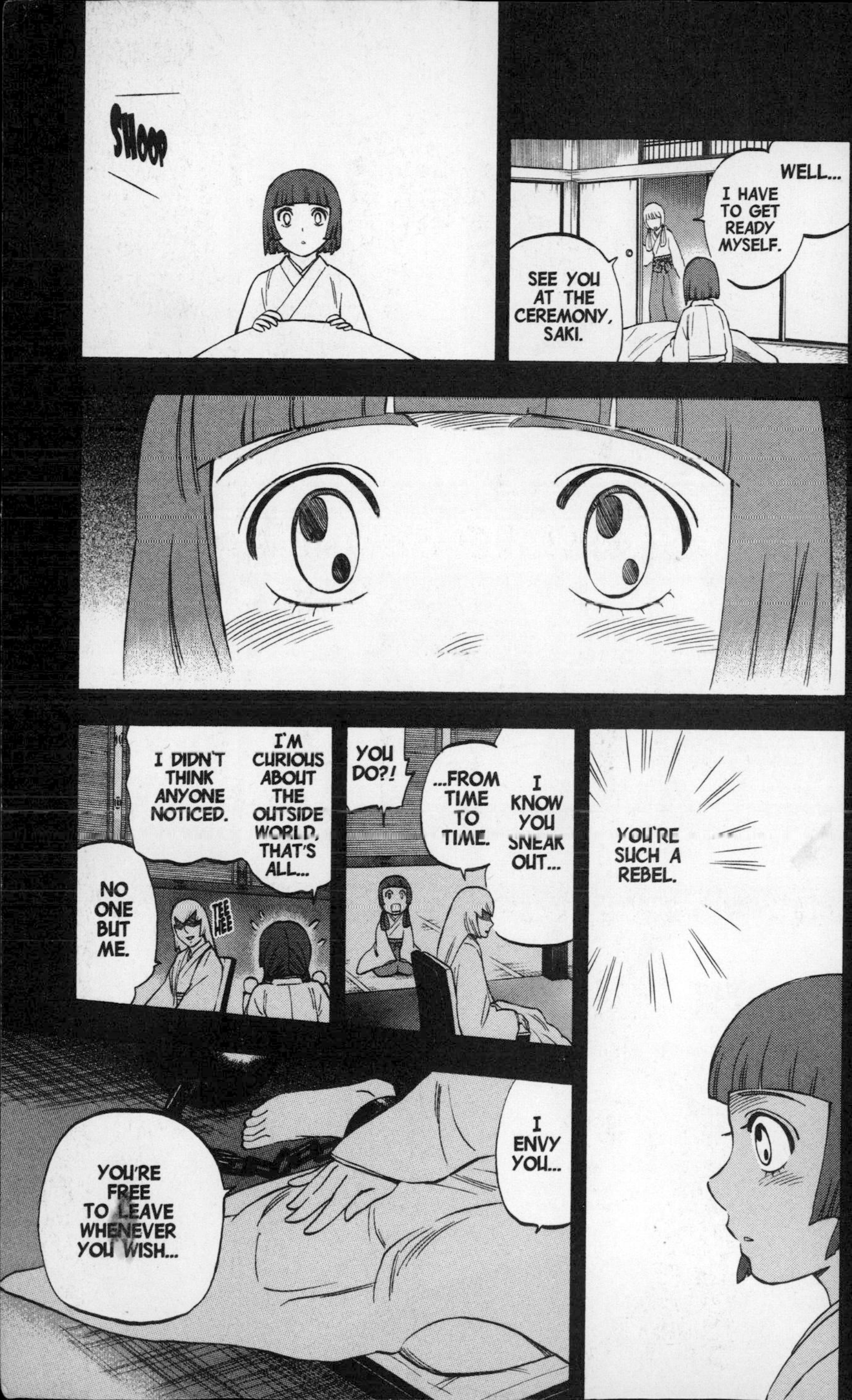
WELL... I HAVE TO GET READY MYSELF.
SEE YOU AT THE CEREMONY, SAKI.
SHOOP
YOU'RE SUCH A REBEL.
I KNOW YOU SNEAK OUT...
...FROM TIME TO TIME.
YOU DO?!
I'M CURIOUS ABOUT THE OUTSIDE WORLD, THAT'S ALL...
I DIDN'T THINK ANYONE NOTICED.
NO ONE BUT ME.
TEE HEE
I ENVY YOU...
YOU'RE FREE TO LEAVE WHENEVER YOU WISH...

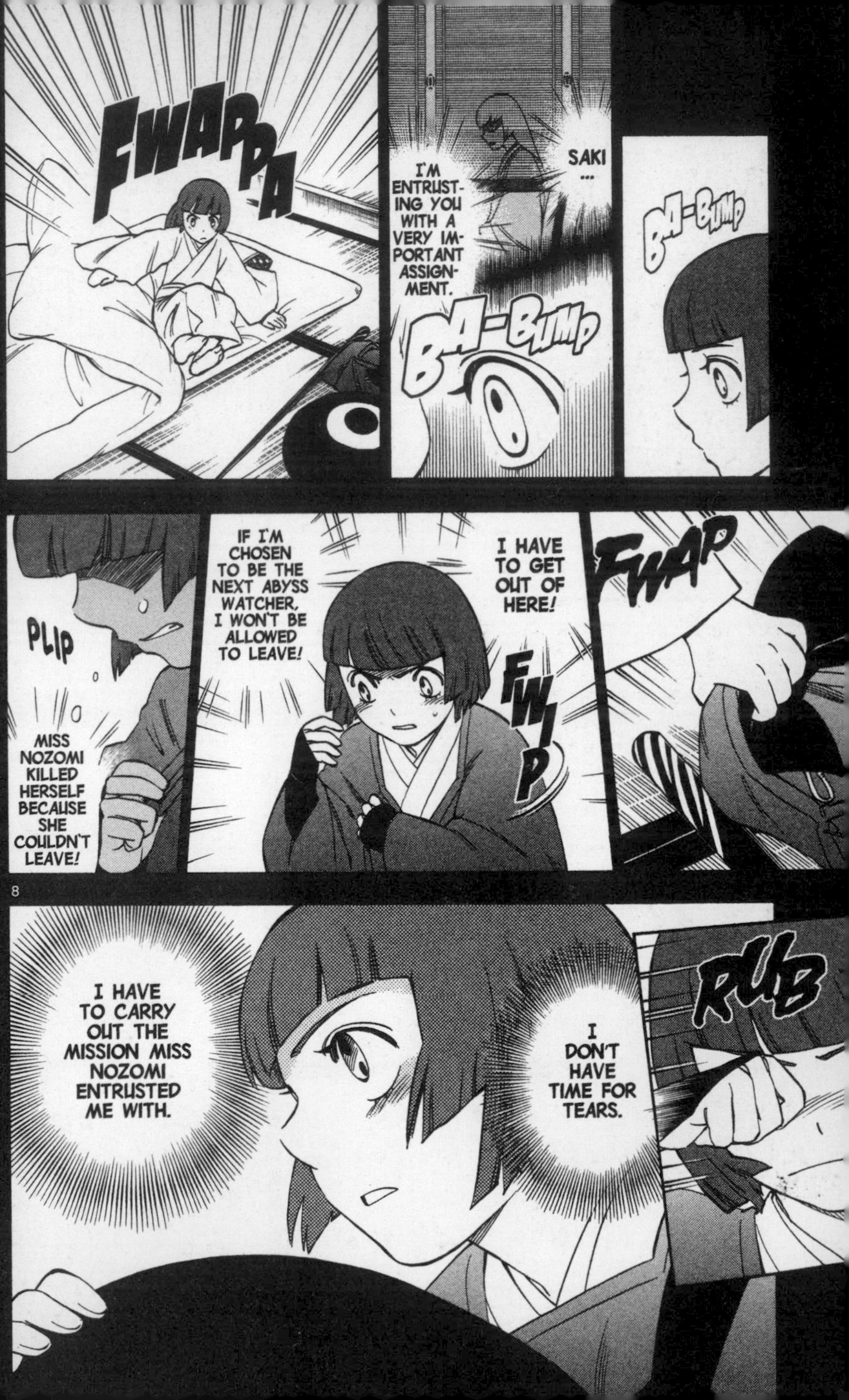
BA-BUMP
SAKI ...
I'M ENTRUSTING YOU WITH A VERY IMPORTANT ASSIGNMENT.
BA-BUMP
FWAPPA
FWAP
I HAVE TO GET OUT OF HERE!
FWIP
IF I'M CHOSEN TO BE THE NEXT ABYSS WATCHER, I WON'T BE ALLOWED TO LEAVE!
PLIP
MISS NOZOMI KILLED HERSELF BECAUSE SHE COULDN'T LEAVE!
RUB
I DON'T HAVE TIME FOR TEARS.
I HAVE TO CARRY OUT THE MISSION MISS NOZOMI ENTRUSTED ME WITH.

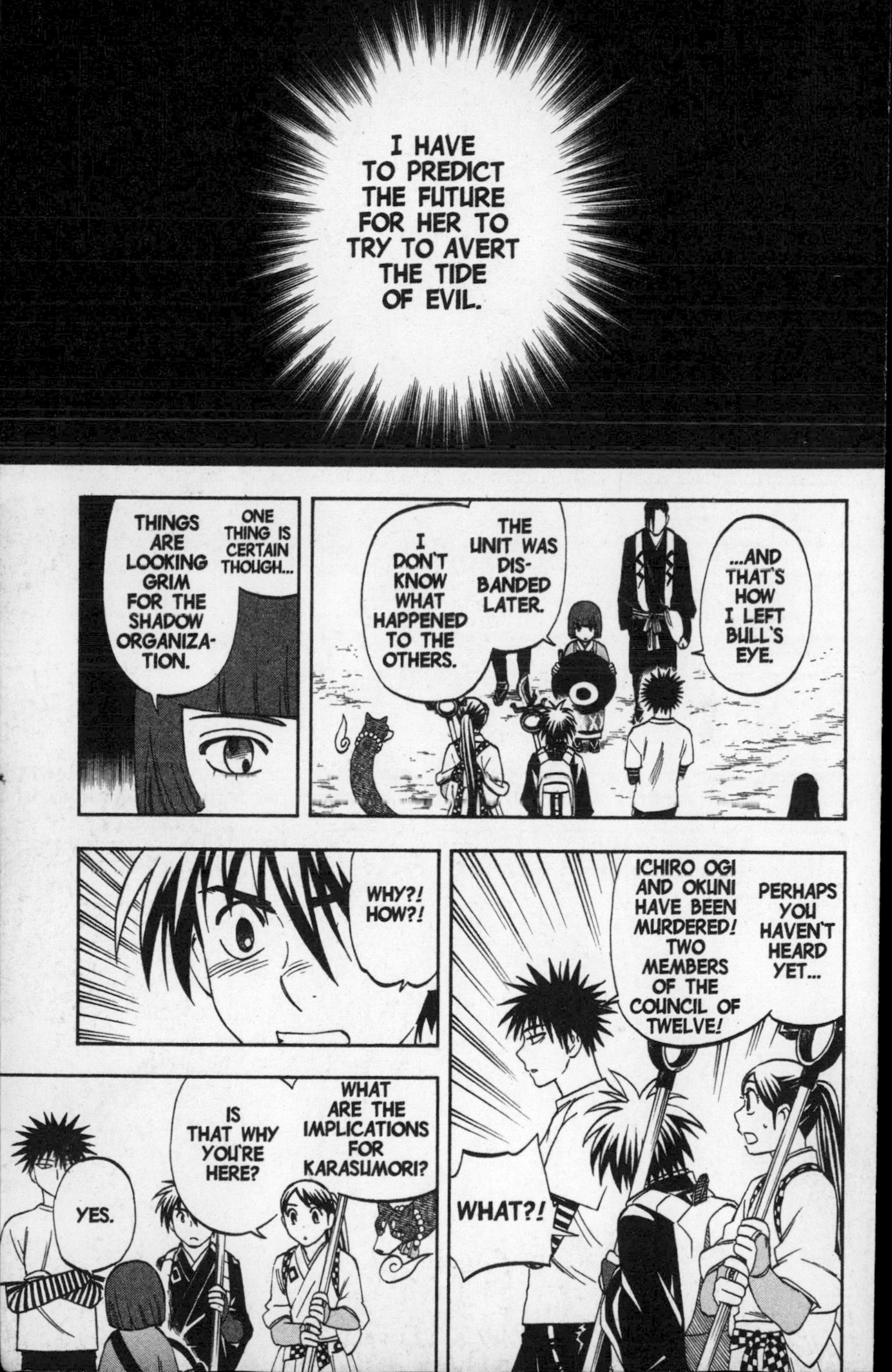

I HAVE TO PREDICT THE FUTURE FOR HER TO TRY TO AVERT THE TIDE OF EVIL.
...AND THAT'S HOW I LEFT BULL'S EYE.
THE UNIT WAS DIS-BANDED LATER.
I DON'T KNOW WHAT HAPPENED TO THE OTHERS.
ONE THING IS CERTAIN THOUGH...
THINGS ARE LOOKING GRIM FOR THE SHADOW ORGANIZA-TION.
PERHAPS YOU HAVEN'T HEARD YET...
ICHIRO OGI AND OKUNI HAVE BEEN MURDERED! TWO MEMBERS OF THE COUNCIL OF TWELVE!
WHAT?!
WHY?! HOW?!
WHAT ARE THE IMPLICATIONS FOR KARASUMORI?
IS THAT WHY YOU'RE HERE?
YES.

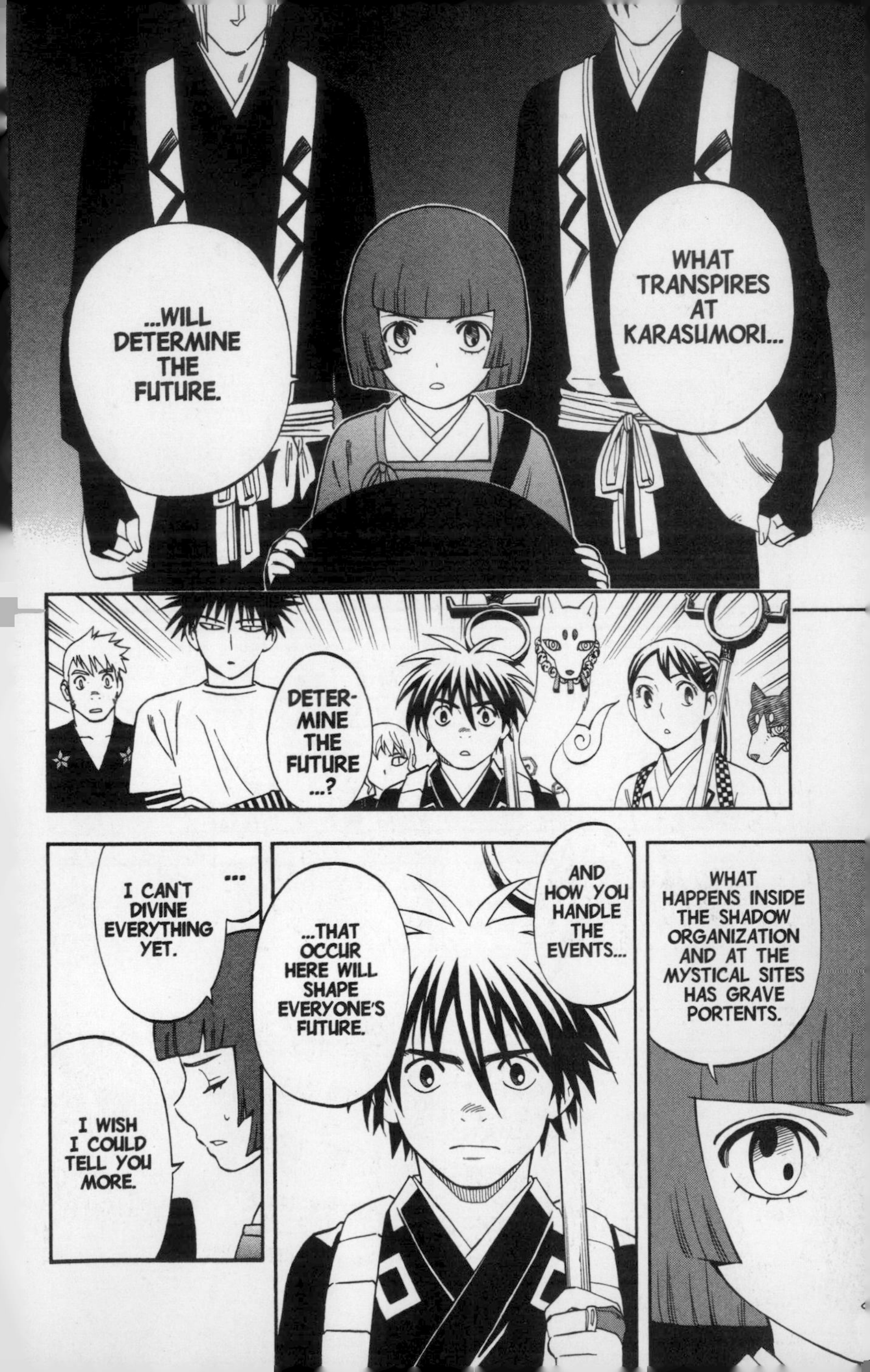
WHAT TRANSPIRES AT KARASUMORI...
...WILL DETERMINE THE FUTURE.
DETER-MINE THE FUTURE ...?
WHAT HAPPENS INSIDE THE SHADOW ORGANIZATION AND AT THE MYSTICAL SITES HAS GRAVE PORTENTS.
AND HOW YOU HANDLE THE EVENTS...
...THAT OCCUR HERE WILL SHAPE EVERYONE'S FUTURE.
...
I CAN'T DIVINE EVERYTHING YET.
I WISH I COULD TELL YOU MORE.

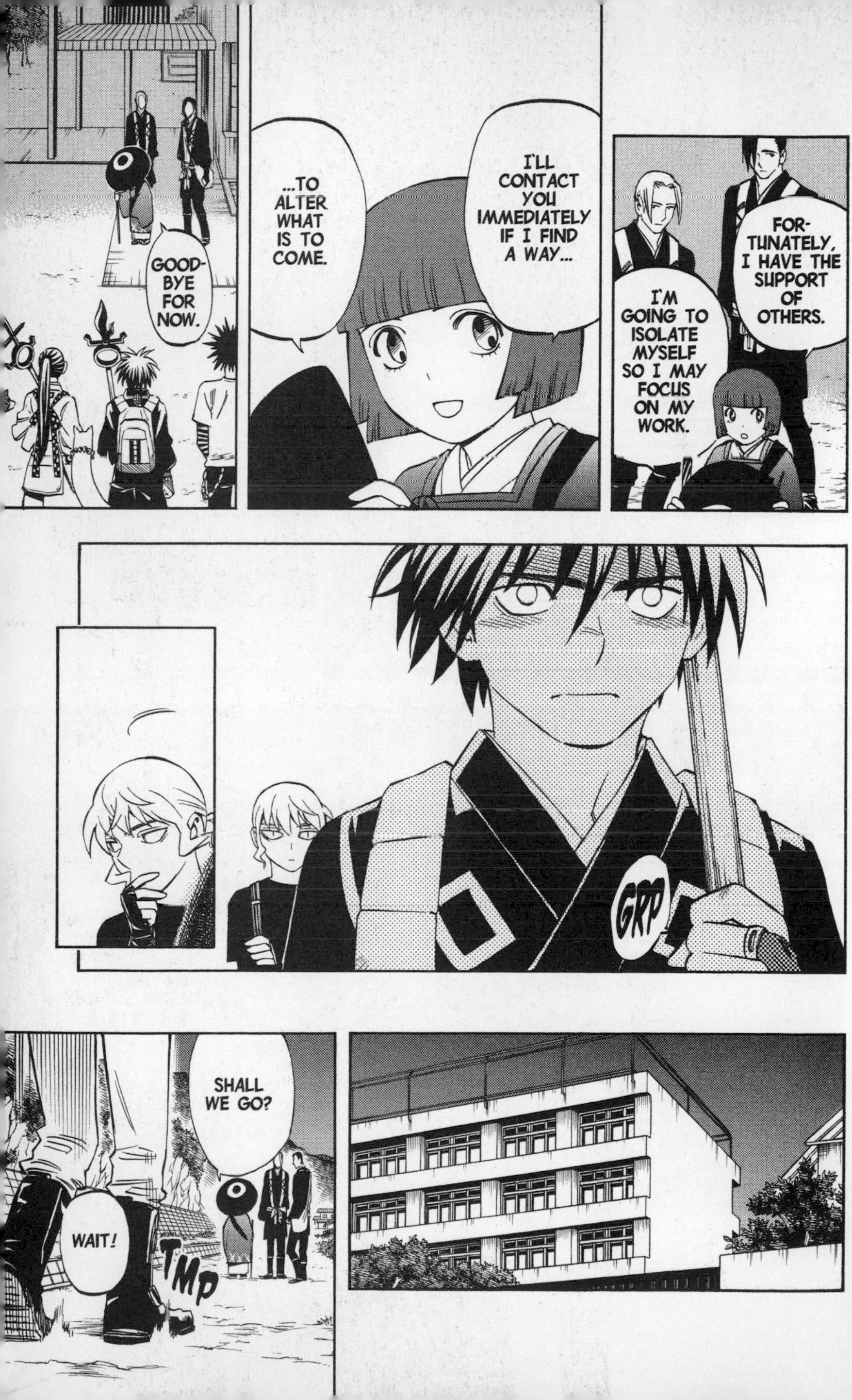
FORTUNATELY, I HAVE THE SUPPORT OF OTHERS.
I'M GOING TO ISOLATE MYSELF SO I MAY FOCUS ON MY WORK.
I'LL CONTACT YOU IMMEDIATELY IF I FIND A WAY...
...TO ALTER WHAT IS TO COME.
GOOD-BYE FOR NOW.
GRP
SHALL WE GO?
WAIT!
TMP

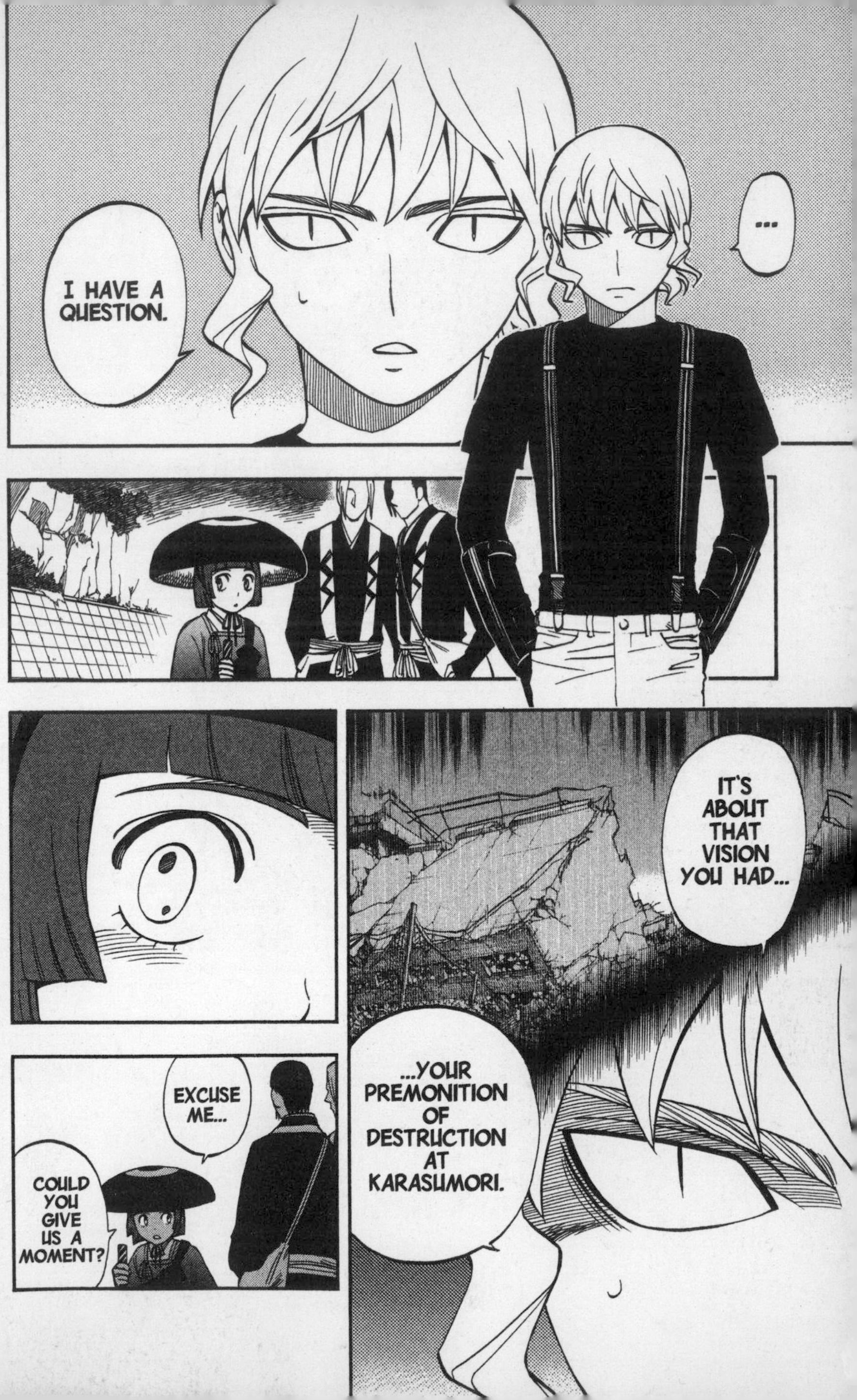
...
I HAVE A QUESTION.
IT'S ABOUT THAT VISION YOU HAD...
...YOUR PREMONITION OF DESTRUCTION AT KARASUMORI.
EXCUSE ME...
COULD YOU GIVE US A MOMENT?

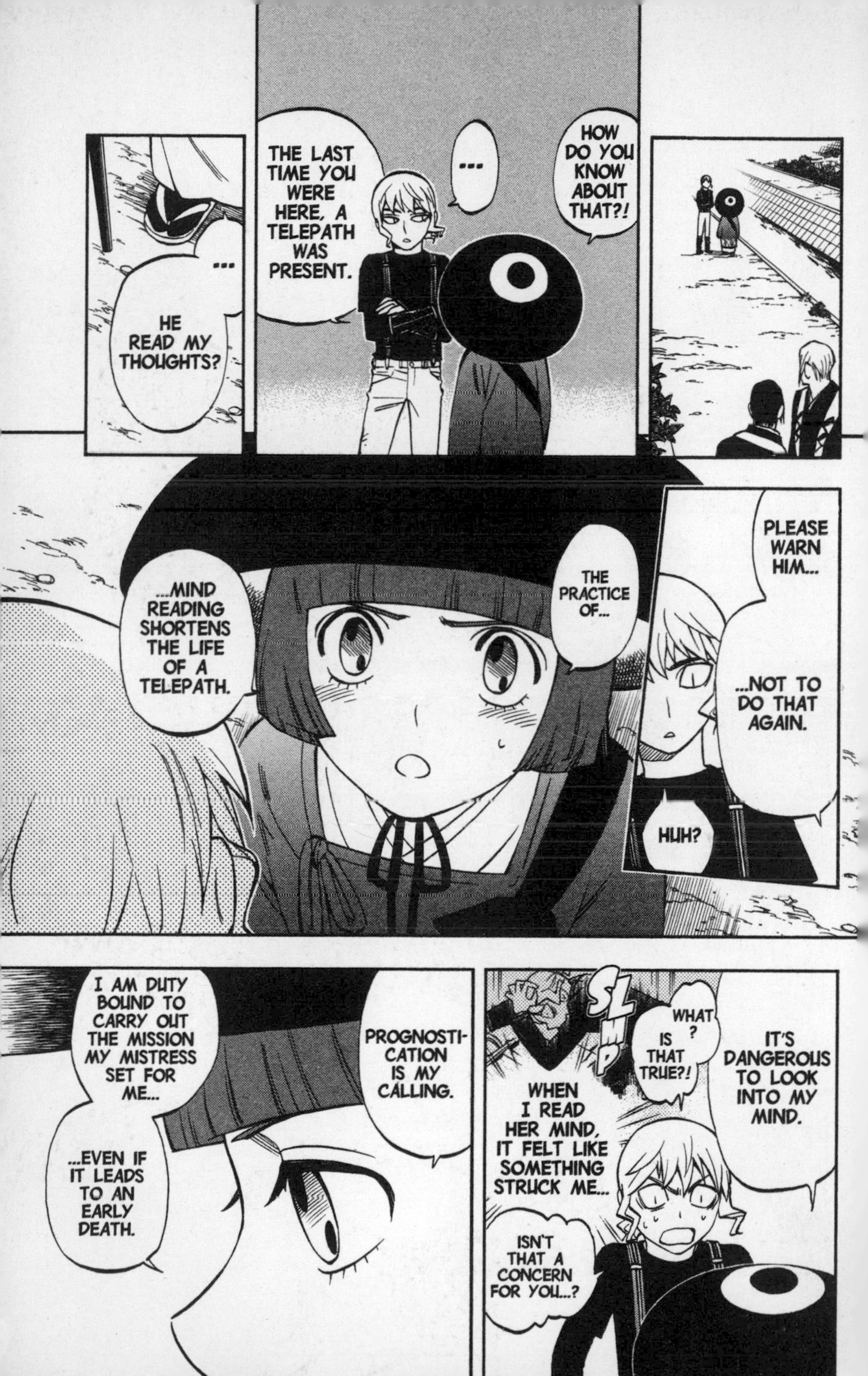

HOW DO YOU KNOW ABOUT THAT?!
...
THE LAST TIME YOU WERE HERE, A TELEPATH WAS PRESENT.
...
HE READ MY THOUGHTS?
PLEASE WARN HIM...
...NOT TO DO THAT AGAIN.
HUH?
THE PRACTICE OF...
...MIND READING SHORTENS THE LIFE OF A TELEPATH.
IT'S DANGEROUS TO LOOK INTO MY MIND.
WHAT? IS THAT TRUE?!
SLUMP
WHEN I READ HER MIND, IT FELT LIKE SOMETHING STRUCK ME...
ISN'T THAT A CONCERN FOR YOU...?
PROGNOSTI-CATION IS MY CALLING.
I AM DUTY BOUND TO CARRY OUT THE MISSION MY MISTRESS SET FOR ME...
...EVEN IF IT LEADS TO AN EARLY DEATH.

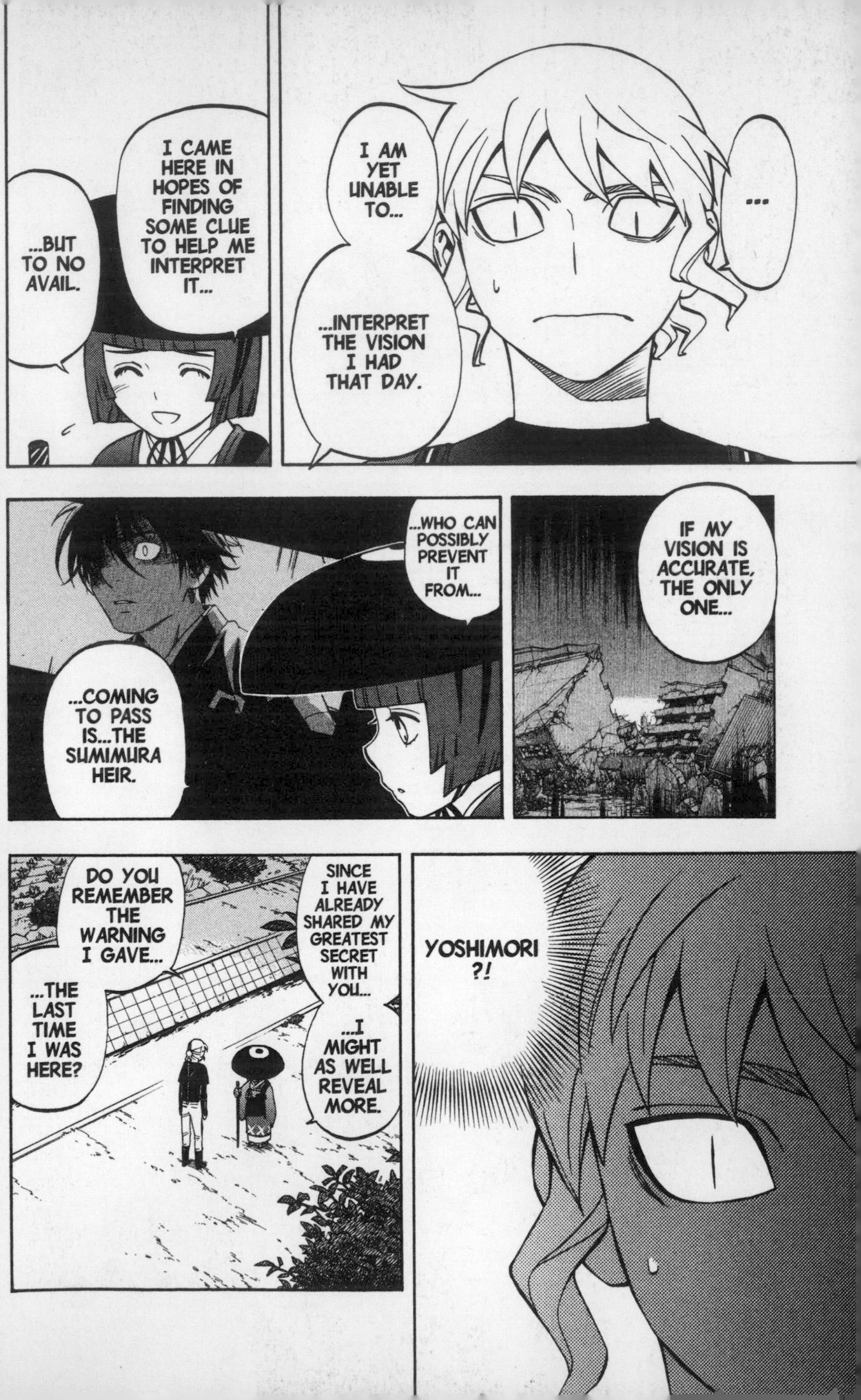
...
I AM YET UNABLE TO...
...INTERPRET THE VISION I HAD THAT DAY.
I CAME HERE IN HOPES OF FINDING SOME CLUE TO HELP ME INTERPRET IT...
...BUT TO NO AVAIL.
IF MY VISION IS ACCURATE, THE ONLY ONE...
...WHO CAN POSSIBLY PREVENT IT FROM...
...COMING TO PASS IS...THE SUMIMURA HEIR.
YOSHIMORI ?!
SINCE I HAVE ALREADY SHARED MY GREATEST SECRET WITH YOU...
...I MIGHT AS WELL REVEAL MORE.
DO YOU REMEMBER THE WARNING I GAVE...
...THE LAST TIME I WAS HERE?

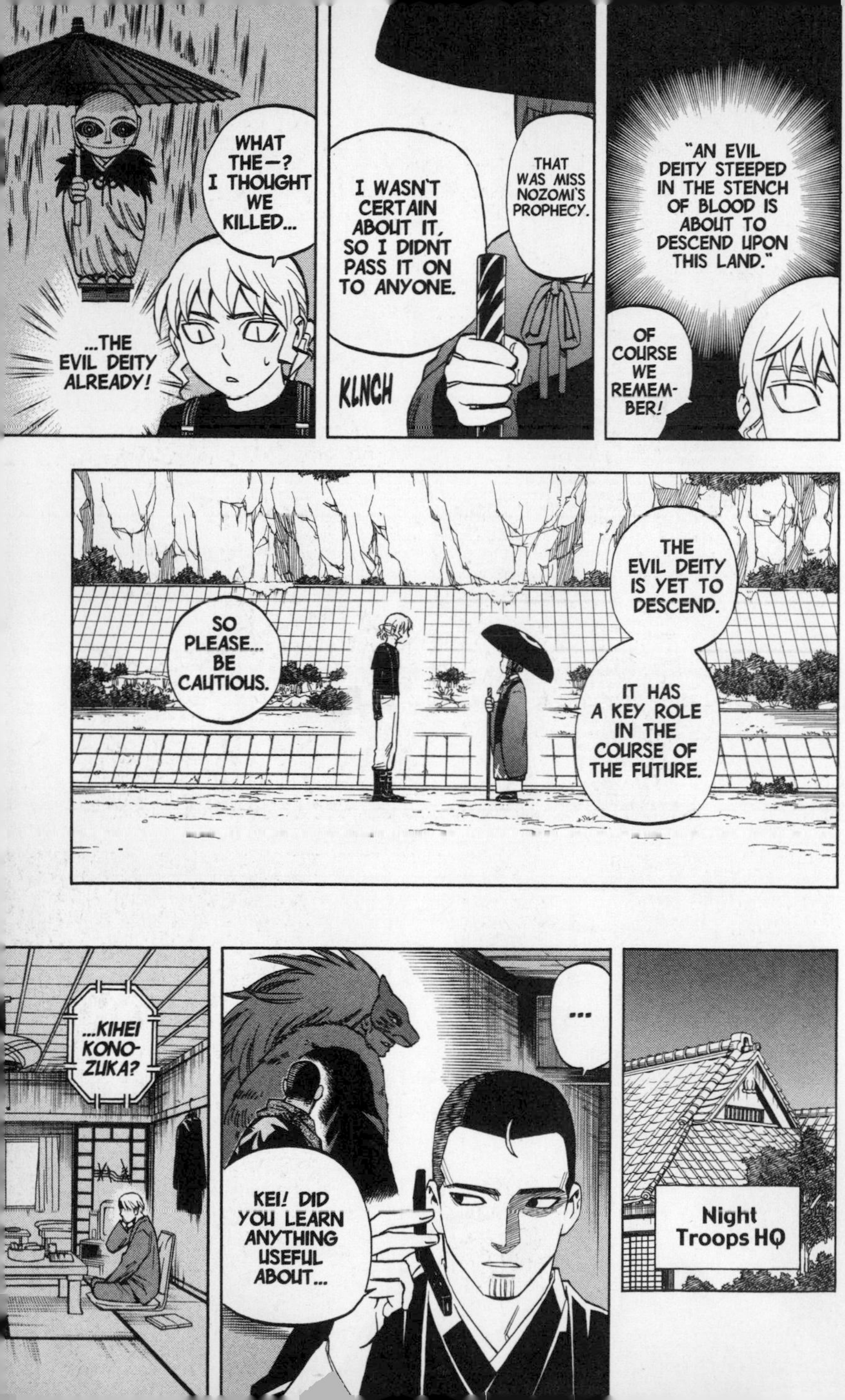
"AN EVIL DEITY STEEPED IN THE STENCH OF BLOOD IS ABOUT TO DESCEND UPON THIS LAND."
OF COURSE WE REMEMBER!
THAT WAS MISS NOZOMI'S PROPHECY.
I WASN'T CERTAIN ABOUT IT, SO I DIDN'T PASS IT ON TO ANYONE.
KLNCH
WHAT THE—? I THOUGHT WE KILLED...
...THE EVIL DEITY ALREADY!
THE EVIL DEITY IS YET TO DESCEND.
IT HAS A KEY ROLE IN THE COURSE OF THE FUTURE.
SO PLEASE... BE CAUTIOUS.
Night Troops HQ
...
KEI! DID YOU LEARN ANYTHING USEFUL ABOUT...
...KIHEI KONOZUKA?

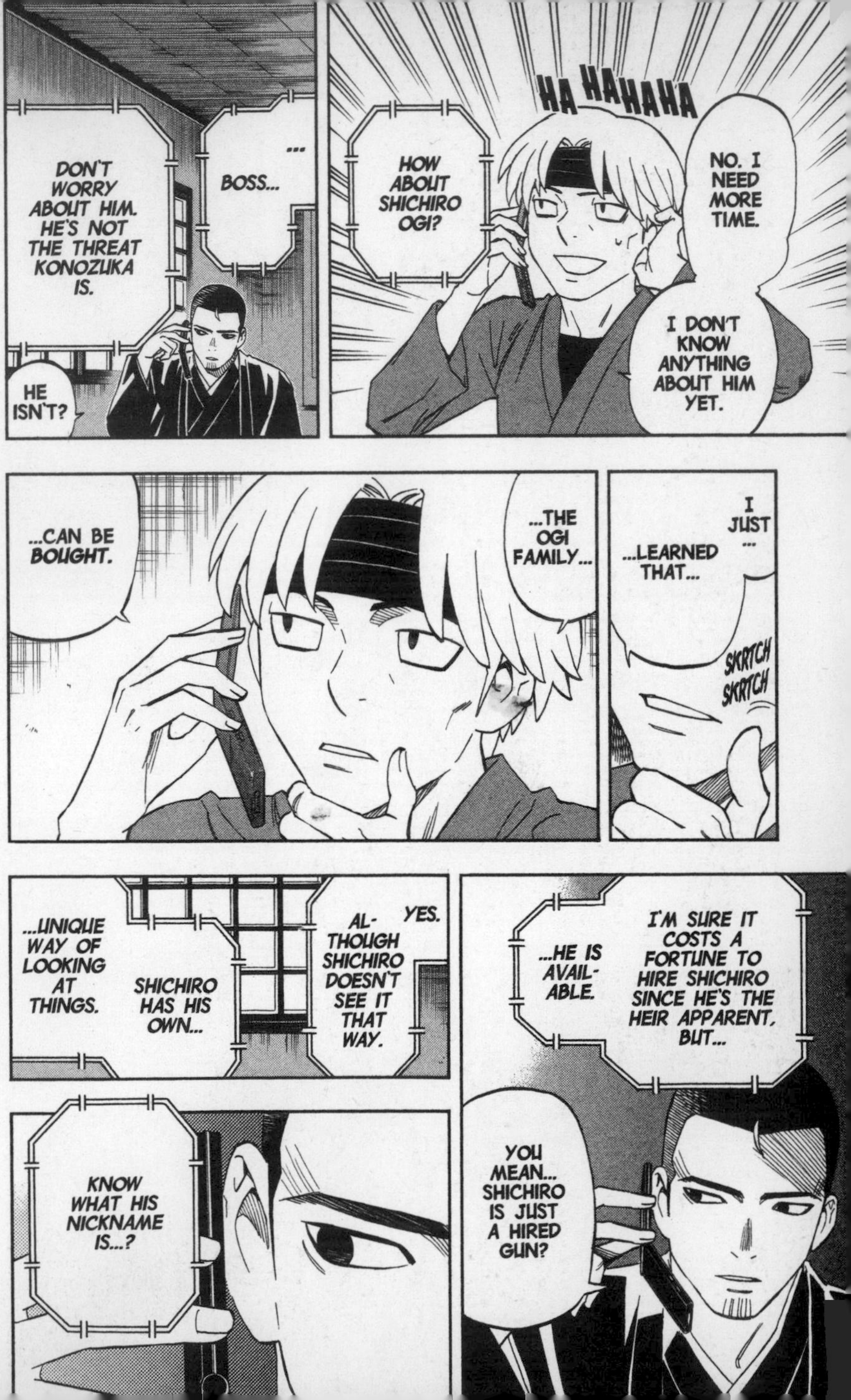
HA HAHAHA
HOW ABOUT SHICHIRO OGI?
NO. I NEED MORE TIME.
I DON'T KNOW ANYTHING ABOUT HIM YET.
...
BOSS...
DON'T WORRY ABOUT HIM. HE'S NOT THE THREAT KONOZUKA IS.
HE ISN'T?
I JUST ...
...LEARNED THAT...
SKRTCH SKRTCH
...THE OGI FAMILY...
...CAN BE BOUGHT.
I'M SURE IT COSTS A FORTUNE TO HIRE SHICHIRO SINCE HE'S THE HEIR APPARENT, BUT...
...HE IS AVAIL- ABLE.
YES.
AL- THOUGH SHICHIRO DOESN'T SEE IT THAT WAY.
SHICHIRO HAS HIS OWN...
...UNIQUE WAY OF LOOKING AT THINGS.
YOU MEAN... SHICHIRO IS JUST A HIRED GUN?
KNOW WHAT HIS NICKNAME IS...?

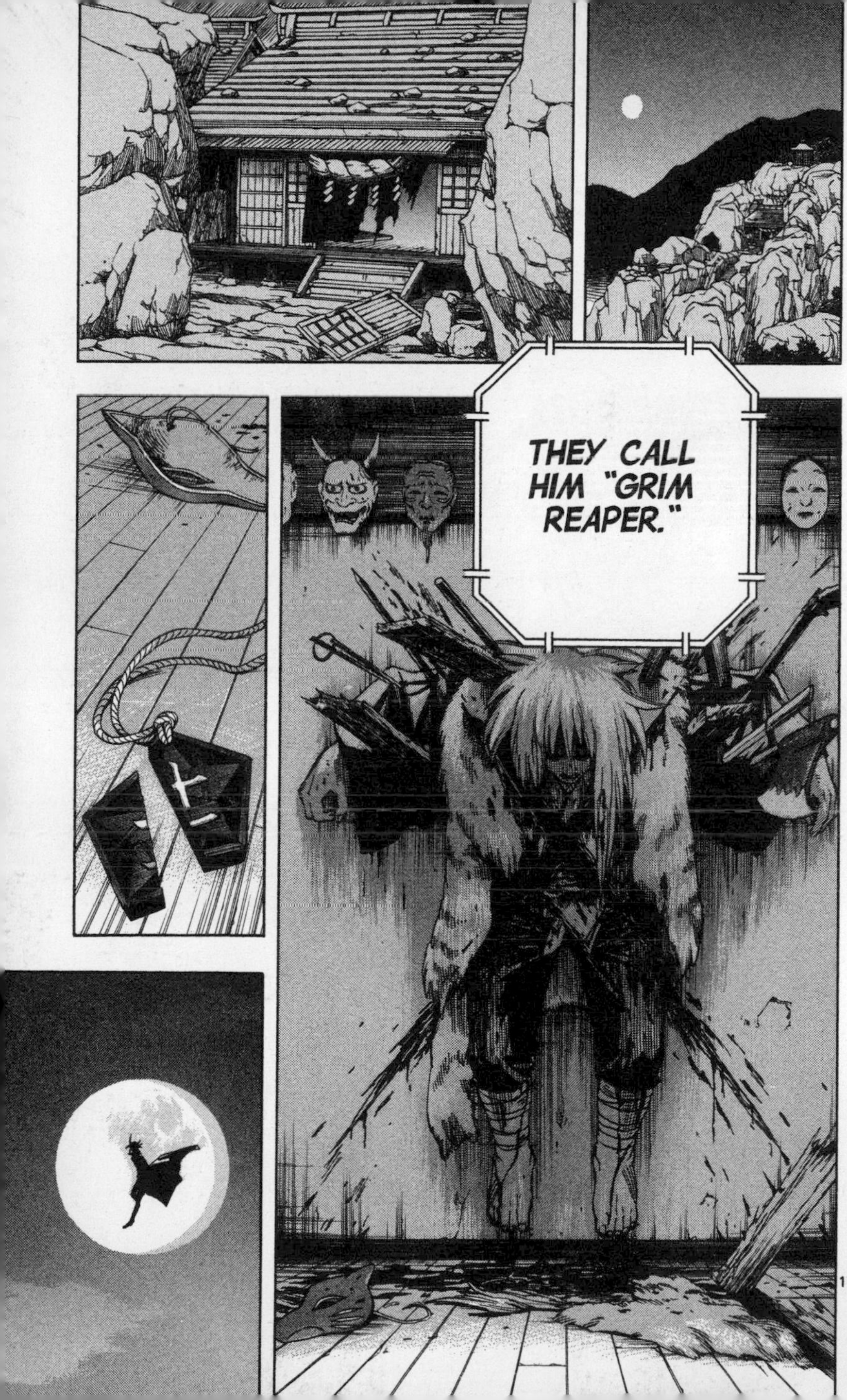
THEY CALL HIM "GRIM REAPER."

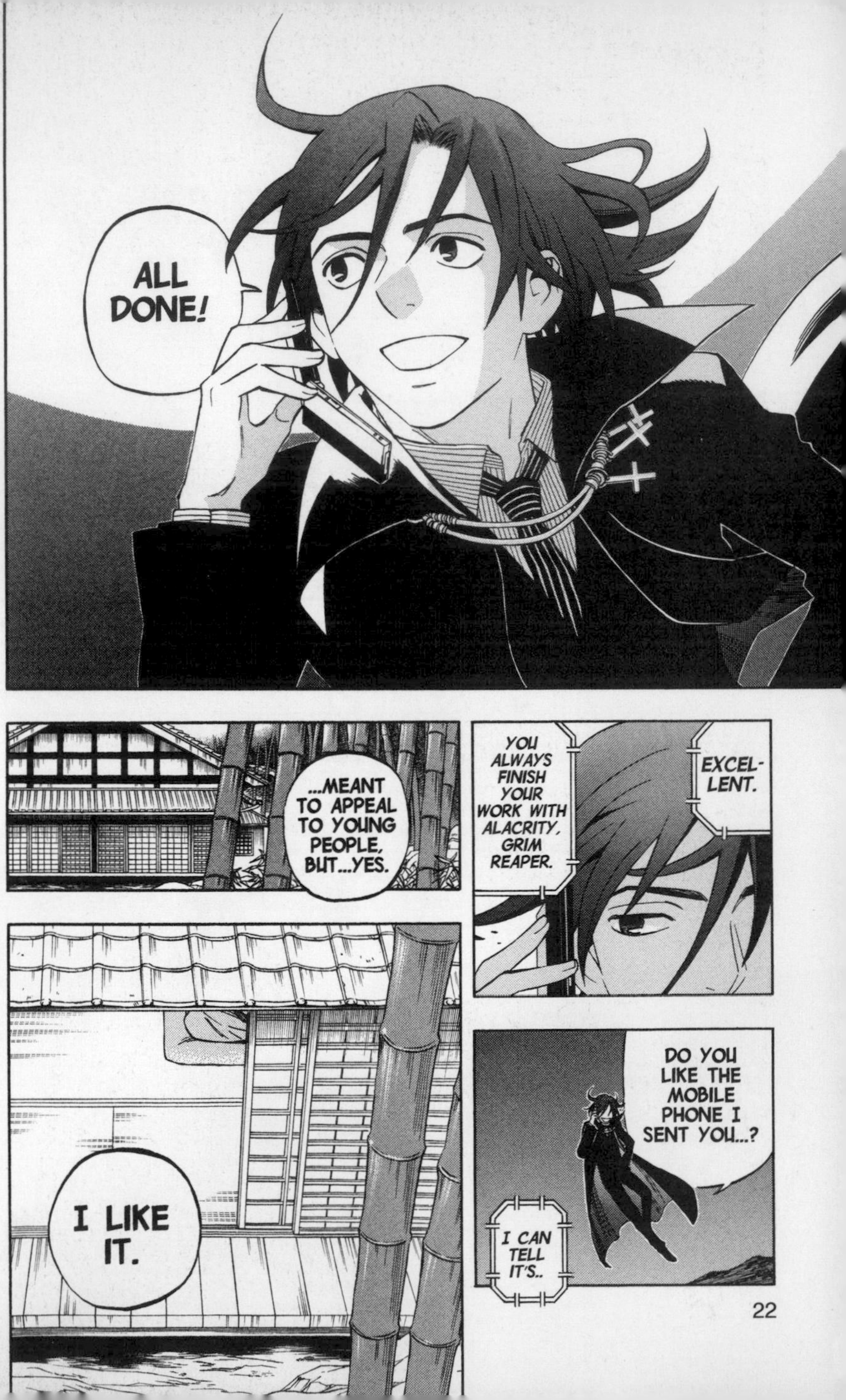
ALL DONE!
EXCEL-LENT.
YOU ALWAYS FINISH YOUR WORK WITH ALACRITY, GRIM REAPER.
DO YOU LIKE THE MOBILE PHONE I SENT YOU...?
I CAN TELL IT'S..
...MEANT TO APPEAL TO YOUNG PEOPLE, BUT...YES.
I LIKE IT.

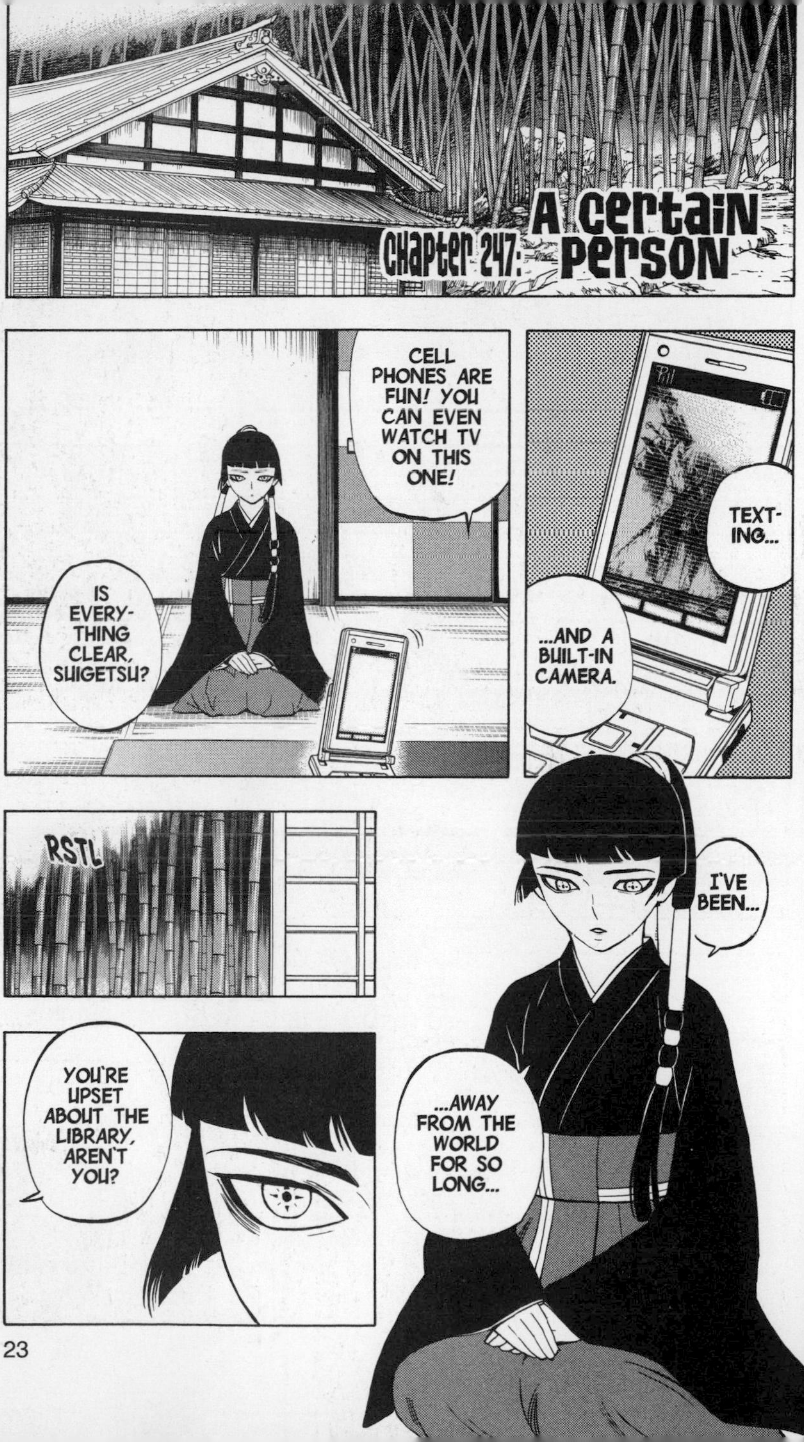

Chapter 247: A Certain Person
TEXT-ING...
...AND A BUILT-IN CAMERA.
CELL PHONES ARE FUN! YOU CAN EVEN WATCH TV ON THIS ONE!
IS EVERY-THING CLEAR, SUIGETSU?
I'VE BEEN...
...AWAY FROM THE WORLD FOR SO LONG...
RSTL
YOU'RE UPSET ABOUT THE LIBRARY, AREN'T YOU?

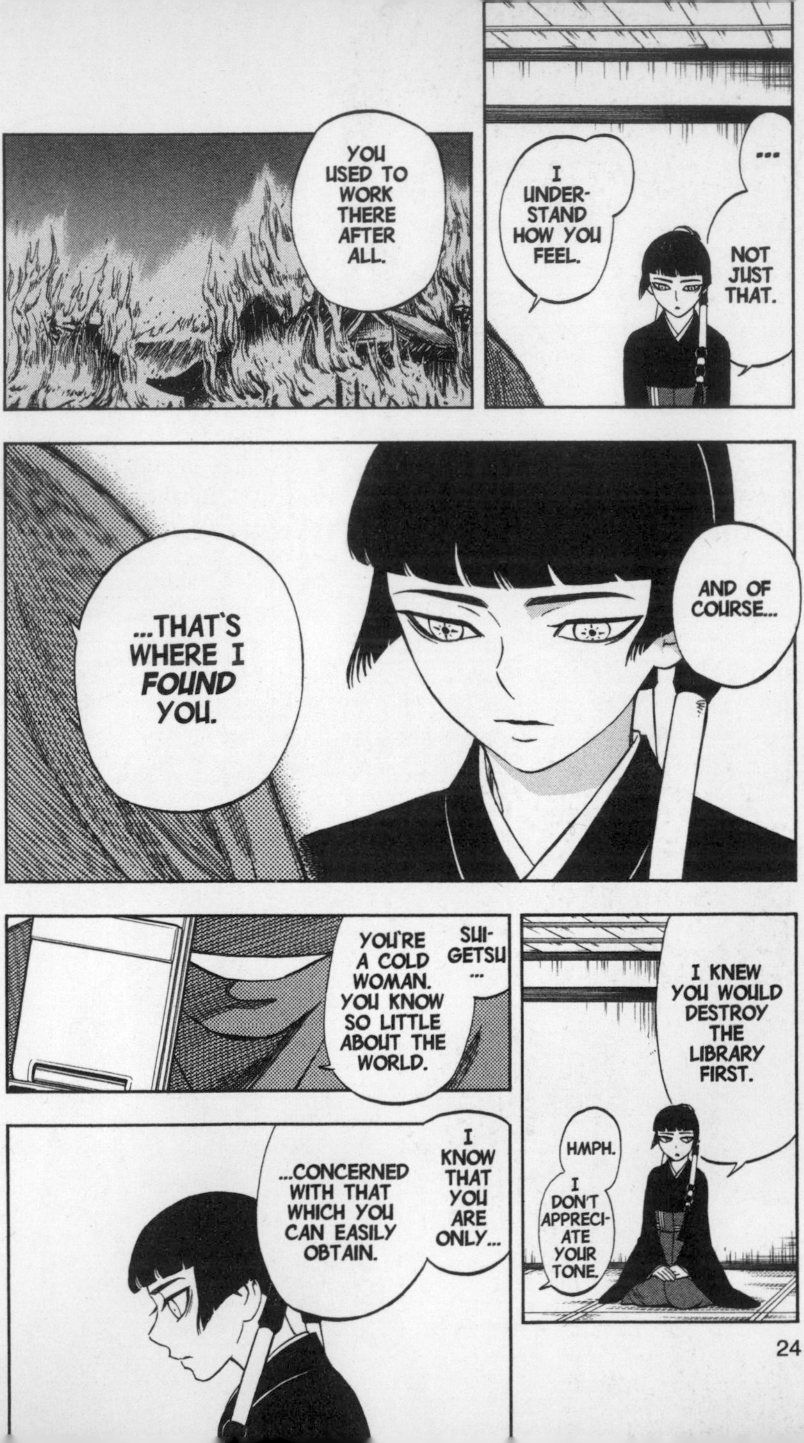
...
NOT JUST THAT.
I UNDER-STAND HOW YOU FEEL.
YOU USED TO WORK THERE AFTER ALL.
AND OF COURSE...
...THAT'S WHERE I *FOUND* YOU.
I KNEW YOU WOULD DESTROY THE LIBRARY FIRST.
HMPH.
I DON'T APPRECI-ATE YOUR TONE.
SUI-GETSU...
YOU'RE A COLD WOMAN. YOU KNOW SO LITTLE ABOUT THE WORLD.
I KNOW THAT YOU ARE ONLY...
...CONCERNED WITH THAT WHICH YOU CAN EASILY OBTAIN.

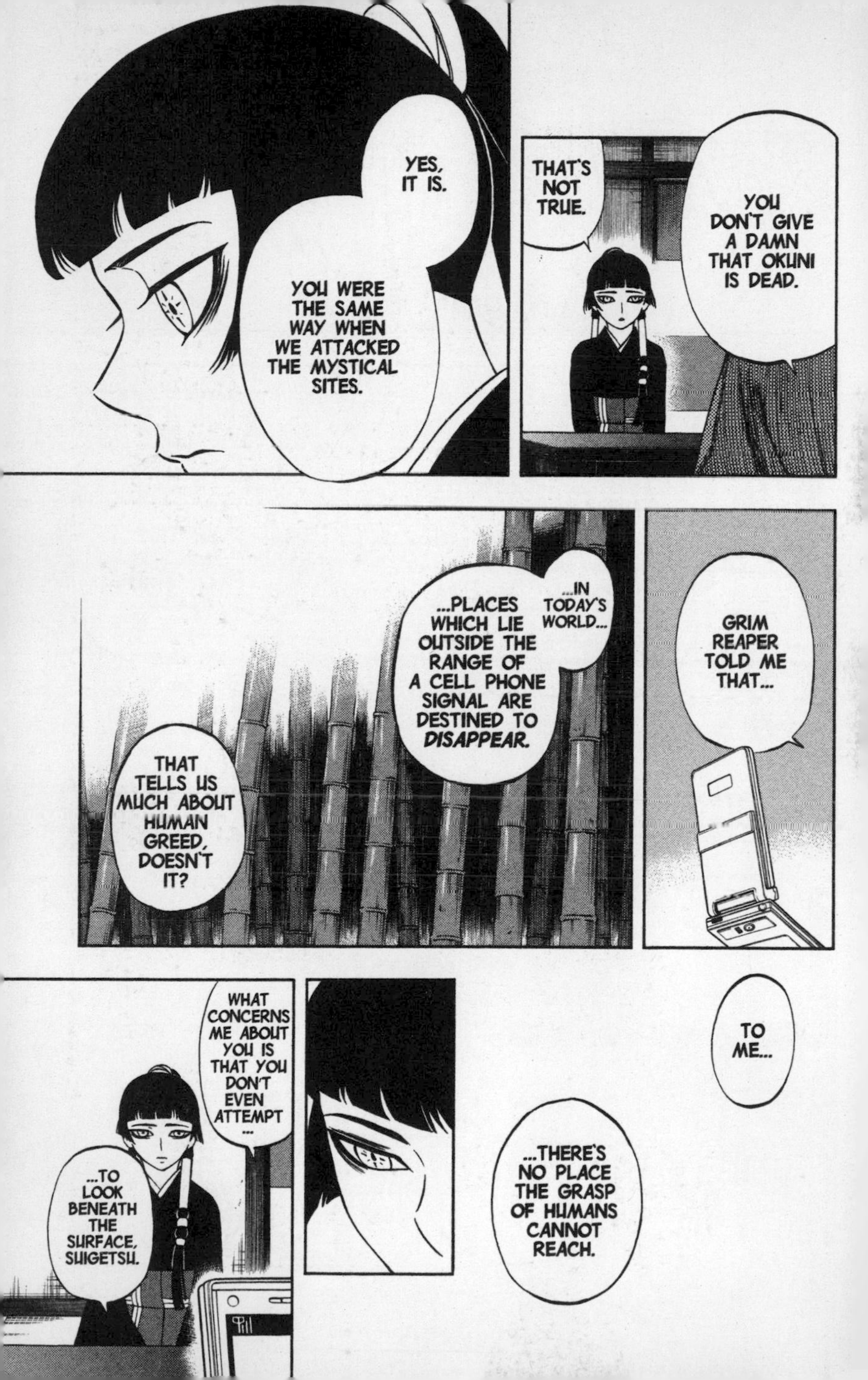
YOU DON'T GIVE A DAMN THAT OKUNI IS DEAD.
THAT'S NOT TRUE.
YES, IT IS.
YOU WERE THE SAME WAY WHEN WE ATTACKED THE MYSTICAL SITES.
GRIM REAPER TOLD ME THAT...
...IN TODAY'S WORLD...
...PLACES WHICH LIE OUTSIDE THE RANGE OF A CELL PHONE SIGNAL ARE DESTINED TO *DISAPPEAR.*
THAT TELLS US MUCH ABOUT HUMAN GREED, DOESN'T IT?
TO ME...
...THERE'S NO PLACE THE GRASP OF HUMANS CANNOT REACH.
WHAT CONCERNS ME ABOUT YOU IS THAT YOU DON'T EVEN ATTEMPT...
...TO LOOK BENEATH THE SURFACE, SUIGETSU.

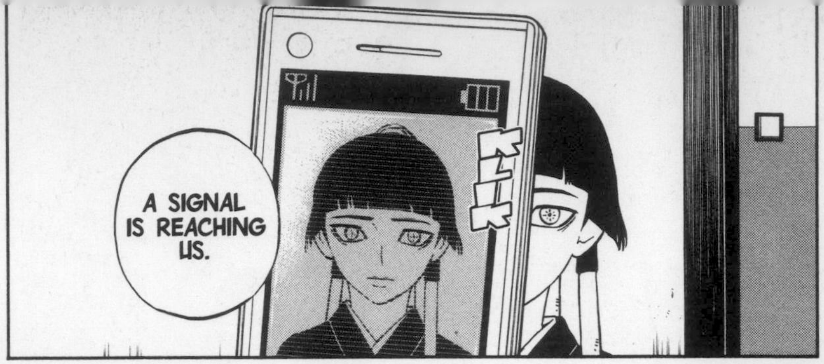
KLIK
A SIGNAL IS REACHING US.

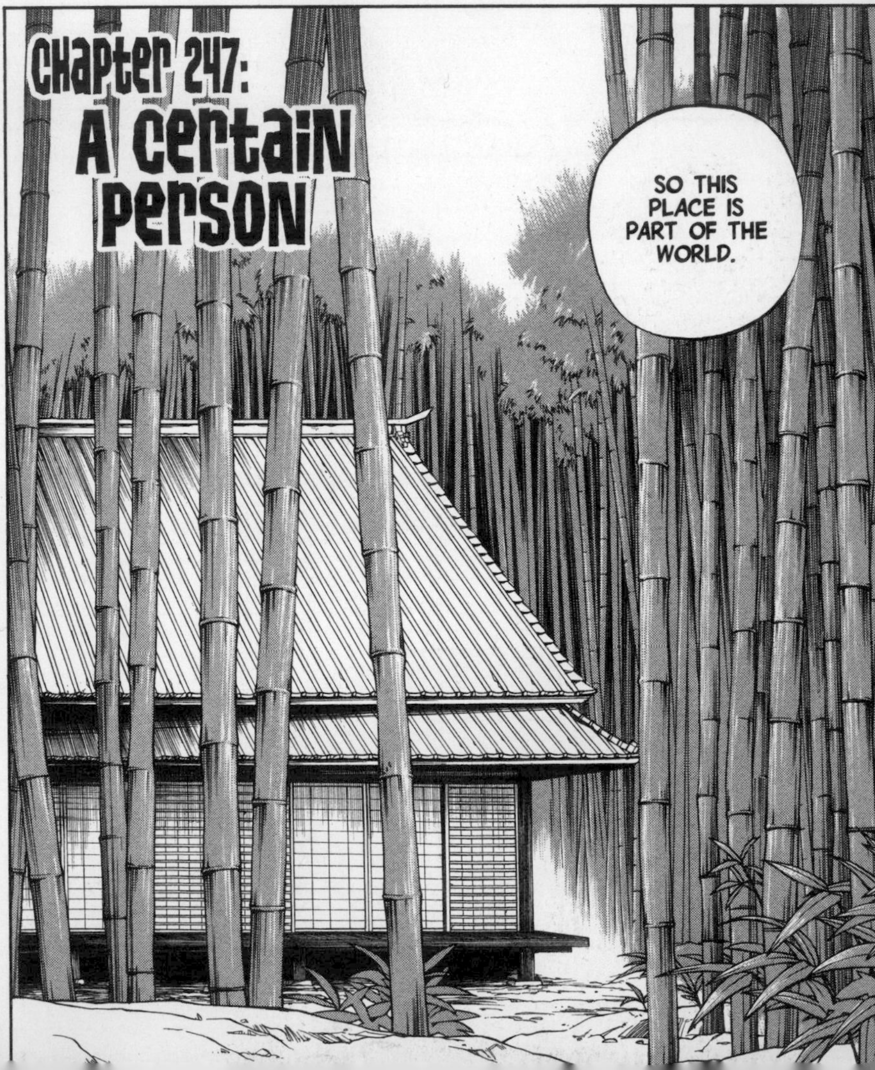
Chapter 247: A Certain Person
SO THIS PLACE IS PART OF THE WORLD.

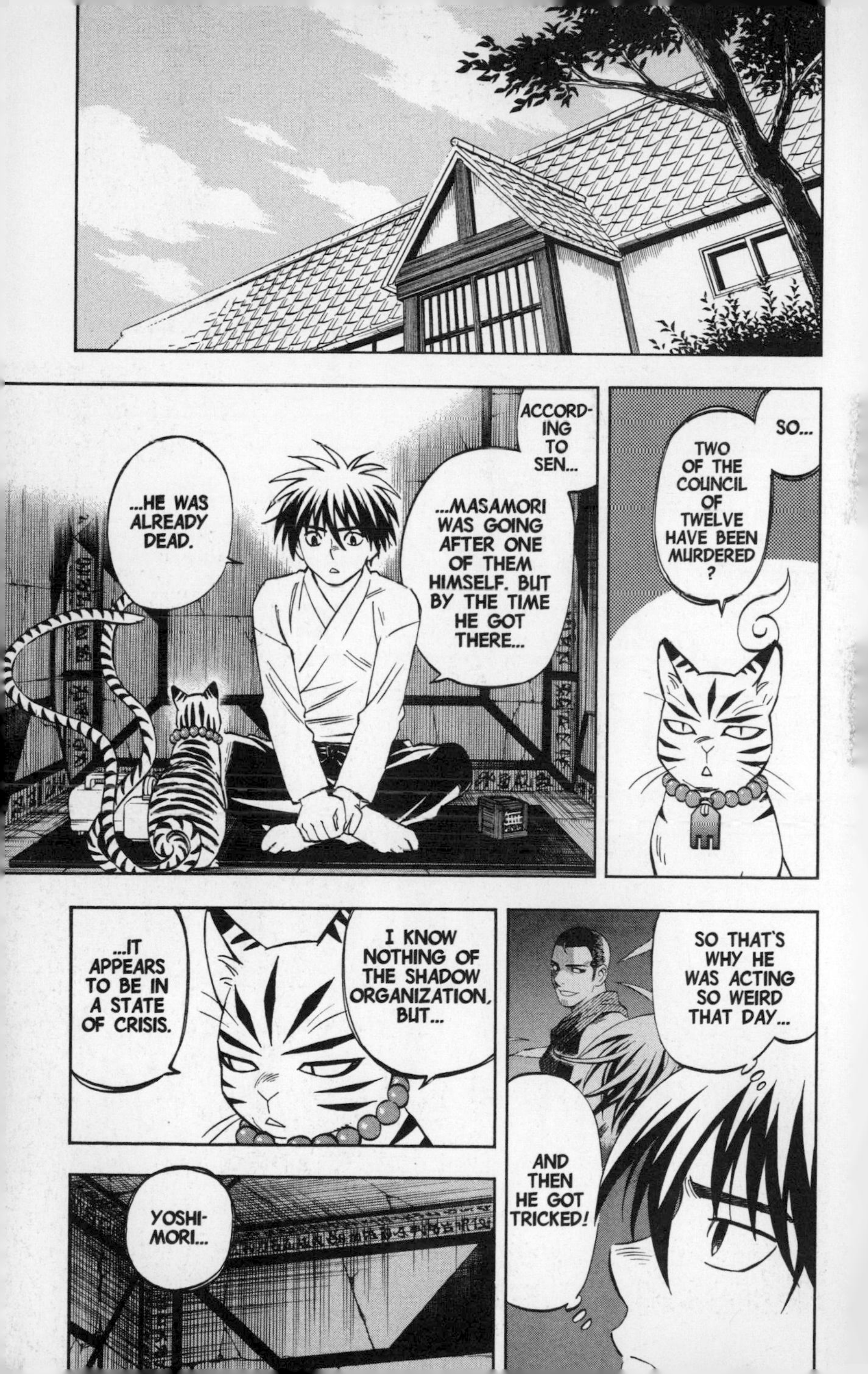
SO...
TWO OF THE COUNCIL OF TWELVE HAVE BEEN MURDERED?
ACCORDING TO SEN...
...MASAMORI WAS GOING AFTER ONE OF THEM HIMSELF. BUT BY THE TIME HE GOT THERE...
...HE WAS ALREADY DEAD.
SO THAT'S WHY HE WAS ACTING SO WEIRD THAT DAY...
AND THEN HE GOT TRICKED!
I KNOW NOTHING OF THE SHADOW ORGANIZATION, BUT...
...IT APPEARS TO BE IN A STATE OF CRISIS.
YOSHIMORI...

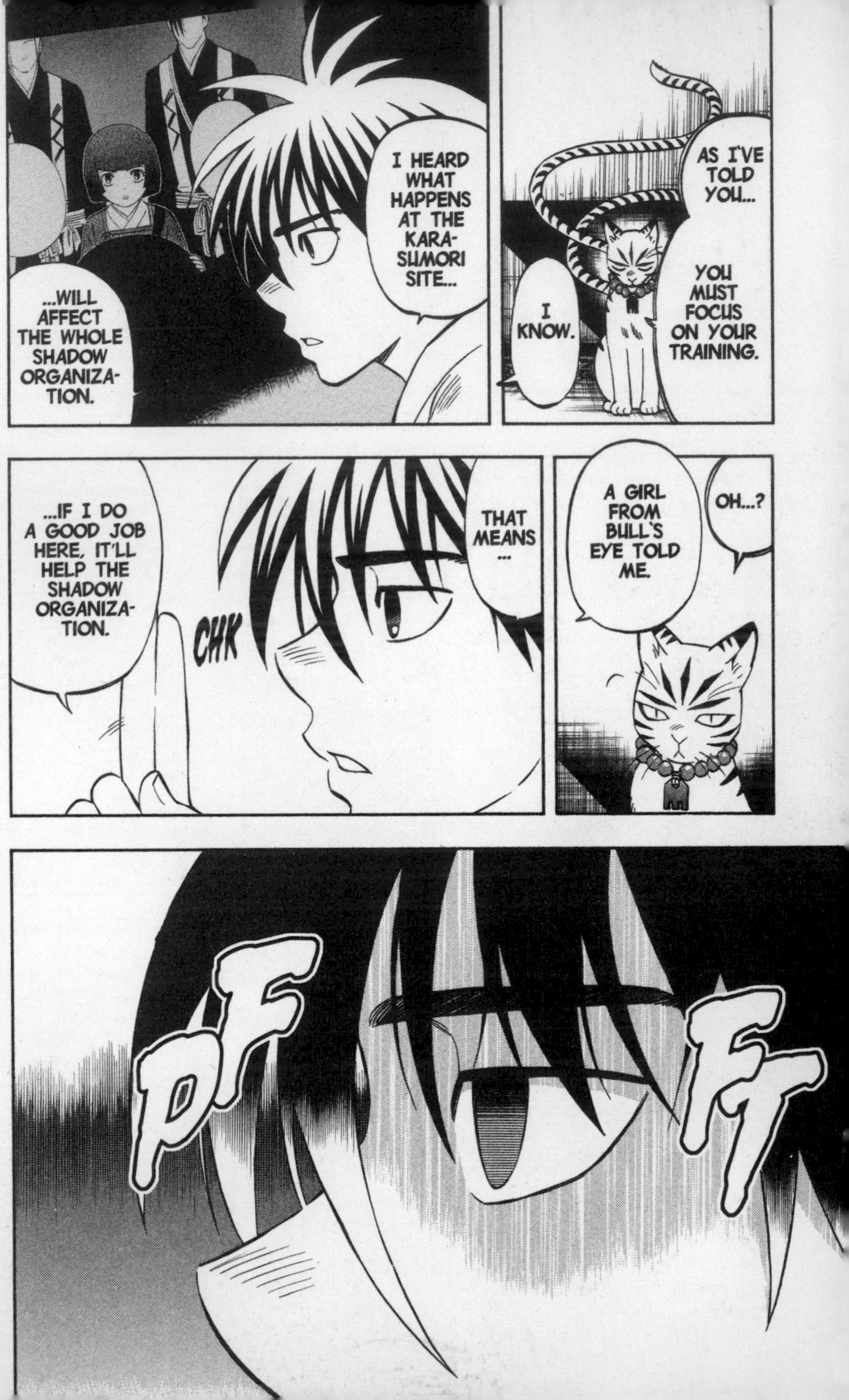
AS I'VE TOLD YOU...
YOU MUST FOCUS ON YOUR TRAINING.
I KNOW.
I HEARD WHAT HAPPENS AT THE KARA-SUMORI SITE...
...WILL AFFECT THE WHOLE SHADOW ORGANIZA-TION.
OH...?
A GIRL FROM BULL'S EYE TOLD ME.
THAT MEANS...
CHK
...IF I DO A GOOD JOB HERE, IT'LL HELP THE SHADOW ORGANIZA-TION.
PFFT

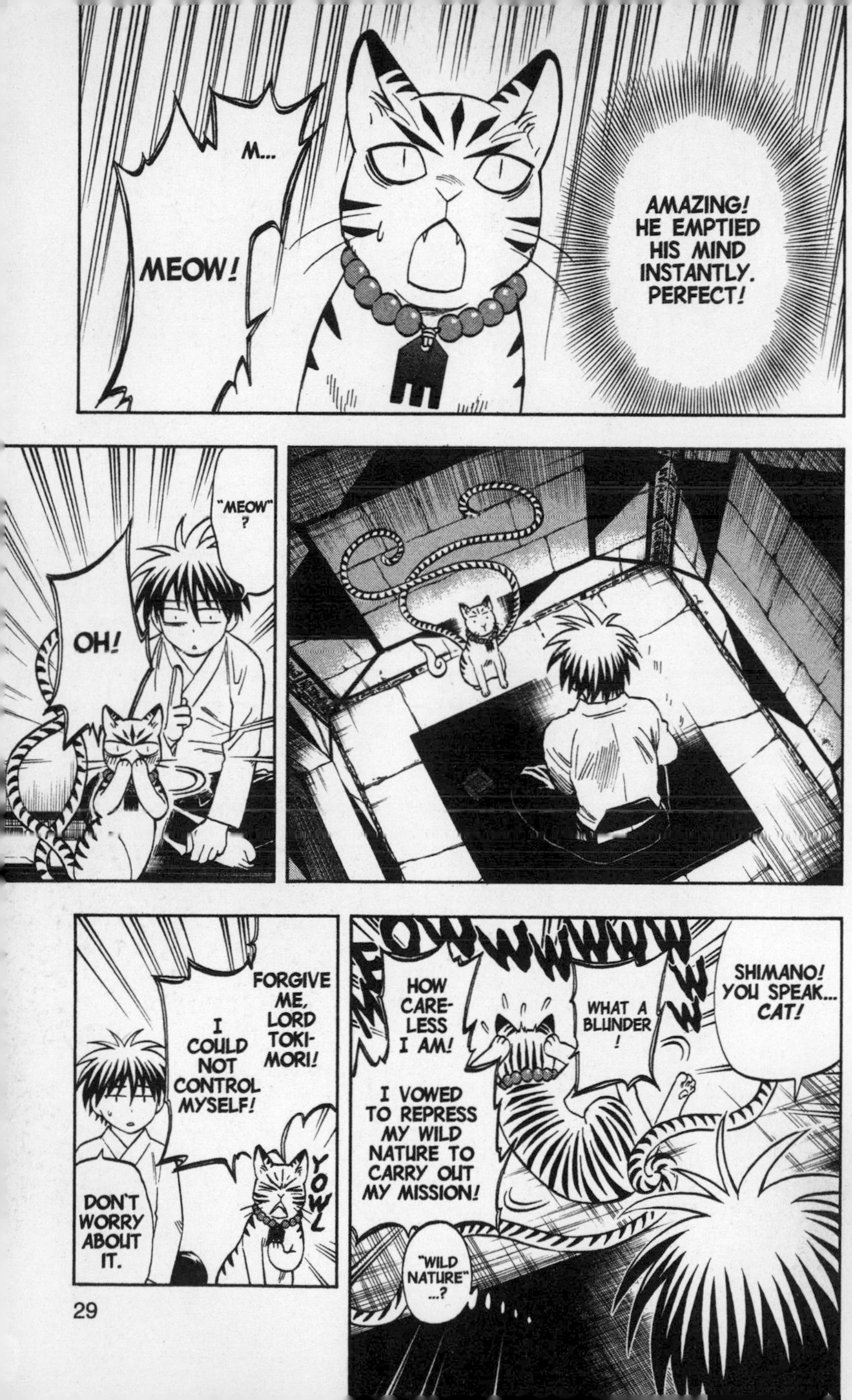
AMAZING! HE EMPTIED HIS MIND INSTANTLY. PERFECT!
M...
MEOW!
"MEOW"?
OH!
SHIMANO! YOU SPEAK... CAT!
WHAT A BLUNDER!
HOW CARELESS I AM!
I VOWED TO REPRESS MY WILD NATURE TO CARRY OUT MY MISSION!
"WILD NATURE"...?
FORGIVE ME, LORD TOKIMORI!
I COULD NOT CONTROL MYSELF!
YOWL
DON'T WORRY ABOUT IT.

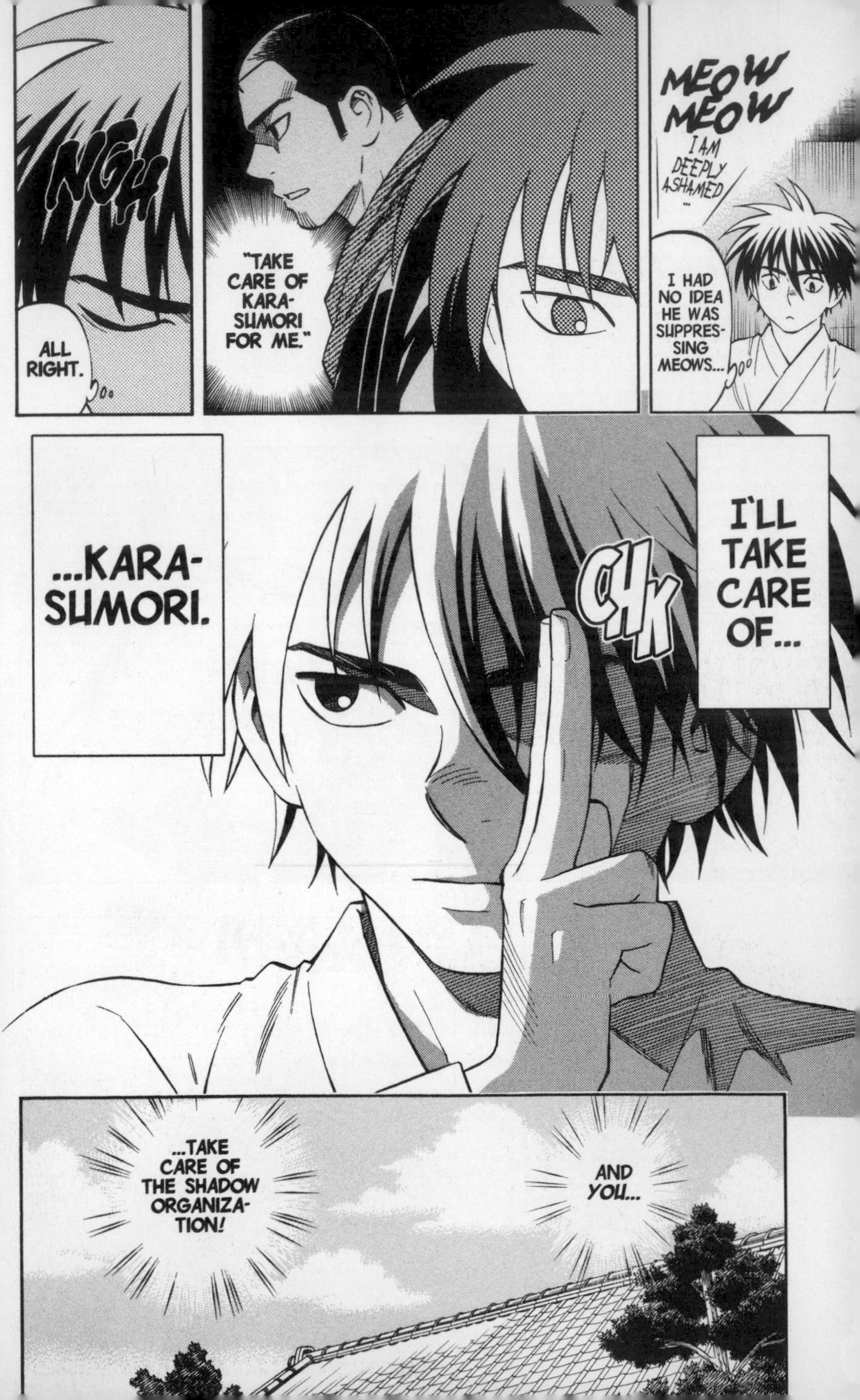
MEOW MEOW
I AM DEEPLY ASHAMED...
I HAD NO IDEA HE WAS SUPPRESSING MEOWS...
"TAKE CARE OF KARASUMORI FOR ME."
NGH
ALL RIGHT.
I'LL TAKE CARE OF...
CHK
...KARASUMORI.
AND YOU...
...TAKE CARE OF THE SHADOW ORGANIZATION!

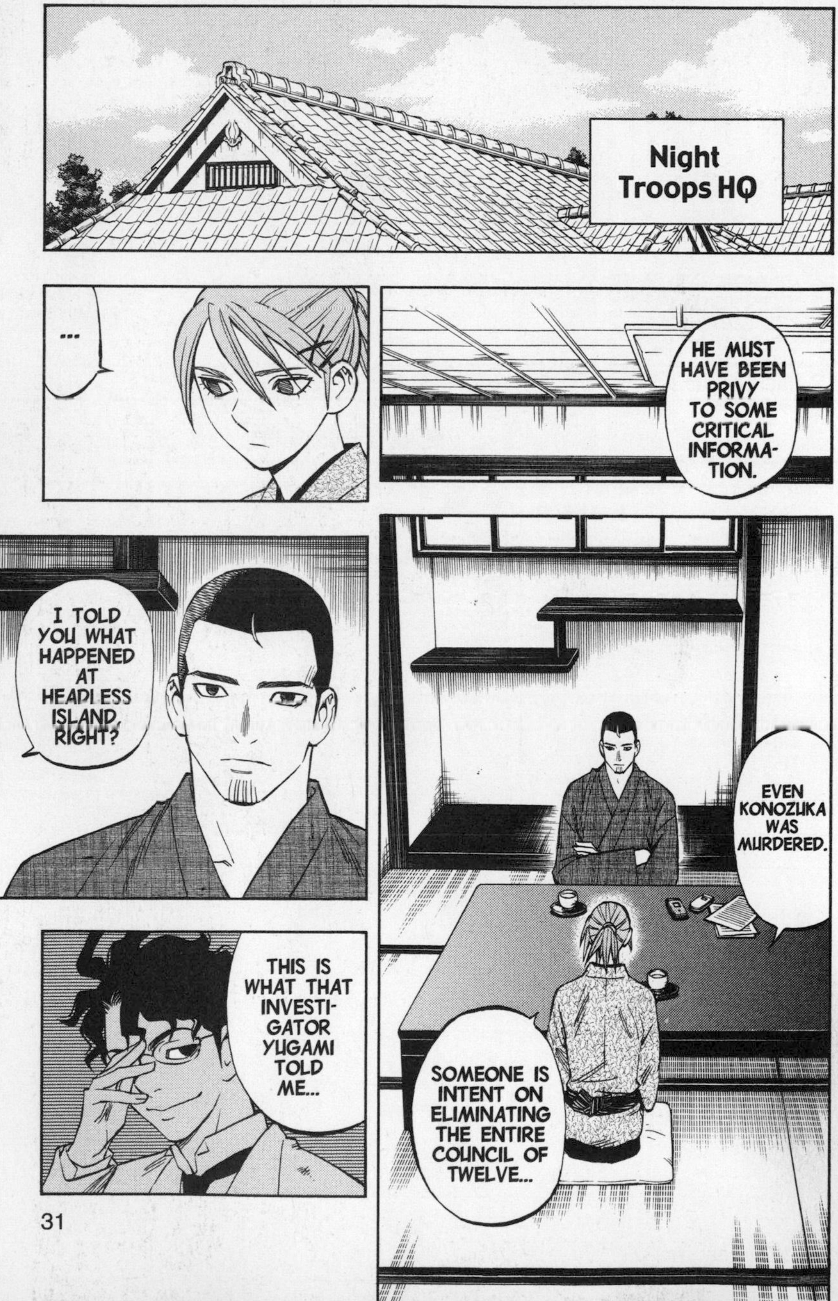
Night Troops HQ
HE MUST HAVE BEEN PRIVY TO SOME CRITICAL INFORMATION.
...
EVEN KONOZUKA WAS MURDERED.
SOMEONE IS INTENT ON ELIMINATING THE ENTIRE COUNCIL OF TWELVE...
I TOLD YOU WHAT HAPPENED AT HEADLESS ISLAND RIGHT?
THIS IS WHAT THAT INVESTIGATOR YUGAMI TOLD ME...

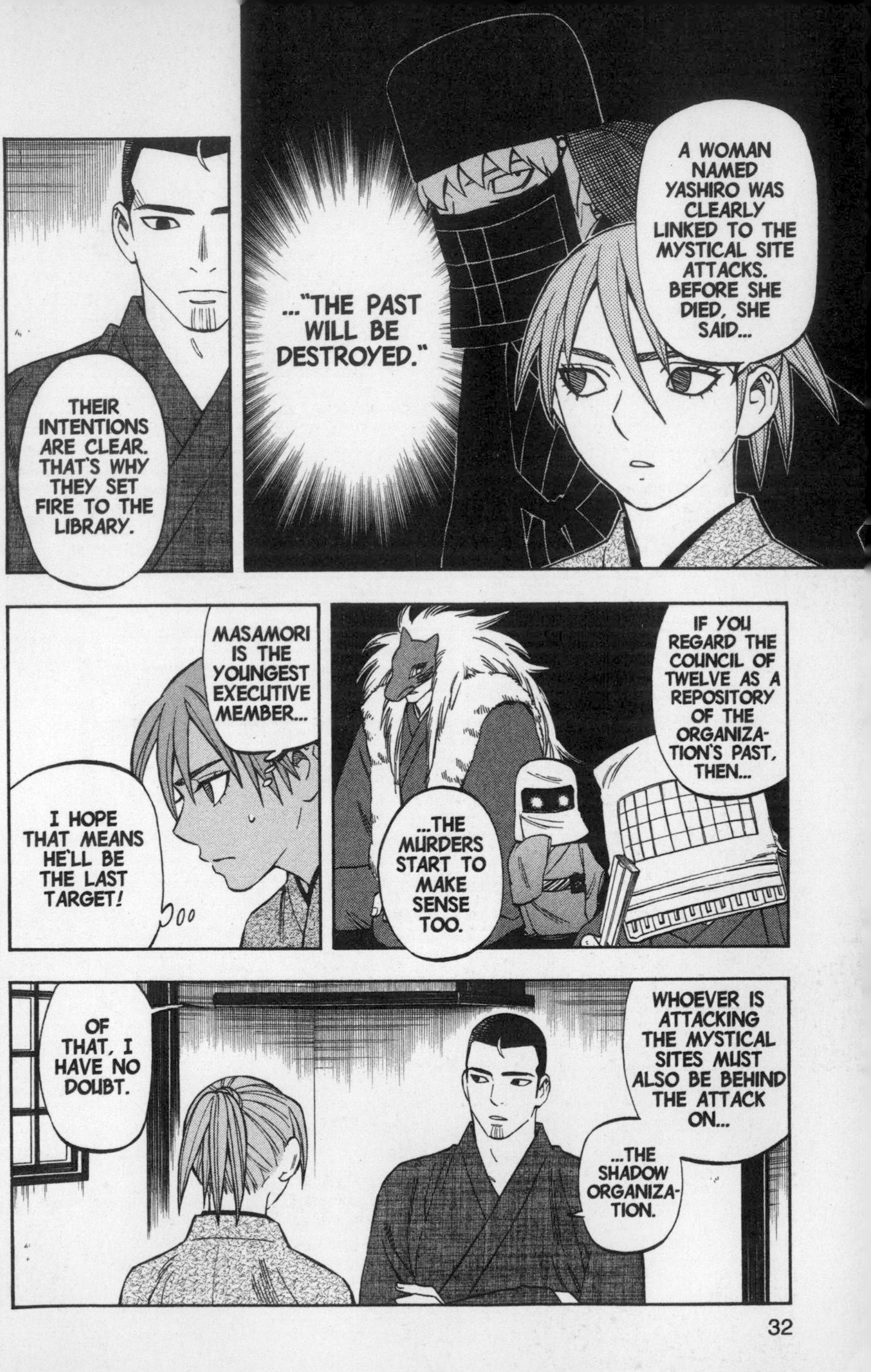
A WOMAN NAMED YASHIRO WAS CLEARLY LINKED TO THE MYSTICAL SITE ATTACKS. BEFORE SHE DIED, SHE SAID...
..."THE PAST WILL BE DESTROYED."
THEIR INTENTIONS ARE CLEAR. THAT'S WHY THEY SET FIRE TO THE LIBRARY.
IF YOU REGARD THE COUNCIL OF TWELVE AS A REPOSITORY OF THE ORGANIZA-TION'S PAST, THEN...
...THE MURDERS START TO MAKE SENSE TOO.
MASAMORI IS THE YOUNGEST EXECUTIVE MEMBER...
I HOPE THAT MEANS HE'LL BE THE LAST TARGET!
WHOEVER IS ATTACKING THE MYSTICAL SITES MUST ALSO BE BEHIND THE ATTACK ON...
...THE SHADOW ORGANIZA-TION.
OF THAT, I HAVE NO DOUBT.

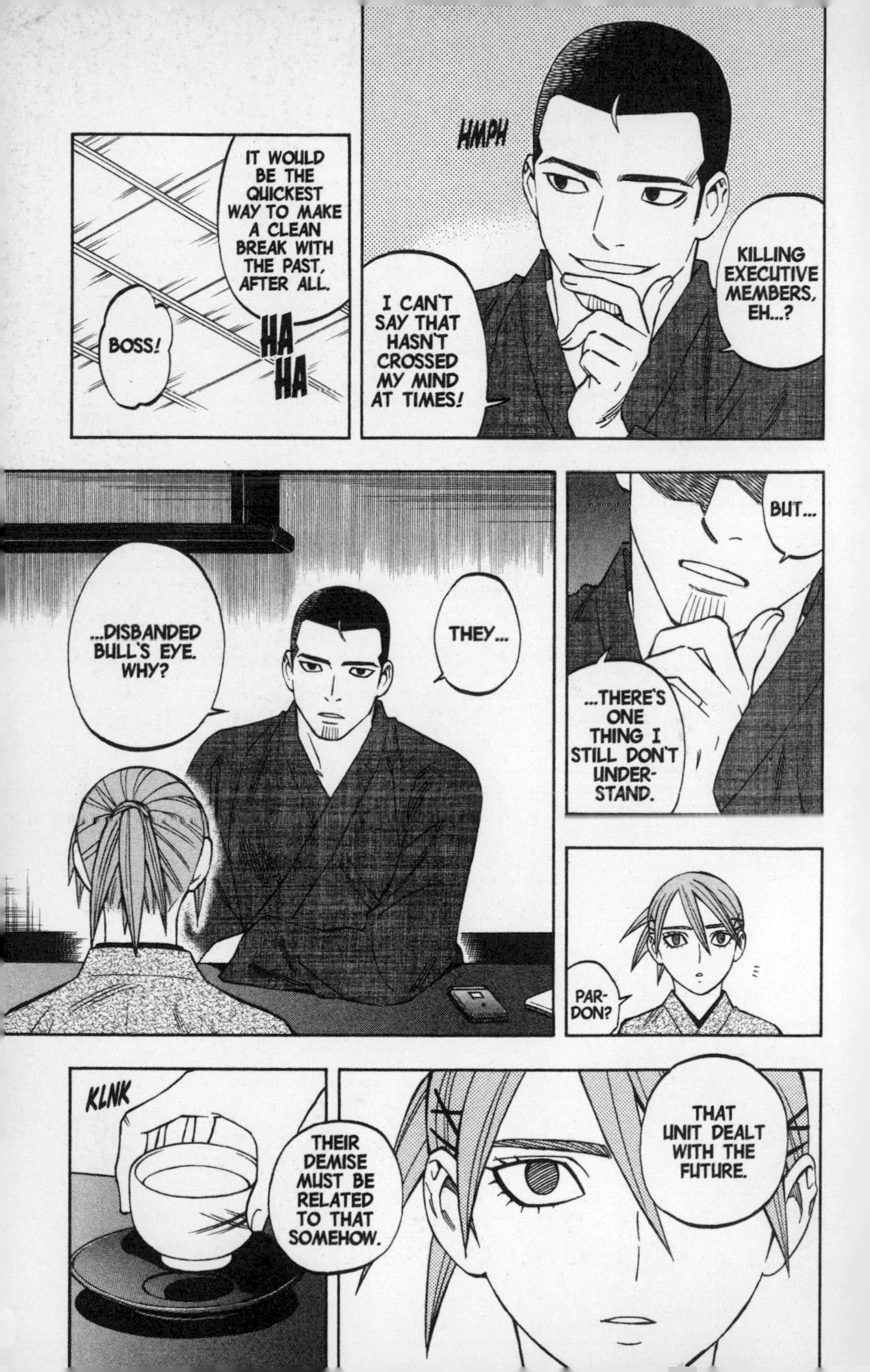
HMPH
KILLING EXECUTIVE MEMBERS, EH...?
I CAN'T SAY THAT HASN'T CROSSED MY MIND AT TIMES!
IT WOULD BE THE QUICKEST WAY TO MAKE A CLEAN BREAK WITH THE PAST, AFTER ALL.
HA HA
BOSS!
BUT...
...THERE'S ONE THING I STILL DON'T UNDER-STAND.
PAR-DON?
THEY...
...DISBANDED BULL'S EYE. WHY?
THAT UNIT DEALT WITH THE FUTURE.
THEIR DEMISE MUST BE RELATED TO THAT SOMEHOW.
KLNK

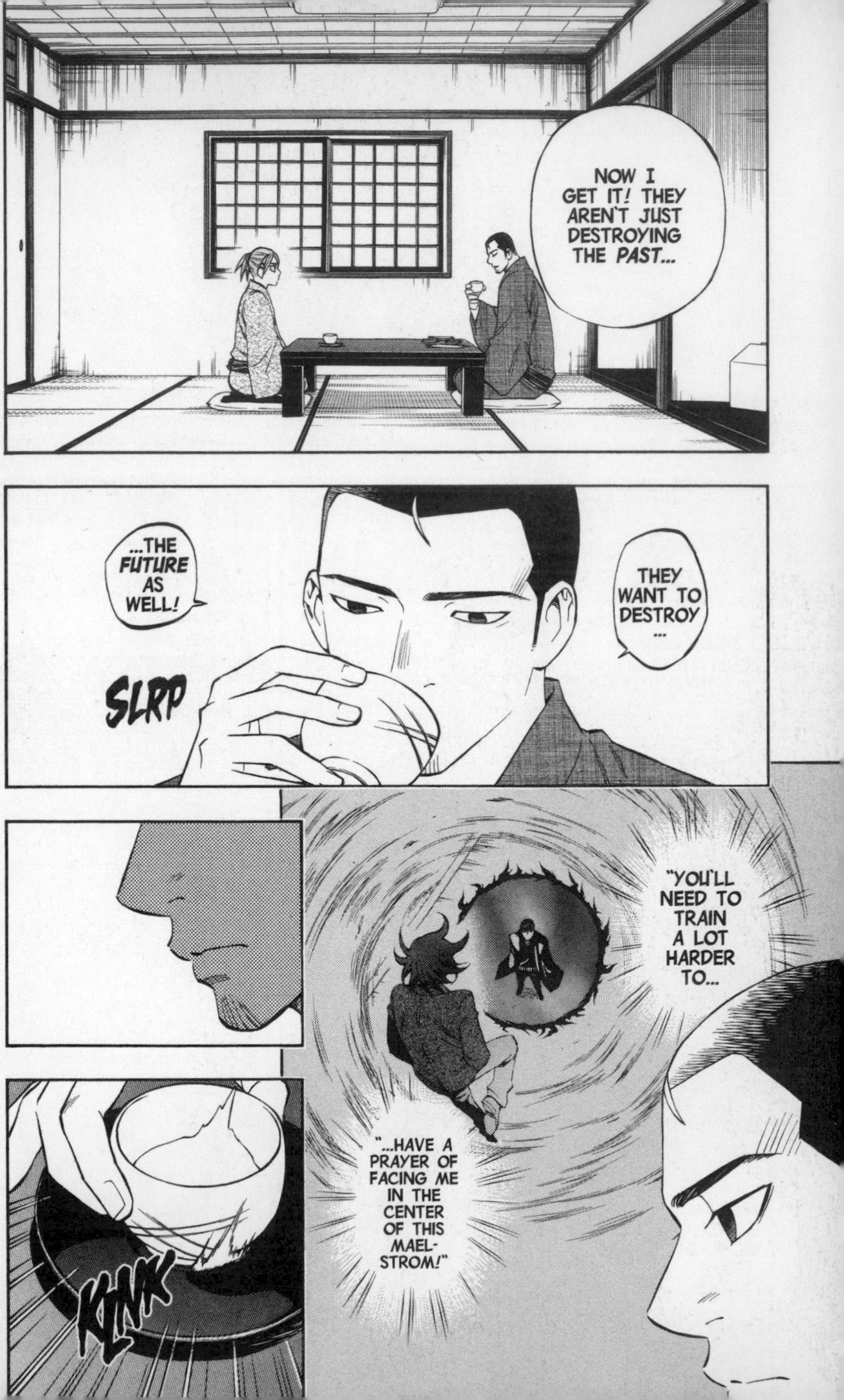
NOW I GET IT! THEY AREN'T JUST DESTROYING THE PAST...
THEY WANT TO DESTROY ...
...THE FUTURE AS WELL!
SLRP
"YOU'LL NEED TO TRAIN A LOT HARDER TO...
"...HAVE A PRAYER OF FACING ME IN THE CENTER OF THIS MAEL-STROM!"
KLINK

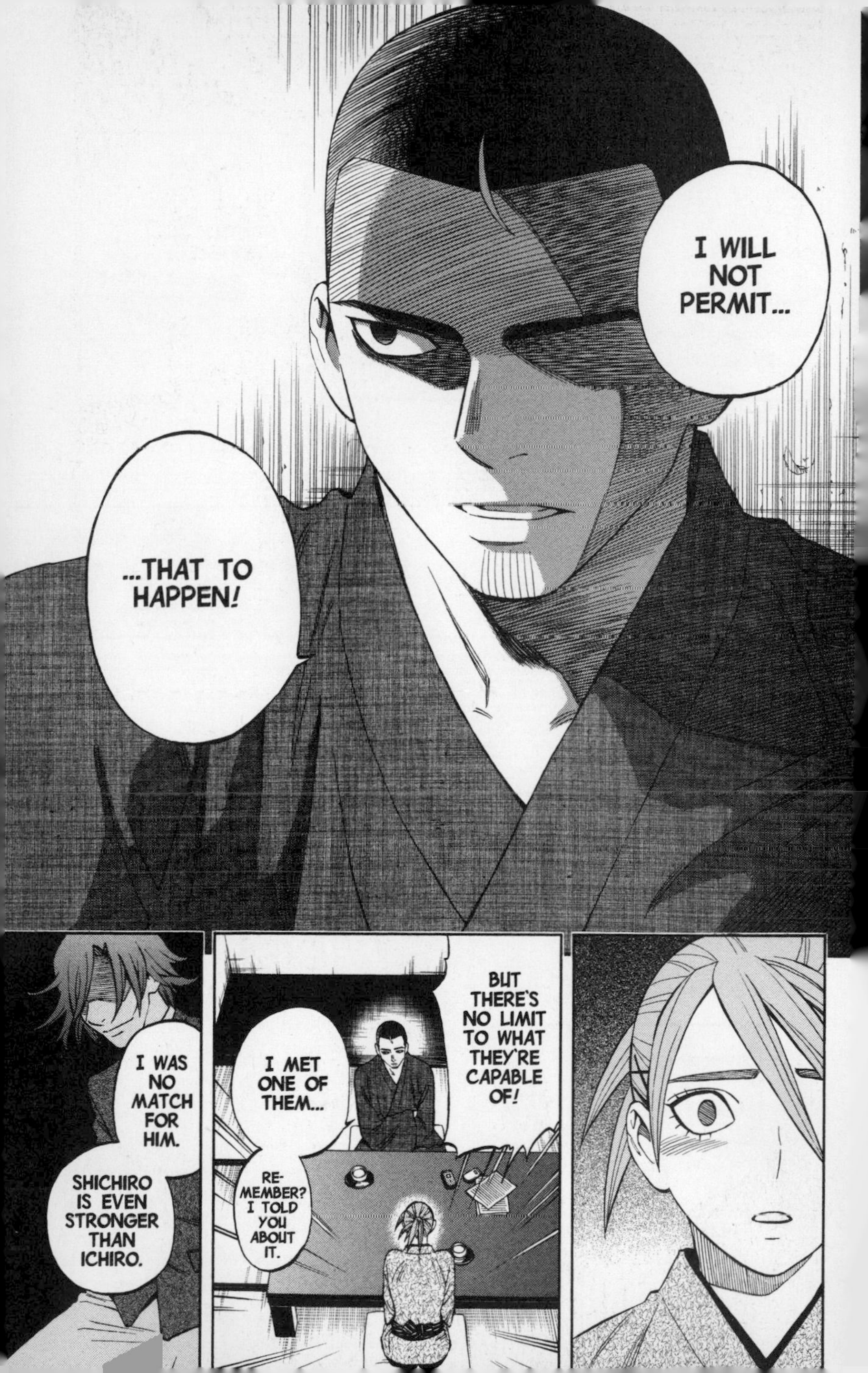
I WILL NOT PERMIT...
...THAT TO HAPPEN!
BUT THERE'S NO LIMIT TO WHAT THEY'RE CAPABLE OF!
I MET ONE OF THEM...
RE-MEMBER? I TOLD YOU ABOUT IT.
I WAS NO MATCH FOR HIM.
SHICHIRO IS EVEN STRONGER THAN ICHIRO.

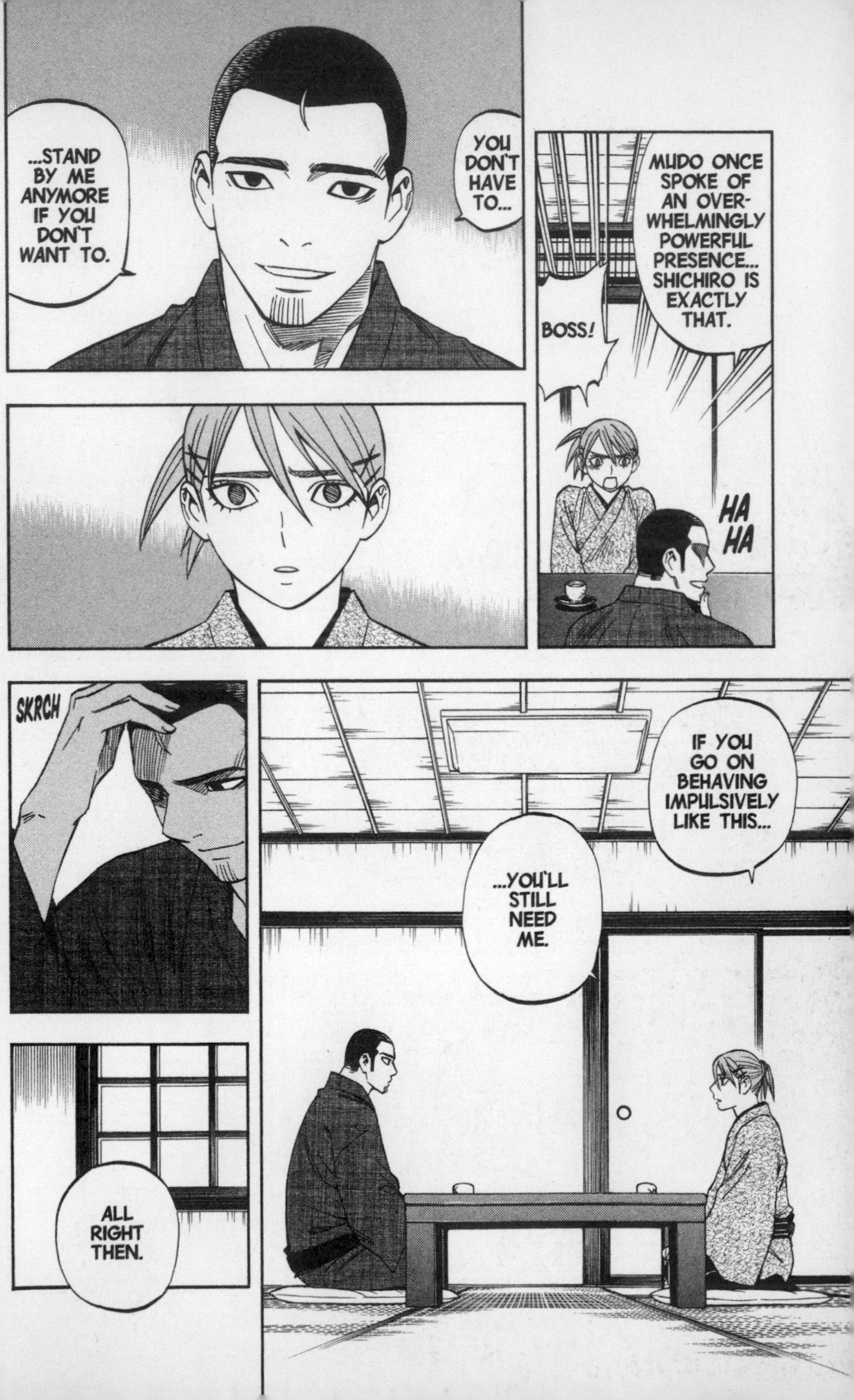
MUDO ONCE SPOKE OF AN OVER-WHELMINGLY POWERFUL PRESENCE... SHICHIRO IS EXACTLY THAT.
BOSS!
HA HA
YOU DON'T HAVE TO...
...STAND BY ME ANYMORE IF YOU DON'T WANT TO.
IF YOU GO ON BEHAVING IMPULSIVELY LIKE THIS...
...YOU'LL STILL NEED ME.
SKRCH
ALL RIGHT THEN.

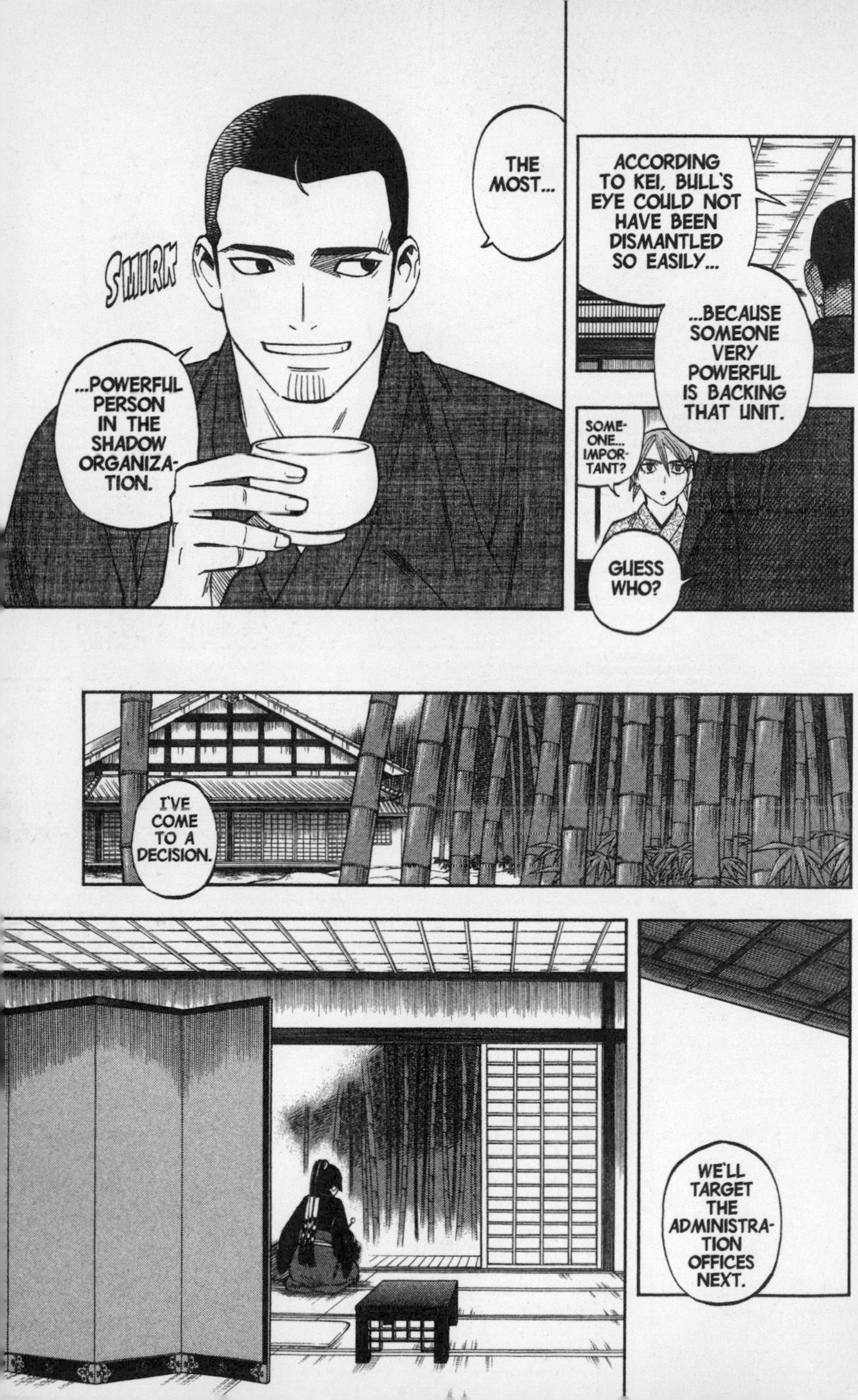
ACCORDING TO KEI, BULL'S EYE COULD NOT HAVE BEEN DISMANTLED SO EASILY...
...BECAUSE SOMEONE VERY POWERFUL IS BACKING THAT UNIT.
SOME-ONE... IMPOR-TANT?
GUESS WHO?
THE MOST...
SMIRK
...POWERFUL PERSON IN THE SHADOW ORGANIZA-TION.
I'VE COME TO A DECISION.
WE'LL TARGET THE ADMINISTRA-TION OFFICES NEXT.

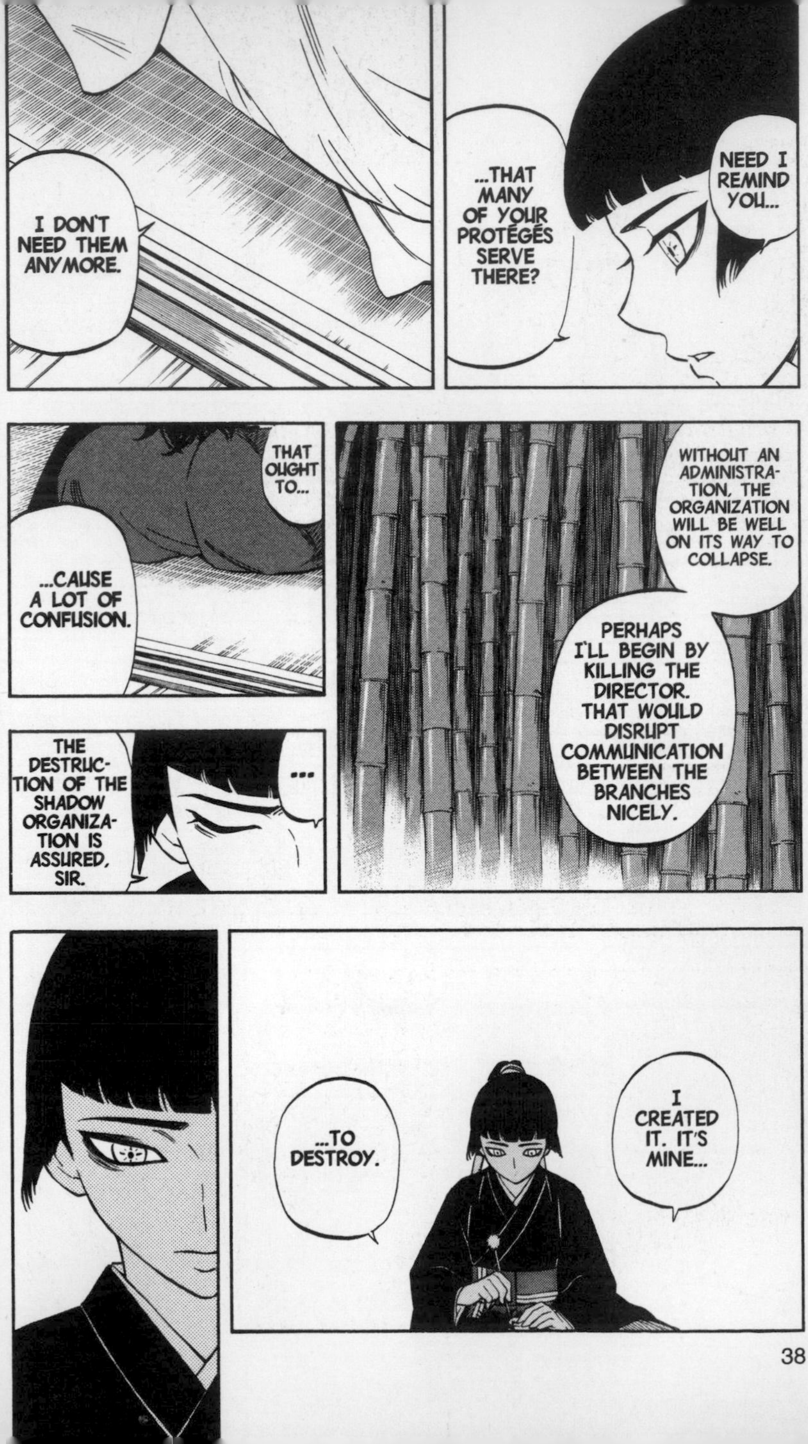
NEED I REMIND YOU...
...THAT MANY OF YOUR PROTÉGÉS SERVE THERE?
I DON'T NEED THEM ANYMORE.
WITHOUT AN ADMINISTRATION, THE ORGANIZATION WILL BE WELL ON ITS WAY TO COLLAPSE.
PERHAPS I'LL BEGIN BY KILLING THE DIRECTOR. THAT WOULD DISRUPT COMMUNICATION BETWEEN THE BRANCHES NICELY.
THAT OUGHT TO...
...CAUSE A LOT OF CONFUSION.
...
THE DESTRUCTION OF THE SHADOW ORGANIZATION IS ASSURED, SIR.
I CREATED IT. IT'S MINE...
...TO DESTROY.

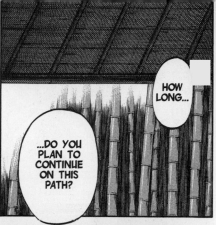

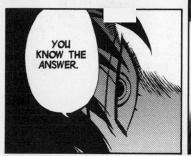

HOW LONG...
...DO YOU PLAN TO CONTINUE ON THIS PATH?
YOU KNOW THE ANSWER.
UNTIL MY WORK IS DONE.
SUIGETSU
...

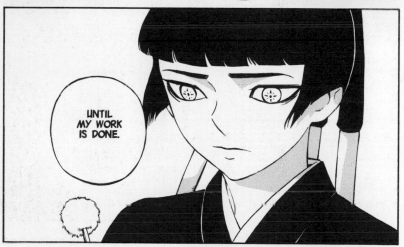

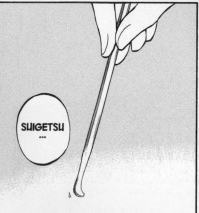

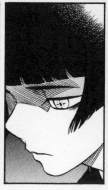

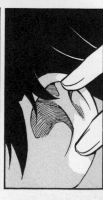

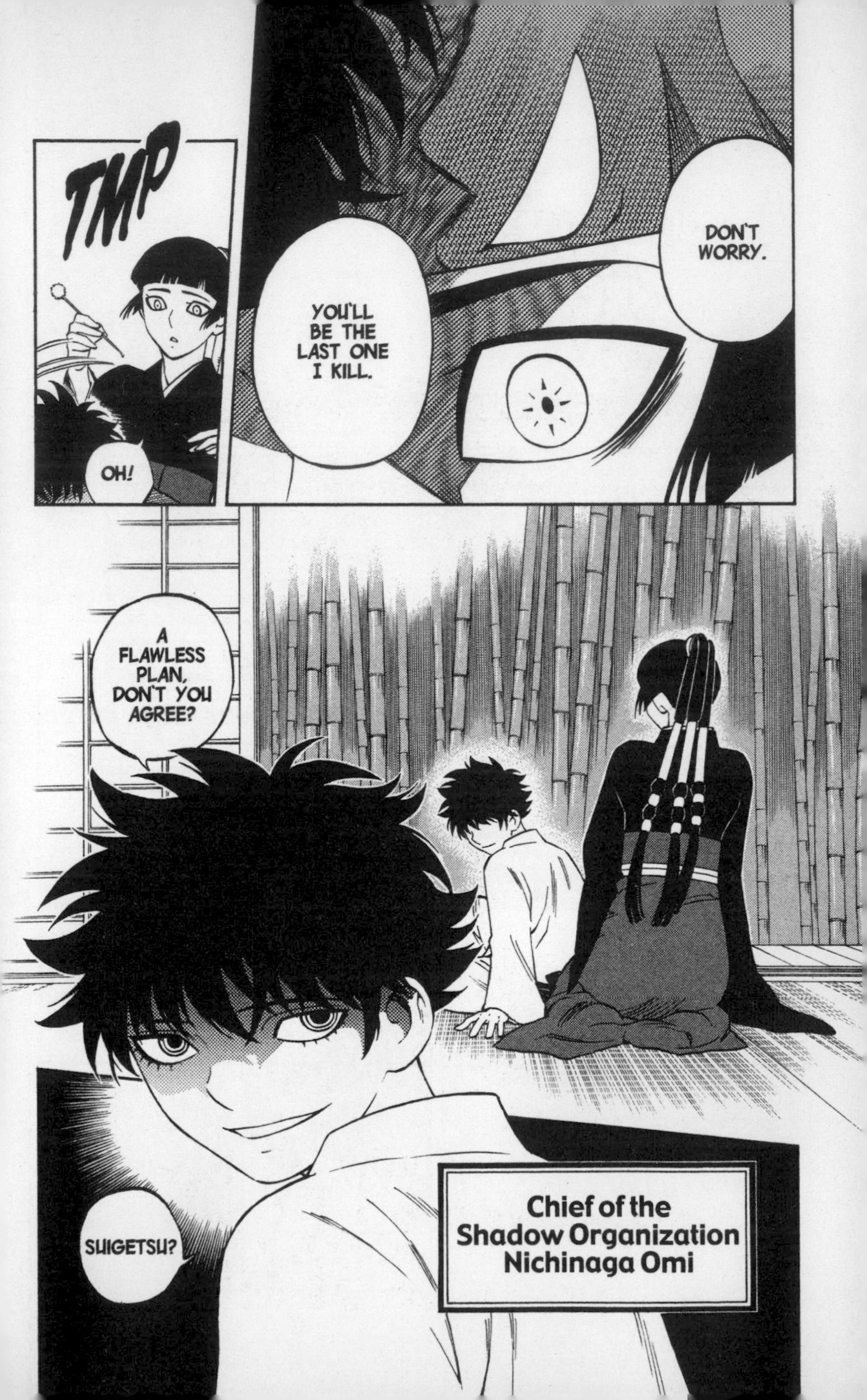
DON'T WORRY.
YOU'LL BE THE LAST ONE I KILL.
TMP
OH!
A FLAWLESS PLAN, DON'T YOU AGREE?
Chief of the Shadow Organization Nichinaga Omi
SUIGETSU?

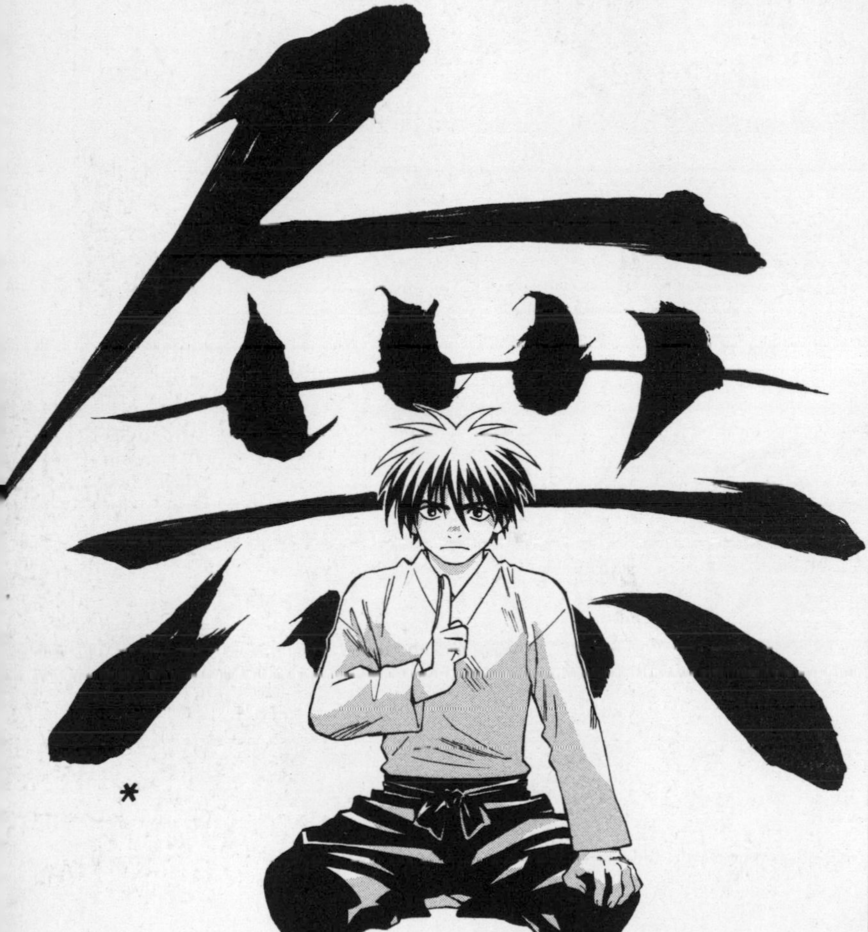
*

Chapter 248: Perfect Form

*NO THOUGHT

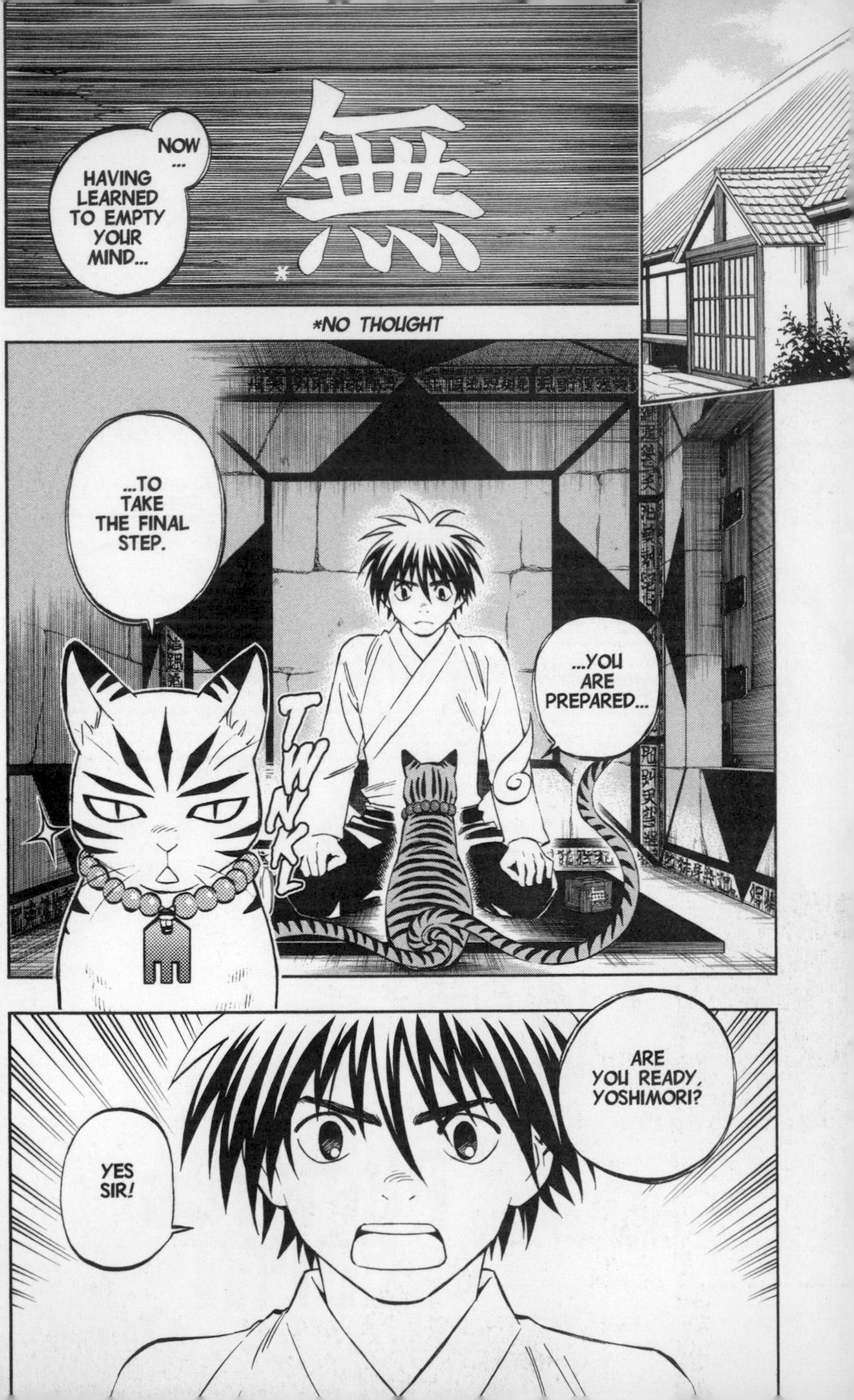

NOW... HAVING LEARNED TO EMPTY YOUR MIND...
無*
*NO THOUGHT
...YOU ARE PREPARED...
...TO TAKE THE FINAL STEP.
TWINKLE
ARE YOU READY, YOSHIMORI?
YES SIR!

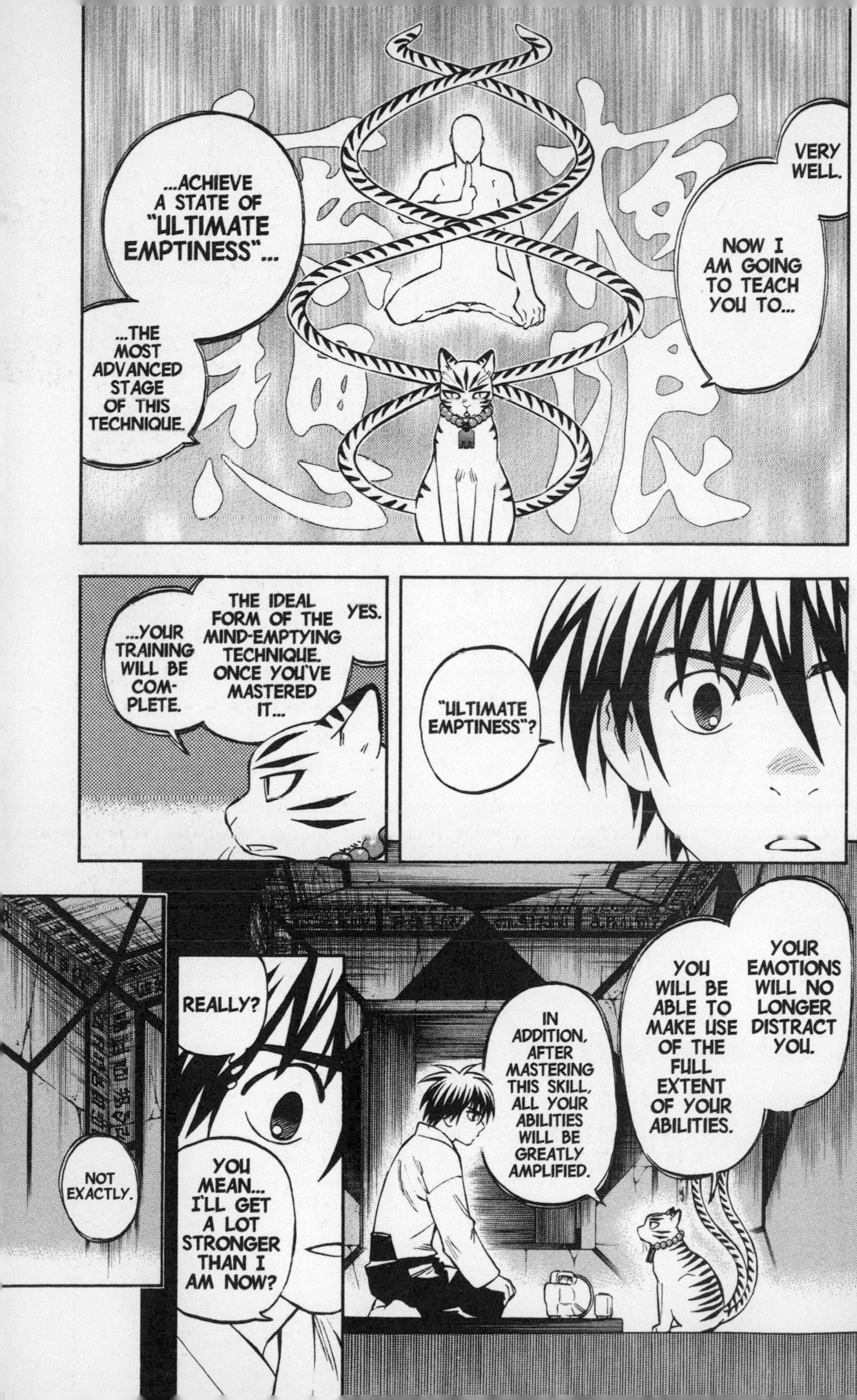
VERY WELL.
NOW I AM GOING TO TEACH YOU TO...
...ACHIEVE A STATE OF "ULTIMATE EMPTINESS"...
...THE MOST ADVANCED STAGE OF THIS TECHNIQUE.
"ULTIMATE EMPTINESS"?
YES.
THE IDEAL FORM OF THE MIND-EMPTYING TECHNIQUE. ONCE YOU'VE MASTERED IT...
...YOUR TRAINING WILL BE COMPLETE.
YOUR EMOTIONS WILL NO LONGER DISTRACT YOU.
YOU WILL BE ABLE TO MAKE USE OF THE FULL EXTENT OF YOUR ABILITIES.
IN ADDITION, AFTER MASTERING THIS SKILL, ALL YOUR ABILITIES WILL BE GREATLY AMPLIFIED.
REALLY?
YOU MEAN... I'LL GET A LOT STRONGER THAN I AM NOW?
NOT EXACTLY.

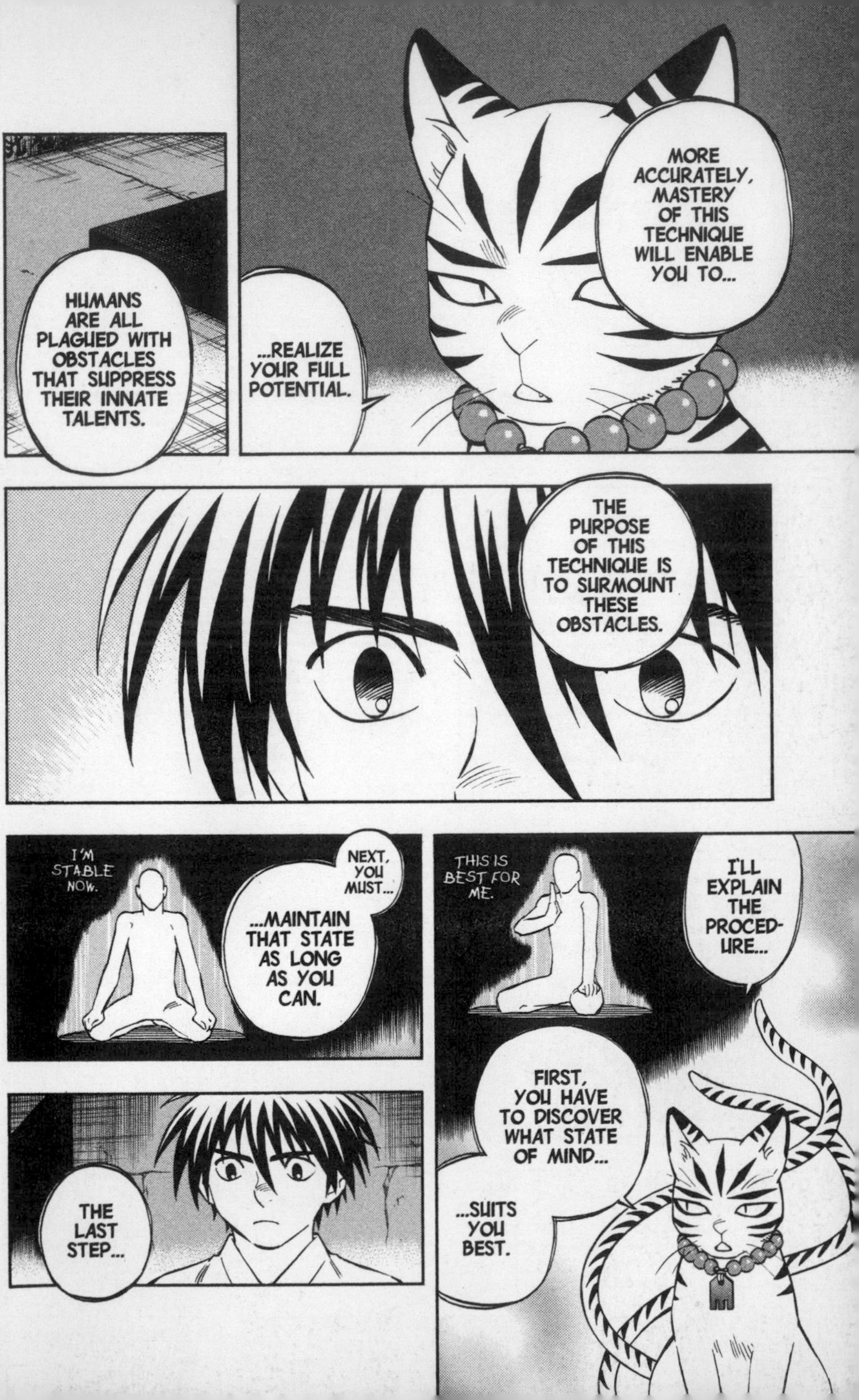
MORE ACCURATELY, MASTERY OF THIS TECHNIQUE WILL ENABLE YOU TO...
...REALIZE YOUR FULL POTENTIAL.
HUMANS ARE ALL PLAGUED WITH OBSTACLES THAT SUPPRESS THEIR INNATE TALENTS.
THE PURPOSE OF THIS TECHNIQUE IS TO SURMOUNT THESE OBSTACLES.
I'LL EXPLAIN THE PROCEDURE...
THIS IS BEST FOR ME.
FIRST, YOU HAVE TO DISCOVER WHAT STATE OF MIND...
...SUITS YOU BEST.
NEXT, YOU MUST...
...MAINTAIN THAT STATE AS LONG AS YOU CAN.
I'M STABLE NOW.
THE LAST STEP...

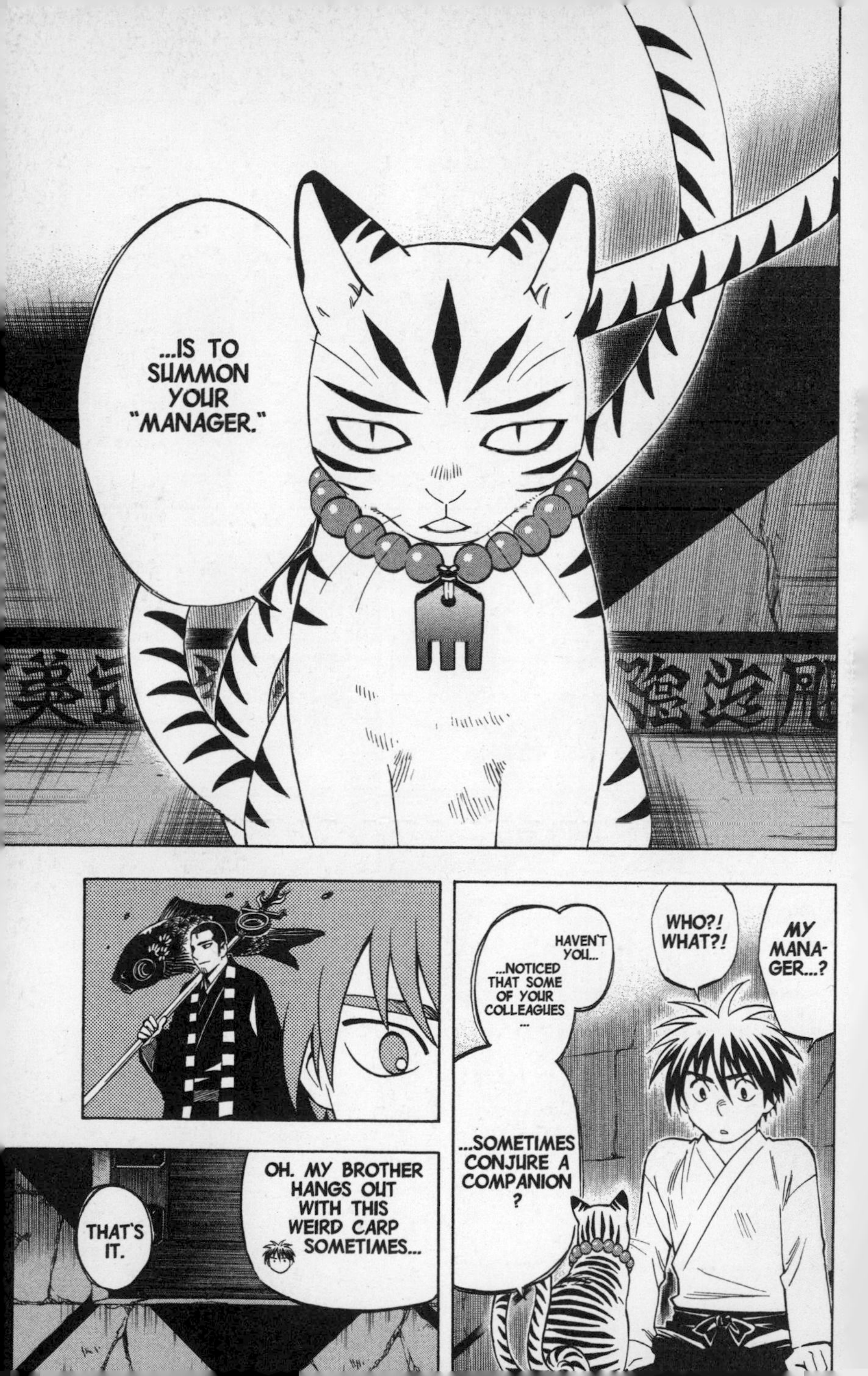
...IS TO SUMMON YOUR "MANAGER."
MY MANA-GER...?
WHO?! WHAT?!
HAVEN'T YOU... ...NOTICED THAT SOME OF YOUR COLLEAGUES ...
...SOMETIMES CONJURE A COMPANION ?
OH. MY BROTHER HANGS OUT WITH THIS WEIRD CARP SOMETIMES...
THAT'S IT.

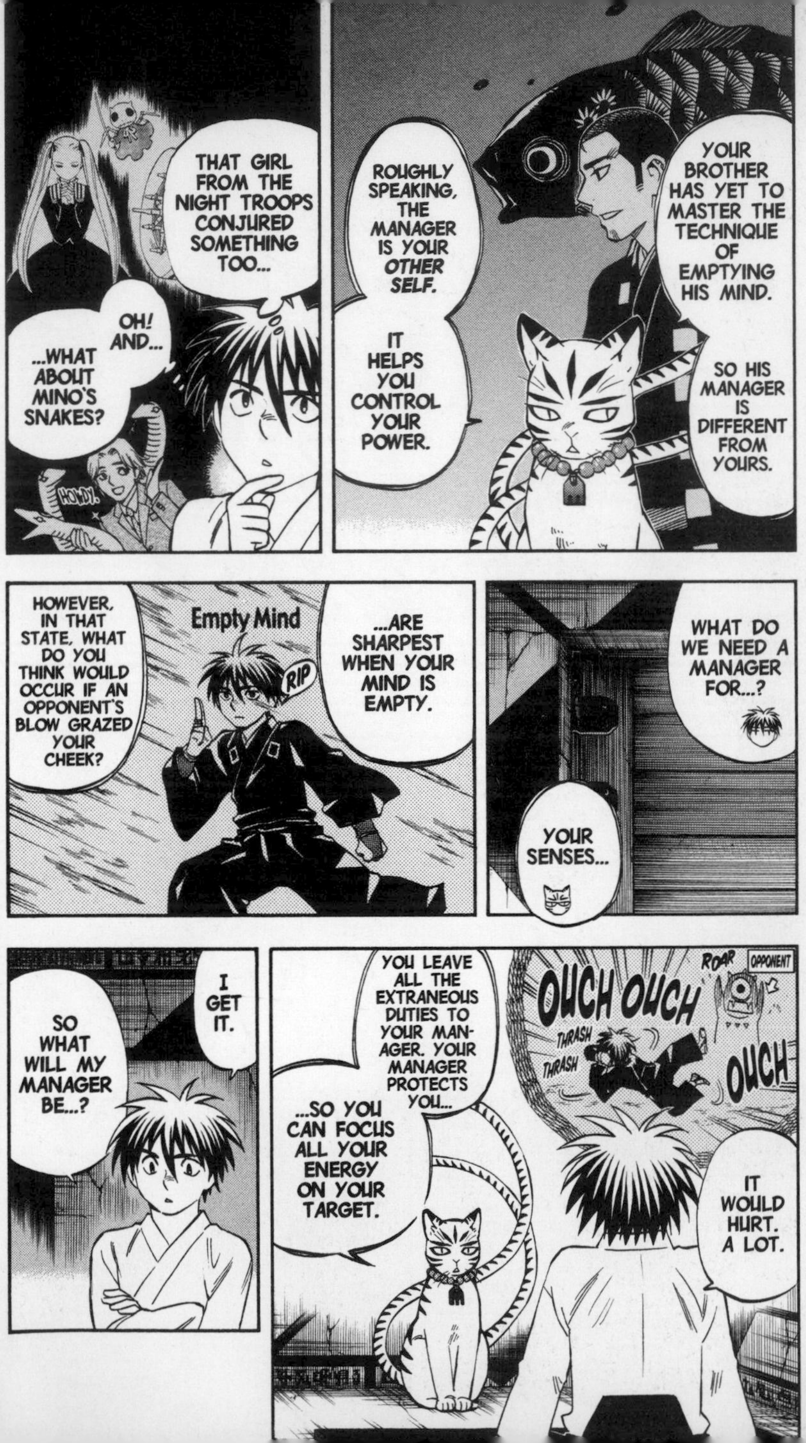
YOUR BROTHER HAS YET TO MASTER THE TECHNIQUE OF EMPTYING HIS MIND.
SO HIS MANAGER IS DIFFERENT FROM YOURS.
ROUGHLY SPEAKING, THE MANAGER IS YOUR *OTHER SELF.*
IT HELPS YOU CONTROL YOUR POWER.
THAT GIRL FROM THE NIGHT TROOPS CONJURED SOMETHING TOO...
OH! AND...
...WHAT ABOUT MINO'S SNAKES?
HOWDY.
WHAT DO WE NEED A MANAGER FOR...?
YOUR SENSES...
...ARE SHARPEST WHEN YOUR MIND IS EMPTY.
Empty Mind
RIP
HOWEVER, IN THAT STATE, WHAT DO YOU THINK WOULD OCCUR IF AN OPPONENT'S BLOW GRAZED YOUR CHEEK?
IT WOULD HURT. A LOT.
ROAR
OPPONENT
OUCH OUCH
THRASH
THRASH
OUCH
YOU LEAVE ALL THE EXTRANEOUS DUTIES TO YOUR MANAGER. YOUR MANAGER PROTECTS YOU...
...SO YOU CAN FOCUS ALL YOUR ENERGY ON YOUR TARGET.
I GET IT.
SO WHAT WILL MY MANAGER BE...?

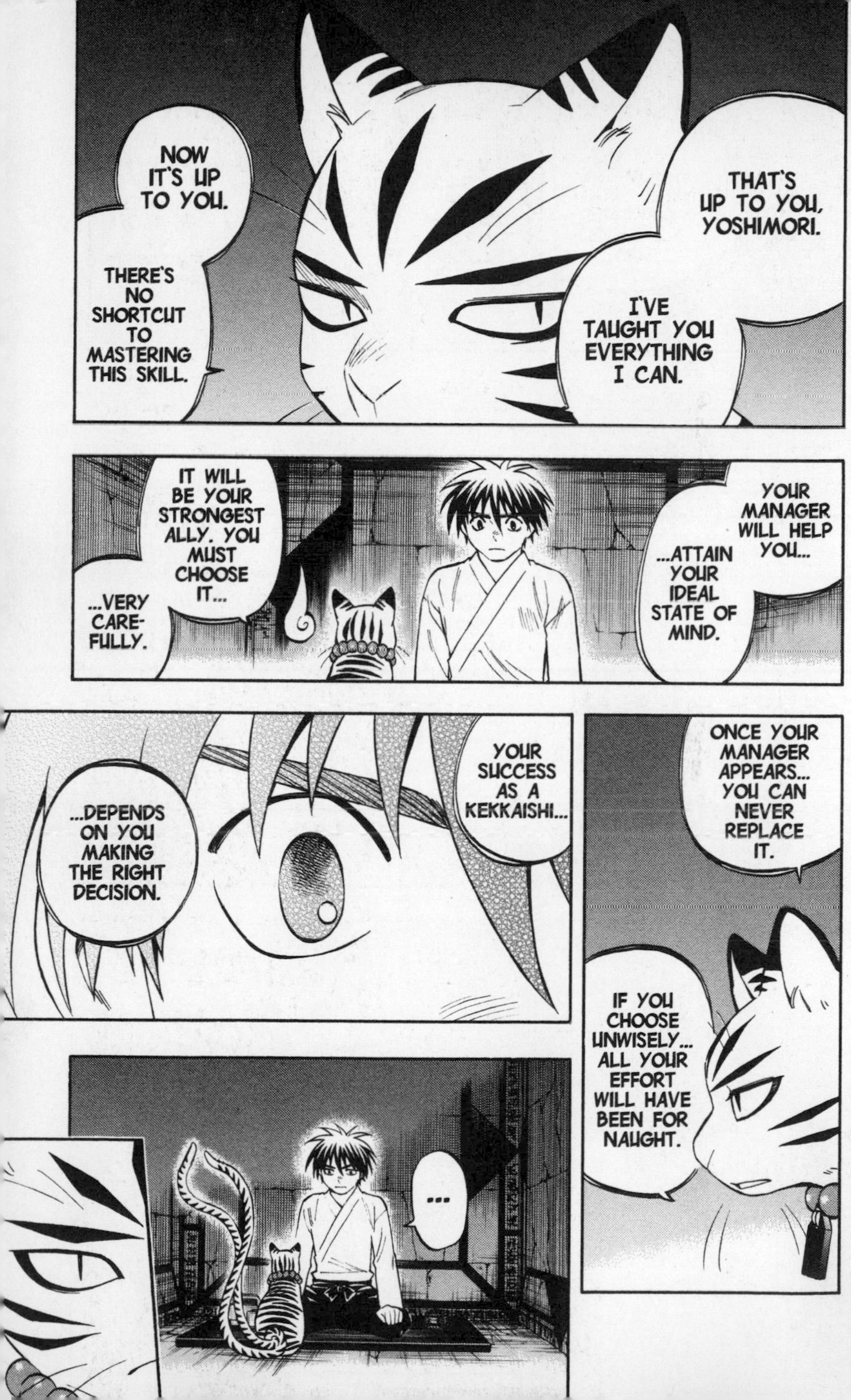
THAT'S UP TO YOU, YOSHIMORI.
I'VE TAUGHT YOU EVERYTHING I CAN.
NOW IT'S UP TO YOU.
THERE'S NO SHORTCUT TO MASTERING THIS SKILL.
YOUR MANAGER WILL HELP YOU...
...ATTAIN YOUR IDEAL STATE OF MIND.
IT WILL BE YOUR STRONGEST ALLY. YOU MUST CHOOSE IT...
...VERY CARE-FULLY.
ONCE YOUR MANAGER APPEARS... YOU CAN NEVER REPLACE IT.
IF YOU CHOOSE UNWISELY... ALL YOUR EFFORT WILL HAVE BEEN FOR NAUGHT.
YOUR SUCCESS AS A KEKKAISHI...
...DEPENDS ON YOU MAKING THE RIGHT DECISION.
...

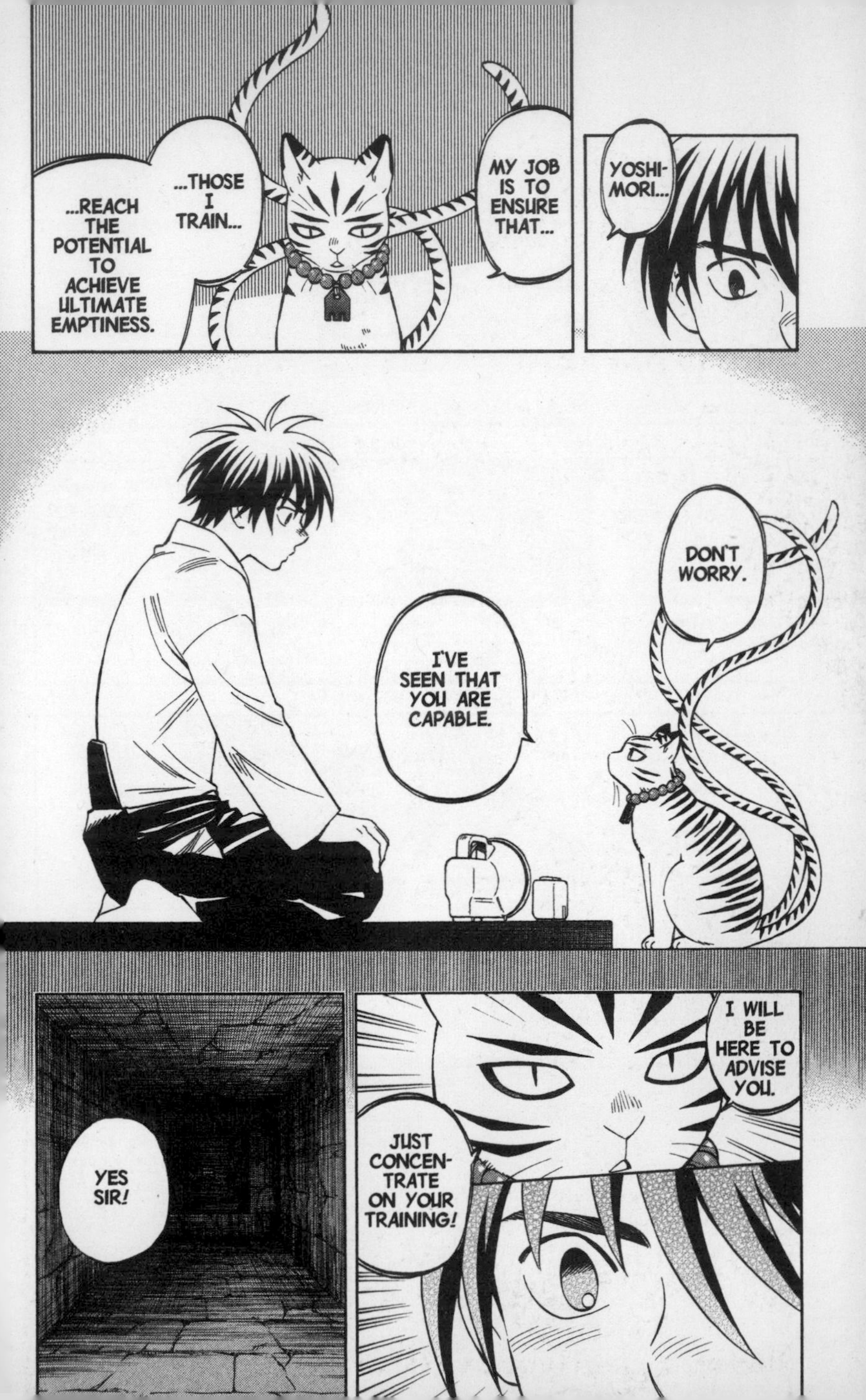
YOSHI-MORI...
MY JOB IS TO ENSURE THAT...
...THOSE I TRAIN...
...REACH THE POTENTIAL TO ACHIEVE ULTIMATE EMPTINESS.
DON'T WORRY.
I'VE SEEN THAT YOU ARE CAPABLE.
I WILL BE HERE TO ADVISE YOU.
JUST CONCEN-TRATE ON YOUR TRAINING!
YES SIR!

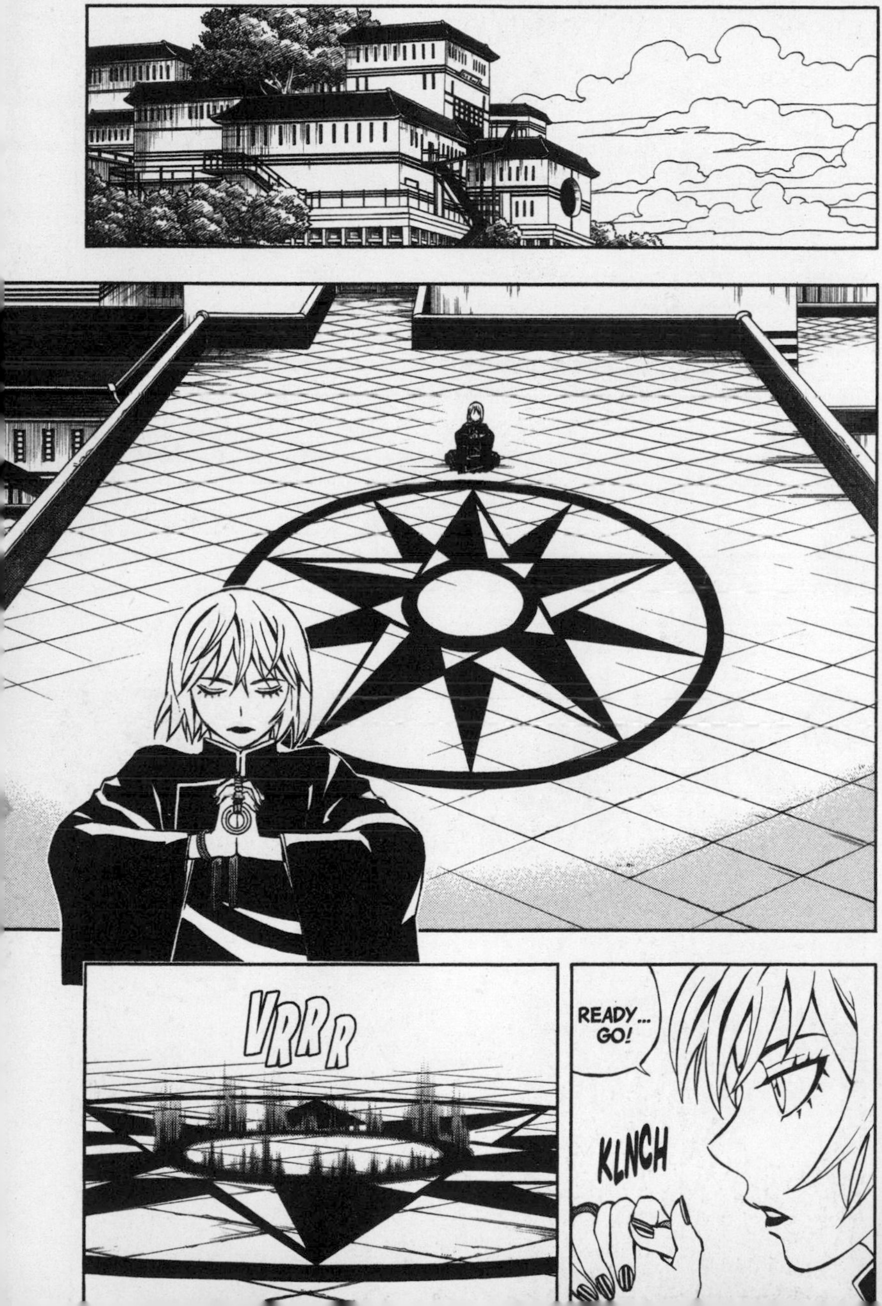
READY... GO!
KLNCH
VRRR

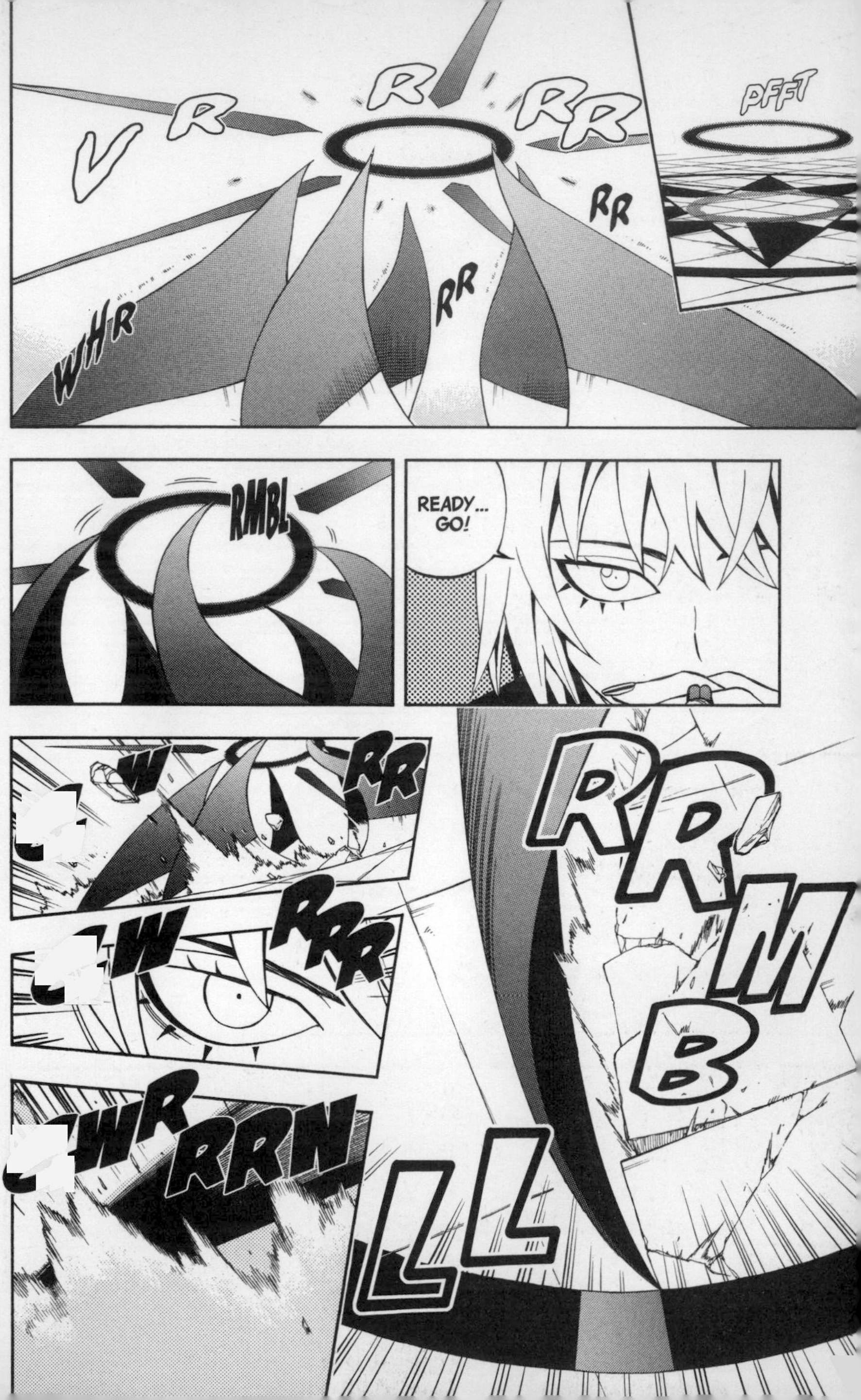
PFFT
V R R RR
RR
RR
WHR
READY... GO!
RMBL
RRRMBLL
W RR
W RRR
WR RRN

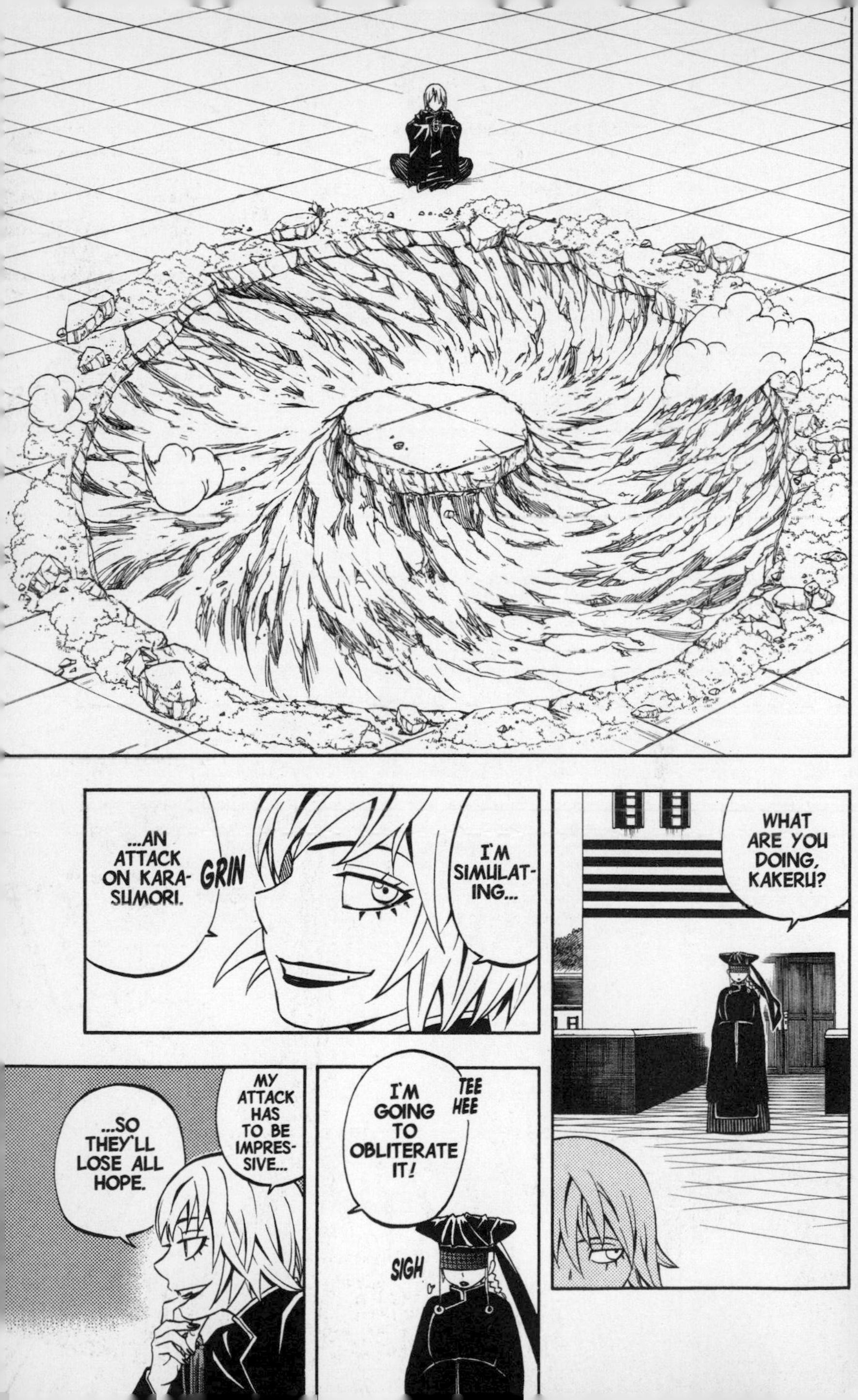
WHAT ARE YOU DOING, KAKERU?
I'M SIMULATING...
GRIN
...AN ATTACK ON KARASUMORI.
TEE HEE
I'M GOING TO OBLITERATE IT!
SIGH
MY ATTACK HAS TO BE IMPRESSIVE...
...SO THEY'LL LOSE ALL HOPE.

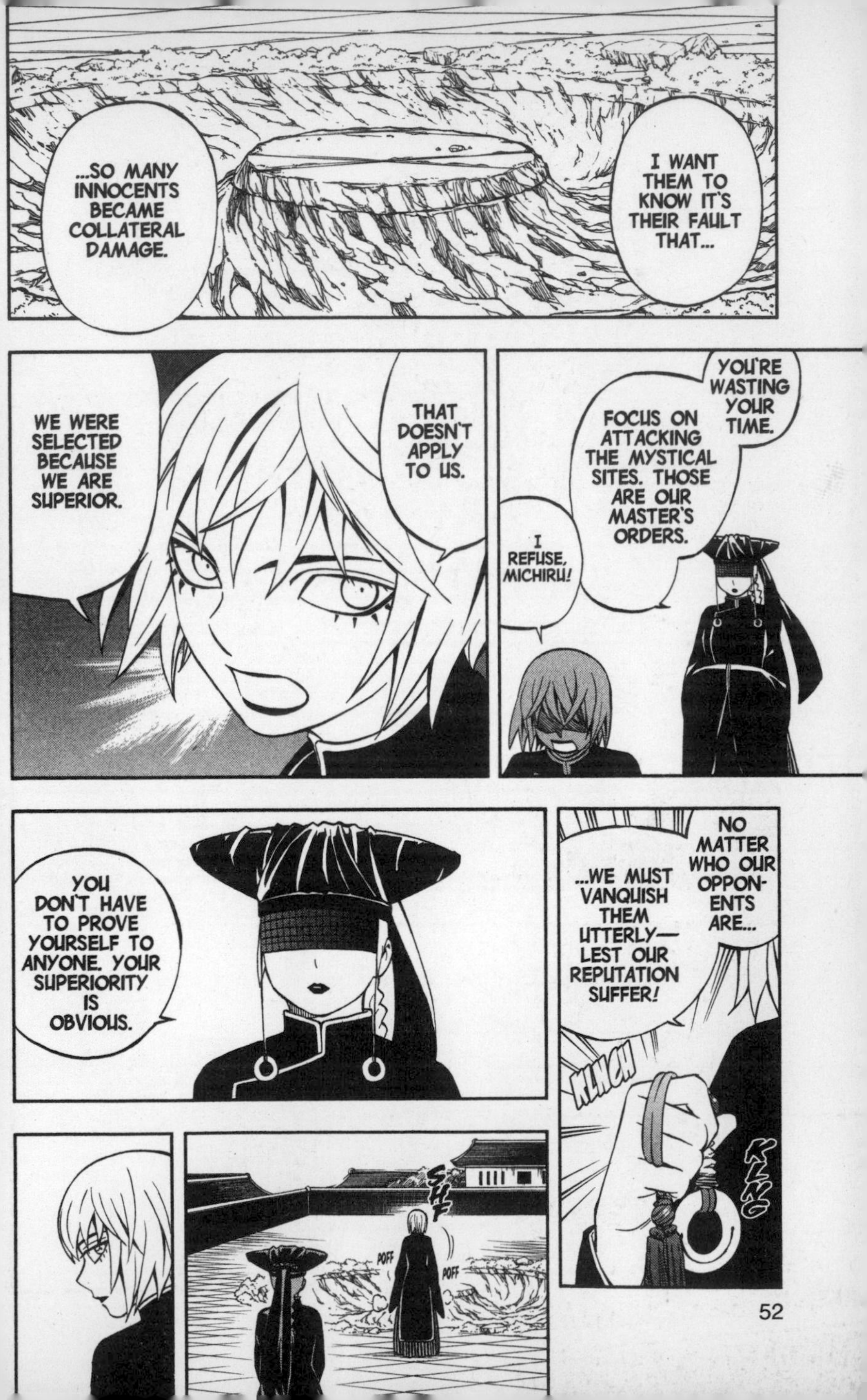
I WANT THEM TO KNOW IT'S THEIR FAULT THAT...
...SO MANY INNOCENTS BECAME COLLATERAL DAMAGE.
YOU'RE WASTING YOUR TIME.
FOCUS ON ATTACKING THE MYSTICAL SITES. THOSE ARE OUR MASTER'S ORDERS.
I REFUSE, MICHIRU!
THAT DOESN'T APPLY TO US.
WE WERE SELECTED BECAUSE WE ARE SUPERIOR.
NO MATTER WHO OUR OPPONENTS ARE...
...WE MUST VANQUISH THEM UTTERLY—LEST OUR REPUTATION SUFFER!
KLNCH
KLING
YOU DON'T HAVE TO PROVE YOURSELF TO ANYONE. YOUR SUPERIORITY IS OBVIOUS.
SHF
POFF
POFF

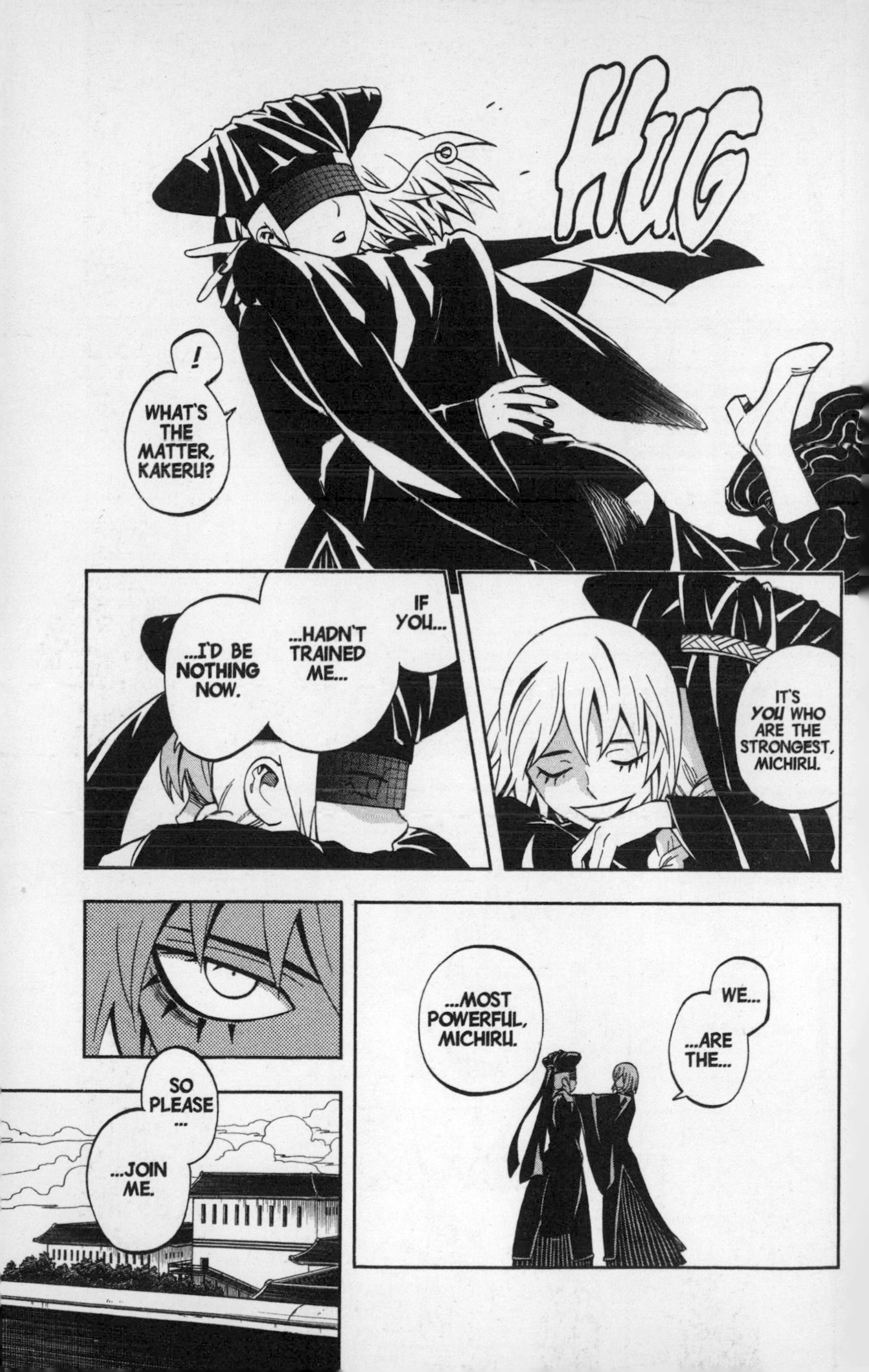
HUG
!
WHAT'S THE MATTER, KAKERU?
IT'S *YOU* WHO ARE THE STRONGEST, MICHIRU.
IF YOU...
...HADN'T TRAINED ME...
...I'D BE NOTHING NOW.
WE...
...ARE THE...
...MOST POWERFUL, MICHIRU.
SO PLEASE...
...JOIN ME.

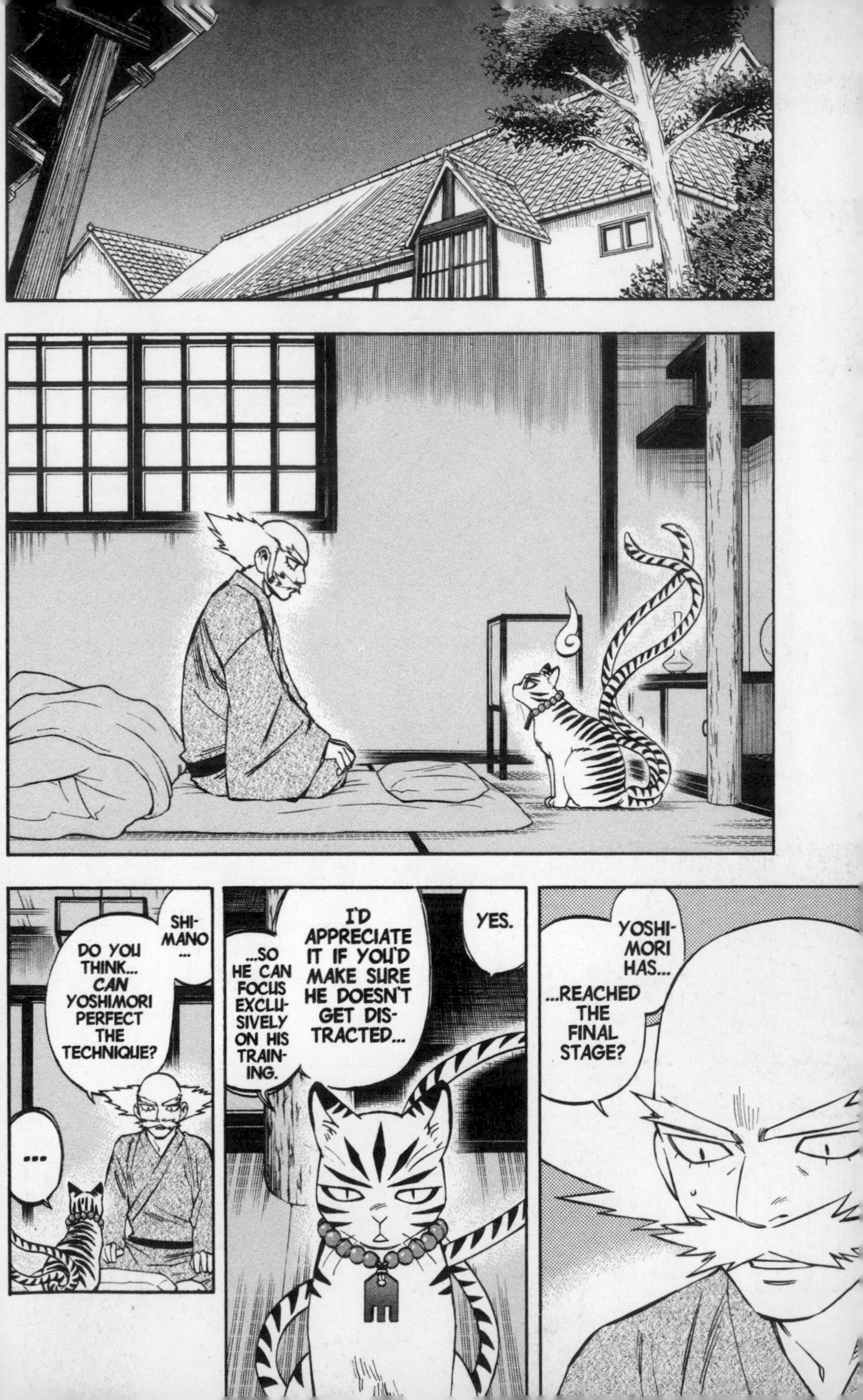
YOSHI-
MORI
HAS...
...REACHED THE FINAL STAGE?
YES.
I'D APPRECIATE IT IF YOU'D MAKE SURE HE DOESN'T GET DIS-
TRACTED...
...SO HE CAN FOCUS EXCLU-
SIVELY ON HIS TRAIN-
ING.
SHI-
MANO
...
DO YOU THINK... CAN YOSHIMORI PERFECT THE TECHNIQUE?
...

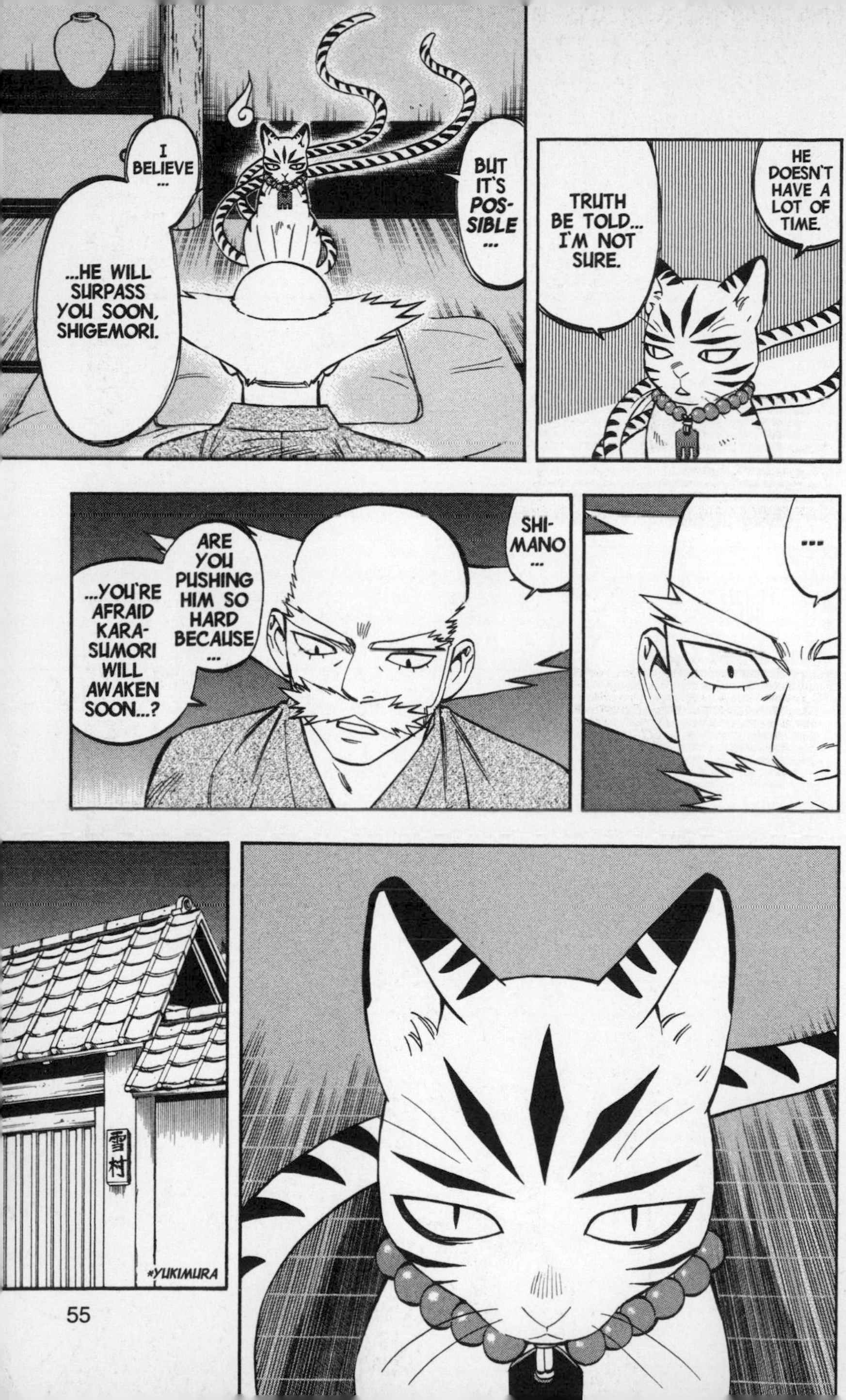
HE DOESN'T HAVE A LOT OF TIME.
TRUTH BE TOLD... I'M NOT SURE.
BUT IT'S POSSIBLE...
I BELIEVE...
...HE WILL SURPASS YOU SOON, SHIGEMORI.
...
SHIMANO...
ARE YOU PUSHING HIM SO HARD BECAUSE...
...YOU'RE AFRAID KARASUMORI WILL AWAKEN SOON...?
雪村
*YUKIMURA

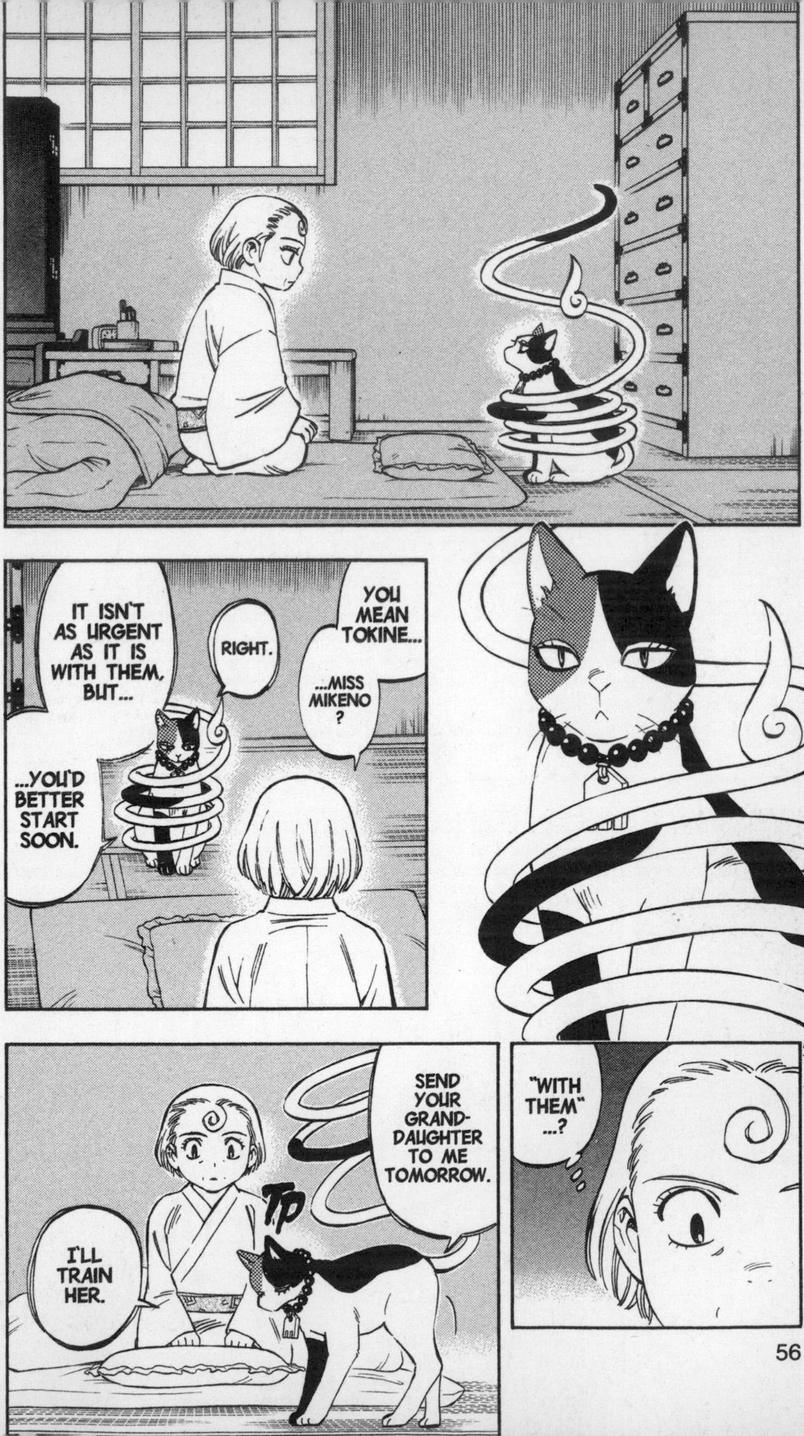
YOU MEAN TOKINE...
...MISS MIKENO?
RIGHT.
IT ISN'T AS URGENT AS IT IS WITH THEM, BUT...
...YOU'D BETTER START SOON.
"WITH THEM" ...?
SEND YOUR GRAND-DAUGHTER TO ME TOMORROW.
TP
I'LL TRAIN HER.

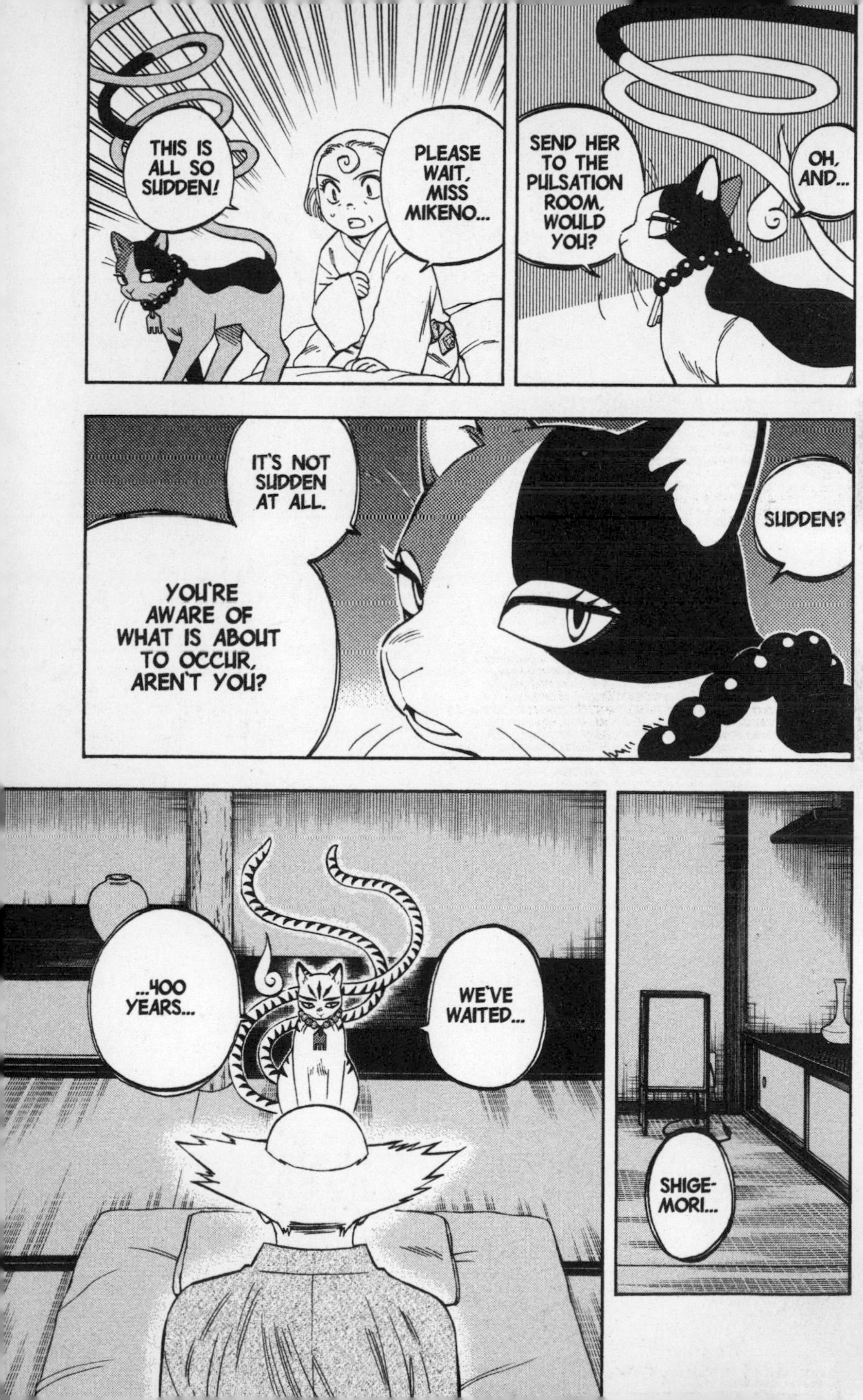
OH, AND...
SEND HER TO THE PULSATION ROOM, WOULD YOU?
PLEASE WAIT, MISS MIKENO...
THIS IS ALL SO SUDDEN!
SUDDEN?
IT'S NOT SUDDEN AT ALL.
YOU'RE AWARE OF WHAT IS ABOUT TO OCCUR, AREN'T YOU?
SHIGE-MORI...
WE'VE WAITED...
...400 YEARS...

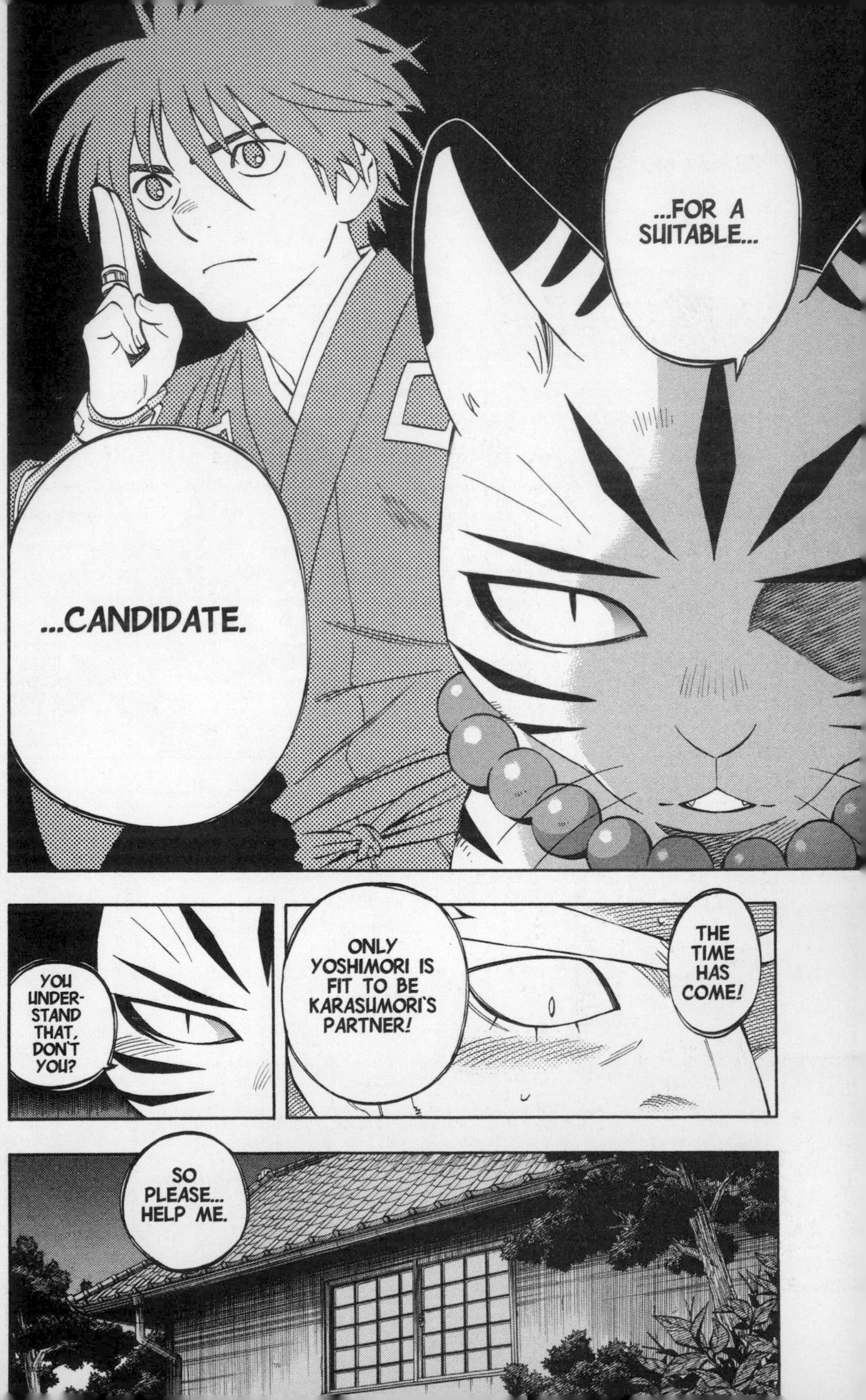
...FOR A SUITABLE...
...CANDIDATE.
THE TIME HAS COME!
ONLY YOSHIMORI IS FIT TO BE KARASUMORI'S PARTNER!
YOU UNDER-STAND THAT, DON'T YOU?
SO PLEASE... HELP ME.

Chapter 249: GRiM Reaper

VROOM

VROOM

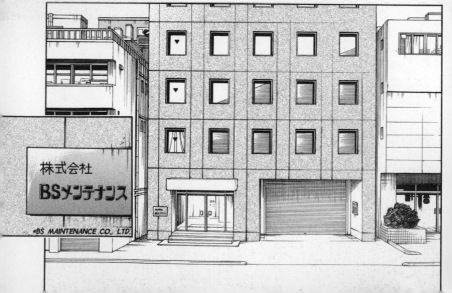

株式会社
BSメンテナンス

*BS MAINTENANCE .CO., LTD.

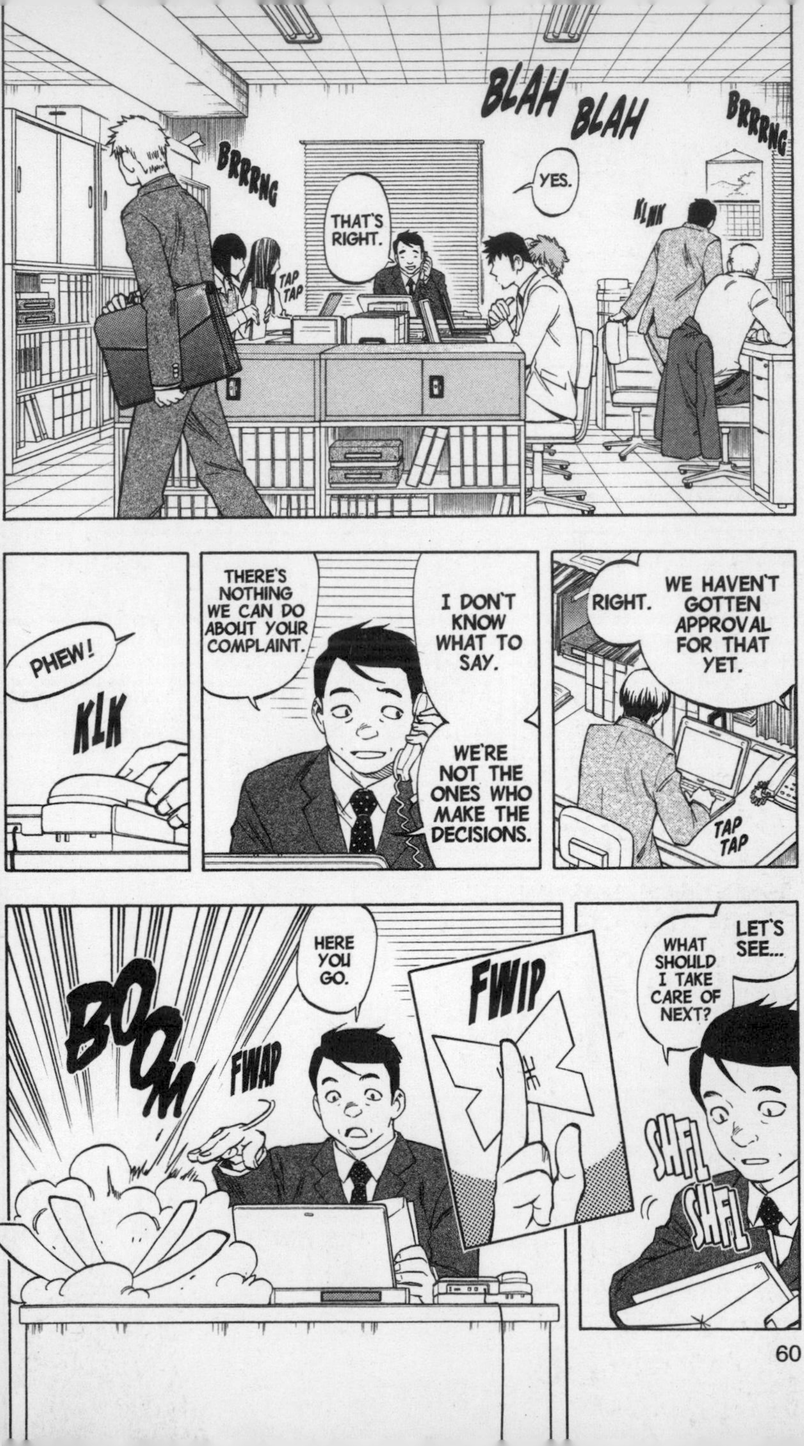
BRRRNG
KLNK
YES.
BLAH
BLAH
THAT'S RIGHT.
TAP TAP
BRRRNG
WE HAVEN'T GOTTEN APPROVAL FOR THAT YET.
RIGHT.
TAP TAP
I DON'T KNOW WHAT TO SAY.
THERE'S NOTHING WE CAN DO ABOUT YOUR COMPLAINT.
WE'RE NOT THE ONES WHO MAKE THE DECISIONS.
PHEW!
KLK
LET'S SEE...
WHAT SHOULD I TAKE CARE OF NEXT?
SHFL
SHFL
FWIP
HERE YOU GO.
FWAP
BOOM

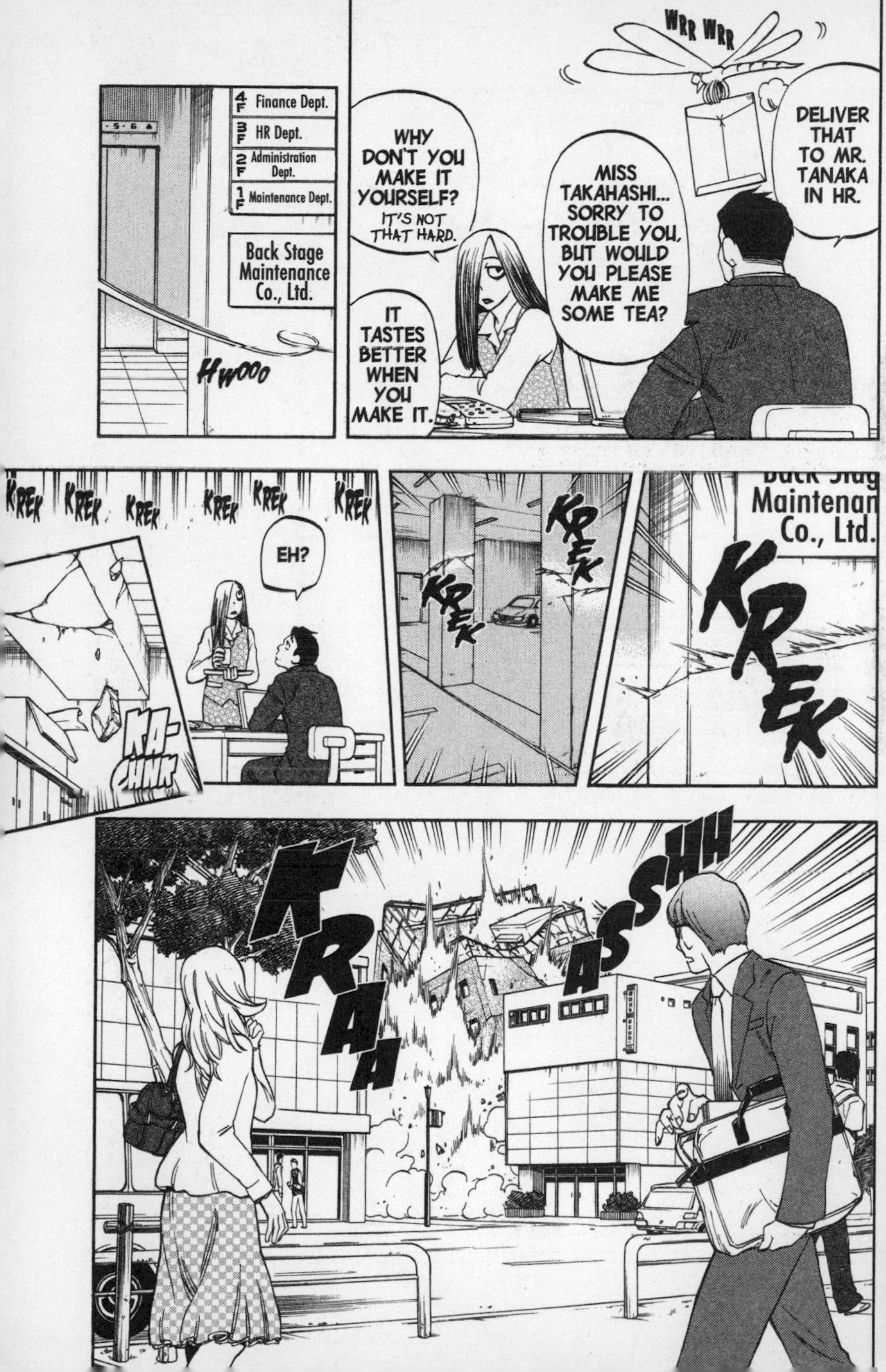
WRR WRR
DELIVER THAT TO MR. TANAKA IN HR.
MISS TAKAHASHI... SORRY TO TROUBLE YOU, BUT WOULD YOU PLEASE MAKE ME SOME TEA?
WHY DON'T YOU MAKE IT YOURSELF? IT'S NOT THAT HARD.
IT TASTES BETTER WHEN YOU MAKE IT.
4F Finance Dept.
3F HR Dept.
2F Administration Dept.
1F Maintenance Dept.
Back Stage Maintenance Co., Ltd.
HWOOO
Maintenan
Co., Ltd.
KREK
KREK
KREK
KREK KREK KREK KREK KREK KREK
EH?
KA-CHNK
KRAASSHH

Chapter 249: Grim Reaper

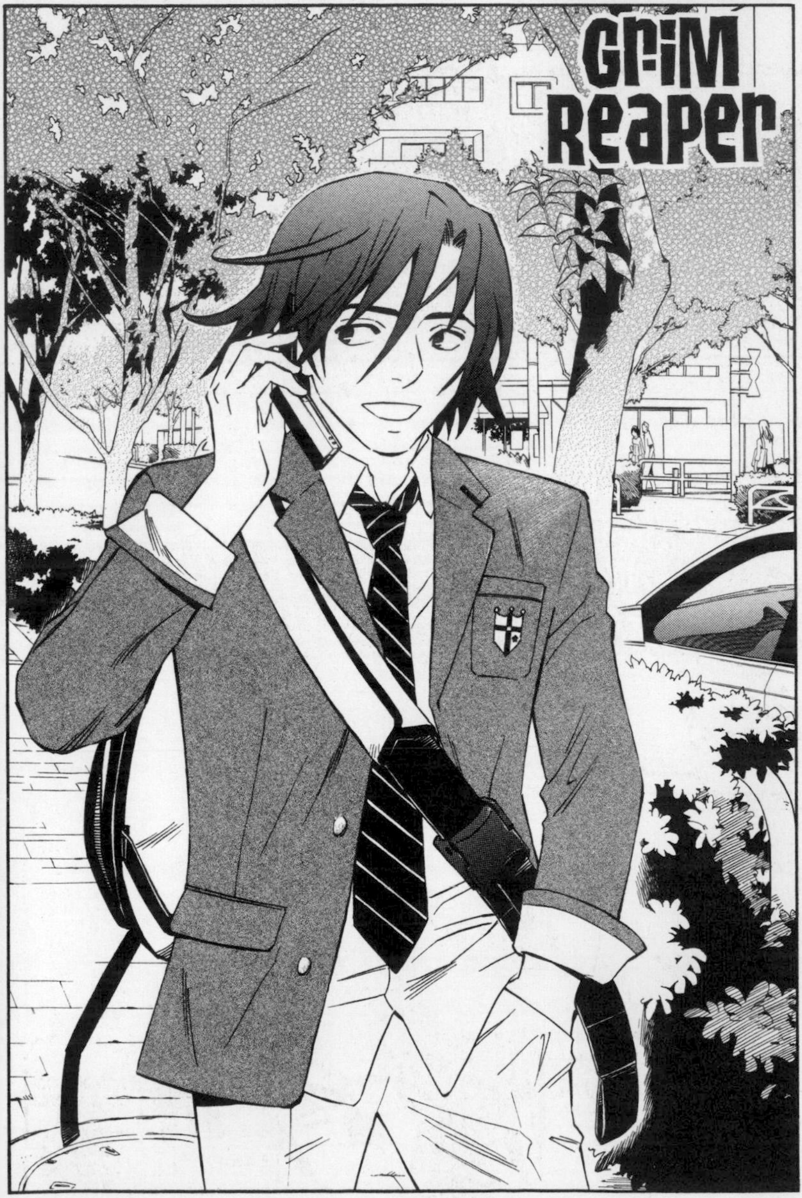

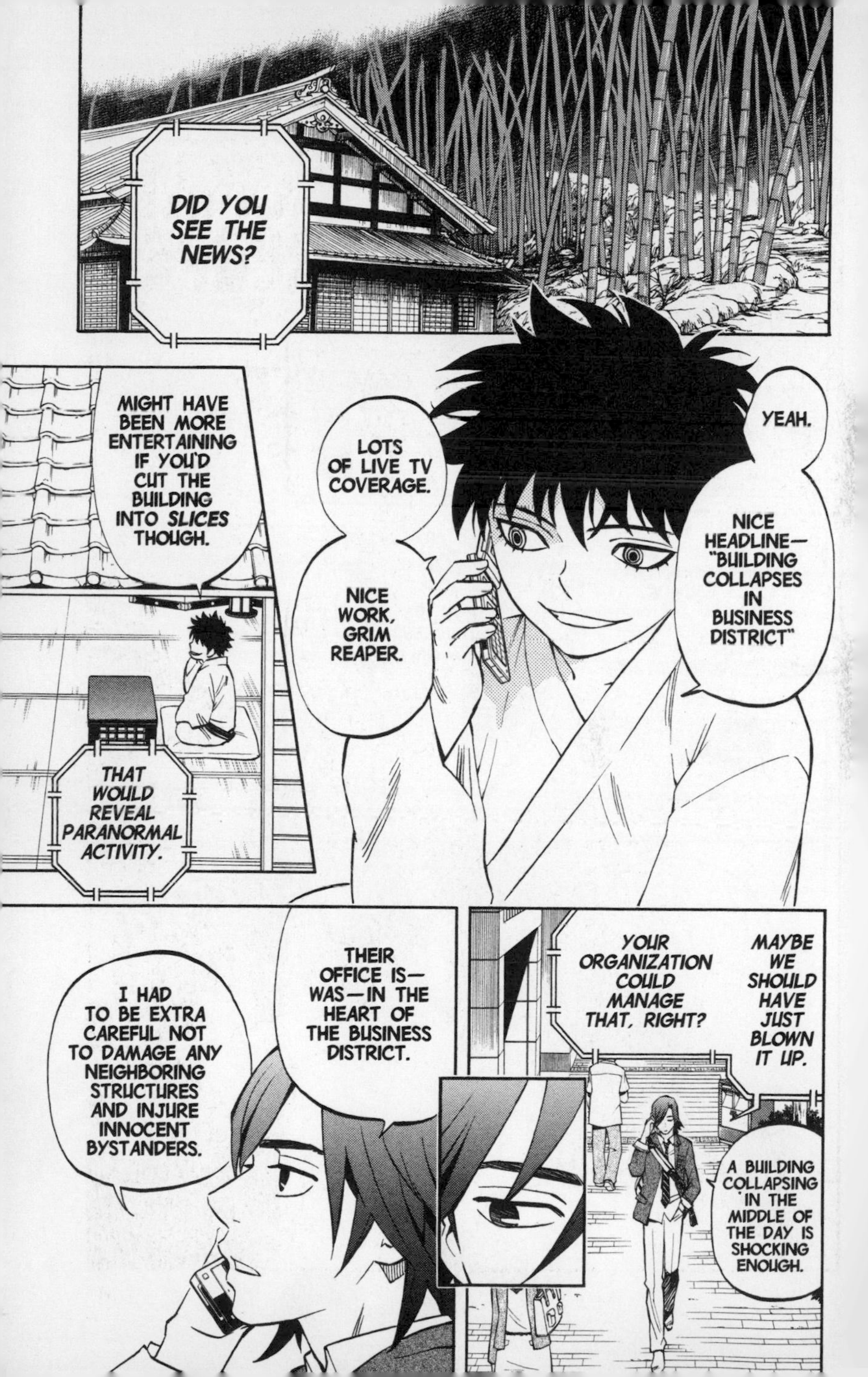
DID YOU SEE THE NEWS?
YEAH.
NICE HEADLINE— "BUILDING COLLAPSES IN BUSINESS DISTRICT"
LOTS OF LIVE TV COVERAGE.
NICE WORK, GRIM REAPER.
MIGHT HAVE BEEN MORE ENTERTAINING IF YOU'D CUT THE BUILDING INTO *SLICES* THOUGH.
THAT WOULD REVEAL PARANORMAL ACTIVITY.
MAYBE WE SHOULD HAVE JUST BLOWN IT UP.
YOUR ORGANIZATION COULD MANAGE THAT, RIGHT?
A BUILDING COLLAPSING IN THE MIDDLE OF THE DAY IS SHOCKING ENOUGH.
THEIR OFFICE IS—WAS—IN THE HEART OF THE BUSINESS DISTRICT.
I HAD TO BE EXTRA CAREFUL NOT TO DAMAGE ANY NEIGHBORING STRUCTURES AND INJURE INNOCENT BYSTANDERS.

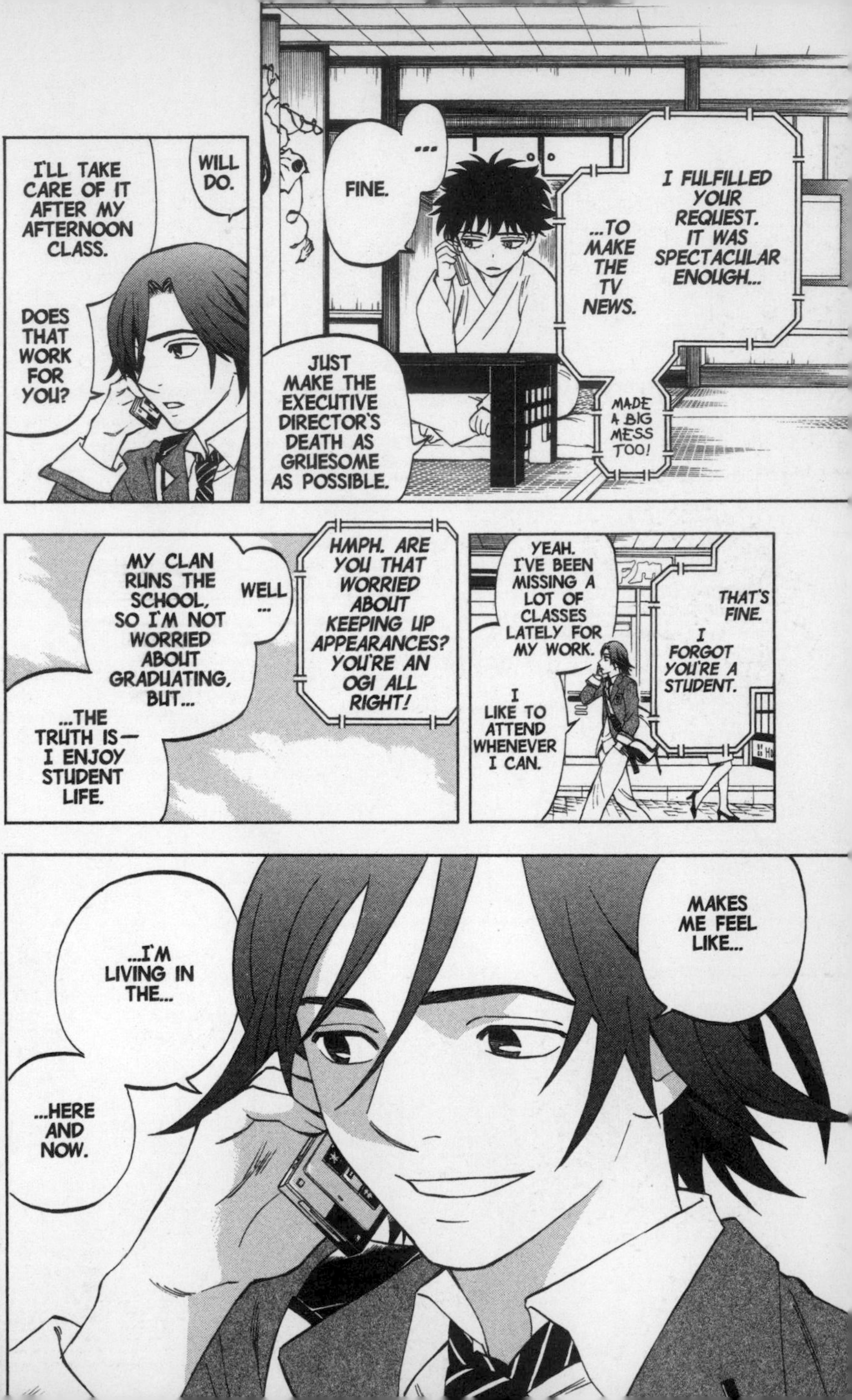
I FULFILLED YOUR REQUEST. IT WAS SPECTACULAR ENOUGH...
...TO MAKE THE TV NEWS.
MADE A BIG MESS TOO!
...
FINE.
JUST MAKE THE EXECUTIVE DIRECTOR'S DEATH AS GRUESOME AS POSSIBLE.
WILL DO.
I'LL TAKE CARE OF IT AFTER MY AFTERNOON CLASS.
DOES THAT WORK FOR YOU?
THAT'S FINE.
I FORGOT YOU'RE A STUDENT.
YEAH. I'VE BEEN MISSING A LOT OF CLASSES LATELY FOR MY WORK.
I LIKE TO ATTEND WHENEVER I CAN.
HMPH. ARE YOU THAT WORRIED ABOUT KEEPING UP APPEARANCES? YOU'RE AN OGI ALL RIGHT!
WELL...
MY CLAN RUNS THE SCHOOL, SO I'M NOT WORRIED ABOUT GRADUATING, BUT...
...THE TRUTH IS— I ENJOY STUDENT LIFE.
MAKES ME FEEL LIKE...
...I'M LIVING IN THE...
...HERE AND NOW.

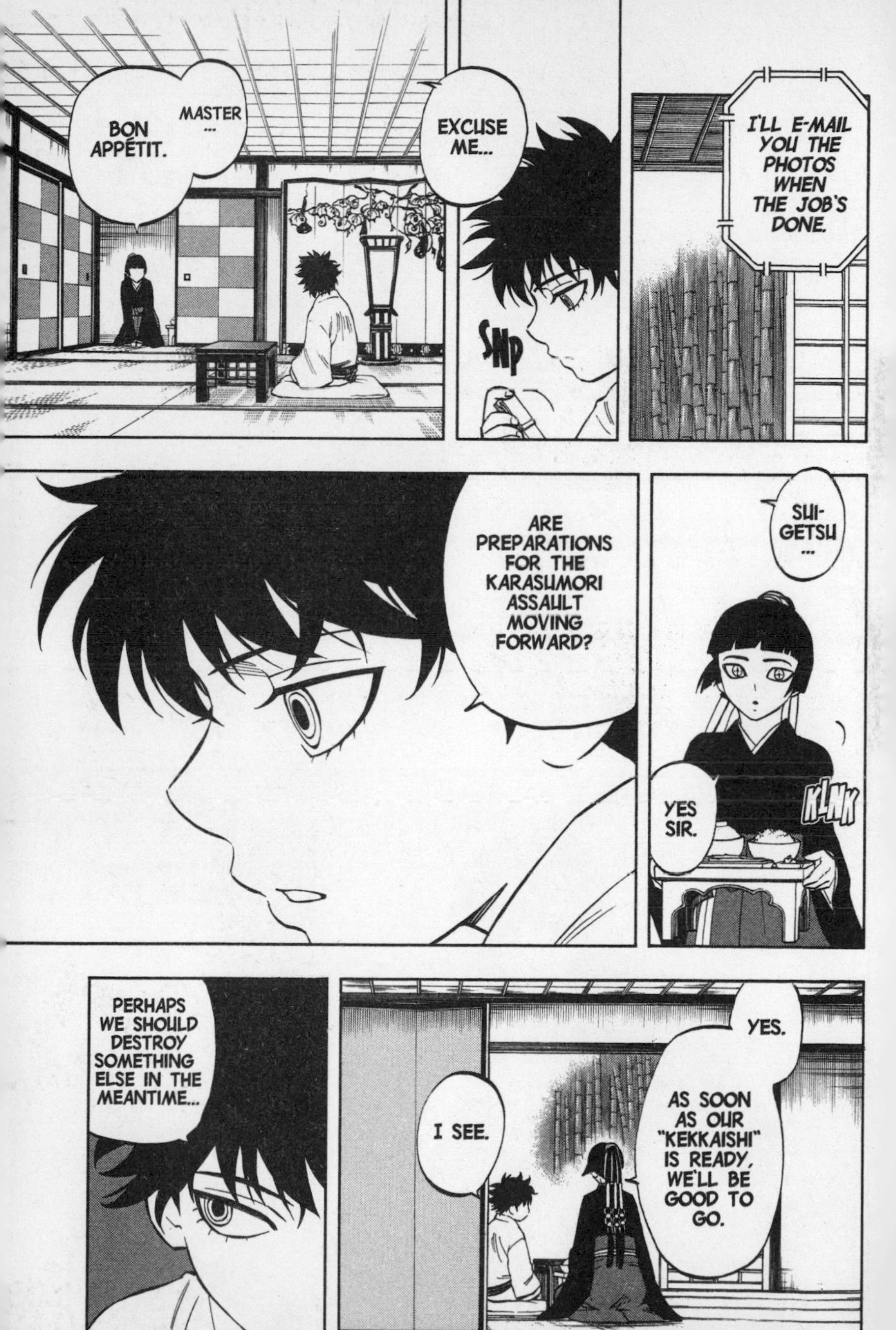
I'LL E-MAIL YOU THE PHOTOS WHEN THE JOB'S DONE.
EXCUSE ME...
SNP
MASTER ...
BON APPÉTIT.
SUI-GETSU ...
YES SIR.
KLINK
ARE PREPARATIONS FOR THE KARASUMORI ASSAULT MOVING FORWARD?
YES.
AS SOON AS OUR "KEKKAISHI" IS READY, WE'LL BE GOOD TO GO.
I SEE.
PERHAPS WE SHOULD DESTROY SOMETHING ELSE IN THE MEANTIME...

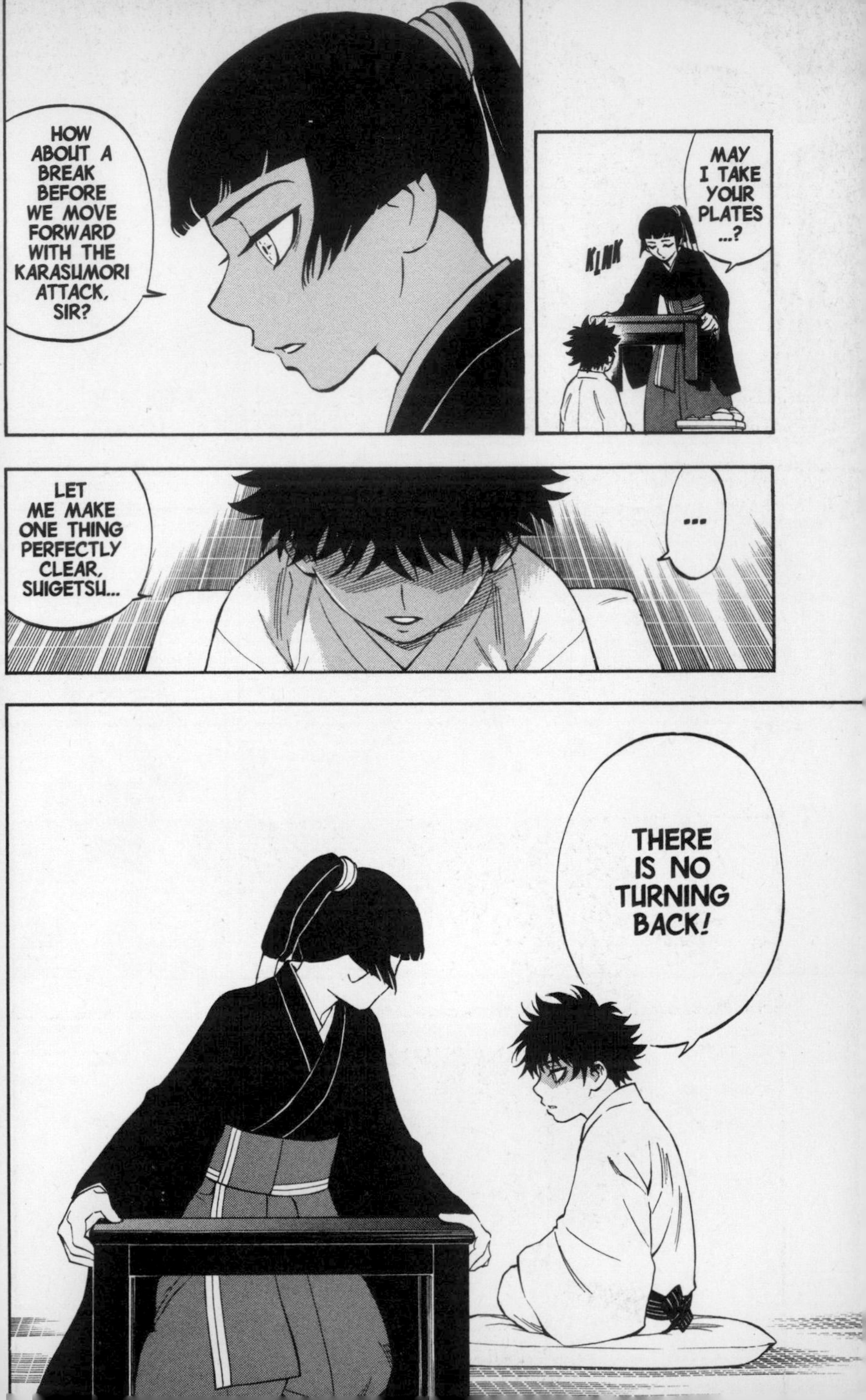
MAY I TAKE YOUR PLATES ...?
KLNK
HOW ABOUT A BREAK BEFORE WE MOVE FORWARD WITH THE KARASUMORI ATTACK, SIR?
...
LET ME MAKE ONE THING PERFECTLY CLEAR, SHIGETSU...
THERE IS NO TURNING BACK!

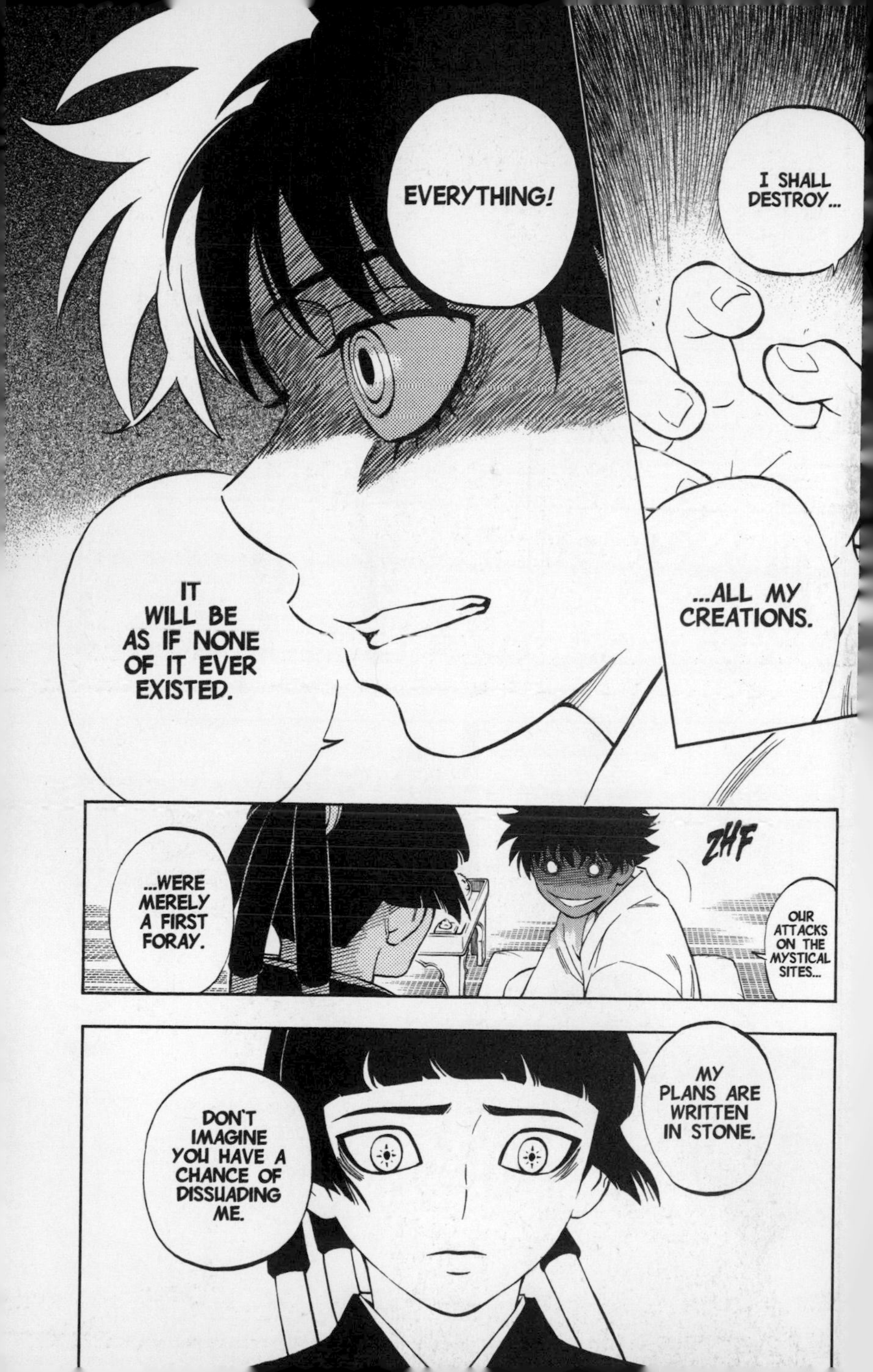
I SHALL DESTROY...
...ALL MY CREATIONS.
EVERYTHING!
IT WILL BE AS IF NONE OF IT EVER EXISTED.
ZHF
OUR ATTACKS ON THE MYSTICAL SITES...
...WERE MERELY A FIRST FORAY.
MY PLANS ARE WRITTEN IN STONE.
DON'T IMAGINE YOU HAVE A CHANCE OF DISSUADING ME.

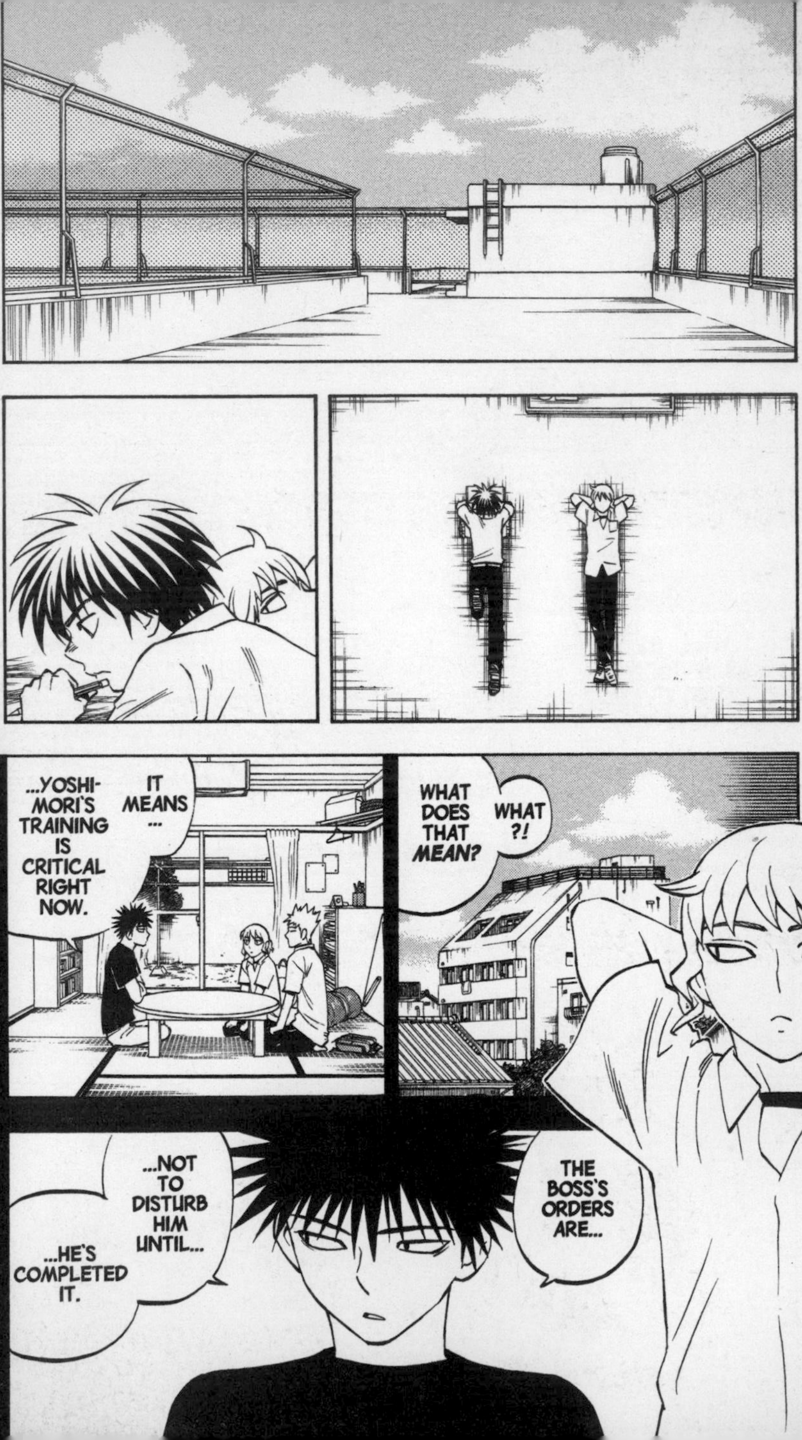
WHAT?!
WHAT DOES THAT *MEAN?*
IT MEANS...
...YOSHIMORI'S TRAINING IS CRITICAL RIGHT NOW.
THE BOSS'S ORDERS ARE...
...NOT TO DISTURB HIM UNTIL...
...HE'S COMPLETED IT.

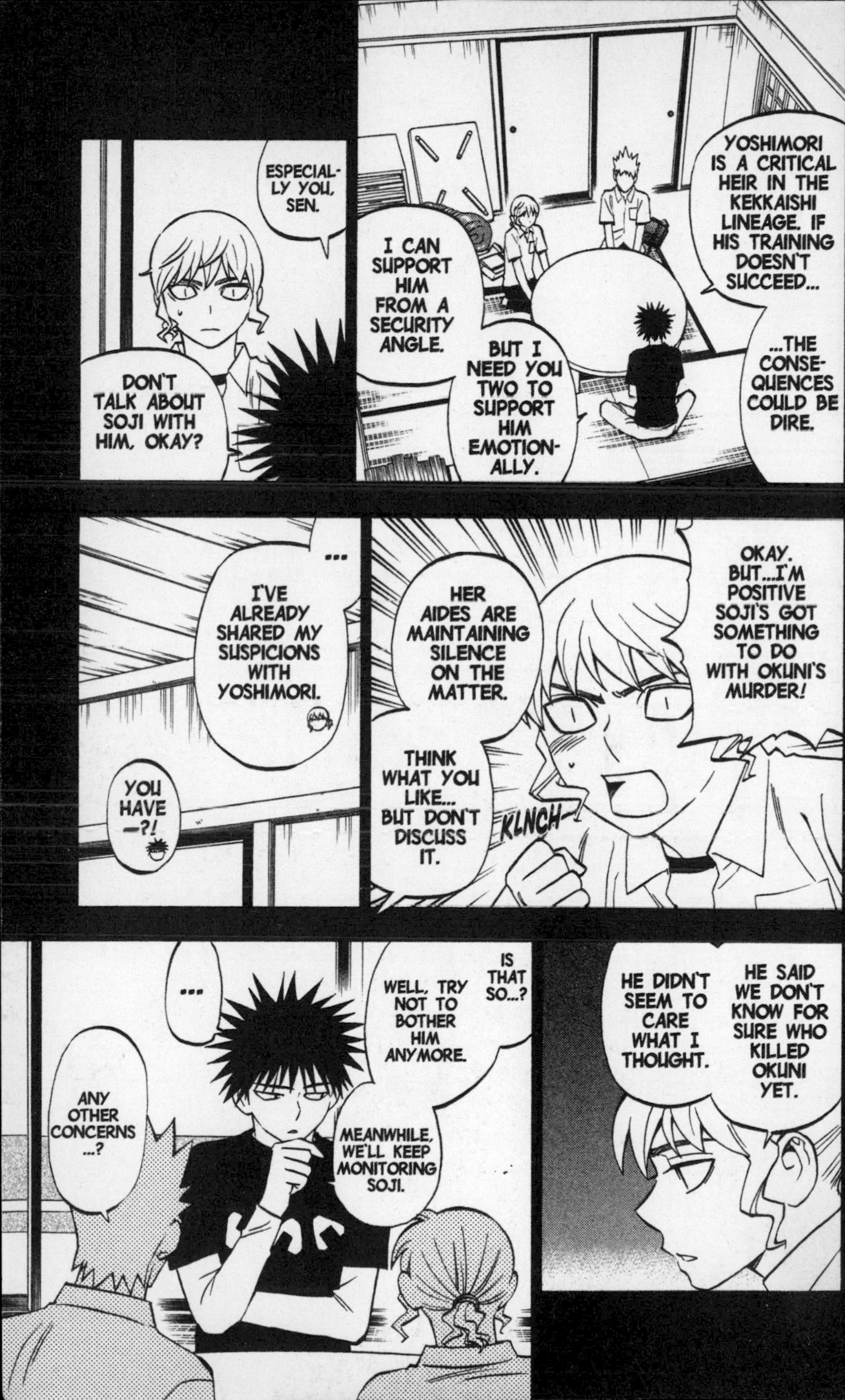
YOSHIMORI IS A CRITICAL HEIR IN THE KEKKAISHI LINEAGE. IF HIS TRAINING DOESN'T SUCCEED...
...THE CONSEQUENCES COULD BE DIRE.
I CAN SUPPORT HIM FROM A SECURITY ANGLE.
BUT I NEED YOU TWO TO SUPPORT HIM EMOTIONALLY.
ESPECIALLY YOU, SEN.
DON'T TALK ABOUT SOJI WITH HIM, OKAY?
OKAY. BUT...I'M POSITIVE SOJI'S GOT SOMETHING TO DO WITH OKUNI'S MURDER!
HER AIDES ARE MAINTAINING SILENCE ON THE MATTER.
KLNCH
THINK WHAT YOU LIKE... BUT DON'T DISCUSS IT.
...
I'VE ALREADY SHARED MY SUSPICIONS WITH YOSHIMORI.
YOU HAVE—?!
HE SAID WE DON'T KNOW FOR SURE WHO KILLED OKUNI YET.
HE DIDN'T SEEM TO CARE WHAT I THOUGHT.
IS THAT SO...?
WELL, TRY NOT TO BOTHER HIM ANYMORE.
...
MEANWHILE, WE'LL KEEP MONITORING SOJI.
ANY OTHER CONCERNS...?

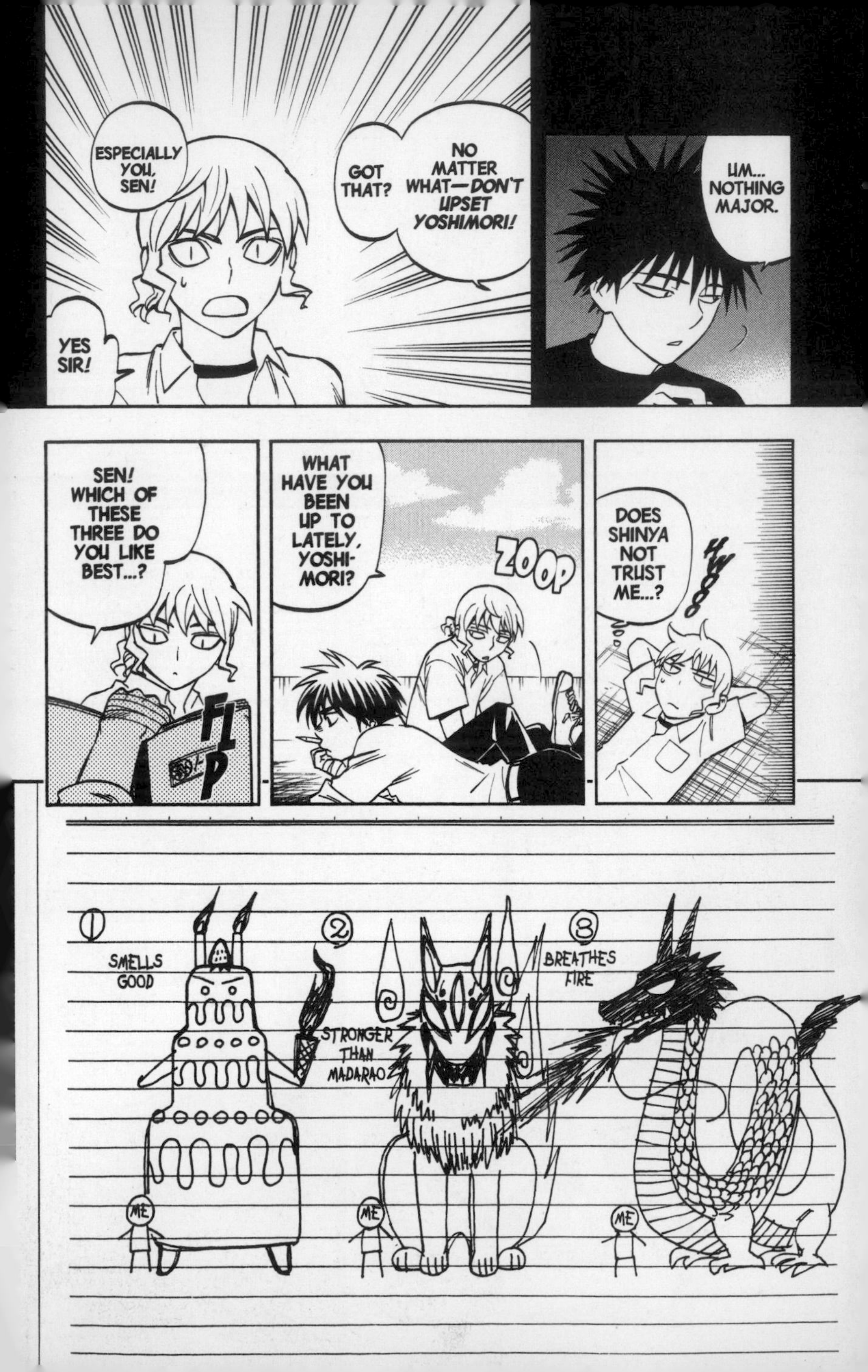
UM... NOTHING MAJOR.
NO MATTER WHAT—DON'T UPSET YOSHIMORI!
GOT THAT?
ESPECIALLY YOU, SEN!
YES SIR!
DOES SHINYA NOT TRUST ME...?
HWOOO
ZOOP
WHAT HAVE YOU BEEN UP TO LATELY, YOSHI-MORI?
SEN! WHICH OF THESE THREE DO YOU LIKE BEST...?
FLIP
3
BREATHES FIRE
ME
2
STRONGER THAN MADARAO
ME
1
SMELLS GOOD
ME

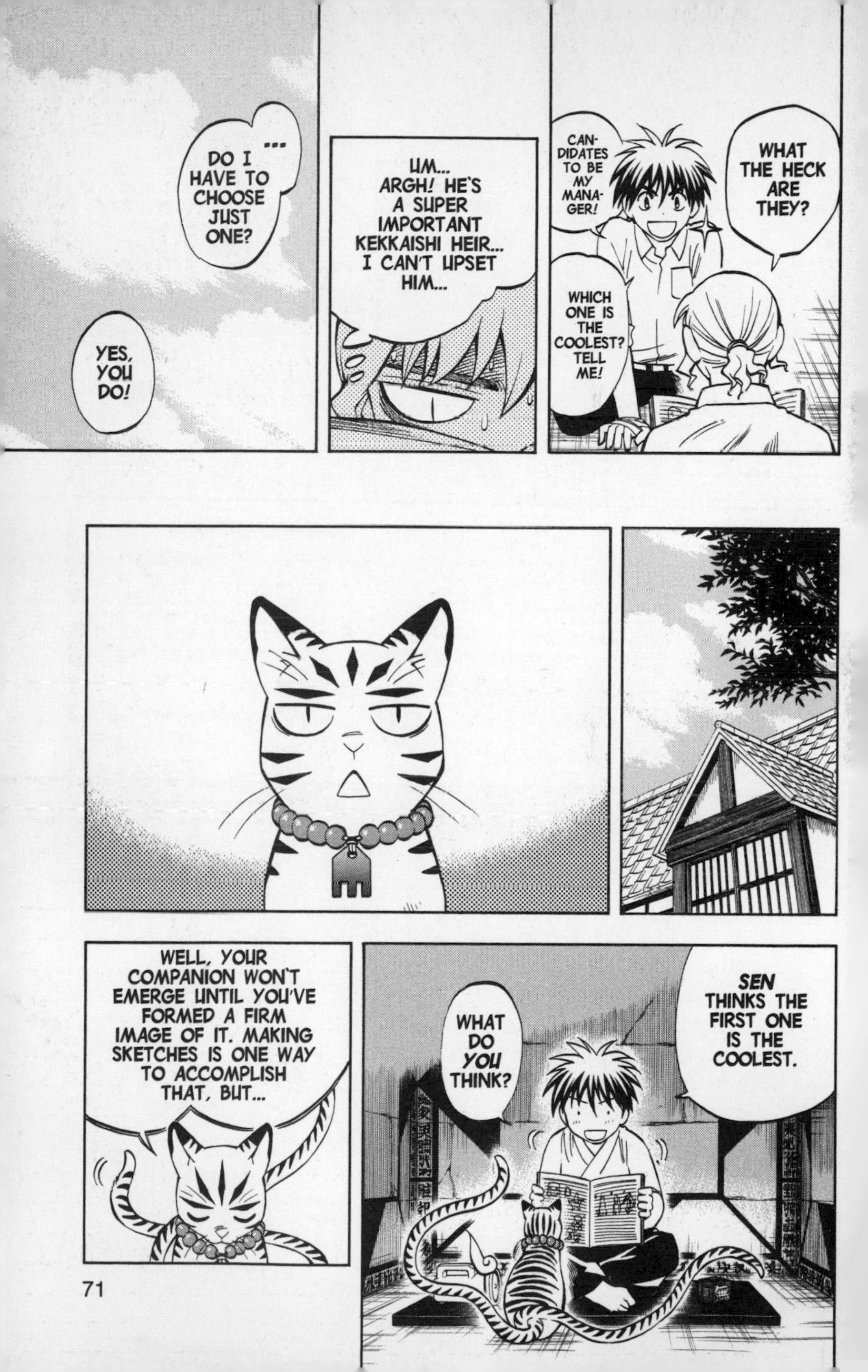
WHAT THE HECK ARE THEY?
CAN-DIDATES TO BE MY MANA-GER!
WHICH ONE IS THE COOLEST? TELL ME!
UM... ARGH! HE'S A SUPER IMPORTANT KEKKAISHI HEIR... I CAN'T UPSET HIM...
... DO I HAVE TO CHOOSE JUST ONE?
YES, YOU DO!
SEN THINKS THE FIRST ONE IS THE COOLEST.
WHAT DO *YOU* THINK?
WELL, YOUR COMPANION WON'T EMERGE UNTIL YOU'VE FORMED A FIRM IMAGE OF IT. MAKING SKETCHES IS ONE WAY TO ACCOMPLISH THAT, BUT...

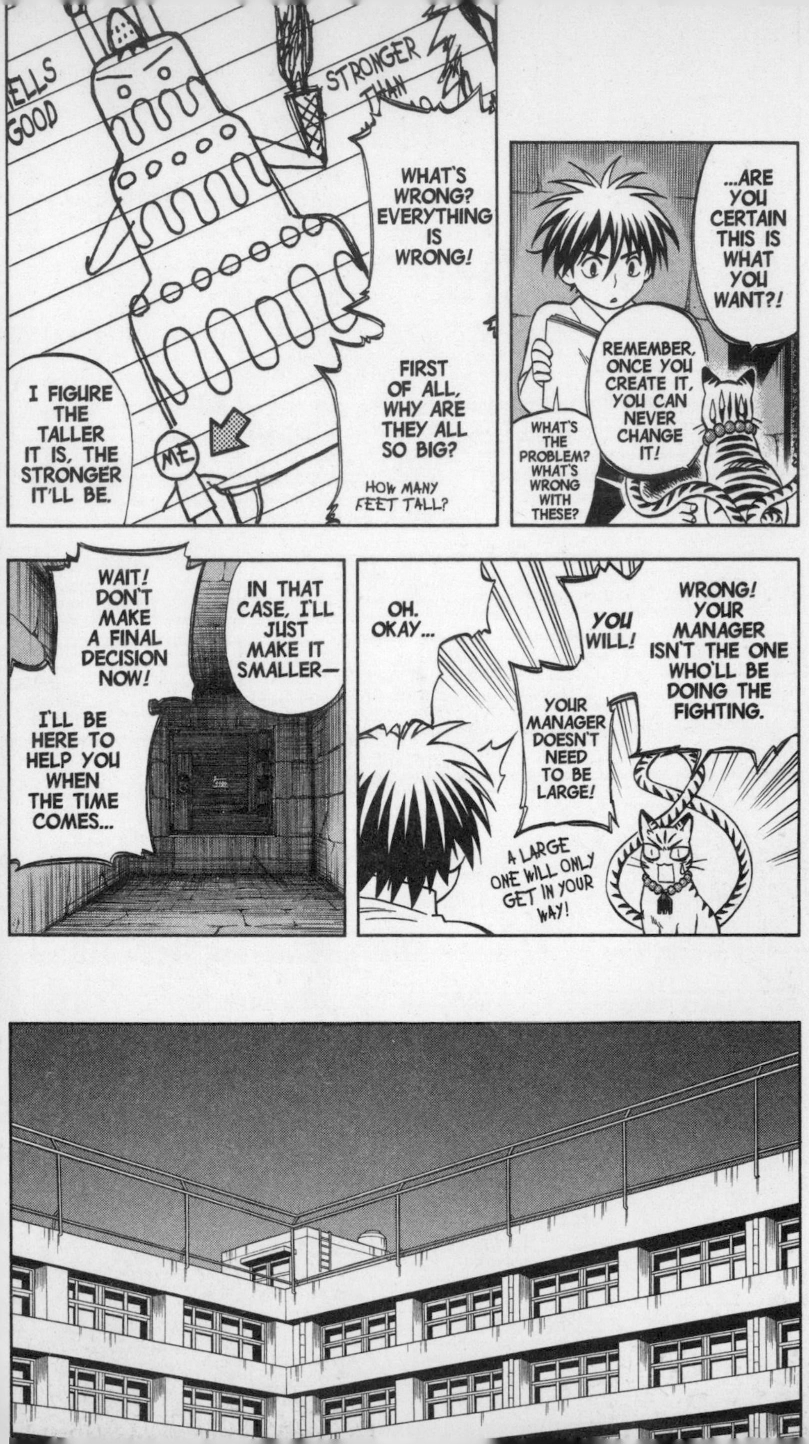
...ARE YOU CERTAIN THIS IS WHAT YOU WANT?!
REMEMBER, ONCE YOU CREATE IT, YOU CAN NEVER CHANGE IT!
WHAT'S THE PROBLEM? WHAT'S WRONG WITH THESE?
WHAT'S WRONG? EVERYTHING IS WRONG!
STRONGER THAN
FIRST OF ALL, WHY ARE THEY ALL SO BIG?
HOW MANY FEET TALL?
ME.
I FIGURE THE TALLER IT IS, THE STRONGER IT'LL BE.
WRONG! YOUR MANAGER ISN'T THE ONE WHO'LL BE DOING THE FIGHTING.
YOU WILL!
OH. OKAY...
YOUR MANAGER DOESN'T NEED TO BE LARGE!
A LARGE ONE WILL ONLY GET IN YOUR WAY!
IN THAT CASE, I'LL JUST MAKE IT SMALLER—
WAIT! DON'T MAKE A FINAL DECISION NOW!
I'LL BE HERE TO HELP YOU WHEN THE TIME COMES...

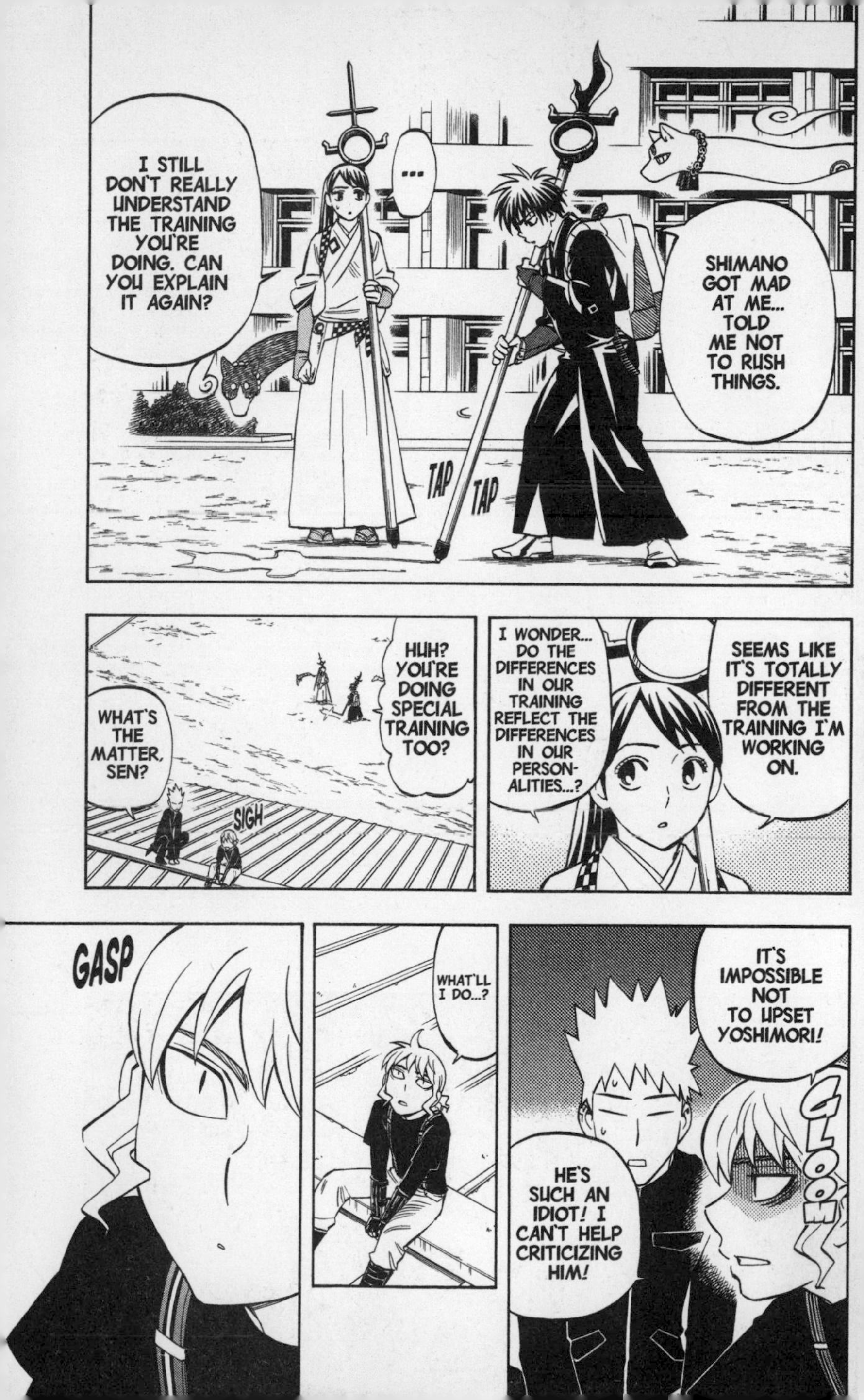
SHIMANO GOT MAD AT ME... TOLD ME NOT TO RUSH THINGS.
...
I STILL DON'T REALLY UNDERSTAND THE TRAINING YOU'RE DOING. CAN YOU EXPLAIN IT AGAIN?
TAP
TAP
SEEMS LIKE IT'S TOTALLY DIFFERENT FROM THE TRAINING I'M WORKING ON.
I WONDER... DO THE DIFFERENCES IN OUR TRAINING REFLECT THE DIFFERENCES IN OUR PERSON-ALITIES...?
HUH? YOU'RE DOING SPECIAL TRAINING TOO?
WHAT'S THE MATTER, SEN?
SIGH
IT'S IMPOSSIBLE NOT TO UPSET YOSHIMORI!
GLOOM
HE'S SUCH AN IDIOT! I CAN'T HELP CRITICIZING HIM!
WHAT'LL I DO...?
GASP

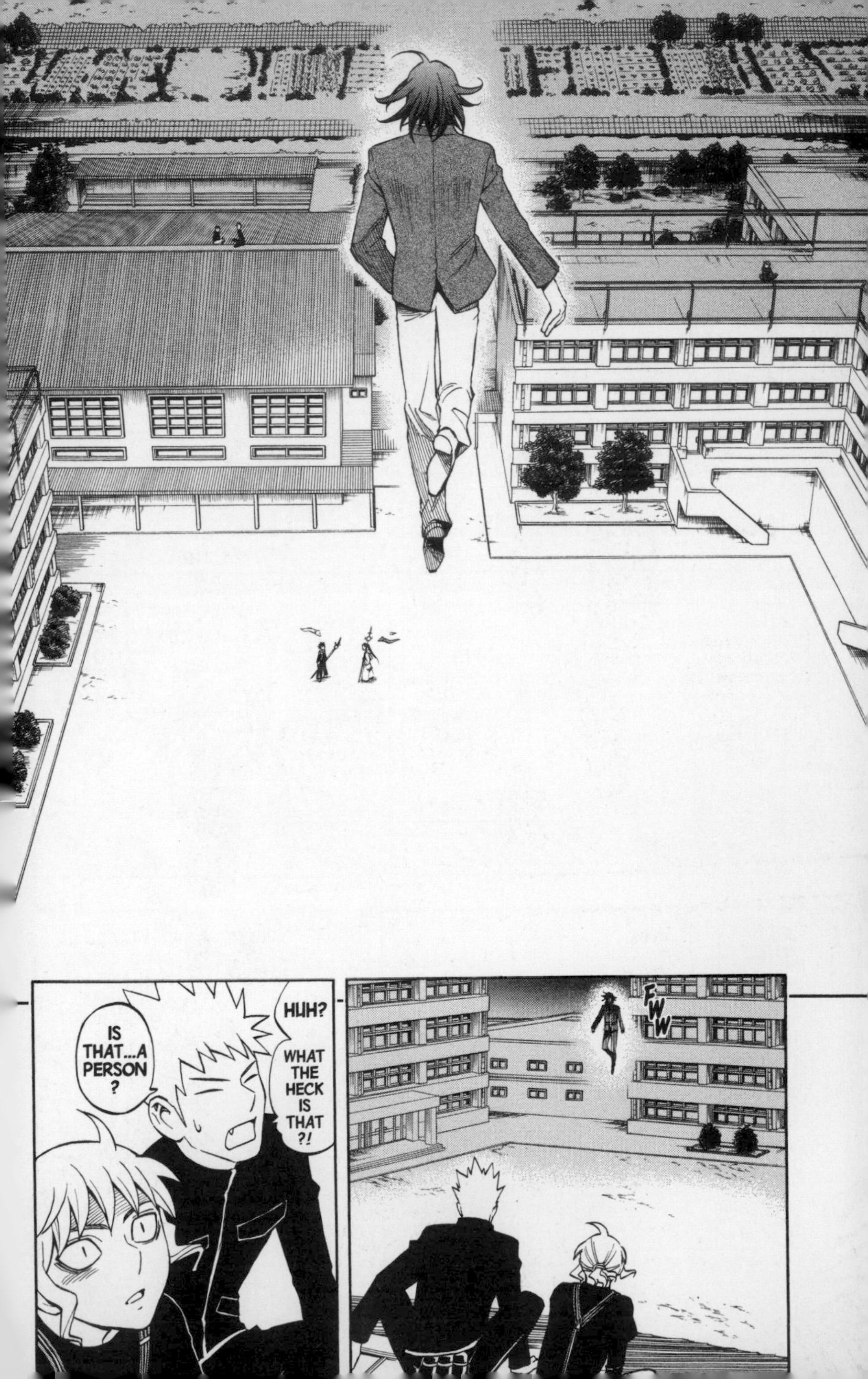
FWW
HUH?
WHAT THE HECK IS THAT?!
IS THAT...A PERSON?

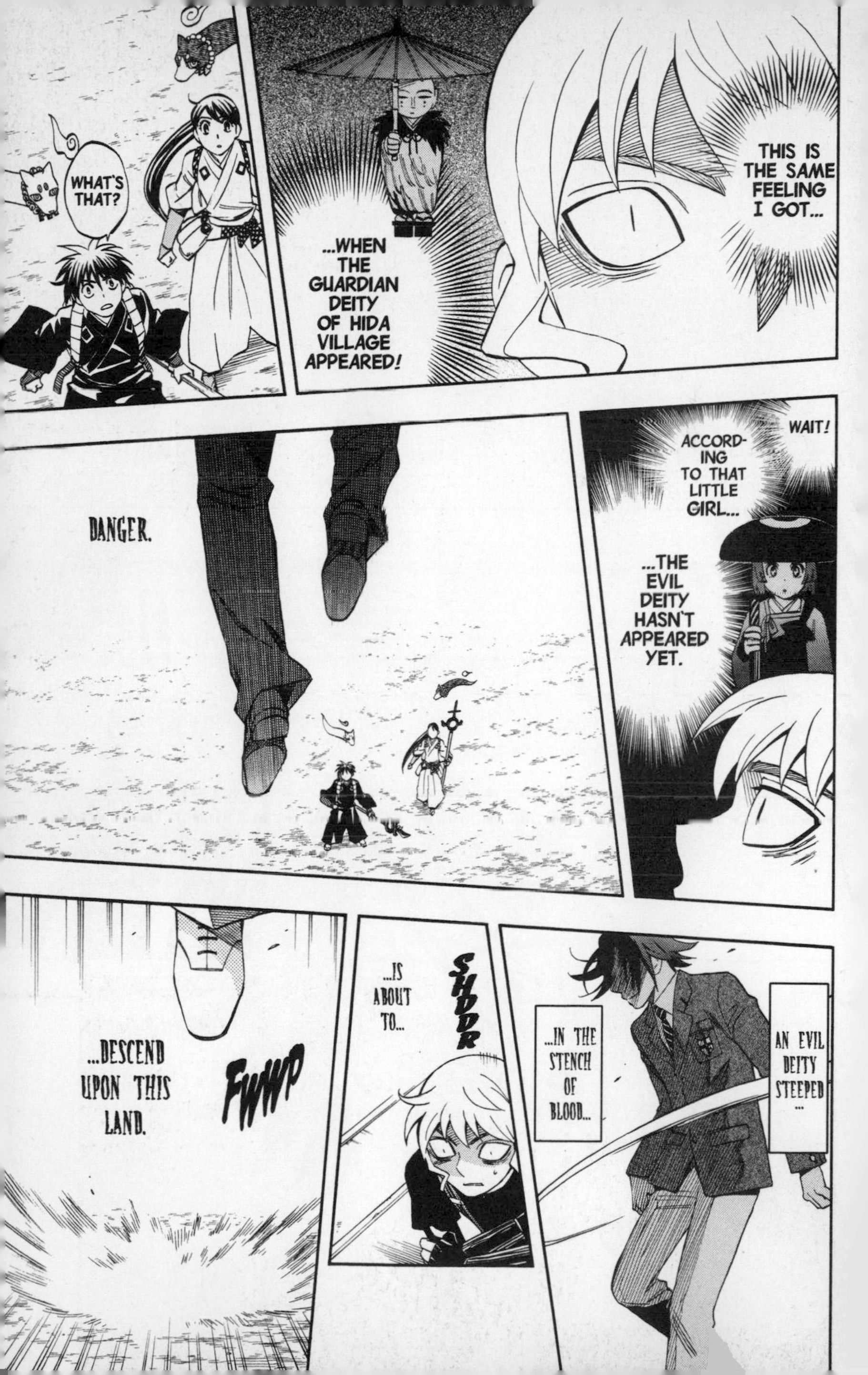
THIS IS THE SAME FEELING I GOT...
...WHEN THE GUARDIAN DEITY OF HIDA VILLAGE APPEARED!
WHAT'S THAT?
WAIT!
ACCORD-ING TO THAT LITTLE GIRL...
...THE EVIL DEITY HASN'T APPEARED YET.
DANGER.
AN EVIL DEITY STEEPED...
...IN THE STENCH OF BLOOD...
SHDDR
...IS ABOUT TO...
...DESCEND UPON THIS LAND.
FWWP

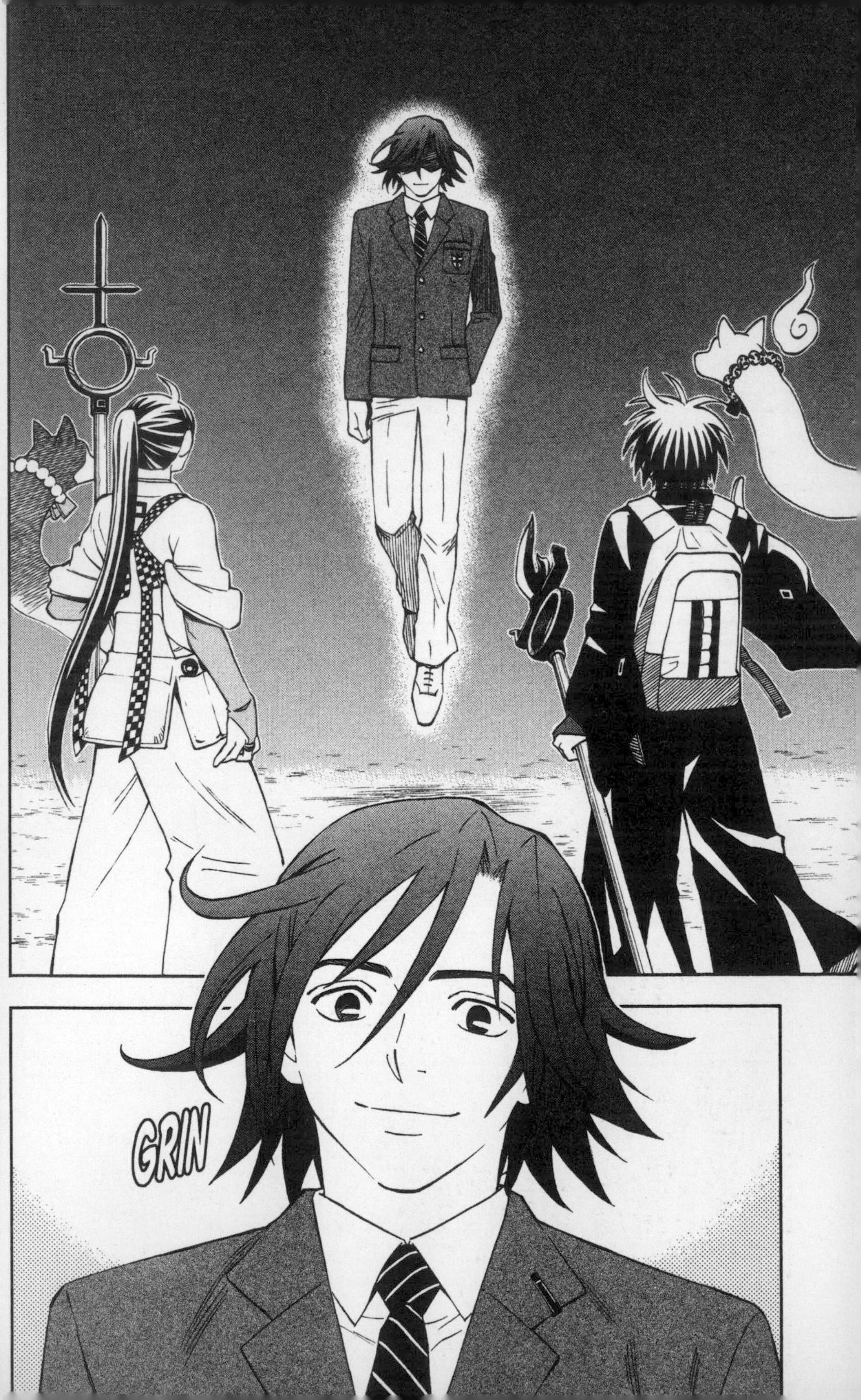
GRIN

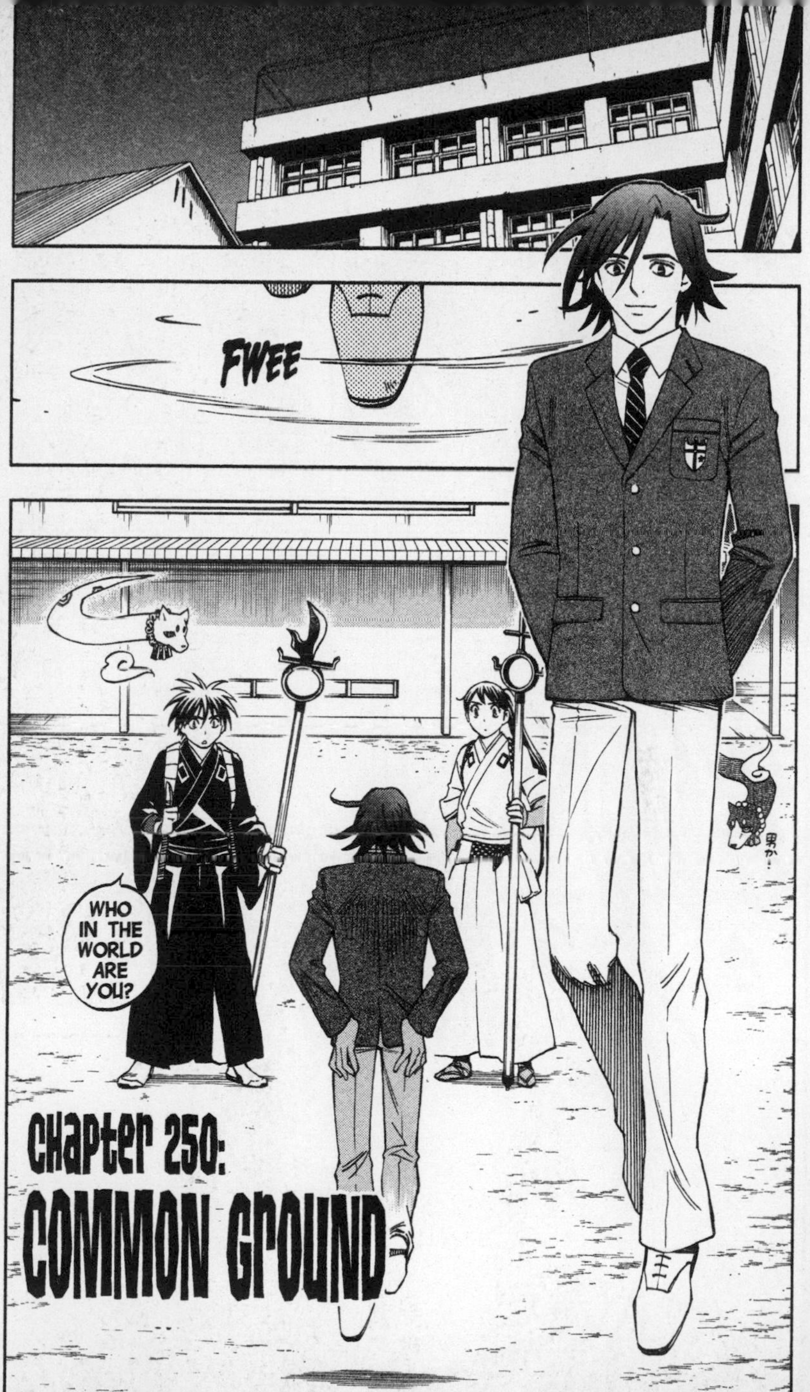
FWEE
男か！
WHO IN THE WORLD ARE YOU?
Chapter 250: Common Ground

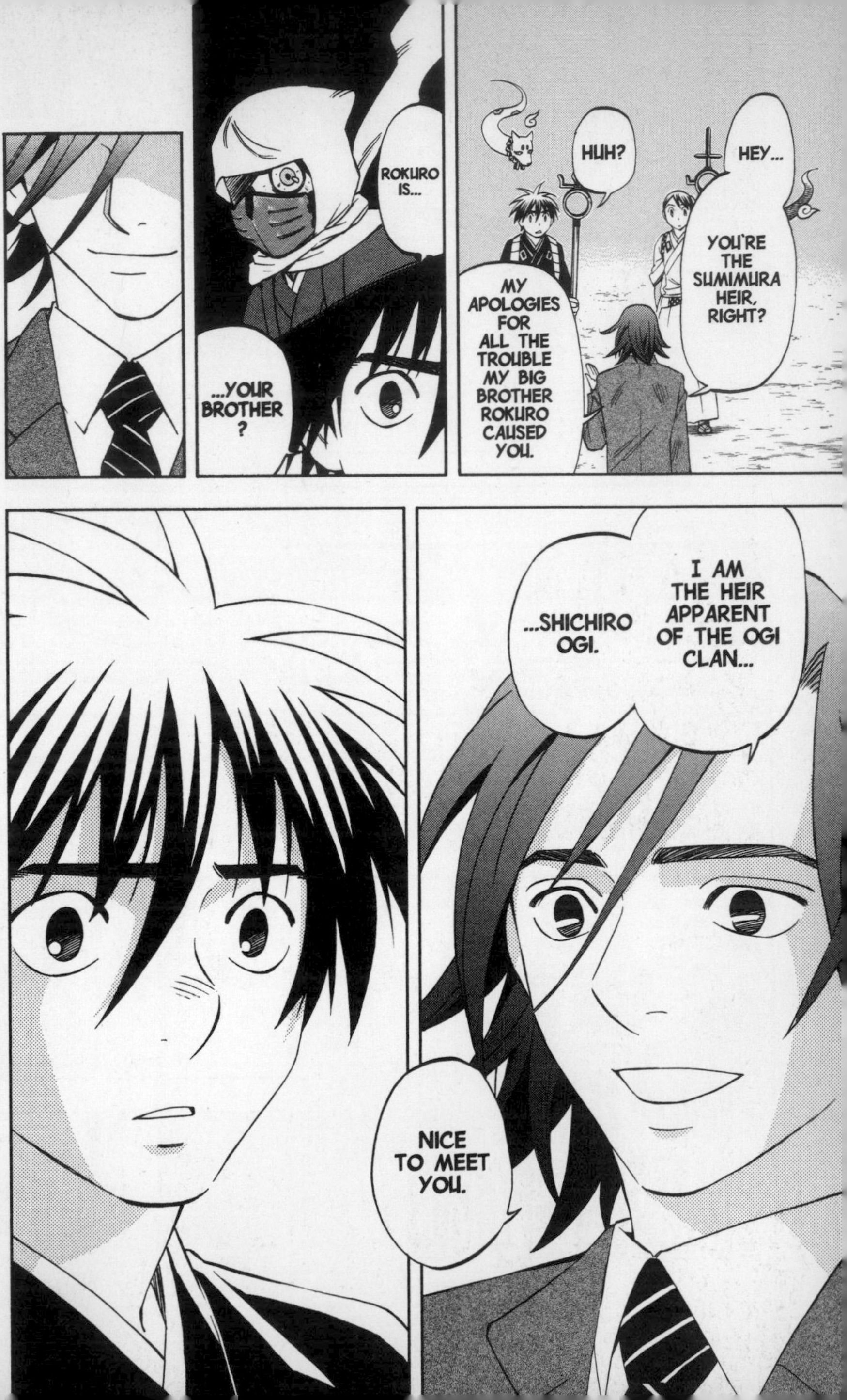
HEY...
YOU'RE THE SUMIMURA HEIR, RIGHT?
HUH?
MY APOLOGIES FOR ALL THE TROUBLE MY BIG BROTHER ROKURO CAUSED YOU.
ROKURO IS...
...YOUR BROTHER?
I AM THE HEIR APPARENT OF THE OGI CLAN...
...SHICHIRO OGI.
NICE TO MEET YOU.

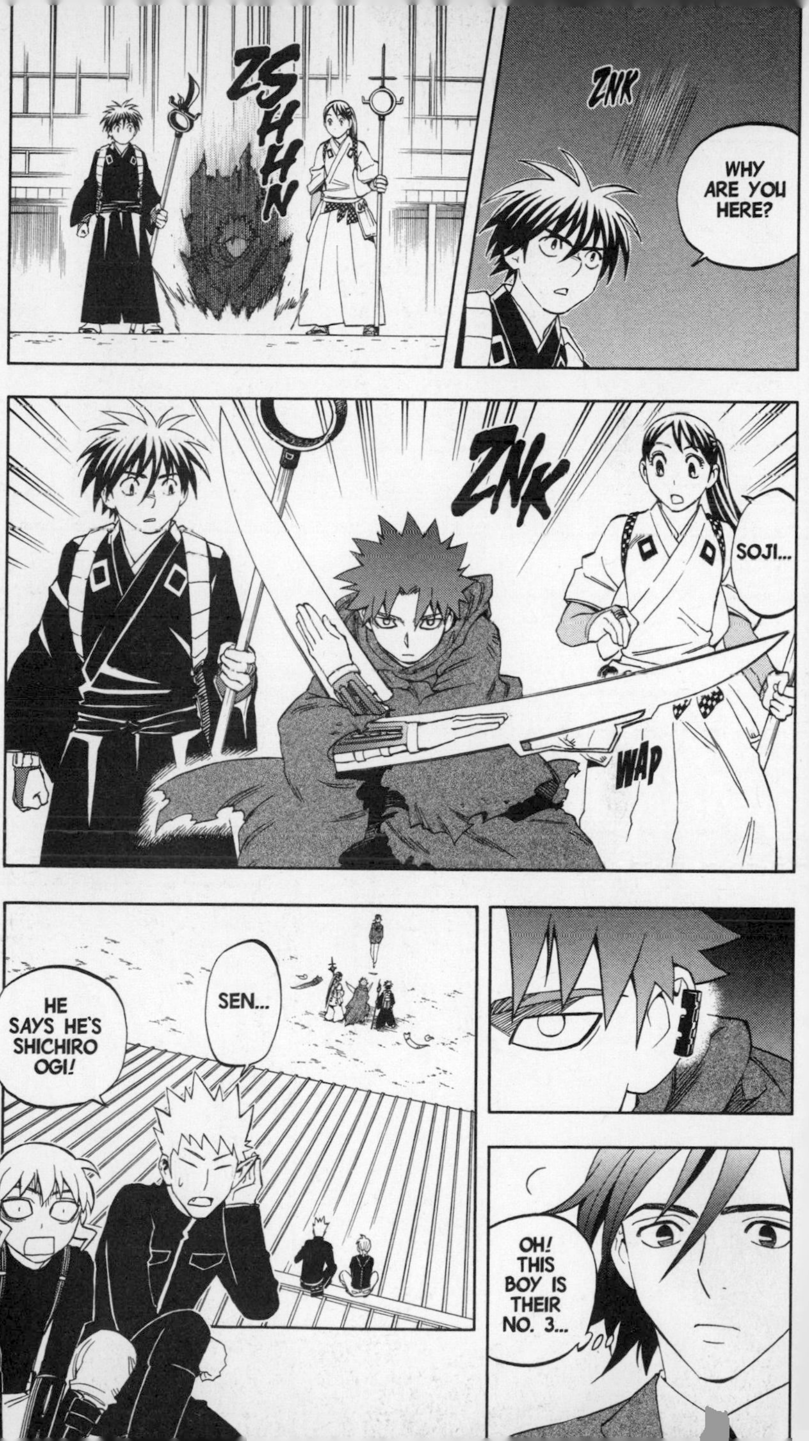
ZNK
WHY ARE YOU HERE?
ZSHHN
ZNK
SOJI...
WAP
OH! THIS BOY IS THEIR NO. 3...
SEN...
HE SAYS HE'S SHICHIRO OGI!

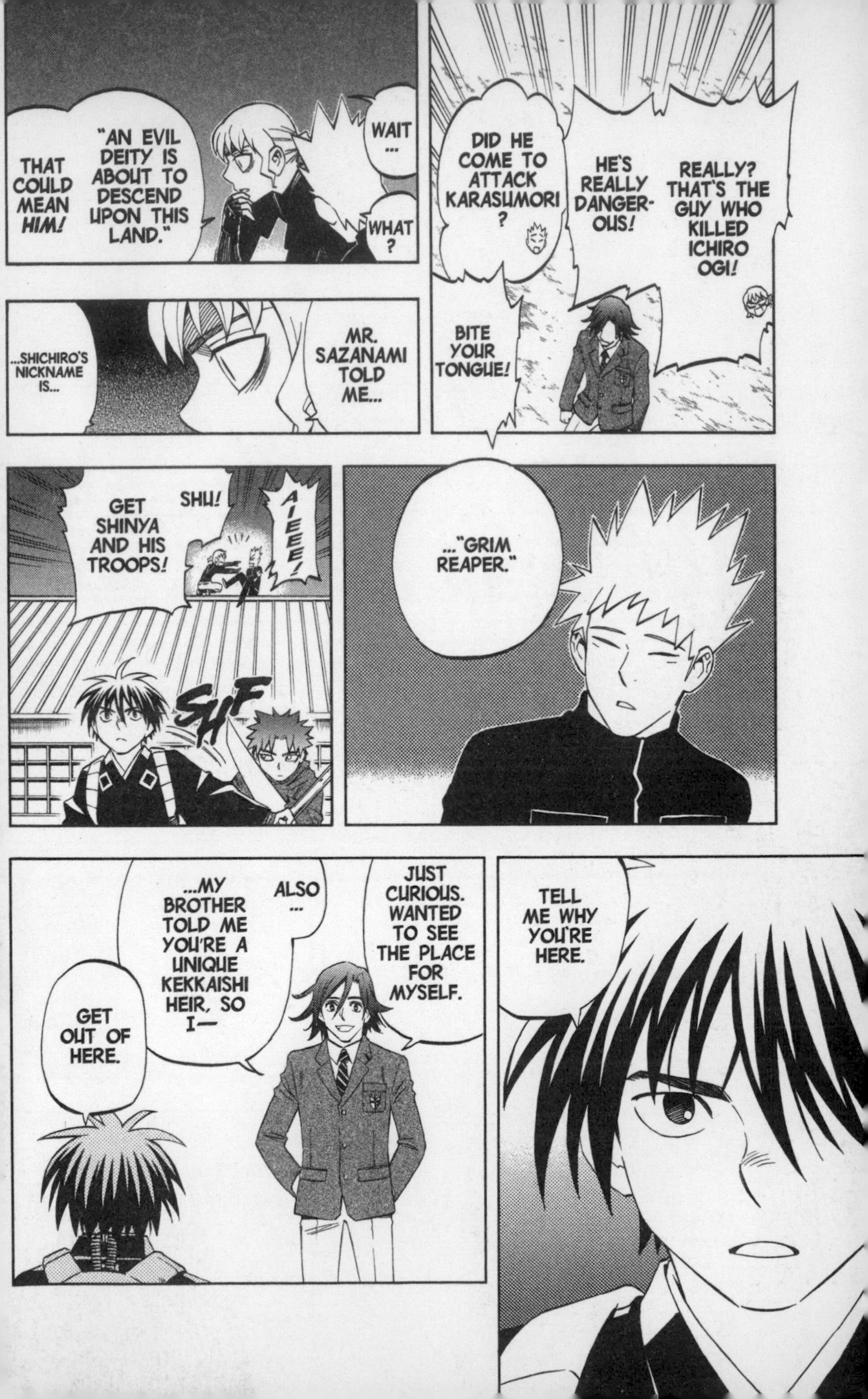
REALLY? THAT'S THE GUY WHO KILLED ICHIRO OGI!
HE'S REALLY DANGER-OUS!
DID HE COME TO ATTACK KARASUMORI?
BITE YOUR TONGUE!
WAIT...
WHAT?
"AN EVIL DEITY IS ABOUT TO DESCEND UPON THIS LAND."
THAT COULD MEAN *HIM!*
MR. SAZANAMI TOLD ME...
...SHICHIRO'S NICKNAME IS...
..."GRIM REAPER."
AIEEE!
SHU!
GET SHINYA AND HIS TROOPS!
SHF
TELL ME WHY YOU'RE HERE.
JUST CURIOUS. WANTED TO SEE THE PLACE FOR MYSELF.
ALSO...
...MY BROTHER TOLD ME YOU'RE A UNIQUE KEKKAISHI HEIR, SO I—
GET OUT OF HERE.

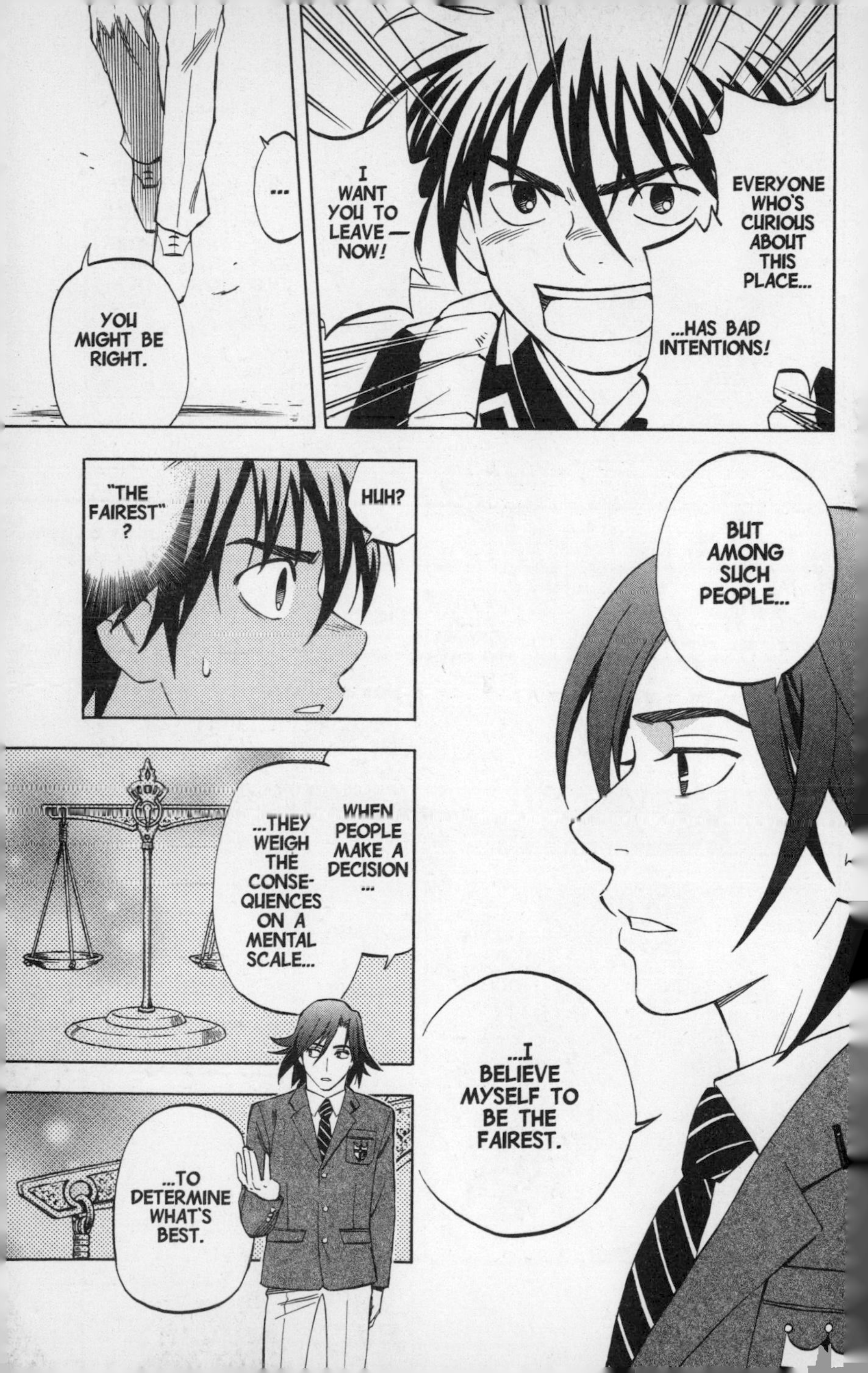
EVERYONE WHO'S CURIOUS ABOUT THIS PLACE...
...HAS BAD INTENTIONS!
I WANT YOU TO LEAVE— NOW!
...
YOU MIGHT BE RIGHT.
BUT AMONG SUCH PEOPLE...
...I BELIEVE MYSELF TO BE THE FAIREST.
HUH?
"THE FAIREST"?
WHEN PEOPLE MAKE A DECISION...
...THEY WEIGH THE CONSE-QUENCES ON A MENTAL SCALE...
...TO DETERMINE WHAT'S BEST.

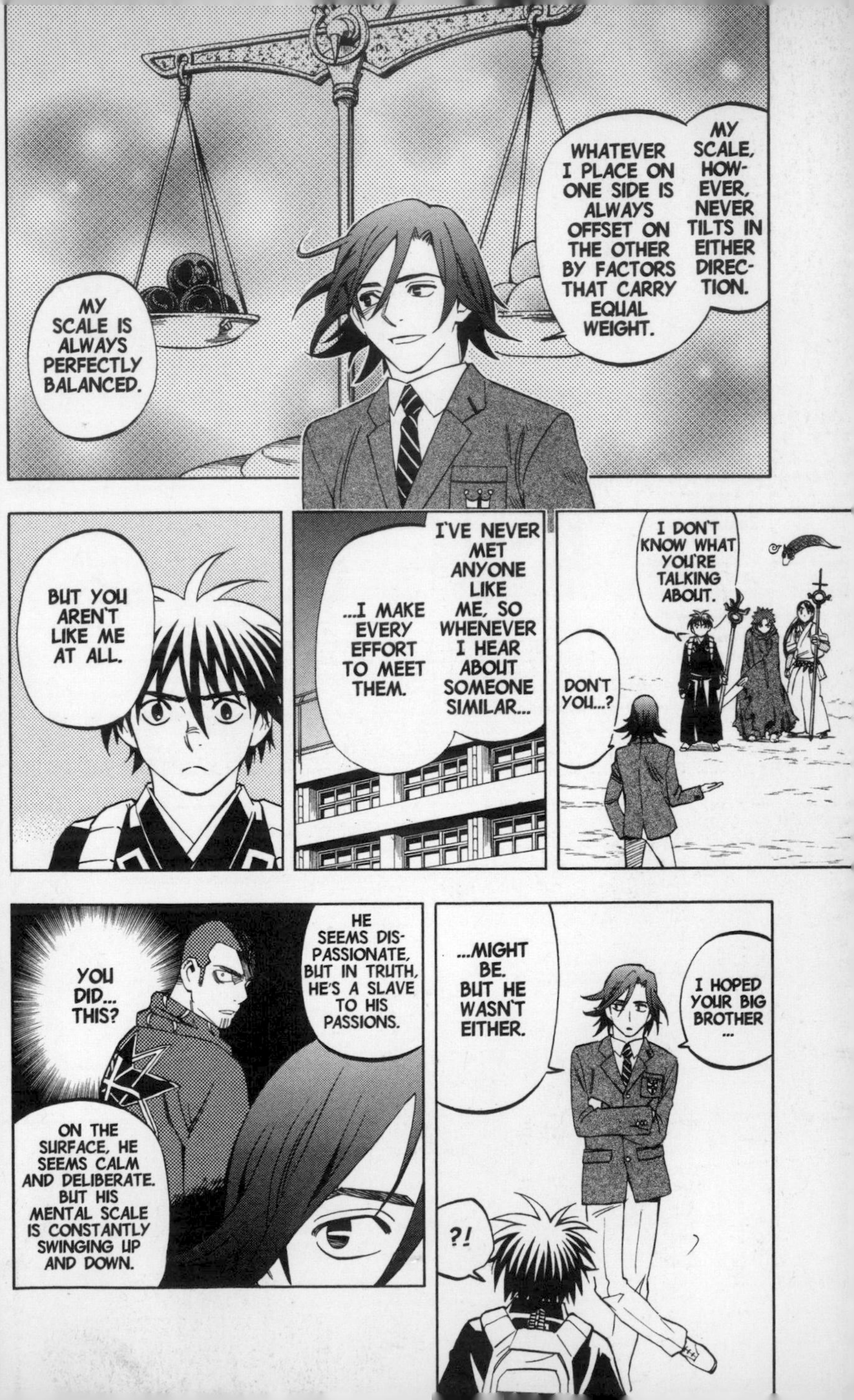
MY SCALE, HOWEVER, NEVER TILTS IN EITHER DIRECTION.
WHATEVER I PLACE ON ONE SIDE IS ALWAYS OFFSET ON THE OTHER BY FACTORS THAT CARRY EQUAL WEIGHT.
MY SCALE IS ALWAYS PERFECTLY BALANCED.
I DON'T KNOW WHAT YOU'RE TALKING ABOUT.
DON'T YOU...?
I'VE NEVER MET ANYONE LIKE ME, SO WHENEVER I HEAR ABOUT SOMEONE SIMILAR...
...I MAKE EVERY EFFORT TO MEET THEM.
BUT YOU AREN'T LIKE ME AT ALL.
I HOPED YOUR BIG BROTHER...
...MIGHT BE. BUT HE WASN'T EITHER.
?!
HE SEEMS DISPASSIONATE, BUT IN TRUTH, HE'S A SLAVE TO HIS PASSIONS.
YOU DID... THIS?
ON THE SURFACE, HE SEEMS CALM AND DELIBERATE. BUT HIS MENTAL SCALE IS CONSTANTLY SWINGING UP AND DOWN.

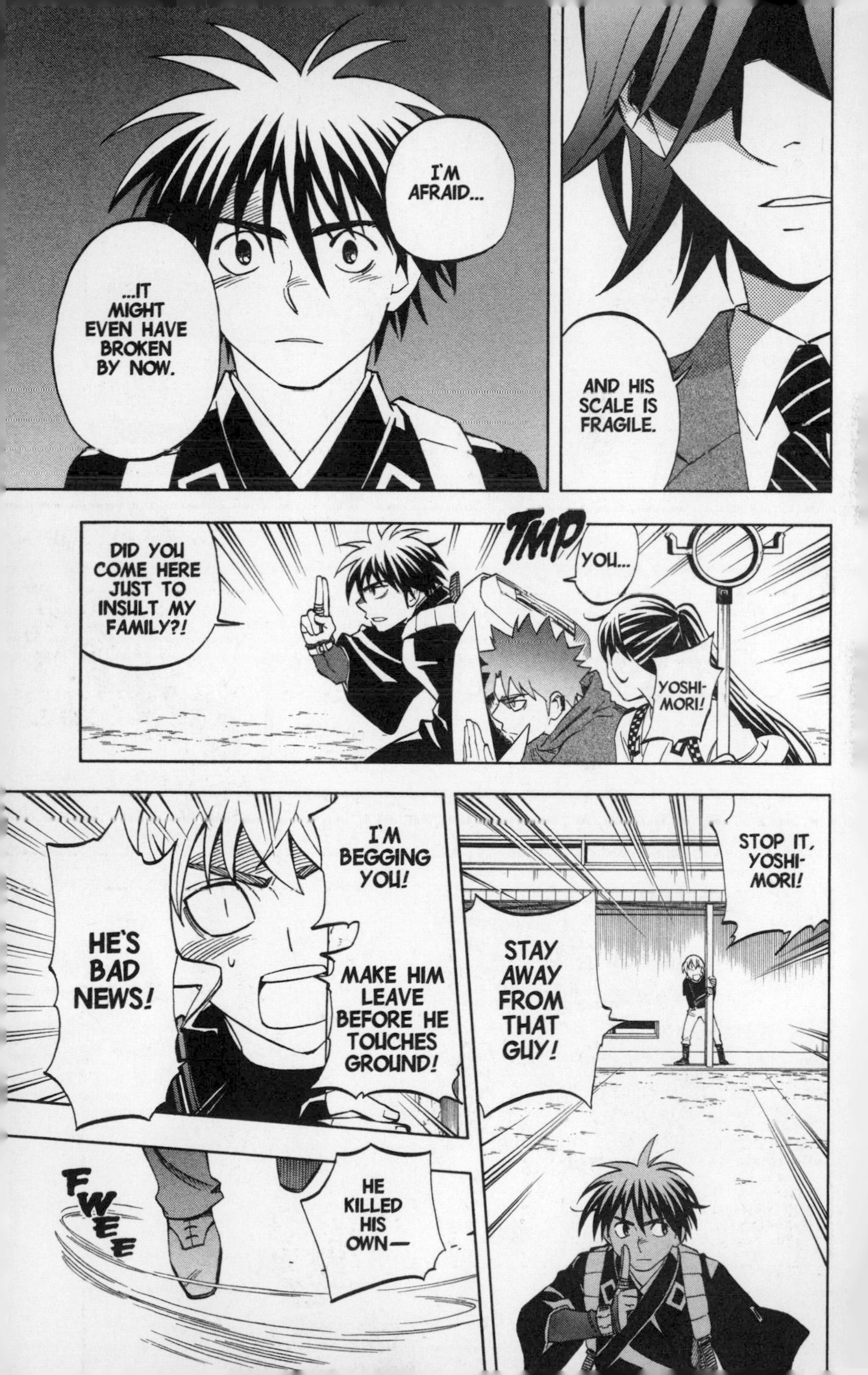
AND HIS SCALE IS FRAGILE.
I'M AFRAID...
...IT MIGHT EVEN HAVE BROKEN BY NOW.
YOU...
TMP
DID YOU COME HERE JUST TO INSULT MY FAMILY?!
YOSHI-MORI!
STOP IT, YOSHI-MORI!
STAY AWAY FROM THAT GUY!
I'M BEGGING YOU!
MAKE HIM LEAVE BEFORE HE TOUCHES GROUND!
HE'S BAD NEWS!
HE KILLED HIS OWN—
FWEE

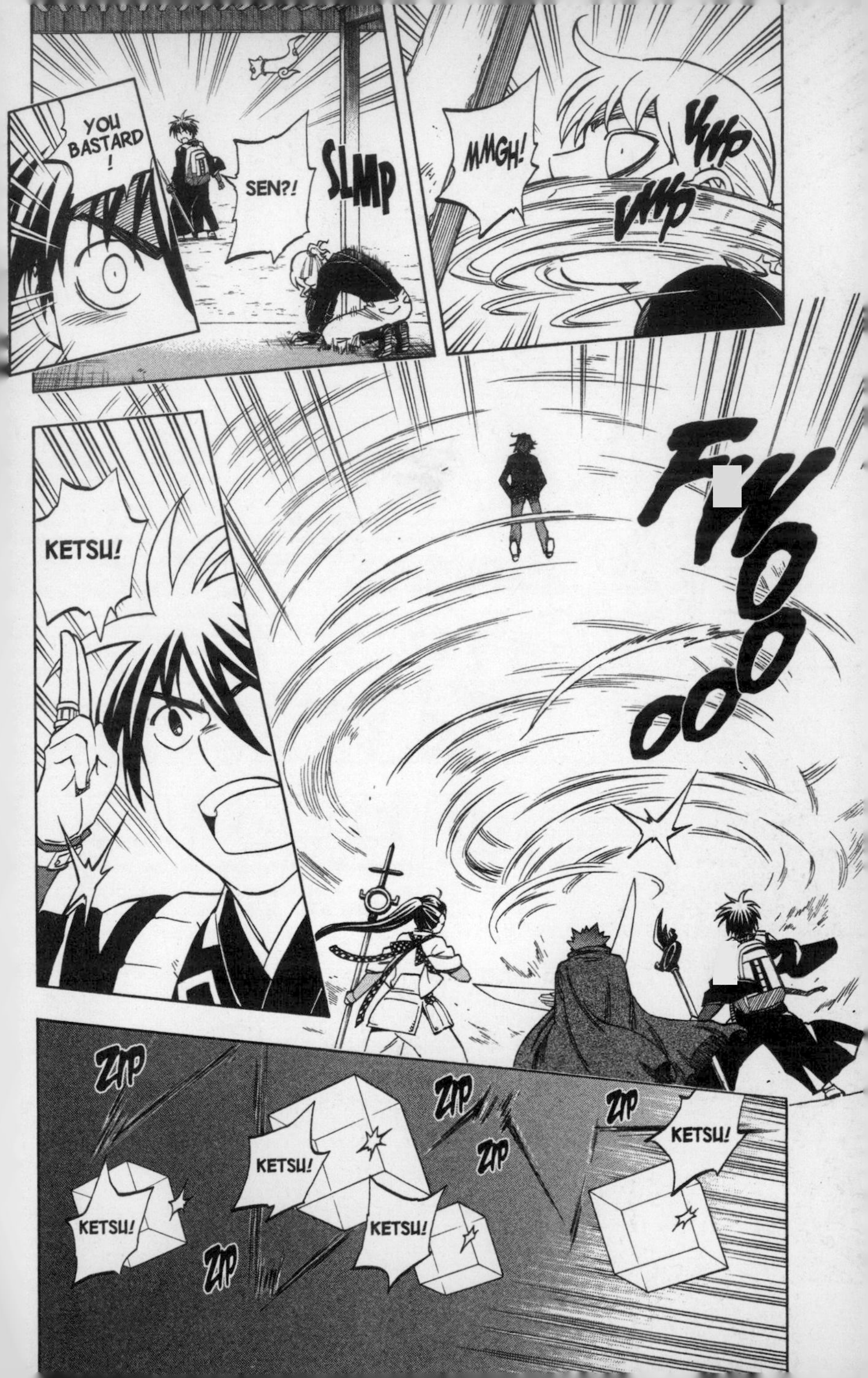
MMGH!
VWIP
VWIP
SLMP
SEN?!
YOU BASTARD!
FWOOOOO
KETSU!
KETSU!
ZIP
ZIP
KETSU!
ZIP
ZIP
KETSU!
KETSU!
ZIP

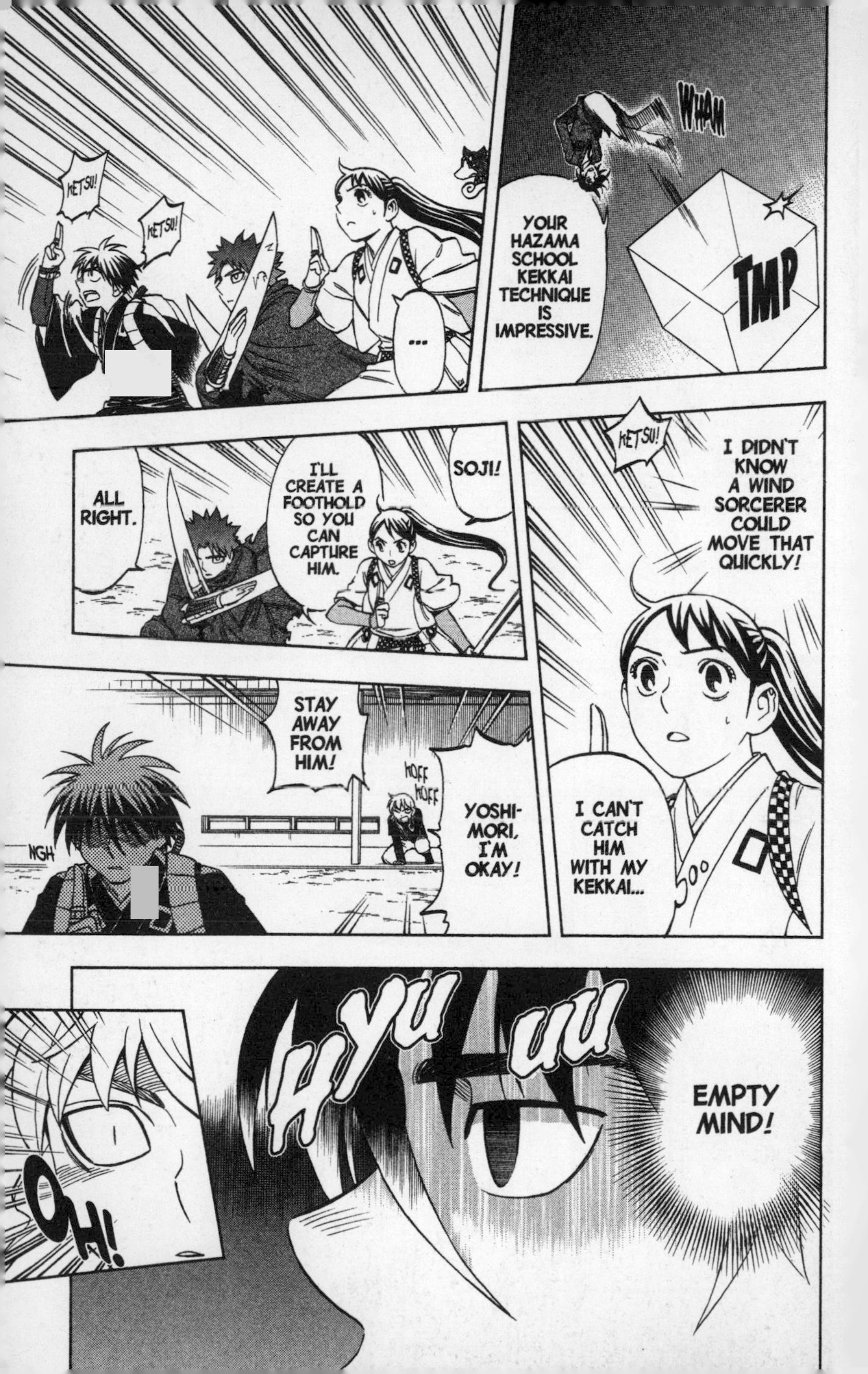
WHAM
TMP
YOUR HAZAMA SCHOOL KEKKAI TECHNIQUE IS IMPRESSIVE.
...
KETSU!
KETSU!
KETSU!
I DIDN'T KNOW A WIND SORCERER COULD MOVE THAT QUICKLY!
I CAN'T CATCH HIM WITH MY KEKKAI...
SOJI!
I'LL CREATE A FOOTHOLD SO YOU CAN CAPTURE HIM.
ALL RIGHT.
YOSHI-MORI, I'M OKAY!
HOFF HOFF
STAY AWAY FROM HIM!
NGH
HYUUU
EMPTY MIND!
OH!

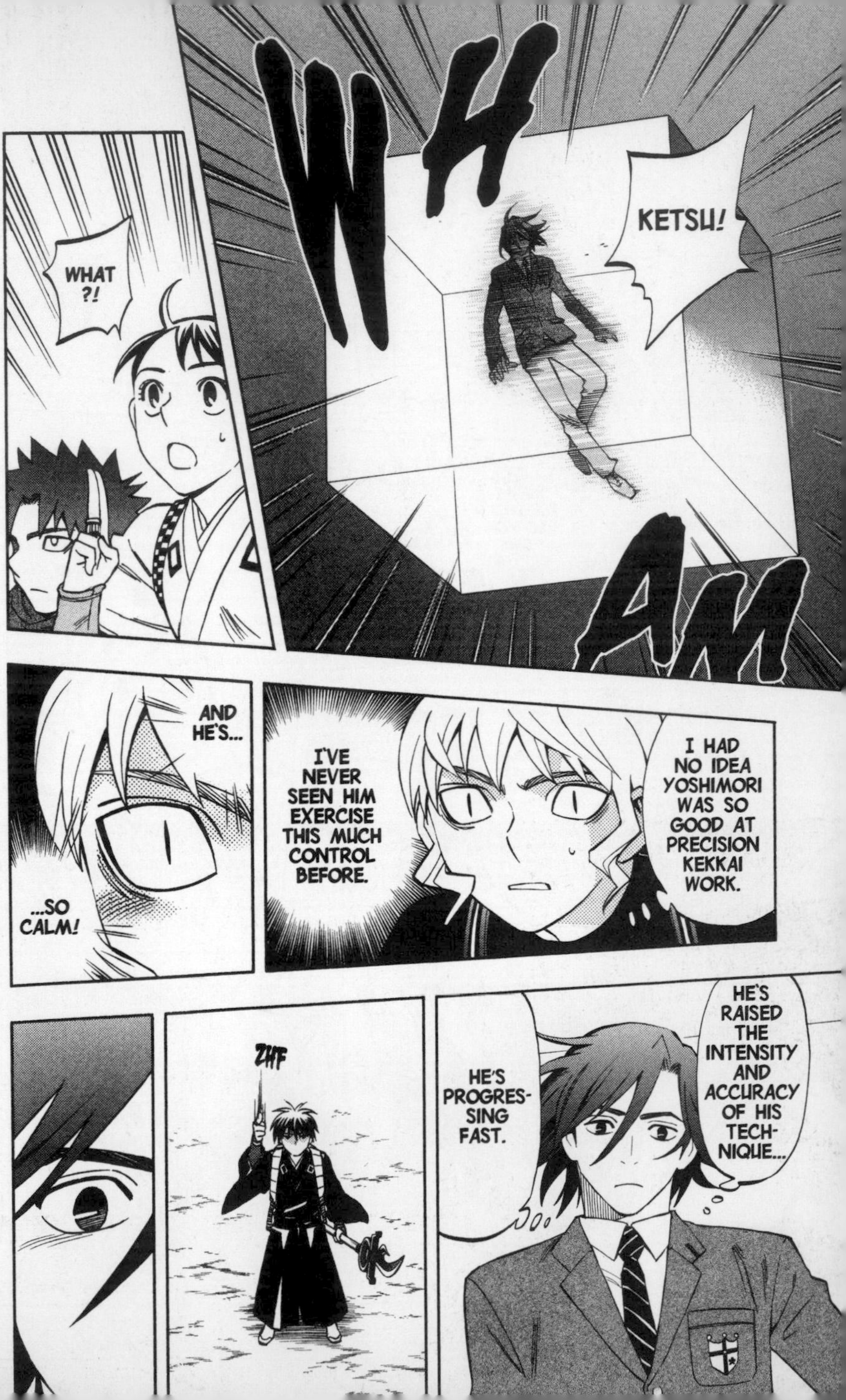
WHAM
KETSU!
WHAT ?!
I HAD NO IDEA YOSHIMORI WAS SO GOOD AT PRECISION KEKKAI WORK.
I'VE NEVER SEEN HIM EXERCISE THIS MUCH CONTROL BEFORE.
AND HE'S...
...SO CALM!
HE'S RAISED THE INTENSITY AND ACCURACY OF HIS TECH-NIQUE...
HE'S PROGRES-SING FAST.
ZHF

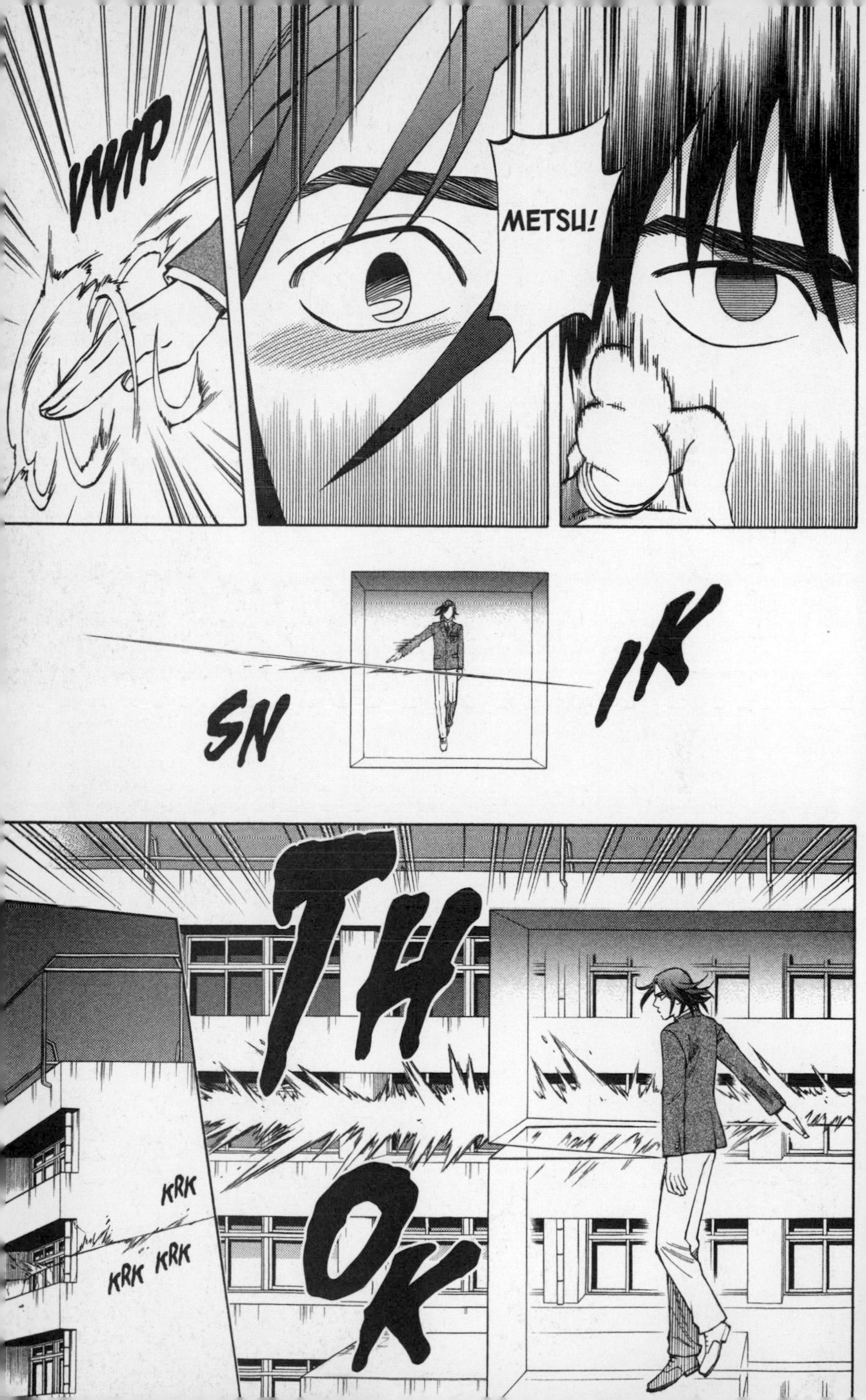
METSU!
VWIP
SN
IK
THOK
KRK
KRK KRK

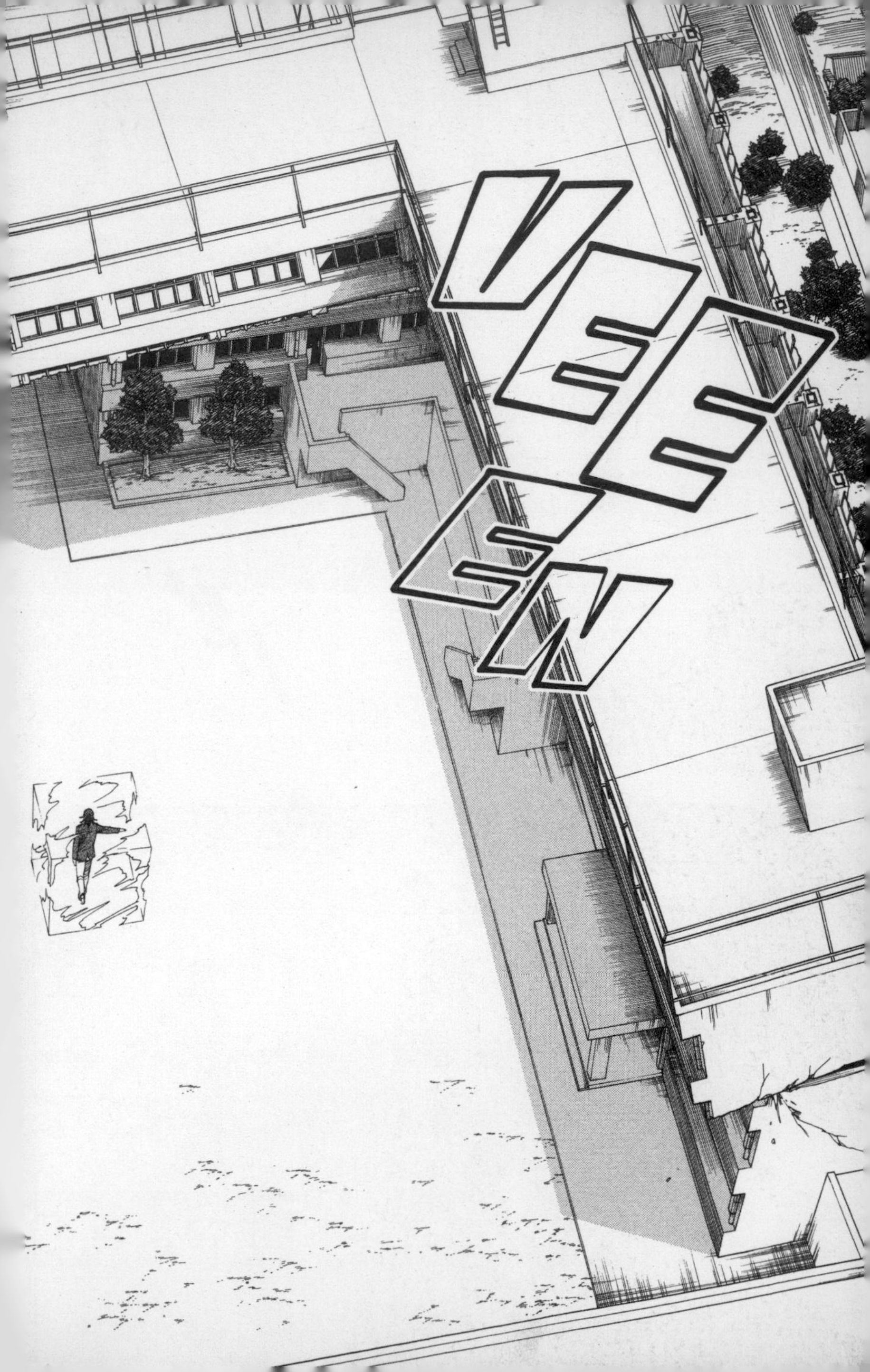
VEEEN

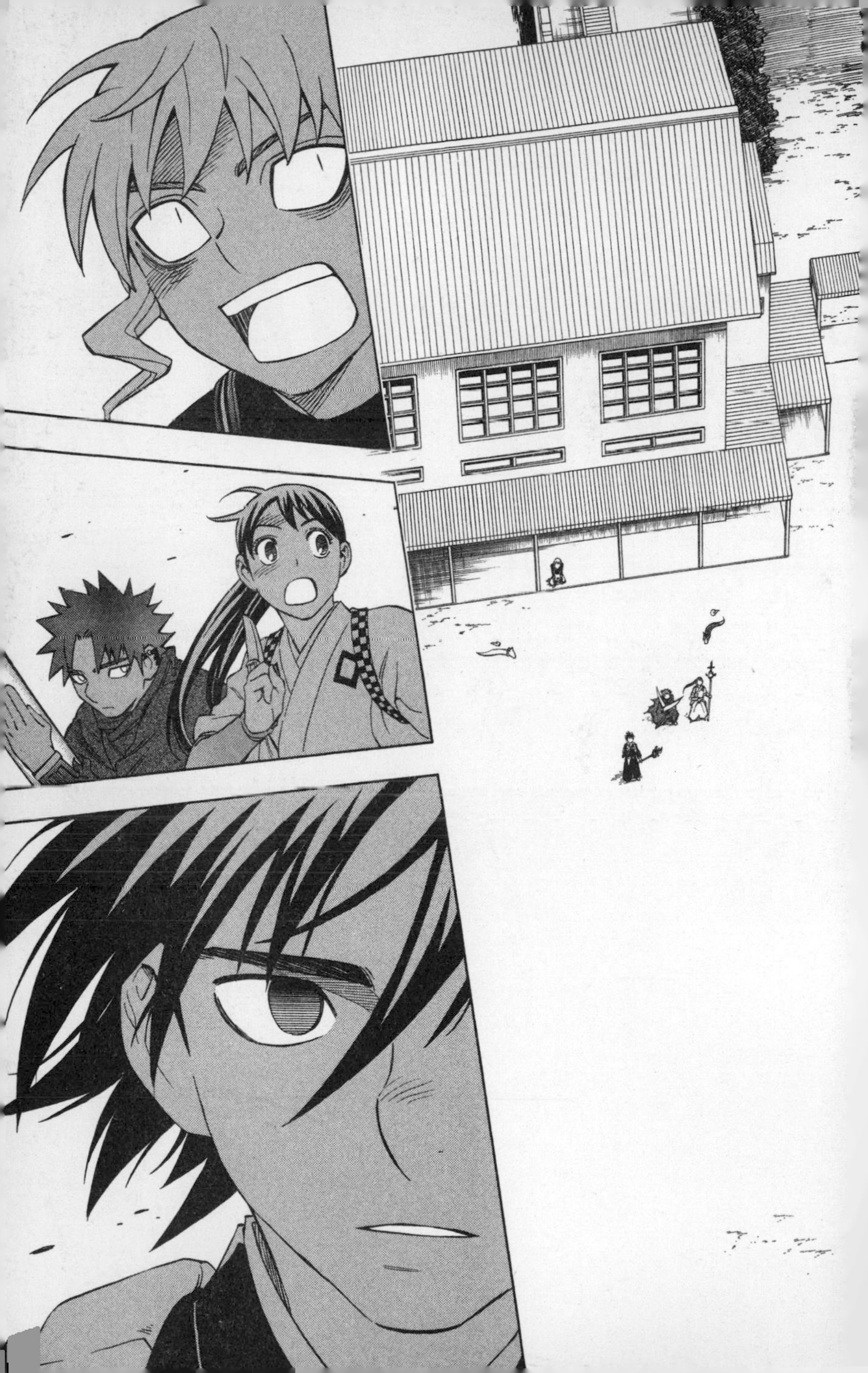

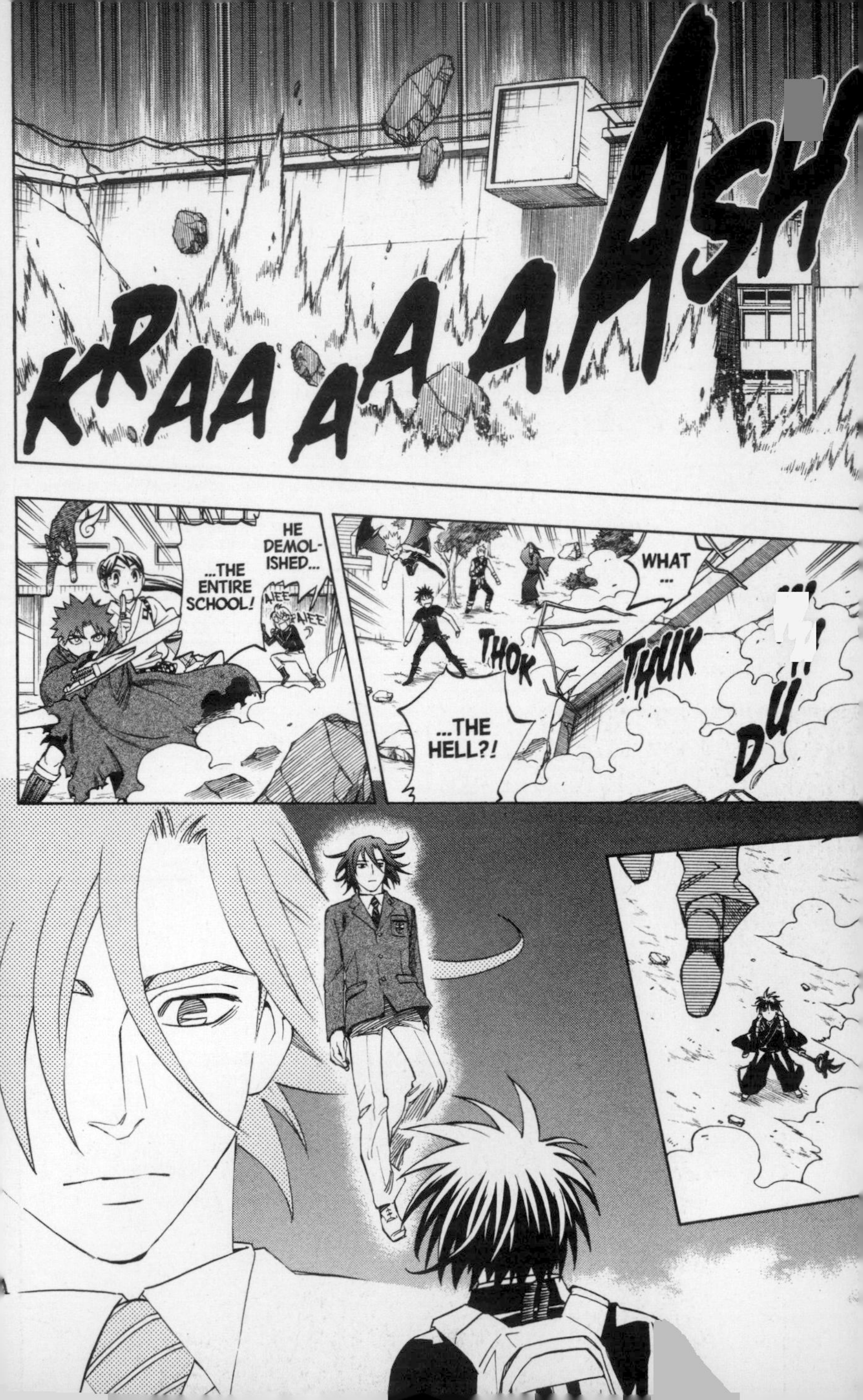
KRAAAAAAASH
DUU!!
WHAT ...
...THE HELL?!
THUK
THOK
HE DEMOL-ISHED...
...THE ENTIRE SCHOOL!
AIEE
AIEE

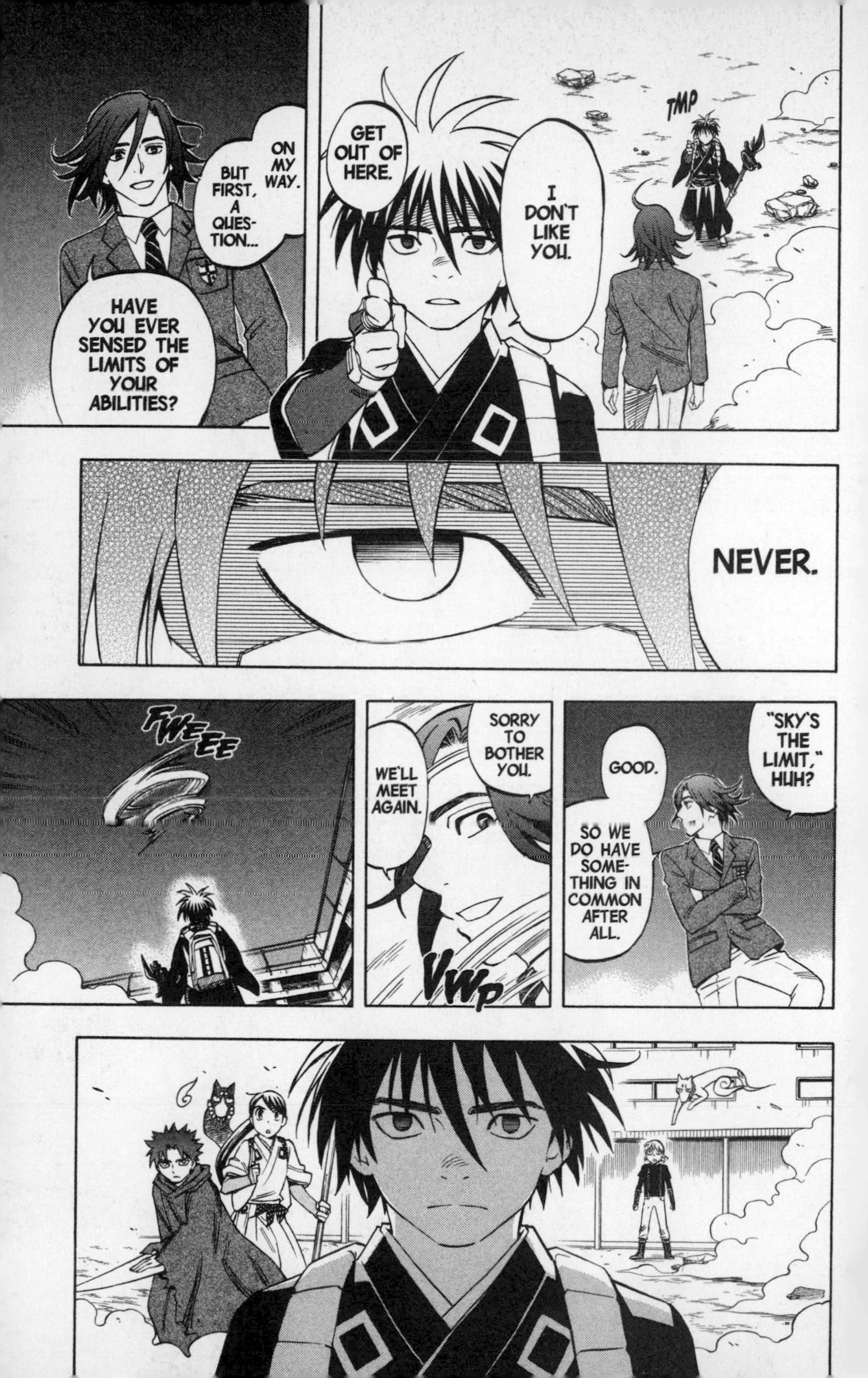
TMP
I DON'T LIKE YOU.
GET OUT OF HERE.
ON MY WAY.
BUT FIRST, A QUES-TION...
HAVE YOU EVER SENSED THE LIMITS OF YOUR ABILITIES?
NEVER.
"SKY'S THE LIMIT," HUH?
GOOD.
SO WE DO HAVE SOME-THING IN COMMON AFTER ALL.
SORRY TO BOTHER YOU.
WE'LL MEET AGAIN.
VWP
FWEEE

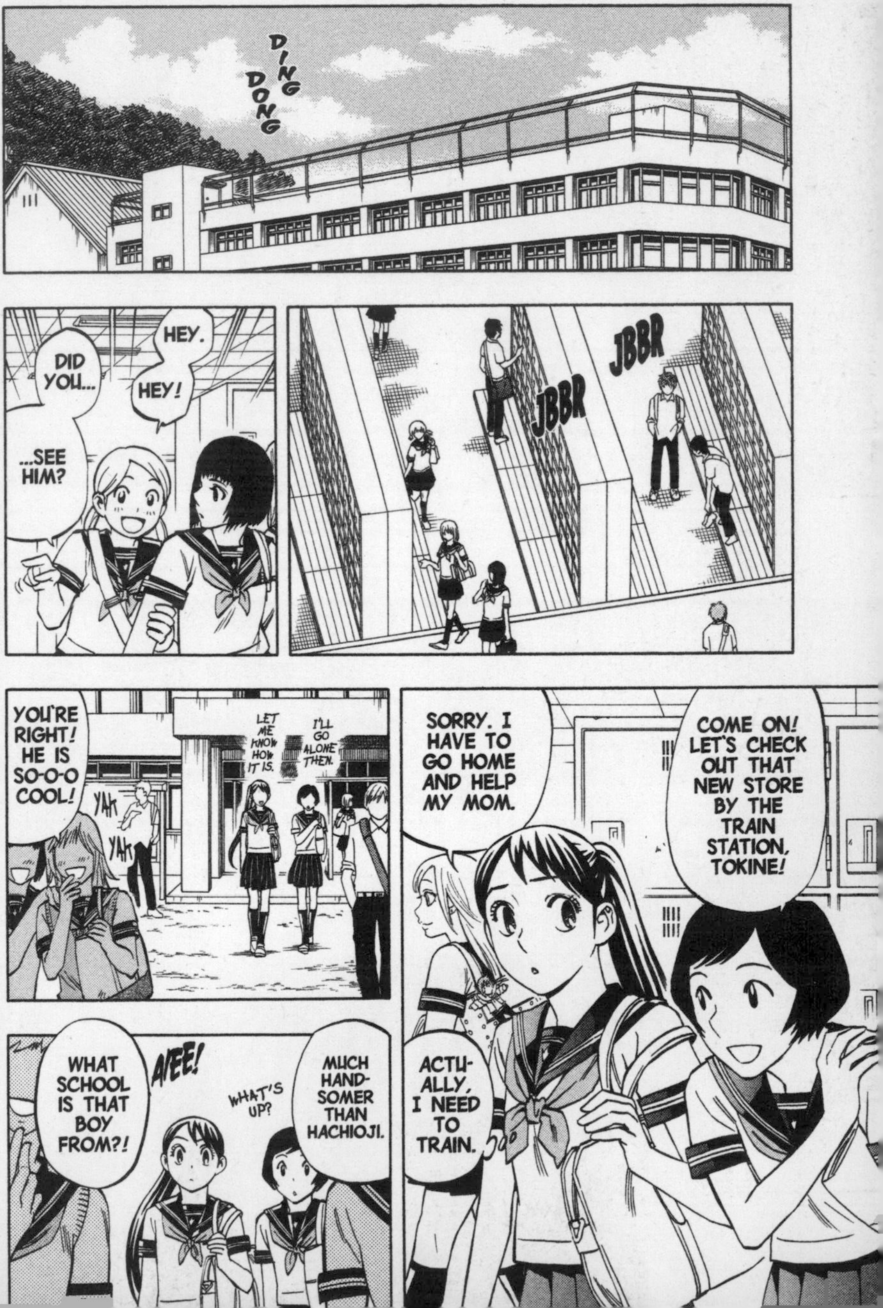
DING DONG
JBBR
JBBR
HEY.
HEY!
DID YOU...
...SEE HIM?
COME ON! LET'S CHECK OUT THAT NEW STORE BY THE TRAIN STATION, TOKINE!
SORRY. I HAVE TO GO HOME AND HELP MY MOM.
ACTU-ALLY, I NEED TO TRAIN.
I'LL GO ALONE THEN.
LET ME KNOW HOW IT IS.
YAK
YAK
YOU'RE RIGHT! HE IS SO-O-O COOL!
MUCH HAND-SOMER THAN HACHIOJI.
WHAT'S UP?
AIEE!
WHAT SCHOOL IS THAT BOY FROM?!

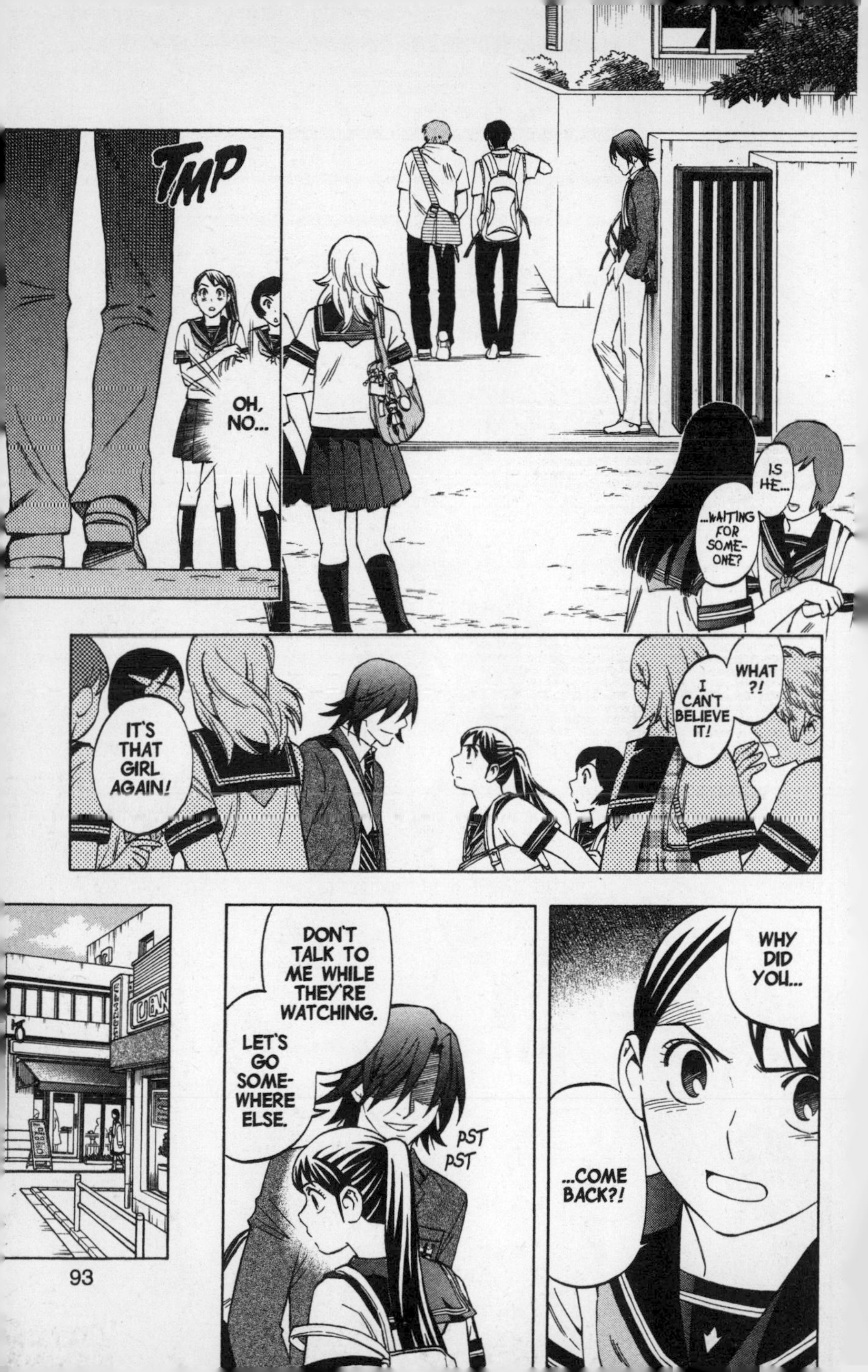
IS HE...
...WAITING FOR SOME-ONE?
TMP
OH, NO...
WHAT?!
I CAN'T BELIEVE IT!
IT'S THAT GIRL AGAIN!
WHY DID YOU...
...COME BACK?!
DON'T TALK TO ME WHILE THEY'RE WATCHING.
LET'S GO SOME-WHERE ELSE.
PST PST

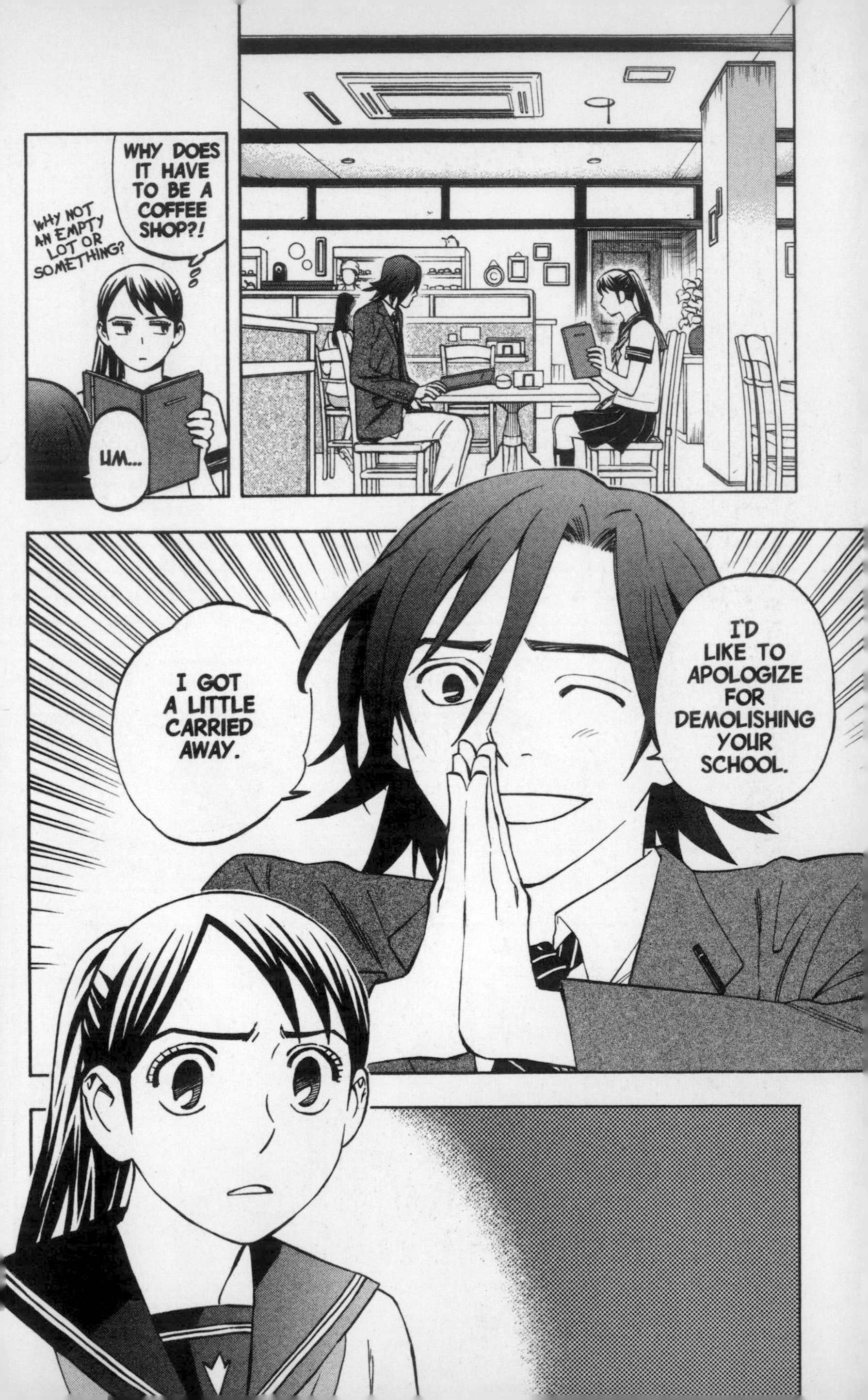
WHY DOES IT HAVE TO BE A COFFEE SHOP?!
WHY NOT AN EMPTY LOT OR SOMETHING?
UM...
I'D LIKE TO APOLOGIZE FOR DEMOLISHING YOUR SCHOOL.
I GOT A LITTLE CARRIED AWAY.

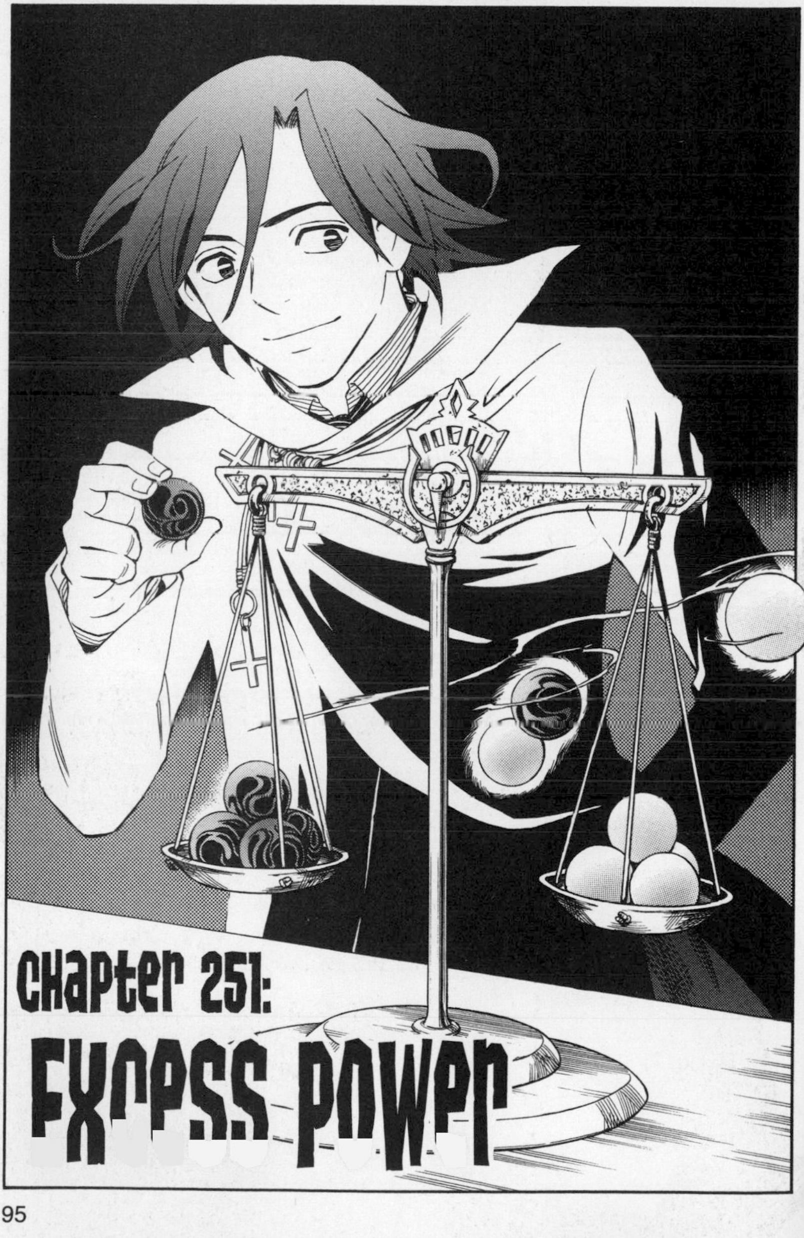
Chapter 251:
Excess Power

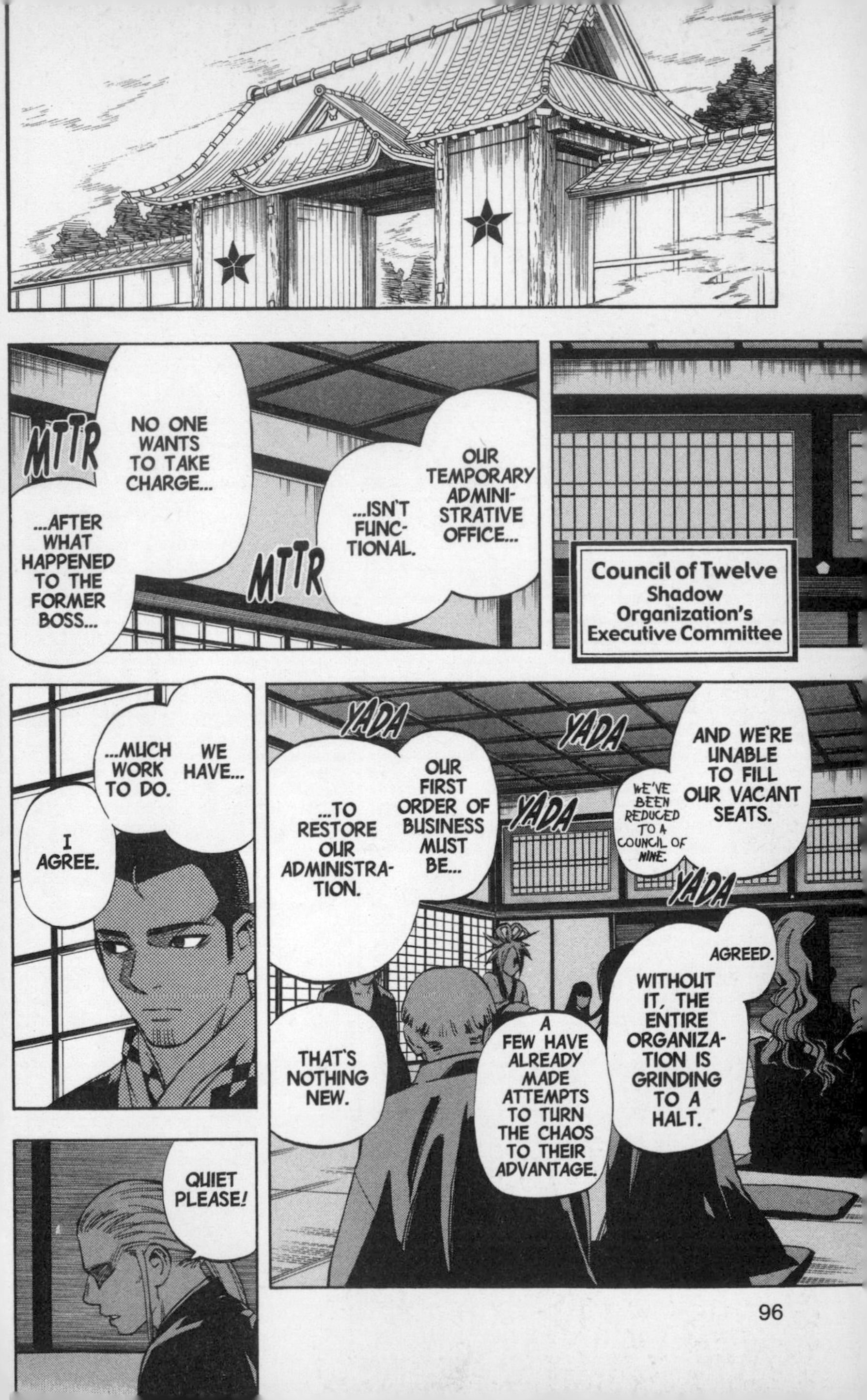
Council of Twelve
Shadow Organization's Executive Committee
OUR TEMPORARY ADMINI-STRATIVE OFFICE...
...ISN'T FUNC-TIONAL.
MTTR
NO ONE WANTS TO TAKE CHARGE...
...AFTER WHAT HAPPENED TO THE FORMER BOSS...
MTTR
YADA
YADA
AND WE'RE UNABLE TO FILL OUR VACANT SEATS.
WE'VE BEEN REDUCED TO A COUNCIL OF NINE.
YADA
OUR FIRST ORDER OF BUSINESS MUST BE...
...TO RESTORE OUR ADMINISTRA-TION.
YADA
AGREED.
WITHOUT IT, THE ENTIRE ORGANIZA-TION IS GRINDING TO A HALT.
A FEW HAVE ALREADY MADE ATTEMPTS TO TURN THE CHAOS TO THEIR ADVANTAGE.
THAT'S NOTHING NEW.
WE HAVE...
...MUCH WORK TO DO.
I AGREE.
QUIET PLEASE!

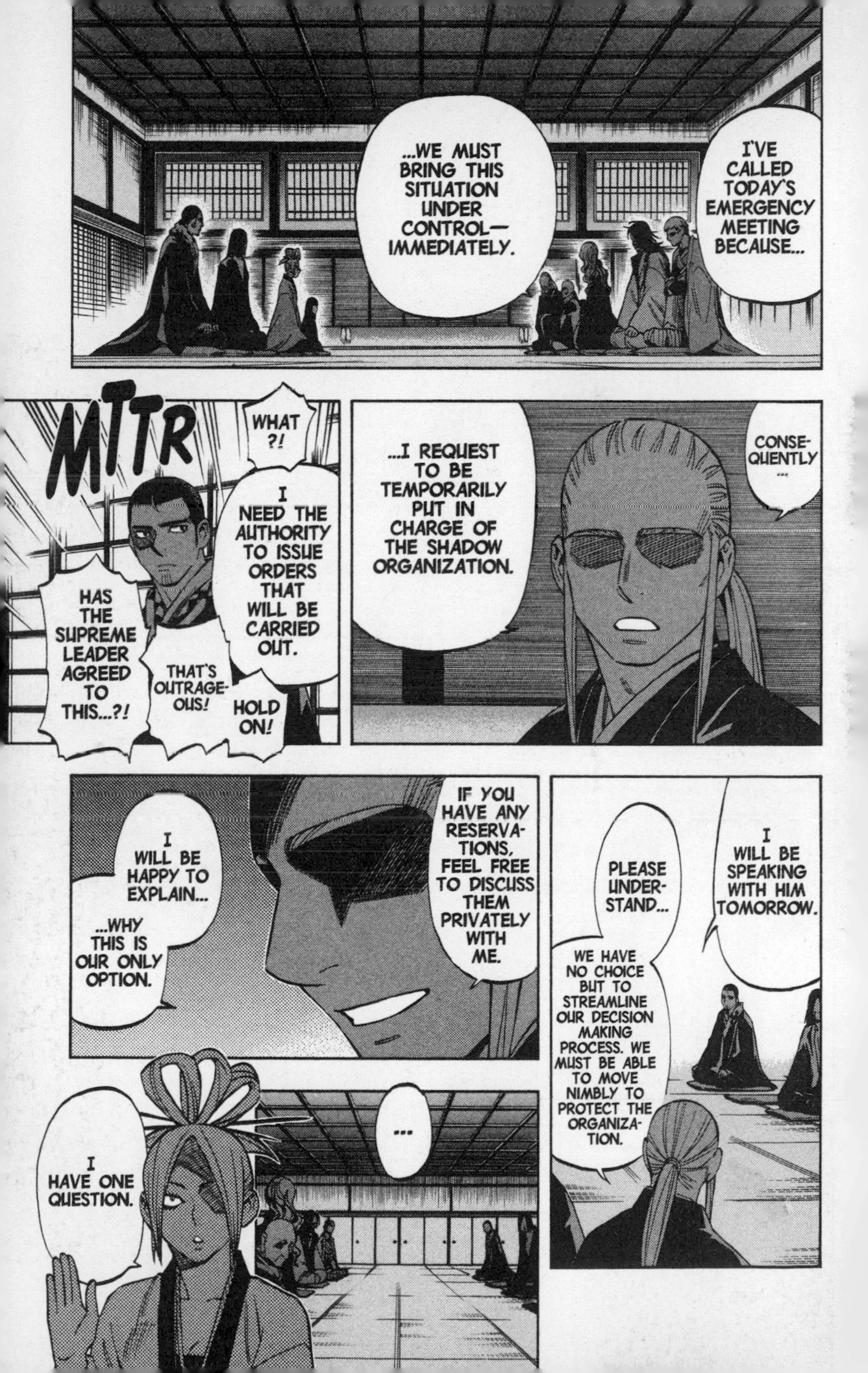
I'VE CALLED TODAY'S EMERGENCY MEETING BECAUSE...
...WE MUST BRING THIS SITUATION UNDER CONTROL—IMMEDIATELY.
CONSEQUENTLY...
...I REQUEST TO BE TEMPORARILY PUT IN CHARGE OF THE SHADOW ORGANIZATION.
I NEED THE AUTHORITY TO ISSUE ORDERS THAT WILL BE CARRIED OUT.
WHAT?!
MTTR
HOLD ON!
THAT'S OUTRAGEOUS!
HAS THE SUPREME LEADER AGREED TO THIS...?!
I WILL BE SPEAKING WITH HIM TOMORROW.
PLEASE UNDERSTAND...
WE HAVE NO CHOICE BUT TO STREAMLINE OUR DECISION MAKING PROCESS. WE MUST BE ABLE TO MOVE NIMBLY TO PROTECT THE ORGANIZATION.
IF YOU HAVE ANY RESERVATIONS, FEEL FREE TO DISCUSS THEM PRIVATELY WITH ME.
I WILL BE HAPPY TO EXPLAIN...
...WHY THIS IS OUR ONLY OPTION.
...
I HAVE ONE QUESTION.

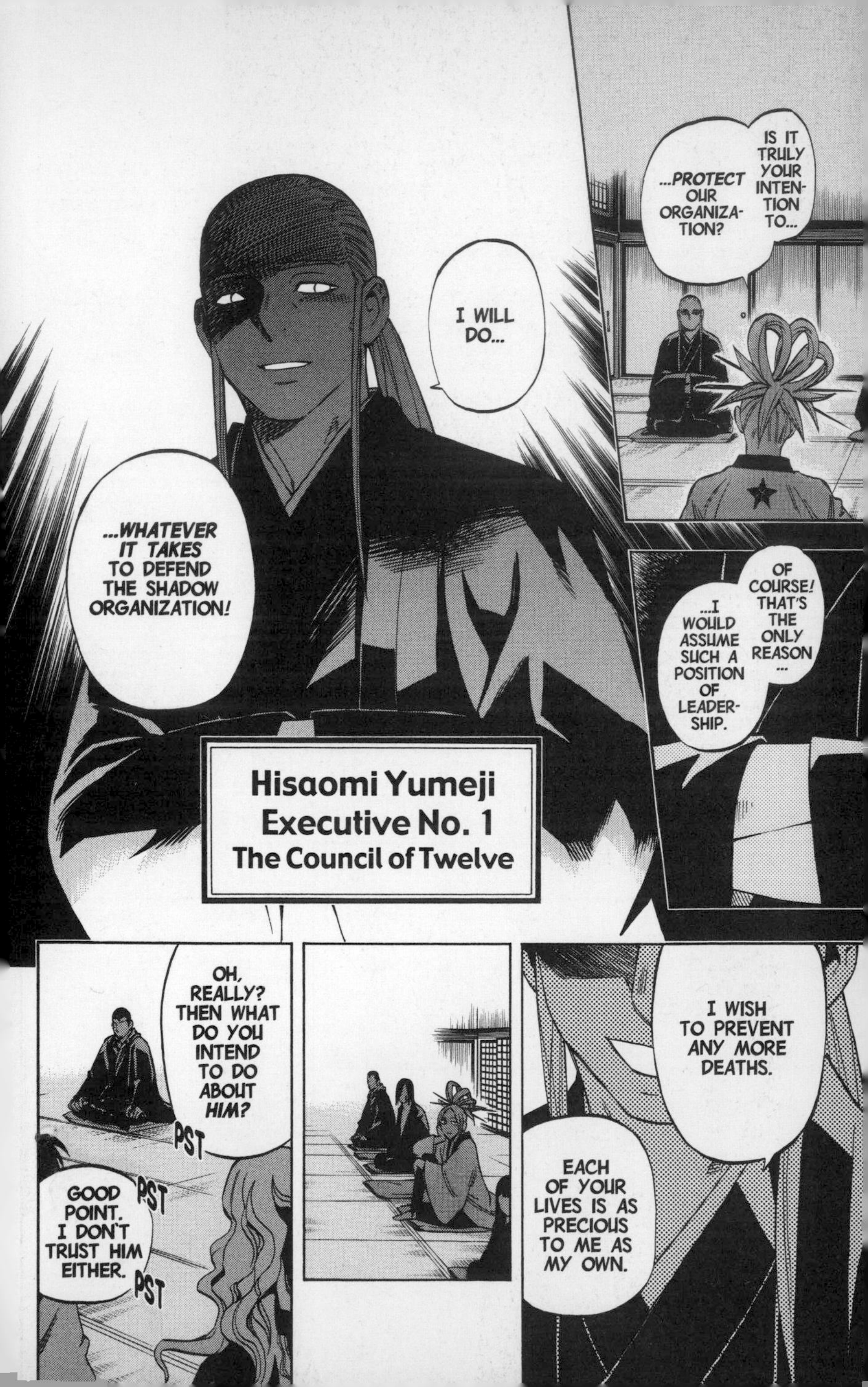
IS IT TRULY YOUR INTENTION TO...
...PROTECT OUR ORGANIZATION?
OF COURSE! THAT'S THE ONLY REASON...
...I WOULD ASSUME SUCH A POSITION OF LEADERSHIP.
I WILL DO...
...WHATEVER IT TAKES TO DEFEND THE SHADOW ORGANIZATION!
Hisaomi Yumeji
Executive No. 1
The Council of Twelve
I WISH TO PREVENT ANY MORE DEATHS.
EACH OF YOUR LIVES IS AS PRECIOUS TO ME AS MY OWN.
OH, REALLY? THEN WHAT DO YOU INTEND TO DO ABOUT HIM?
PST
GOOD POINT. I DON'T TRUST HIM EITHER.
PST
PST

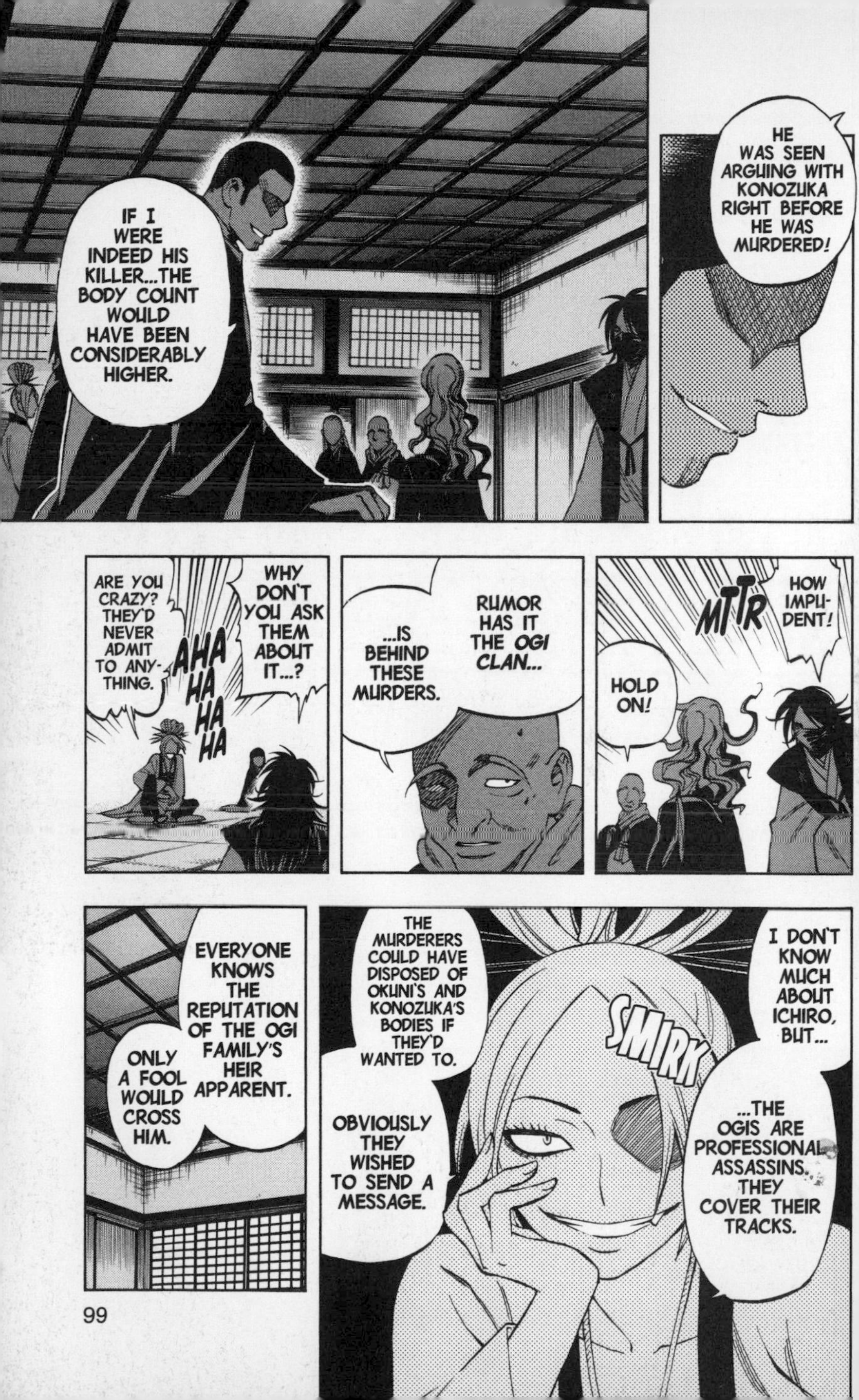
HE WAS SEEN ARGUING WITH KONOZUKA RIGHT BEFORE HE WAS MURDERED!
IF I WERE INDEED HIS KILLER...THE BODY COUNT WOULD HAVE BEEN CONSIDERABLY HIGHER.
HOW IMPU-DENT!
MTTR
HOLD ON!
RUMOR HAS IT THE OGI CLAN...
...IS BEHIND THESE MURDERS.
WHY DON'T YOU ASK THEM ABOUT IT...?
AHA HA HA HA
ARE YOU CRAZY? THEY'D NEVER ADMIT TO ANY-THING.
I DON'T KNOW MUCH ABOUT ICHIRO, BUT...
SMIRK
THE MURDERERS COULD HAVE DISPOSED OF OKUNI'S AND KONOZUKA'S BODIES IF THEY'D WANTED TO.
...THE OGIS ARE PROFESSIONAL ASSASSINS. THEY COVER THEIR TRACKS.
OBVIOUSLY THEY WISHED TO SEND A MESSAGE.
EVERYONE KNOWS THE REPUTATION OF THE OGI FAMILY'S HEIR APPARENT.
ONLY A FOOL WOULD CROSS HIM.

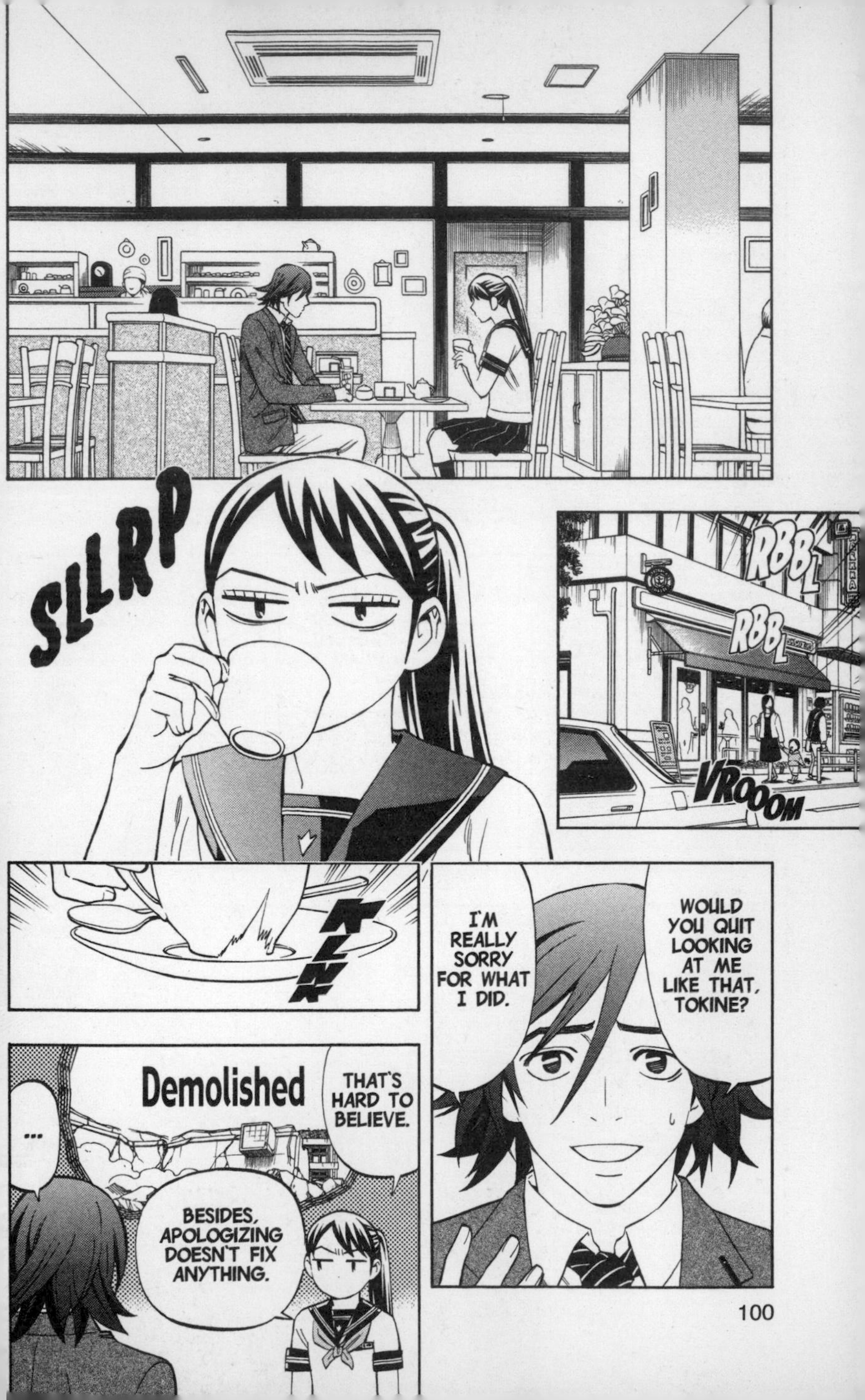
RBBL
RBBL
VROOOM
SLLRP
WOULD YOU QUIT LOOKING AT ME LIKE THAT, TOKINE?
I'M REALLY SORRY FOR WHAT I DID.
KLINK
THAT'S HARD TO BELIEVE.
Demolished
BESIDES, APOLOGIZING DOESN'T FIX ANYTHING.
...

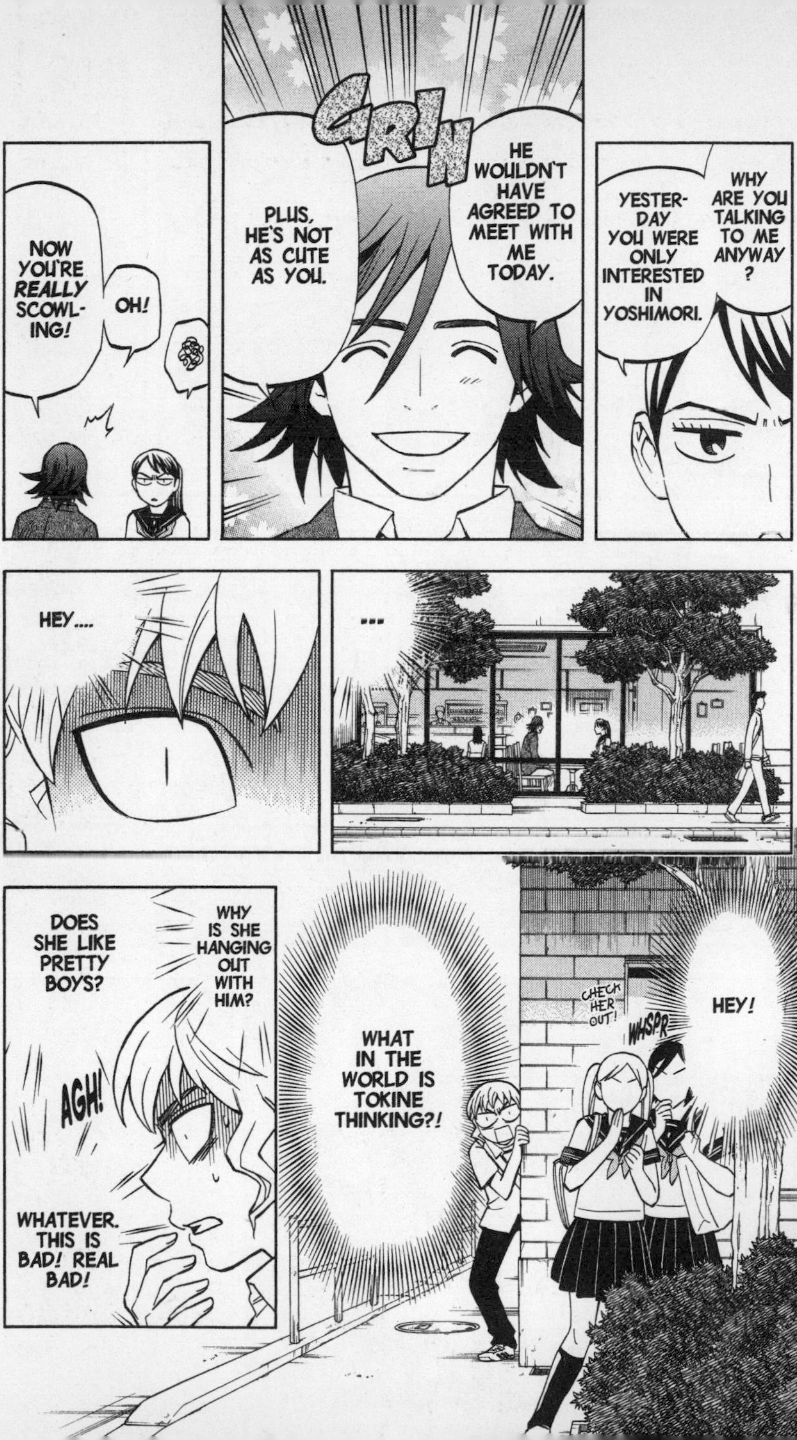
WHY ARE YOU TALKING TO ME ANYWAY?
YESTERDAY YOU WERE ONLY INTERESTED IN YOSHIMORI.
GRIN
HE WOULDN'T HAVE AGREED TO MEET WITH ME TODAY.
PLUS, HE'S NOT AS CUTE AS YOU.
OH!
NOW YOU'RE *REALLY* SCOWLING!
...
HEY....
HEY!
WHSPR
CHECK HER OUT!
WHAT IN THE WORLD IS TOKINE THINKING?!
WHY IS SHE HANGING OUT WITH HIM?
DOES SHE LIKE PRETTY BOYS?
AGH!
WHATEVER. THIS IS BAD! REAL BAD!

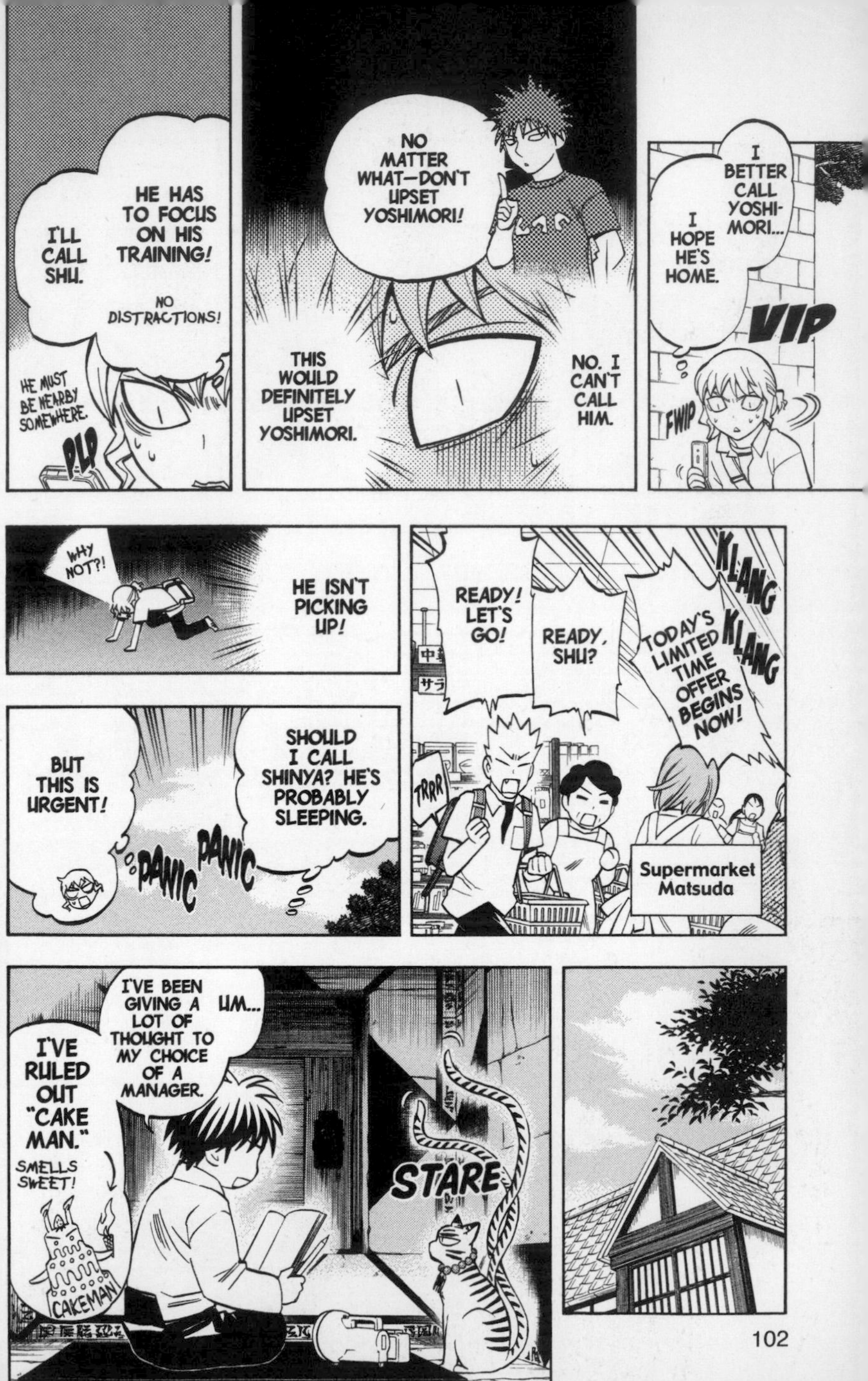
I BETTER CALL YOSHIMORI...
I HOPE HE'S HOME.
VIP
FWIP
NO MATTER WHAT—DON'T UPSET YOSHIMORI!
NO. I CAN'T CALL HIM.
THIS WOULD DEFINITELY UPSET YOSHIMORI.
HE HAS TO FOCUS ON HIS TRAINING!
NO DISTRACTIONS!
I'LL CALL SHU.
HE MUST BE NEARBY SOMEWHERE.
PLP
KLANG
KLANG
TODAY'S LIMITED TIME OFFER BEGINS NOW!
READY, SHU?
READY! LET'S GO!
TRRR
Supermarket Matsuda
HE ISN'T PICKING UP!
WHY NOT?!
SHOULD I CALL SHINYA? HE'S PROBABLY SLEEPING.
BUT THIS IS URGENT!
PANIC
PANIC
UM...
I'VE BEEN GIVING A LOT OF THOUGHT TO MY CHOICE OF A MANAGER.
I'VE RULED OUT "CAKE MAN."
SMELLS SWEET!
CAKEMAN
STARE

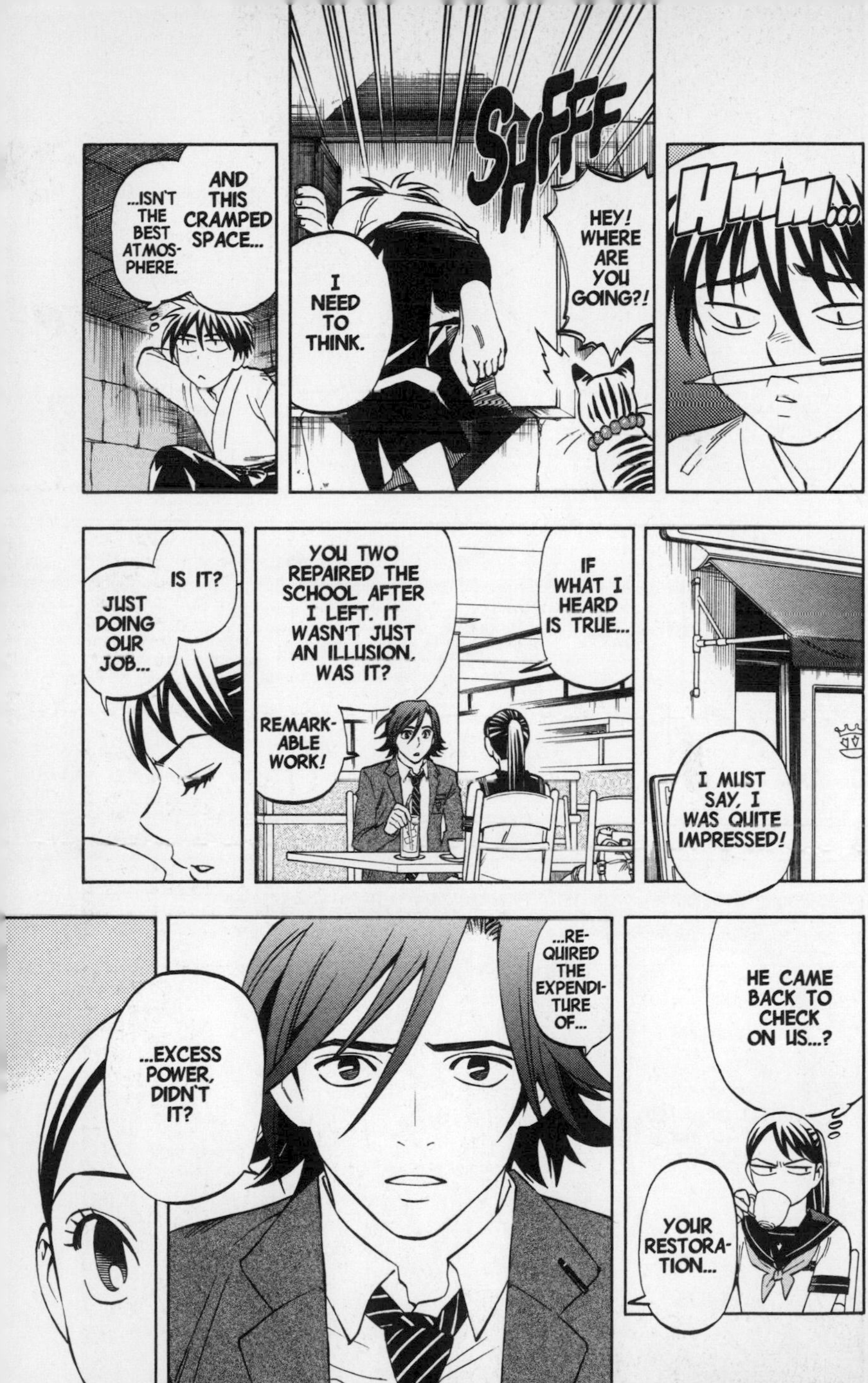
HMM...
SHFFF
HEY! WHERE ARE YOU GOING?!
I NEED TO THINK.
AND THIS CRAMPED SPACE...
...ISN'T THE BEST ATMOSPHERE.
I MUST SAY, I WAS QUITE IMPRESSED!
IF WHAT I HEARD IS TRUE...
YOU TWO REPAIRED THE SCHOOL AFTER I LEFT. IT WASN'T JUST AN ILLUSION, WAS IT?
REMARKABLE WORK!
IS IT?
JUST DOING OUR JOB...
HE CAME BACK TO CHECK ON US...?
YOUR RESTORATION...
...REQUIRED THE EXPENDITURE OF...
...EXCESS POWER, DIDN'T IT?

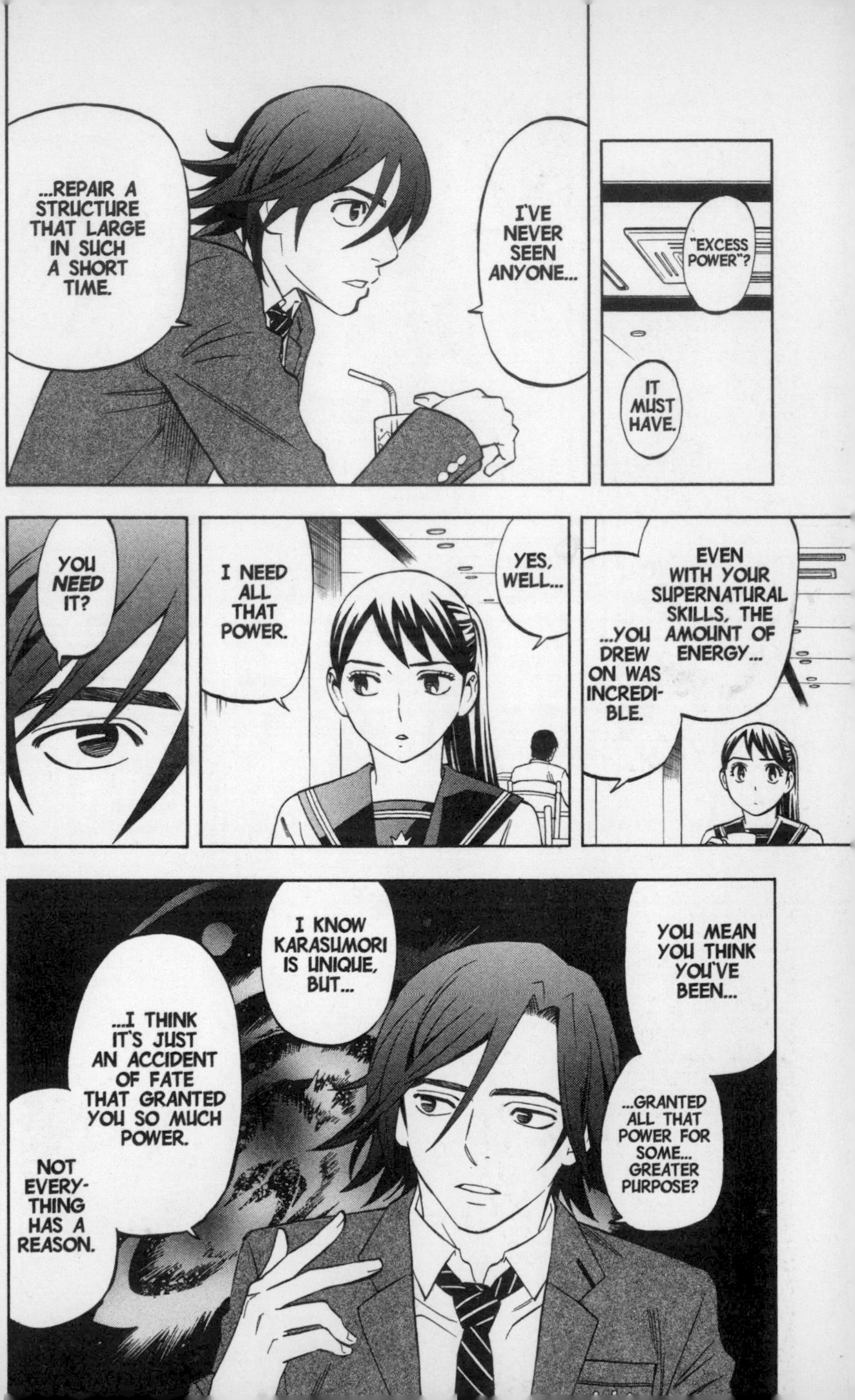
"EXCESS POWER"?
IT MUST HAVE.
I'VE NEVER SEEN ANYONE...
...REPAIR A STRUCTURE THAT LARGE IN SUCH A SHORT TIME.
EVEN WITH YOUR SUPERNATURAL SKILLS, THE AMOUNT OF ENERGY...
...YOU DREW ON WAS INCREDI-BLE.
YES, WELL...
I NEED ALL THAT POWER.
YOU NEED IT?
YOU MEAN YOU THINK YOU'VE BEEN...
...GRANTED ALL THAT POWER FOR SOME... GREATER PURPOSE?
I KNOW KARASUMORI IS UNIQUE, BUT...
...I THINK IT'S JUST AN ACCIDENT OF FATE THAT GRANTED YOU SO MUCH POWER.
NOT EVERY-THING HAS A REASON.

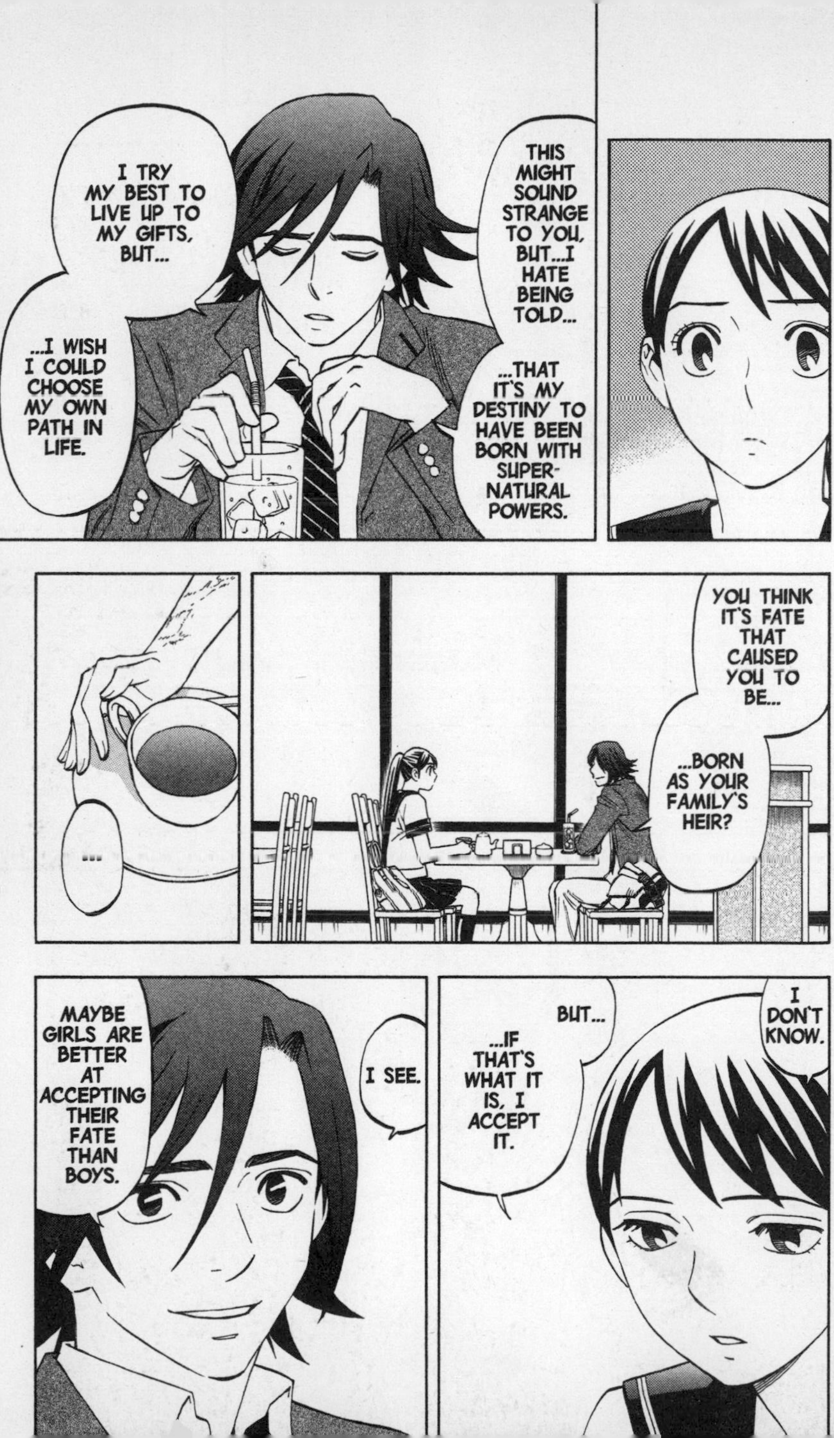
THIS MIGHT SOUND STRANGE TO YOU, BUT...I HATE BEING TOLD...
...THAT IT'S MY DESTINY TO HAVE BEEN BORN WITH SUPER-NATURAL POWERS.
I TRY MY BEST TO LIVE UP TO MY GIFTS, BUT...
...I WISH I COULD CHOOSE MY OWN PATH IN LIFE.
YOU THINK IT'S FATE THAT CAUSED YOU TO BE...
...BORN AS YOUR FAMILY'S HEIR?
...
I DON'T KNOW.
BUT...
...IF THAT'S WHAT IT IS, I ACCEPT IT.
I SEE.
MAYBE GIRLS ARE BETTER AT ACCEPTING THEIR FATE THAN BOYS.

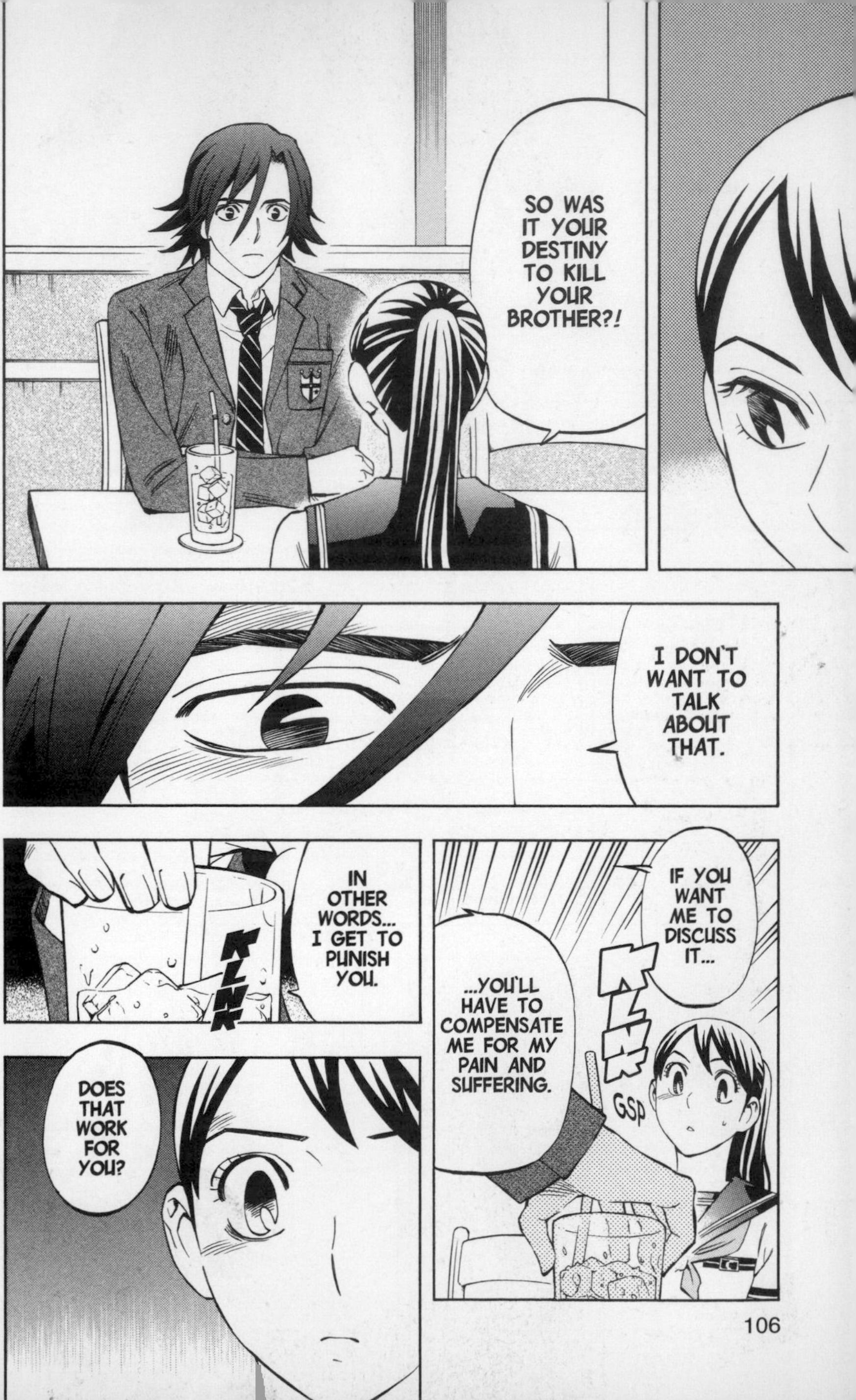
SO WAS IT YOUR DESTINY TO KILL YOUR BROTHER?!
I DON'T WANT TO TALK ABOUT THAT.
IF YOU WANT ME TO DISCUSS IT...
...YOU'LL HAVE TO COMPENSATE ME FOR MY PAIN AND SUFFERING.
KLNK
GSP
IN OTHER WORDS... I GET TO PUNISH YOU.
KLNK
DOES THAT WORK FOR YOU?

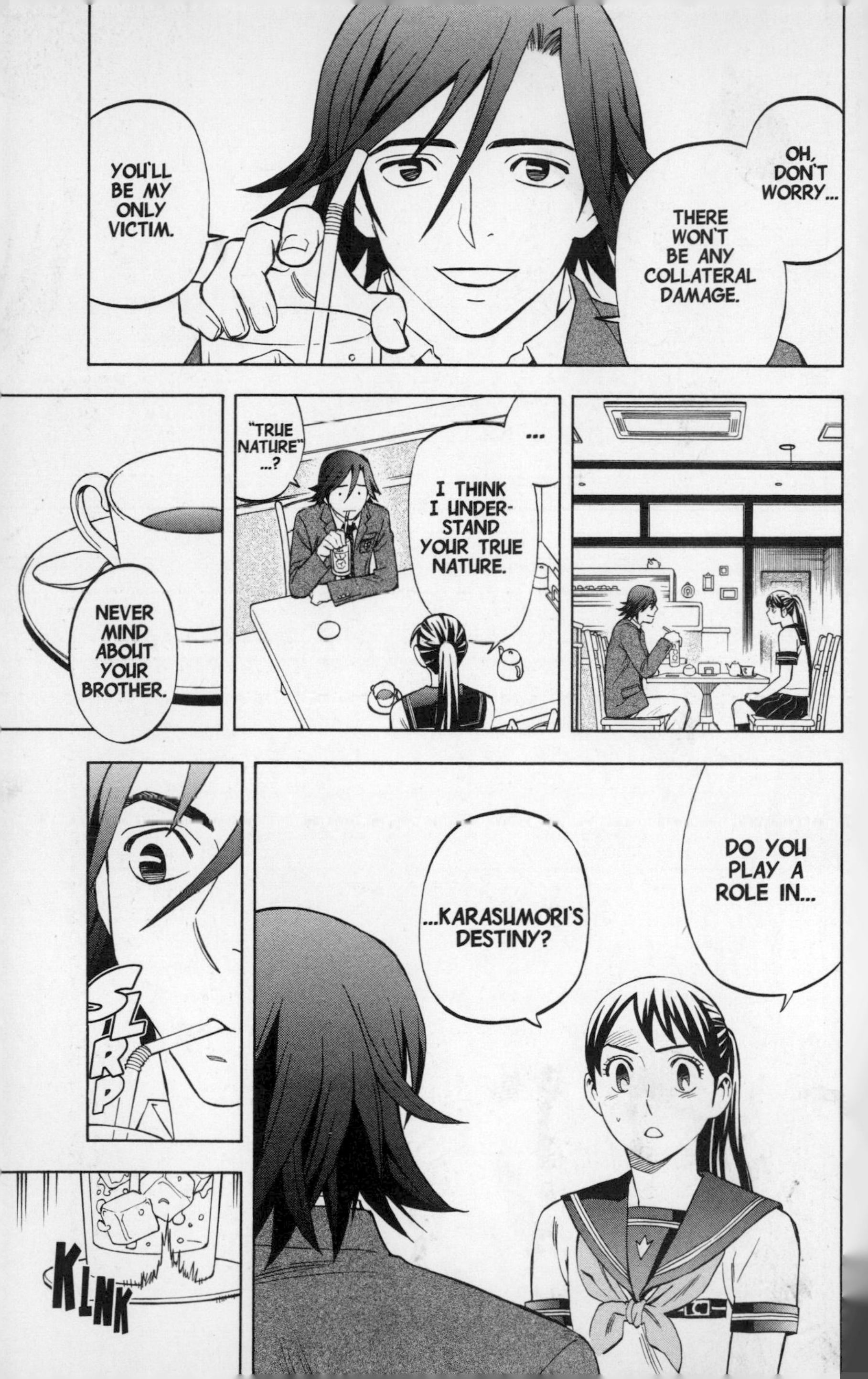
OH, DON'T WORRY...
THERE WON'T BE ANY COLLATERAL DAMAGE.
YOU'LL BE MY ONLY VICTIM.
...
I THINK I UNDER-STAND YOUR TRUE NATURE.
"TRUE NATURE" ...?
NEVER MIND ABOUT YOUR BROTHER.
DO YOU PLAY A ROLE IN...
...KARASUMORI'S DESTINY?
SLRP
KLINK

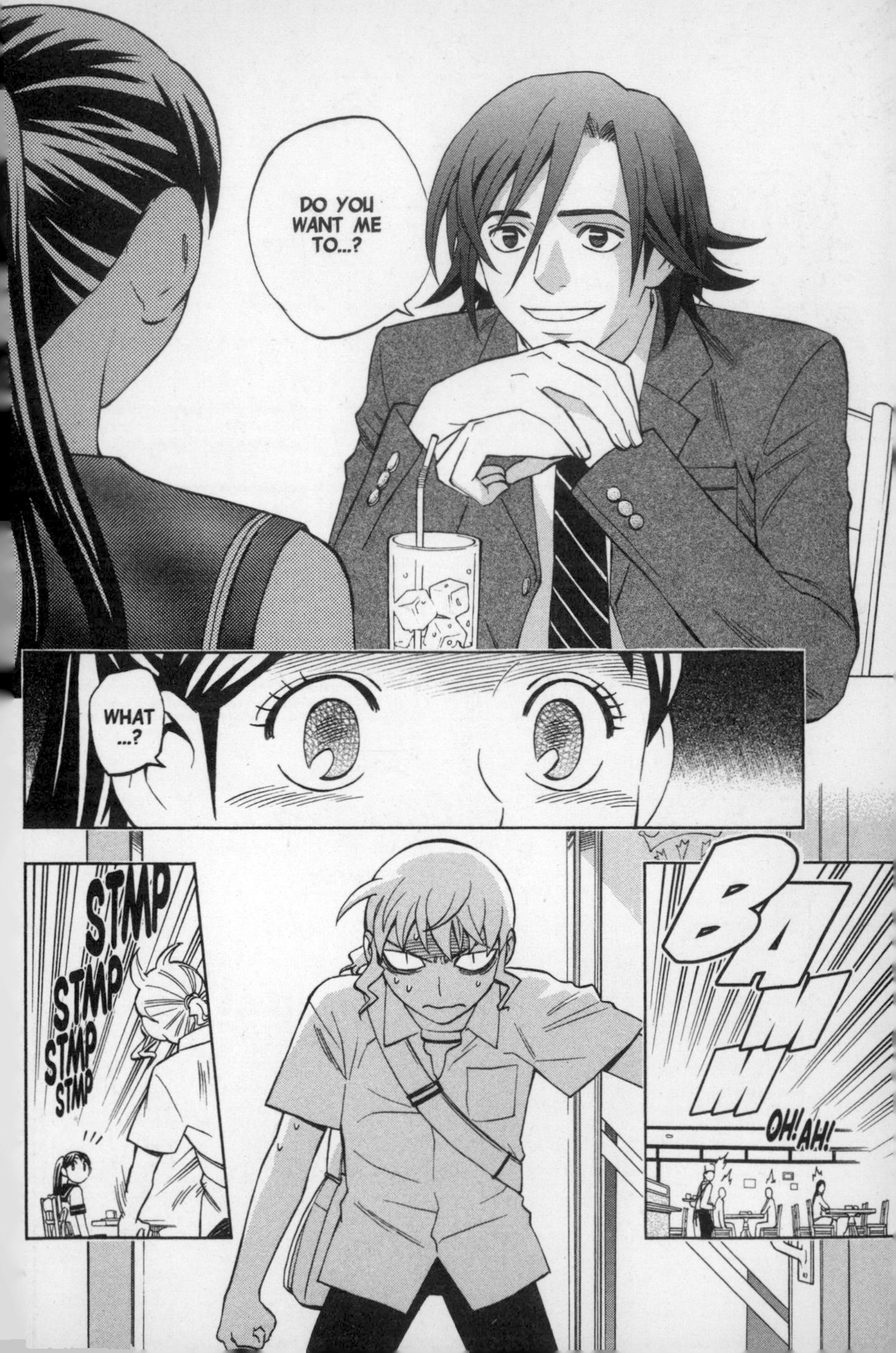
DO YOU WANT ME TO...?
WHAT ...?
BAMM
OH! AH!
STMP STMP STMP STMP

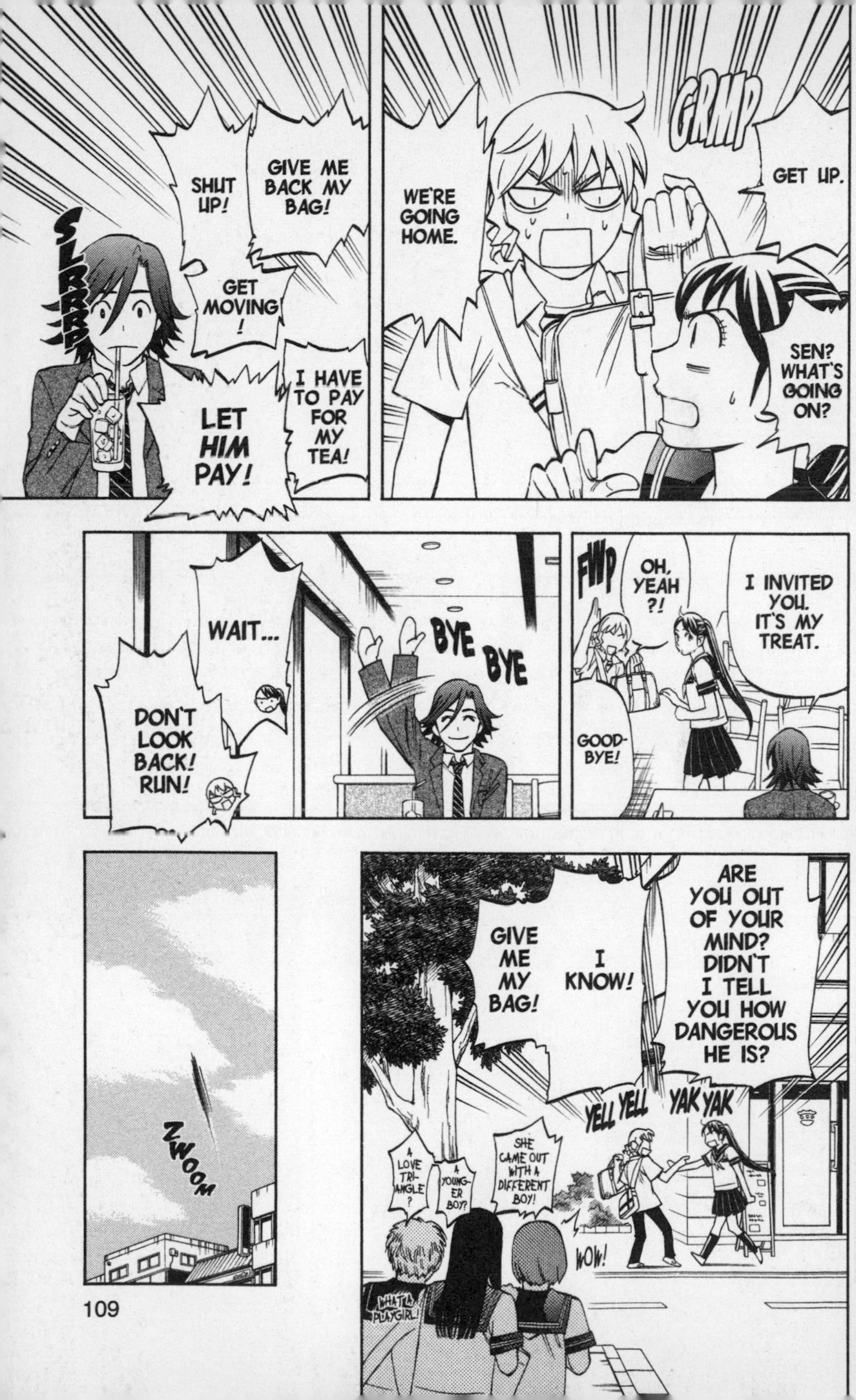
GRMP
GET UP.
SEN? WHAT'S GOING ON?
WE'RE GOING HOME.
GIVE ME BACK MY BAG!
SHUT UP!
I HAVE TO PAY FOR MY TEA!
GET MOVING!
LET HIM PAY!
SLRRRP
I INVITED YOU. IT'S MY TREAT.
OH, YEAH?!
FWP
GOOD-BYE!
WAIT...
BYE BYE
DON'T LOOK BACK! RUN!
ARE YOU OUT OF YOUR MIND? DIDN'T I TELL YOU HOW DANGEROUS HE IS?
I KNOW!
GIVE ME MY BAG!
YAK YAK
YELL YELL
SHE CAME OUT WITH A DIFFERENT BOY!
A YOUNGER BOY?
A LOVE TRIANGLE?
WOW!
WHAT A PLAYGIRL!
ZWOOM

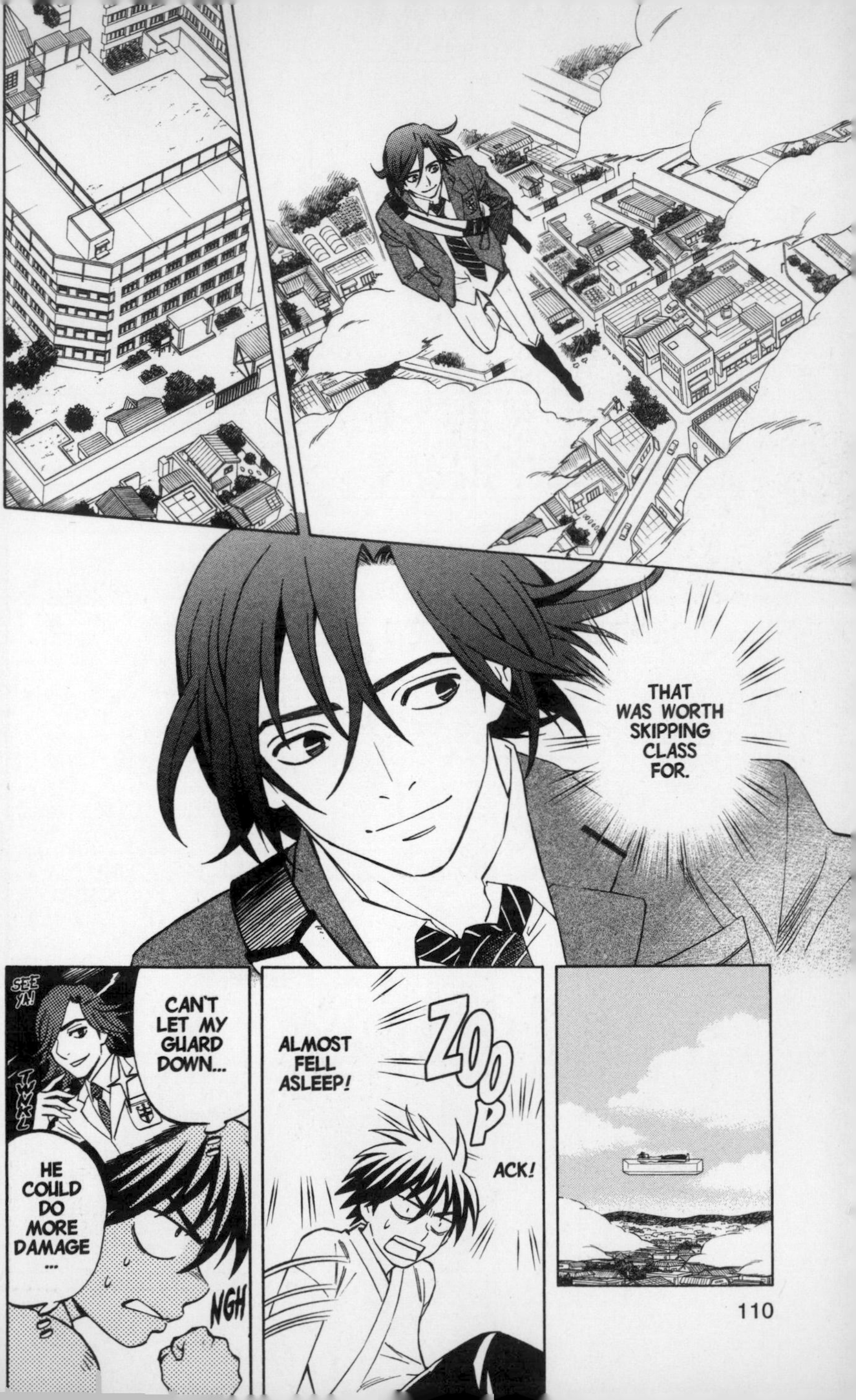
THAT WAS WORTH SKIPPING CLASS FOR.
ZOOP
ALMOST FELL ASLEEP!
ACK!
CAN'T LET MY GUARD DOWN...
SEE YA!
HE COULD DO MORE DAMAGE...
NGH

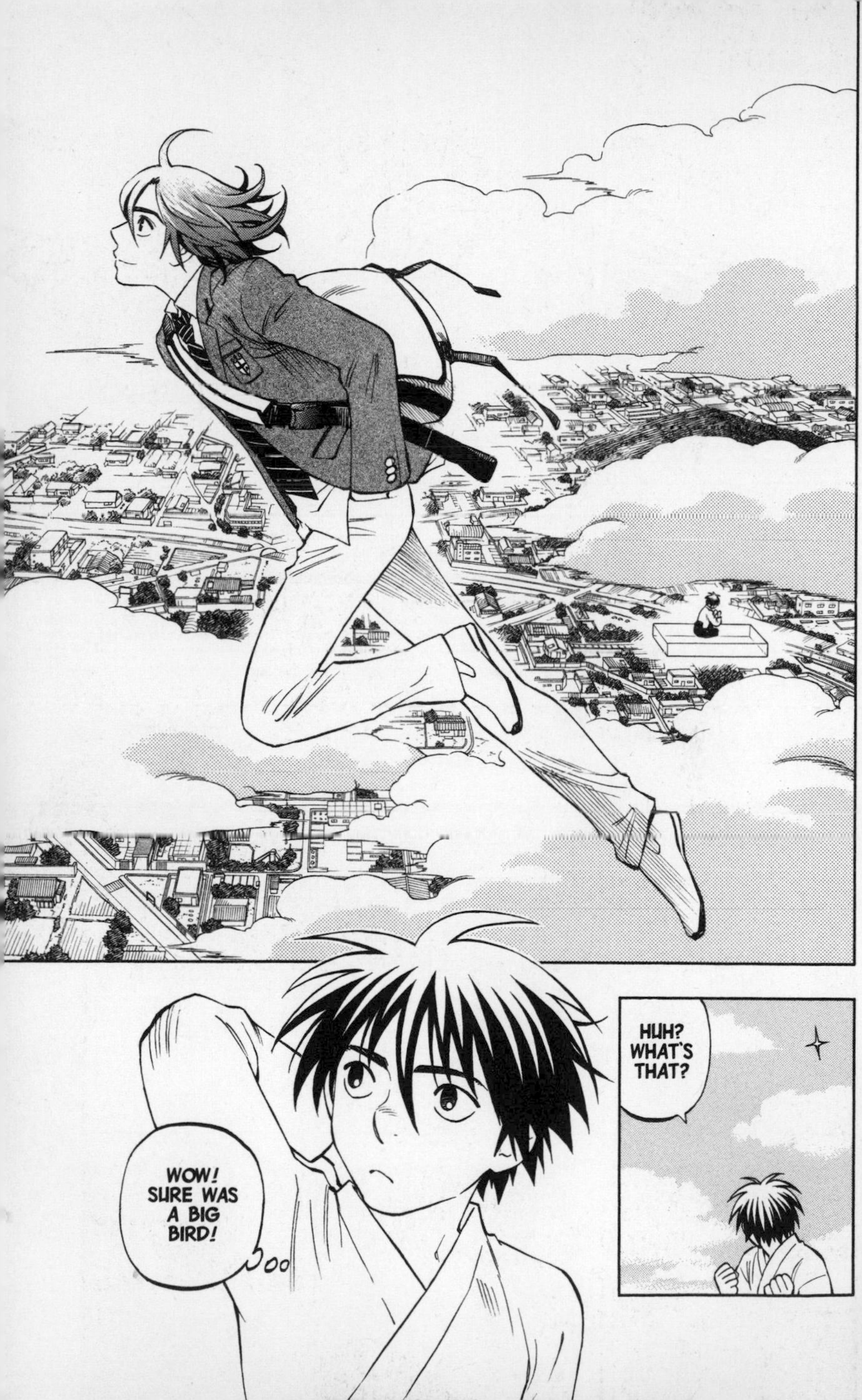
HUH? WHAT'S THAT?
WOW! SURE WAS A BIG BIRD!

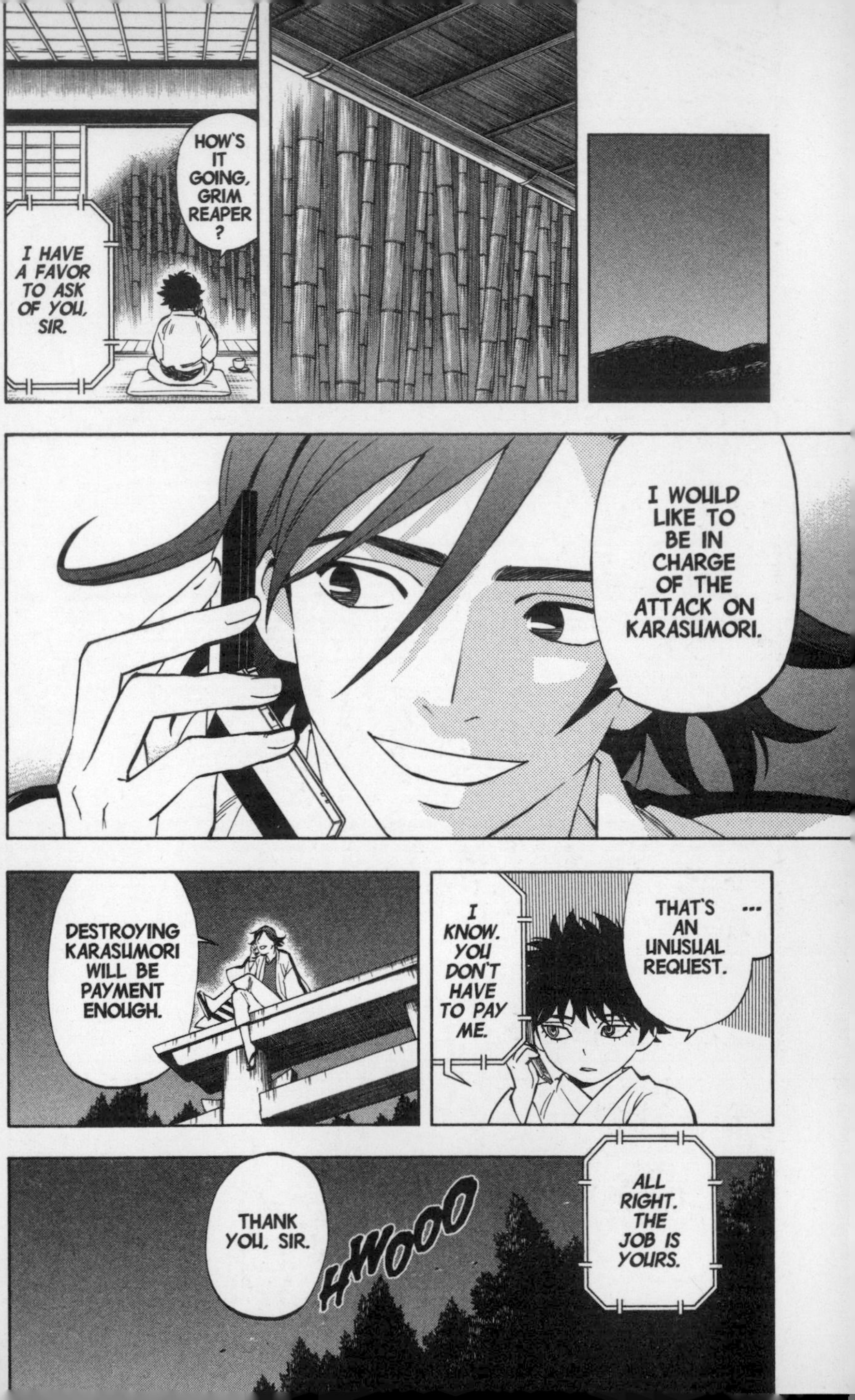
HOW'S IT GOING, GRIM REAPER?
I HAVE A FAVOR TO ASK OF YOU, SIR.
I WOULD LIKE TO BE IN CHARGE OF THE ATTACK ON KARASUMORI.
THAT'S ... AN UNUSUAL REQUEST.
I KNOW. YOU DON'T HAVE TO PAY ME.
DESTROYING KARASUMORI WILL BE PAYMENT ENOUGH.
ALL RIGHT. THE JOB IS YOURS.
HWOOO
THANK YOU, SIR.

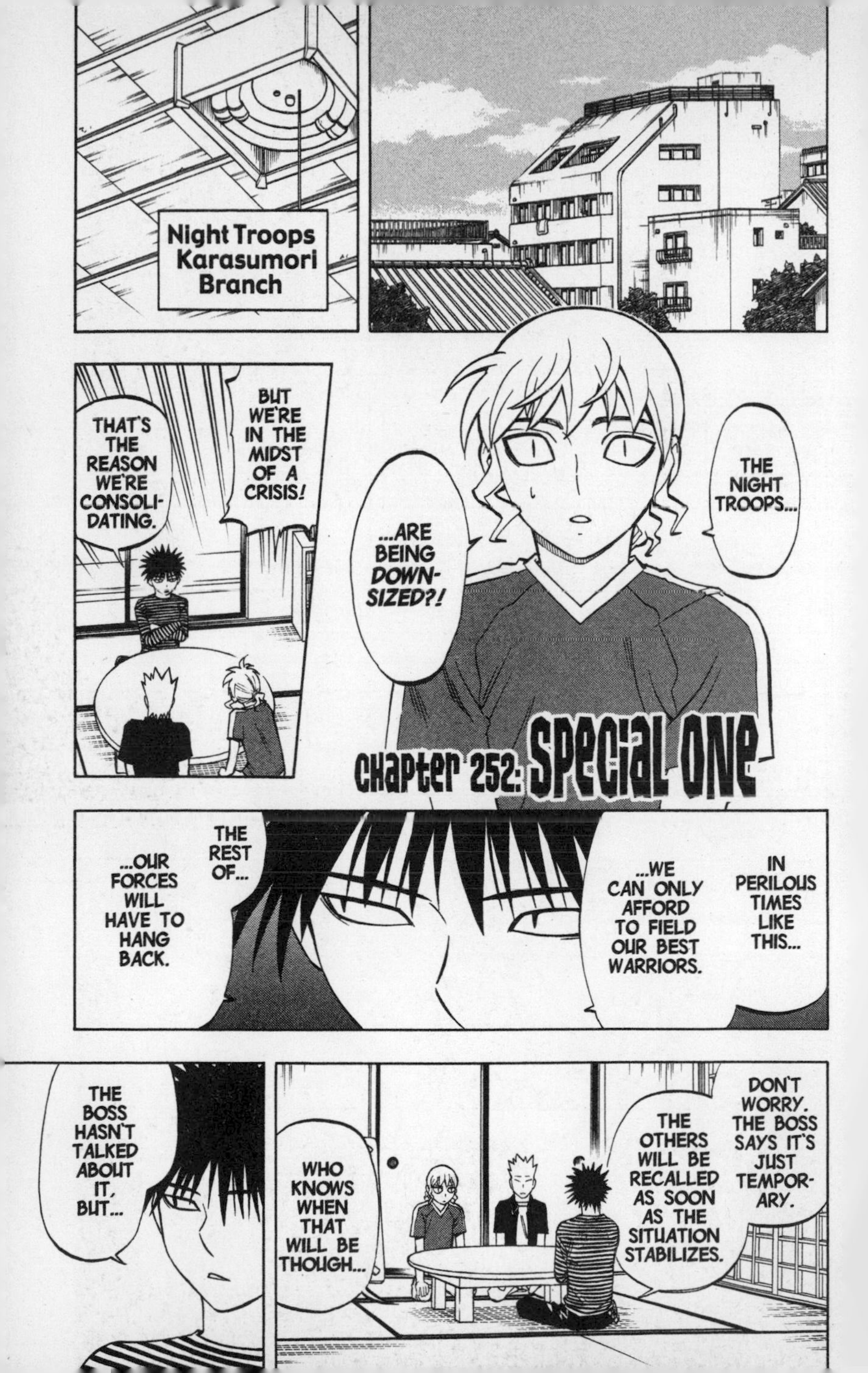
Night Troops Karasumori Branch
THE NIGHT TROOPS...
...ARE BEING DOWNSIZED?!
Chapter 252: Special One
BUT WE'RE IN THE MIDST OF A CRISIS!
THAT'S THE REASON WE'RE CONSOLIDATING.
IN PERILOUS TIMES LIKE THIS...
...WE CAN ONLY AFFORD TO FIELD OUR BEST WARRIORS.
THE REST OF...
...OUR FORCES WILL HAVE TO HANG BACK.
DON'T WORRY. THE BOSS SAYS IT'S JUST TEMPORARY.
THE OTHERS WILL BE RECALLED AS SOON AS THE SITUATION STABILIZES.
WHO KNOWS WHEN THAT WILL BE THOUGH...
THE BOSS HASN'T TALKED ABOUT IT, BUT...

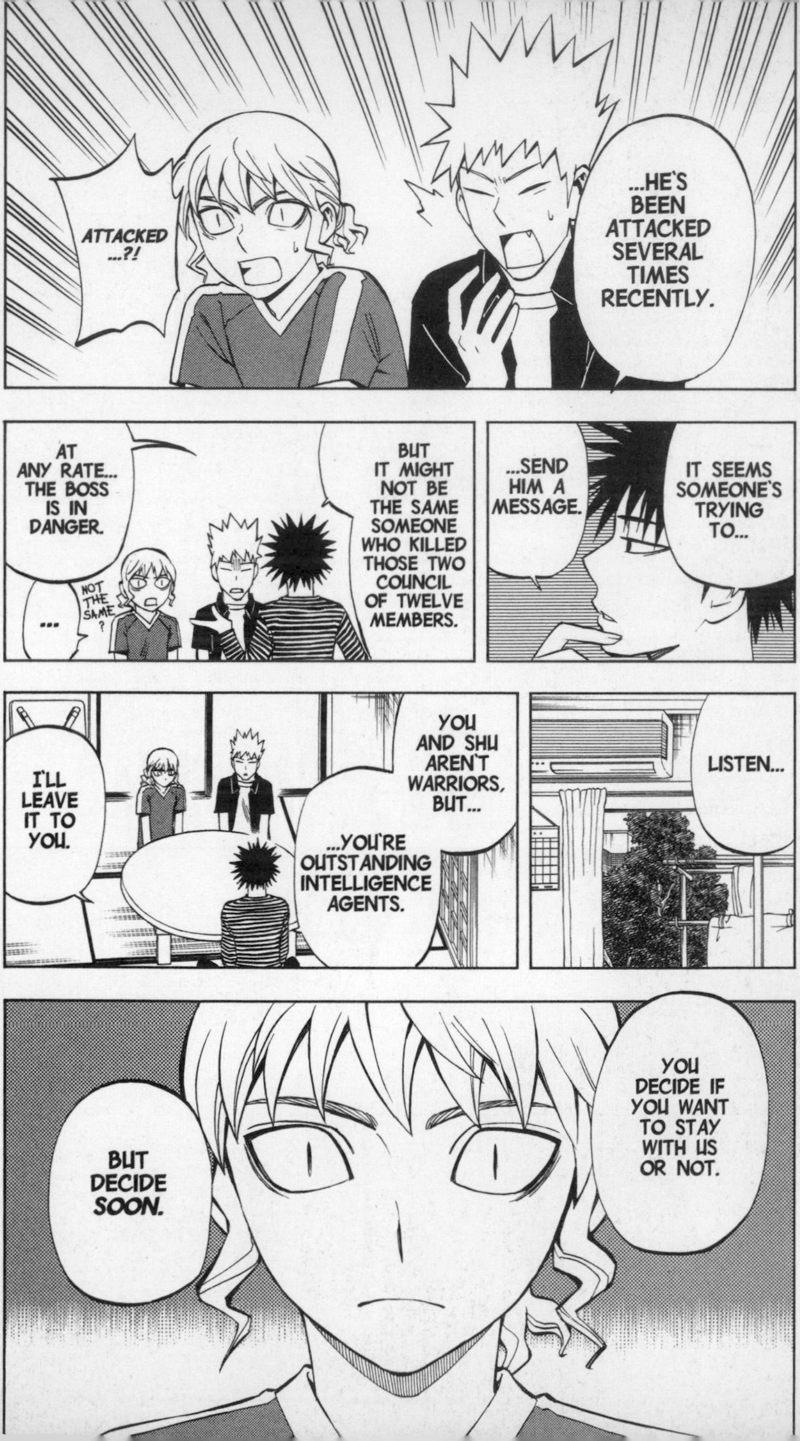
...HE'S BEEN ATTACKED SEVERAL TIMES RECENTLY.
ATTACKED ...?!
IT SEEMS SOMEONE'S TRYING TO...
...SEND HIM A MESSAGE.
BUT IT MIGHT NOT BE THE SAME SOMEONE WHO KILLED THOSE TWO COUNCIL OF TWELVE MEMBERS.
AT ANY RATE... THE BOSS IS IN DANGER.
NOT THE SAME?
...
LISTEN...
YOU AND SHU AREN'T WARRIORS, BUT...
...YOU'RE OUTSTANDING INTELLIGENCE AGENTS.
I'LL LEAVE IT TO YOU.
YOU DECIDE IF YOU WANT TO STAY WITH US OR NOT.
BUT DECIDE SOON.

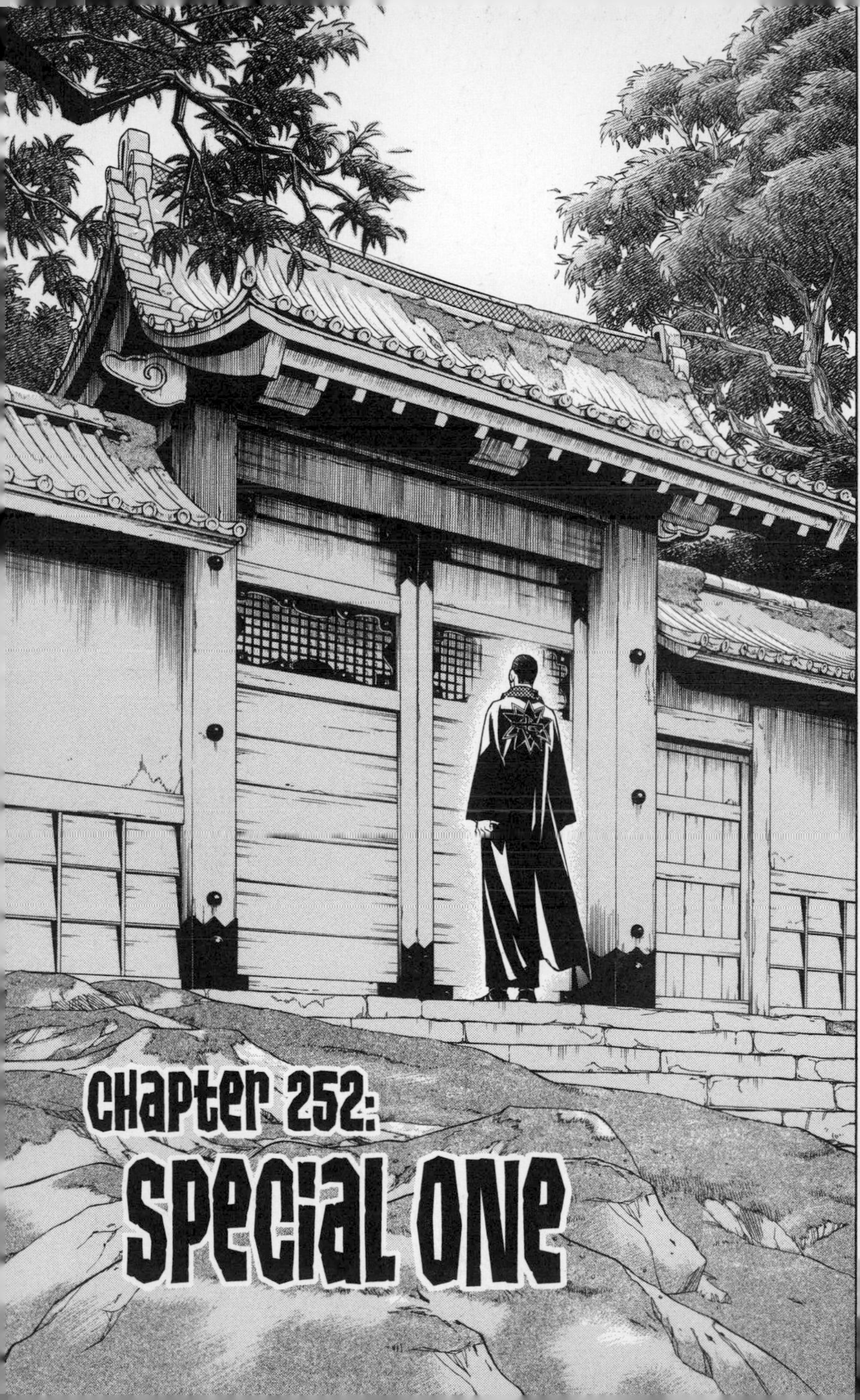
Chapter 252:
Special One

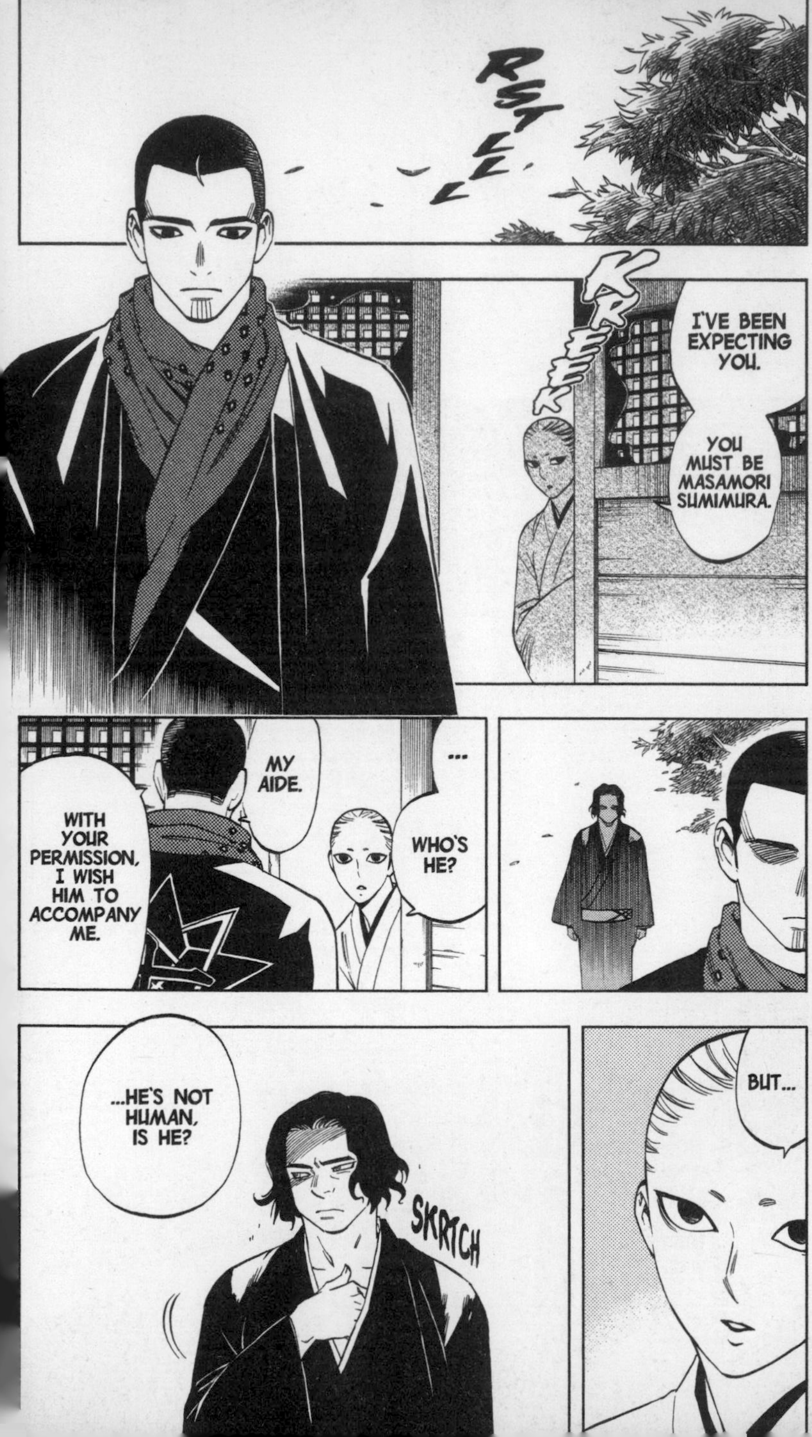
RSTLLL
KREEK
I'VE BEEN EXPECTING YOU.
YOU MUST BE MASAMORI SUMIMURA.
...
WHO'S HE?
MY AIDE.
WITH YOUR PERMISSION, I WISH HIM TO ACCOMPANY ME.
BUT...
...HE'S NOT HUMAN, IS HE?
SKRTCH

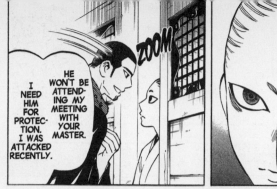

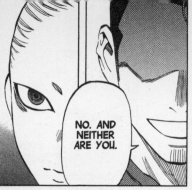

NO. AND NEITHER ARE YOU.
ZOOM
HE WON'T BE ATTENDING MY MEETING WITH YOUR MASTER.
I NEED HIM FOR PROTECTION. I WAS ATTACKED RECENTLY.
CERTAINLY YOU'LL ALLOW ME TO...
...HAVE MY BODYGUARD ACCOMPANY ME.
I'LL HAVE TO ASK MY MASTER'S PERMISSION.
KREEK
PLEASE WAIT HERE.

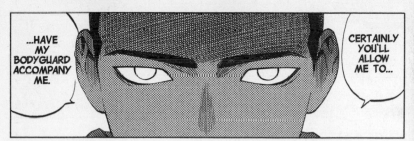

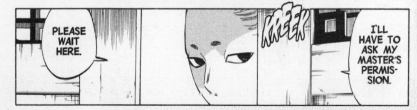

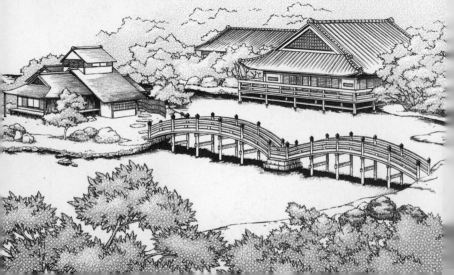

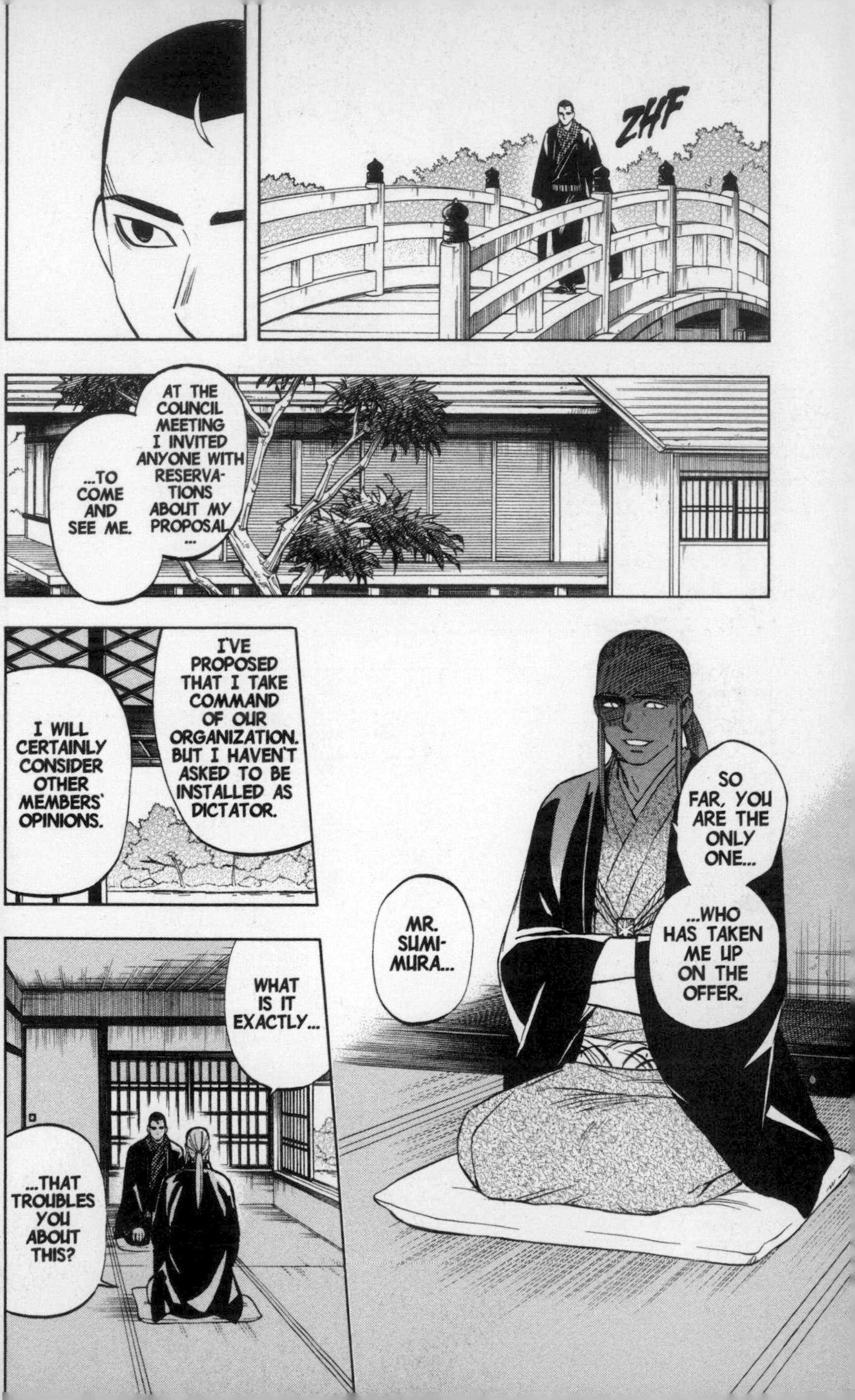
ZHF
AT THE COUNCIL MEETING I INVITED ANYONE WITH RESERVATIONS ABOUT MY PROPOSAL...
...TO COME AND SEE ME.
SO FAR, YOU ARE THE ONLY ONE...
...WHO HAS TAKEN ME UP ON THE OFFER.
MR. SUMIMURA...
I'VE PROPOSED THAT I TAKE COMMAND OF OUR ORGANIZATION. BUT I HAVEN'T ASKED TO BE INSTALLED AS DICTATOR.
I WILL CERTAINLY CONSIDER OTHER MEMBERS' OPINIONS.
WHAT IS IT EXACTLY...
...THAT TROUBLES YOU ABOUT THIS?

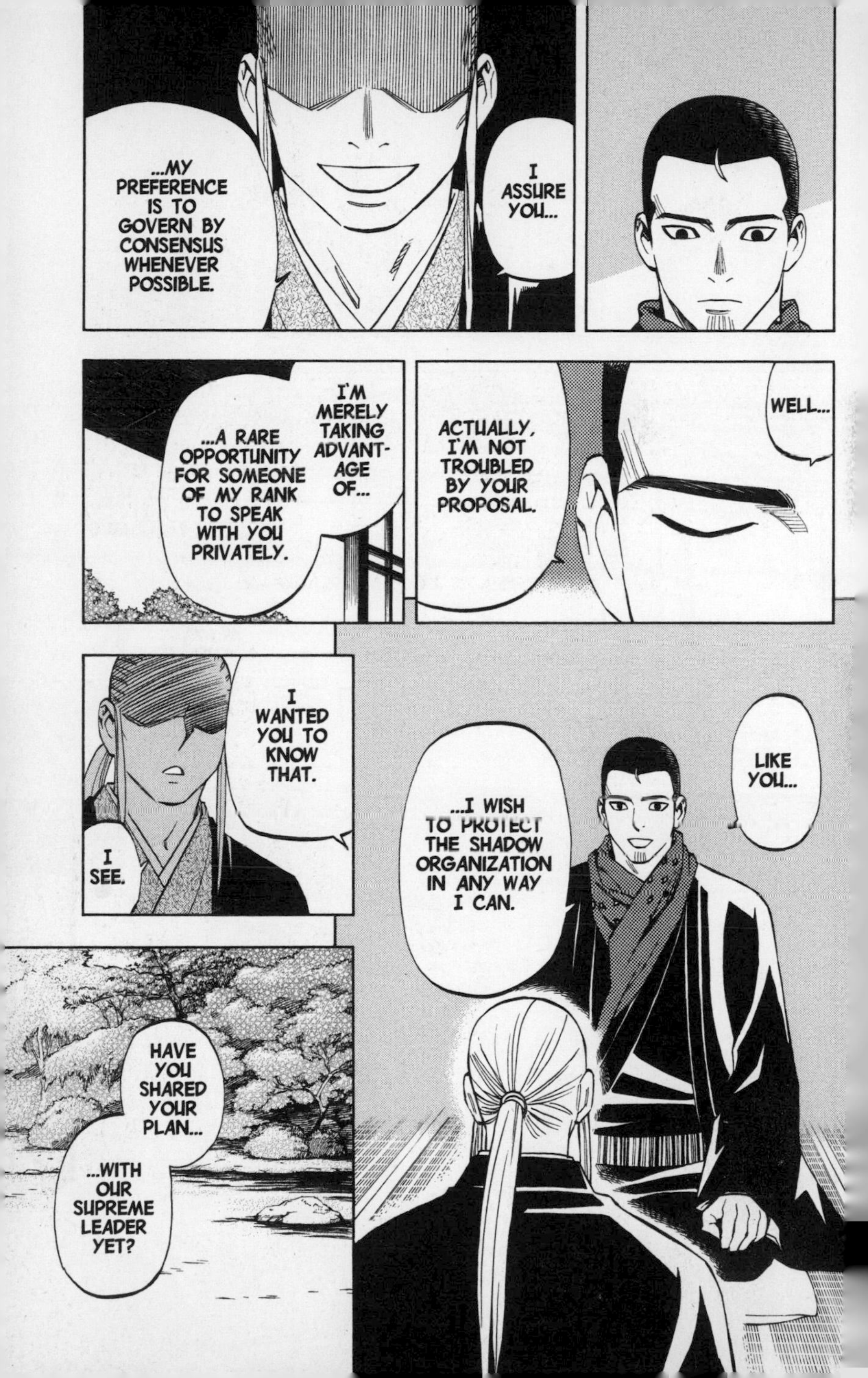
I ASSURE YOU...
...MY PREFERENCE IS TO GOVERN BY CONSENSUS WHENEVER POSSIBLE.
WELL...
ACTUALLY, I'M NOT TROUBLED BY YOUR PROPOSAL.
I'M MERELY TAKING ADVANTAGE OF...
...A RARE OPPORTUNITY FOR SOMEONE OF MY RANK TO SPEAK WITH YOU PRIVATELY.
LIKE YOU...
...I WISH TO PROTECT THE SHADOW ORGANIZATION IN ANY WAY I CAN.
I WANTED YOU TO KNOW THAT.
I SEE.
HAVE YOU SHARED YOUR PLAN...
...WITH OUR SUPREME LEADER YET?

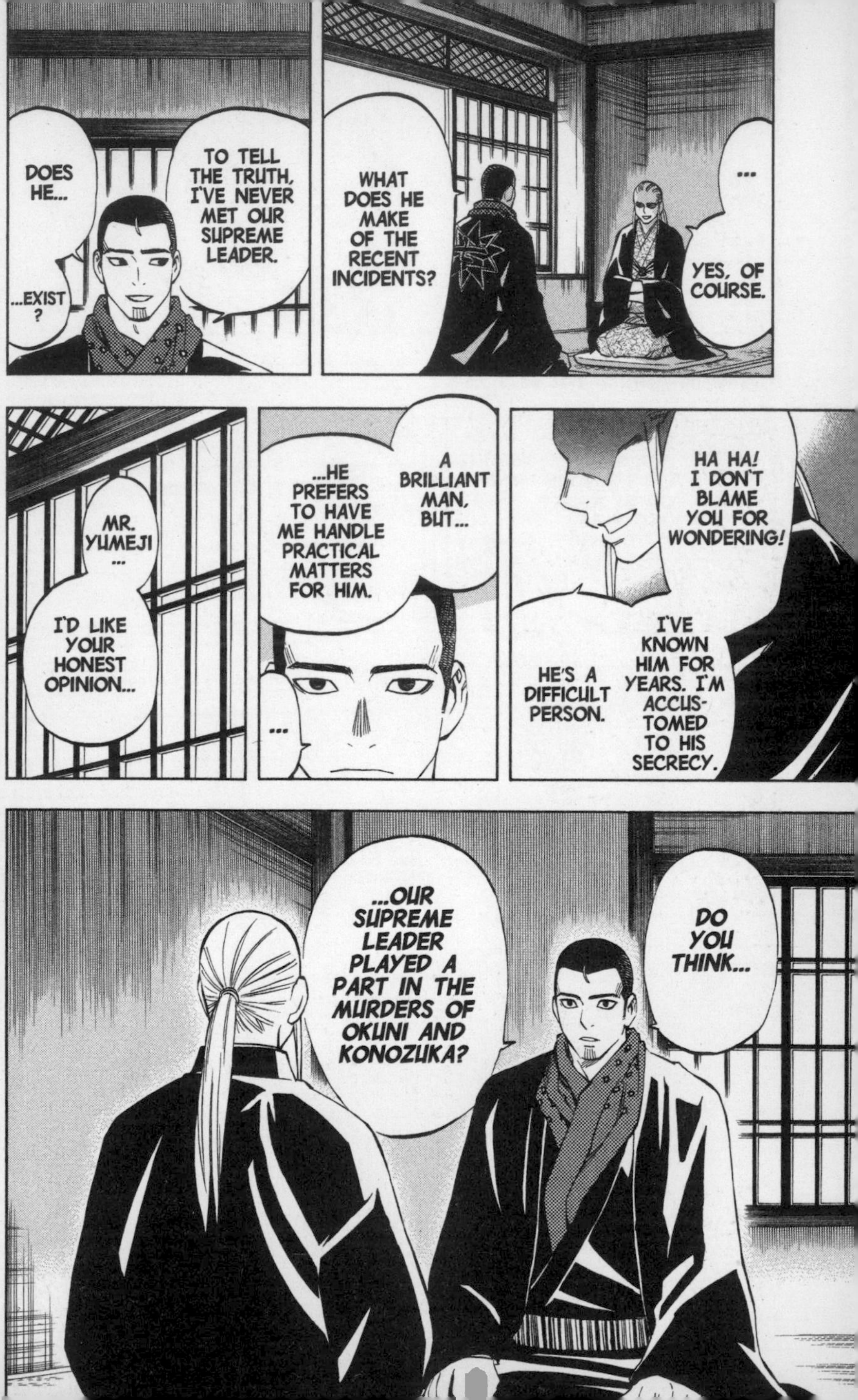
...
YES, OF COURSE.
WHAT DOES HE MAKE OF THE RECENT INCIDENTS?
TO TELL THE TRUTH, I'VE NEVER MET OUR SUPREME LEADER.
DOES HE...
...EXIST?
HA HA! I DON'T BLAME YOU FOR WONDERING!
I'VE KNOWN HIM FOR YEARS. I'M ACCUS-TOMED TO HIS SECRECY.
HE'S A DIFFICULT PERSON.
A BRILLIANT MAN, BUT...
...HE PREFERS TO HAVE ME HANDLE PRACTICAL MATTERS FOR HIM.
...
MR. YUMEJI...
I'D LIKE YOUR HONEST OPINION...
DO YOU THINK...
...OUR SUPREME LEADER PLAYED A PART IN THE MURDERS OF OKUNI AND KONOZUKA?

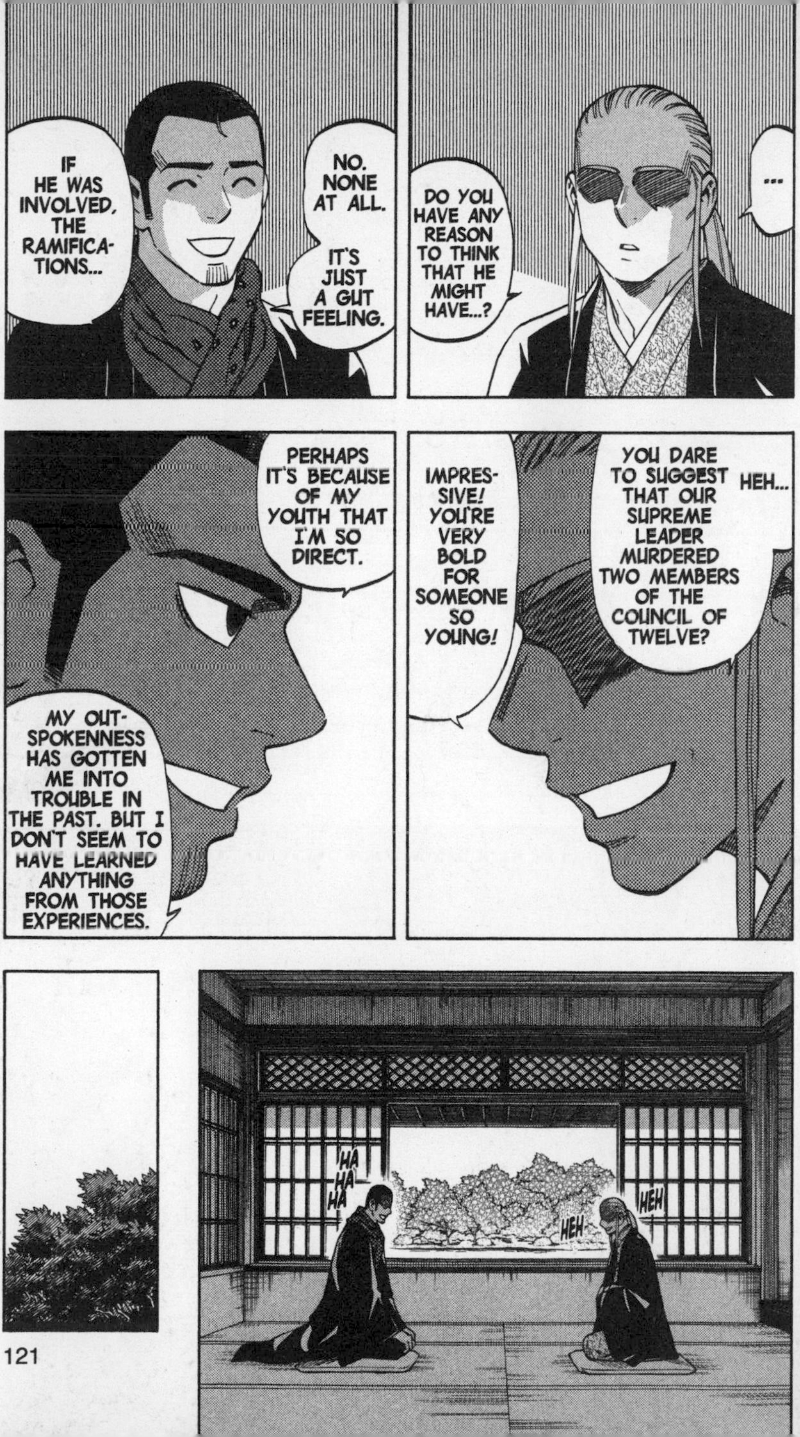
...
DO YOU HAVE ANY REASON TO THINK THAT HE MIGHT HAVE...?
NO. NONE AT ALL.
IT'S JUST A GUT FEELING.
IF HE WAS INVOLVED, THE RAMIFICATIONS...
HEH...
YOU DARE TO SUGGEST THAT OUR SUPREME LEADER MURDERED TWO MEMBERS OF THE COUNCIL OF TWELVE?
IMPRESSIVE! YOU'RE VERY BOLD FOR SOMEONE SO YOUNG!
PERHAPS IT'S BECAUSE OF MY YOUTH THAT I'M SO DIRECT.
MY OUTSPOKENNESS HAS GOTTEN ME INTO TROUBLE IN THE PAST. BUT I DON'T SEEM TO HAVE LEARNED ANYTHING FROM THOSE EXPERIENCES.
HEH
HEH
HA HA HA

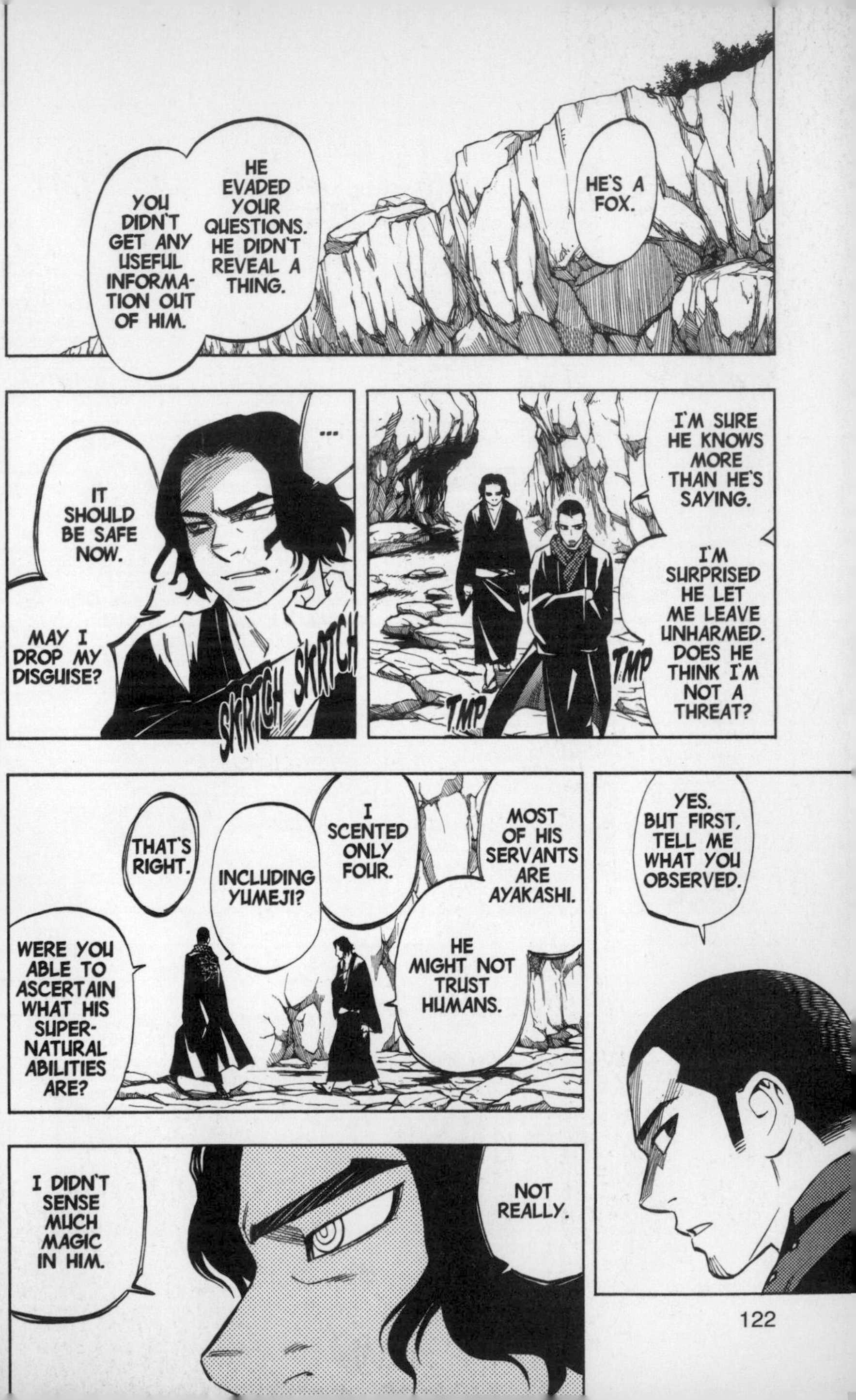

HE'S A FOX.
HE EVADED YOUR QUESTIONS. HE DIDN'T REVEAL A THING.
YOU DIDN'T GET ANY USEFUL INFORMATION OUT OF HIM.
I'M SURE HE KNOWS MORE THAN HE'S SAYING.
I'M SURPRISED HE LET ME LEAVE UNHARMED. DOES HE THINK I'M NOT A THREAT?
TMP
TMP
...
IT SHOULD BE SAFE NOW.
MAY I DROP MY DISGUISE?
SKRTCH SKRTCH
YES. BUT FIRST, TELL ME WHAT YOU OBSERVED.
MOST OF HIS SERVANTS ARE AYAKASHI.
HE MIGHT NOT TRUST HUMANS.
I SCENTED ONLY FOUR.
INCLUDING YUMEJI?
THAT'S RIGHT.
WERE YOU ABLE TO ASCERTAIN WHAT HIS SUPER-NATURAL ABILITIES ARE?
NOT REALLY.
I DIDN'T SENSE MUCH MAGIC IN HIM.

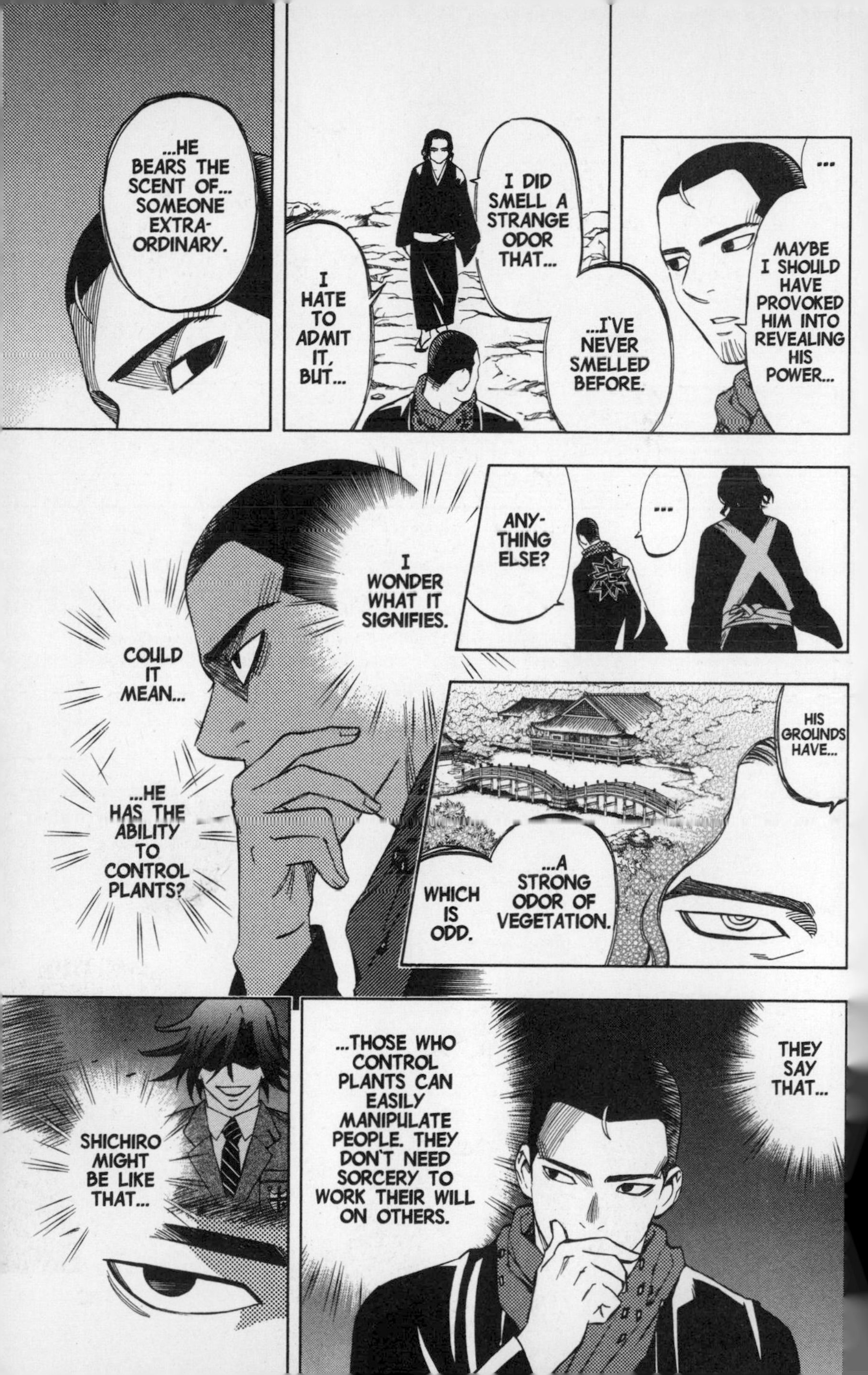
...
MAYBE I SHOULD HAVE PROVOKED HIM INTO REVEALING HIS POWER...
I HATE TO ADMIT IT, BUT...
I DID SMELL A STRANGE ODOR THAT...
...I'VE NEVER SMELLED BEFORE.
...HE BEARS THE SCENT OF... SOMEONE EXTRA-ORDINARY.
...
ANY-THING ELSE?
HIS GROUNDS HAVE...
...A STRONG ODOR OF VEGETATION.
WHICH IS ODD.
I WONDER WHAT IT SIGNIFIES.
COULD IT MEAN...
...HE HAS THE ABILITY TO CONTROL PLANTS?
THEY SAY THAT...
...THOSE WHO CONTROL PLANTS CAN EASILY MANIPULATE PEOPLE. THEY DON'T NEED SORCERY TO WORK THEIR WILL ON OTHERS.
SHICHIRO MIGHT BE LIKE THAT...

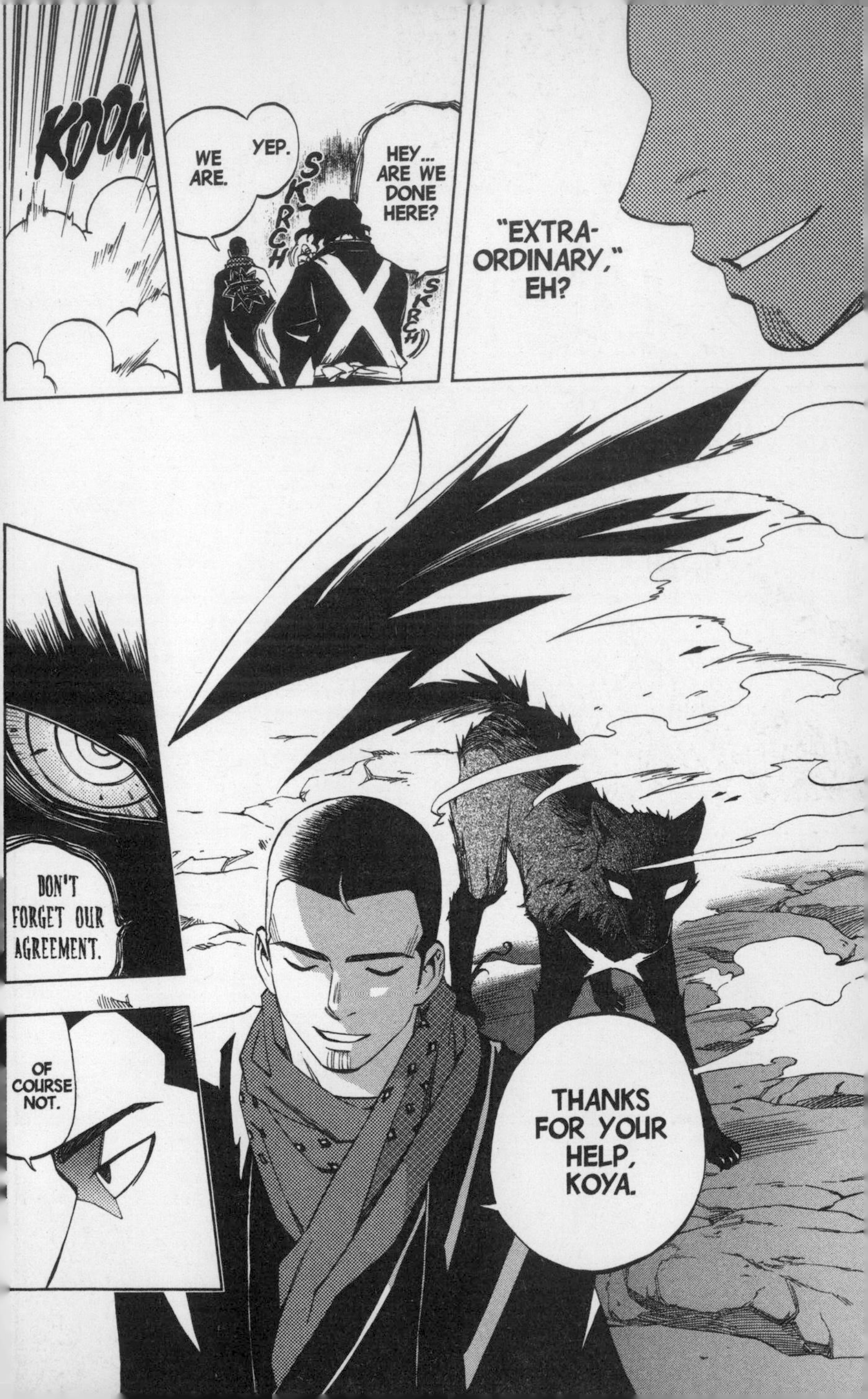
"EXTRA-ORDINARY," EH?
HEY... ARE WE DONE HERE?
SKRCH
SKRCH
YEP.
WE ARE.
KOOM
THANKS FOR YOUR HELP, KOYA.
DON'T FORGET OUR AGREEMENT.
OF COURSE NOT.

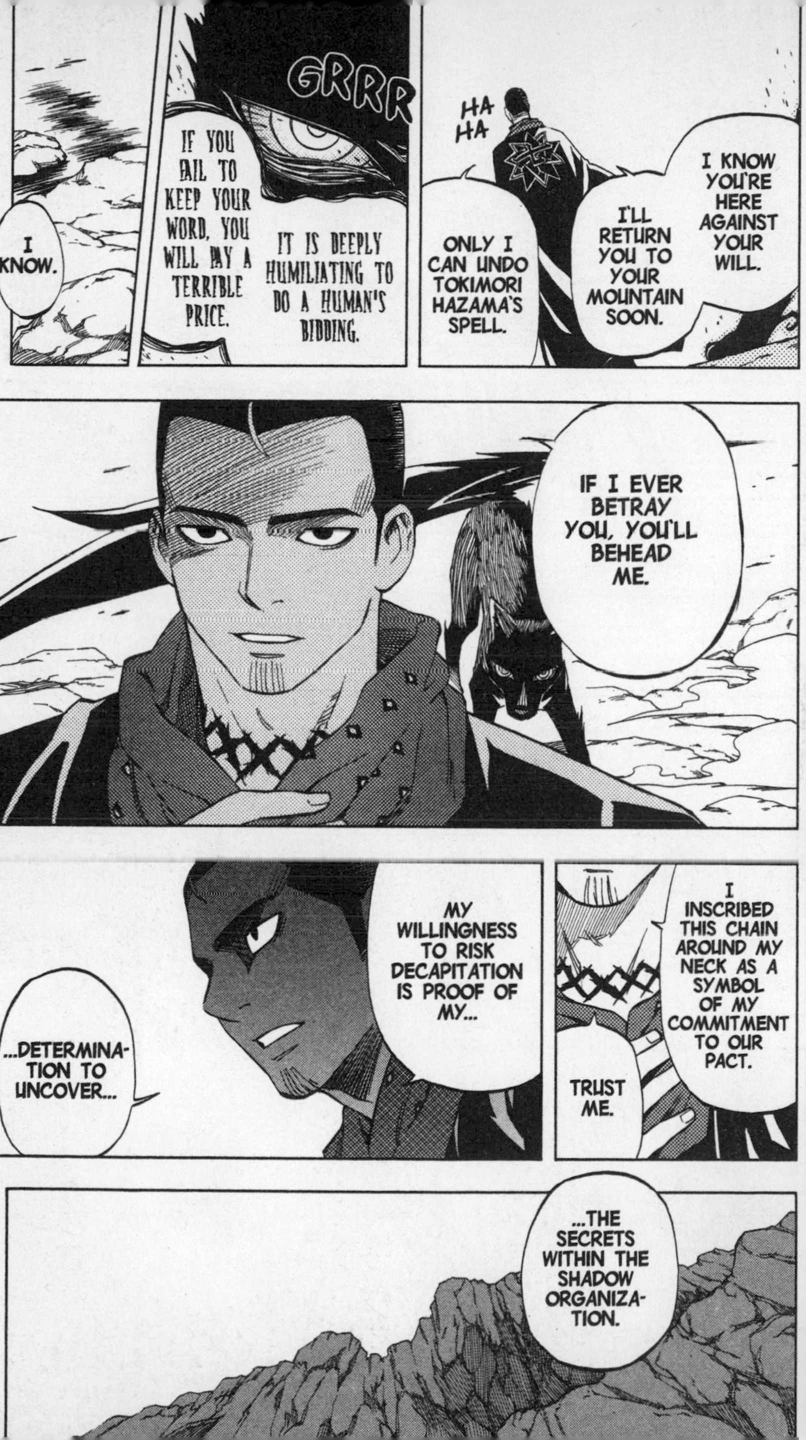

I KNOW YOU'RE HERE AGAINST YOUR WILL.
I'LL RETURN YOU TO YOUR MOUNTAIN SOON.
ONLY I CAN UNDO TOKIMORI HAZAMA'S SPELL.
HA HA
GRRR
IT IS DEEPLY HUMILIATING TO DO A HUMAN'S BIDDING.
IF YOU FAIL TO KEEP YOUR WORD, YOU WILL PAY A TERRIBLE PRICE.
I KNOW.
IF I EVER BETRAY YOU, YOU'LL BEHEAD ME.
I INSCRIBED THIS CHAIN AROUND MY NECK AS A SYMBOL OF MY COMMITMENT TO OUR PACT.
TRUST ME.
MY WILLINGNESS TO RISK DECAPITATION IS PROOF OF MY...
...DETERMINATION TO UNCOVER...
...THE SECRETS WITHIN THE SHADOW ORGANIZATION.

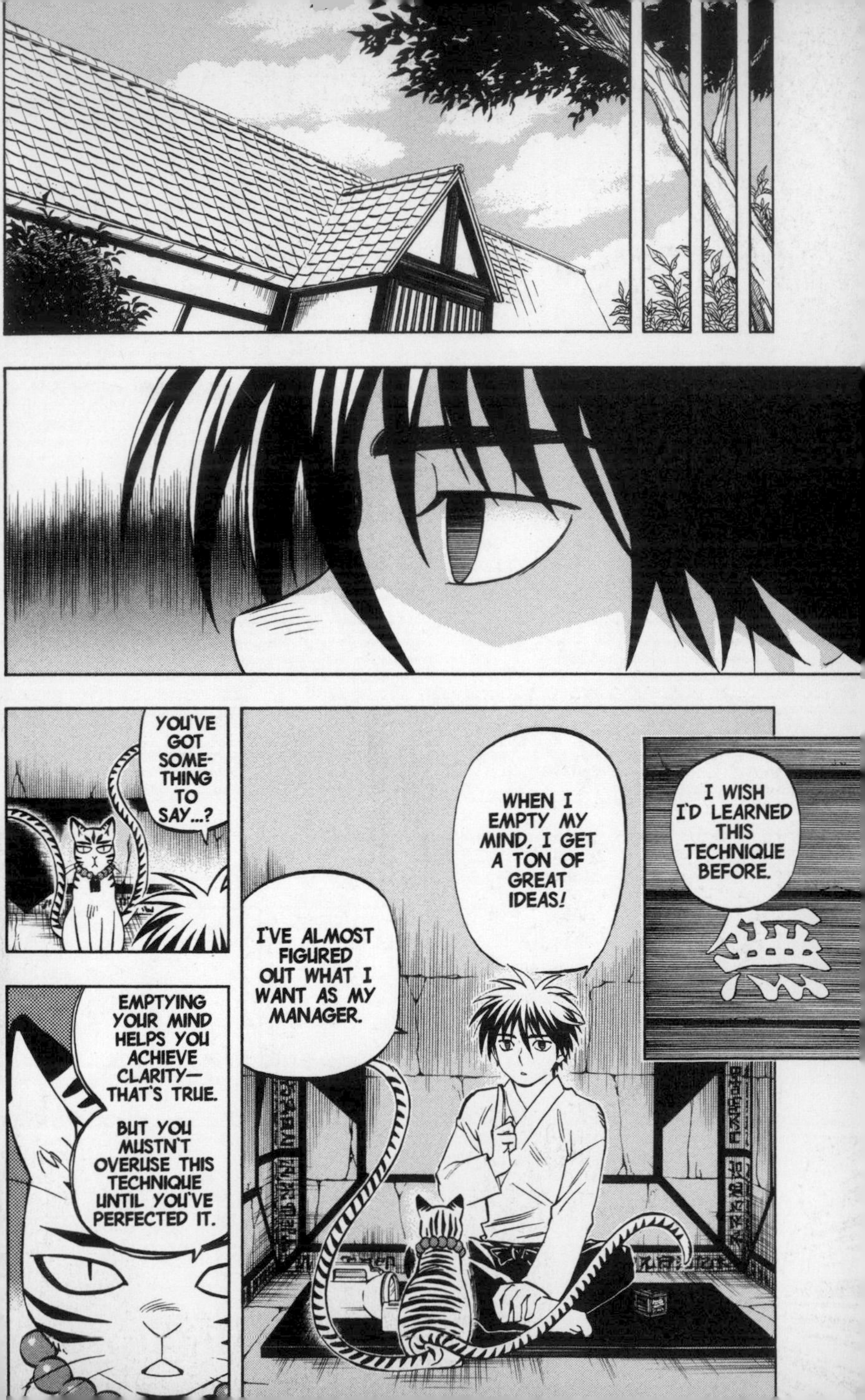
I WISH I'D LEARNED THIS TECHNIQUE BEFORE.
無
WHEN I EMPTY MY MIND, I GET A TON OF GREAT IDEAS!
I'VE ALMOST FIGURED OUT WHAT I WANT AS MY MANAGER.
YOU'VE GOT SOMETHING TO SAY...?
EMPTYING YOUR MIND HELPS YOU ACHIEVE CLARITY—THAT'S TRUE.
BUT YOU MUSTN'T OVERUSE THIS TECHNIQUE UNTIL YOU'VE PERFECTED IT.

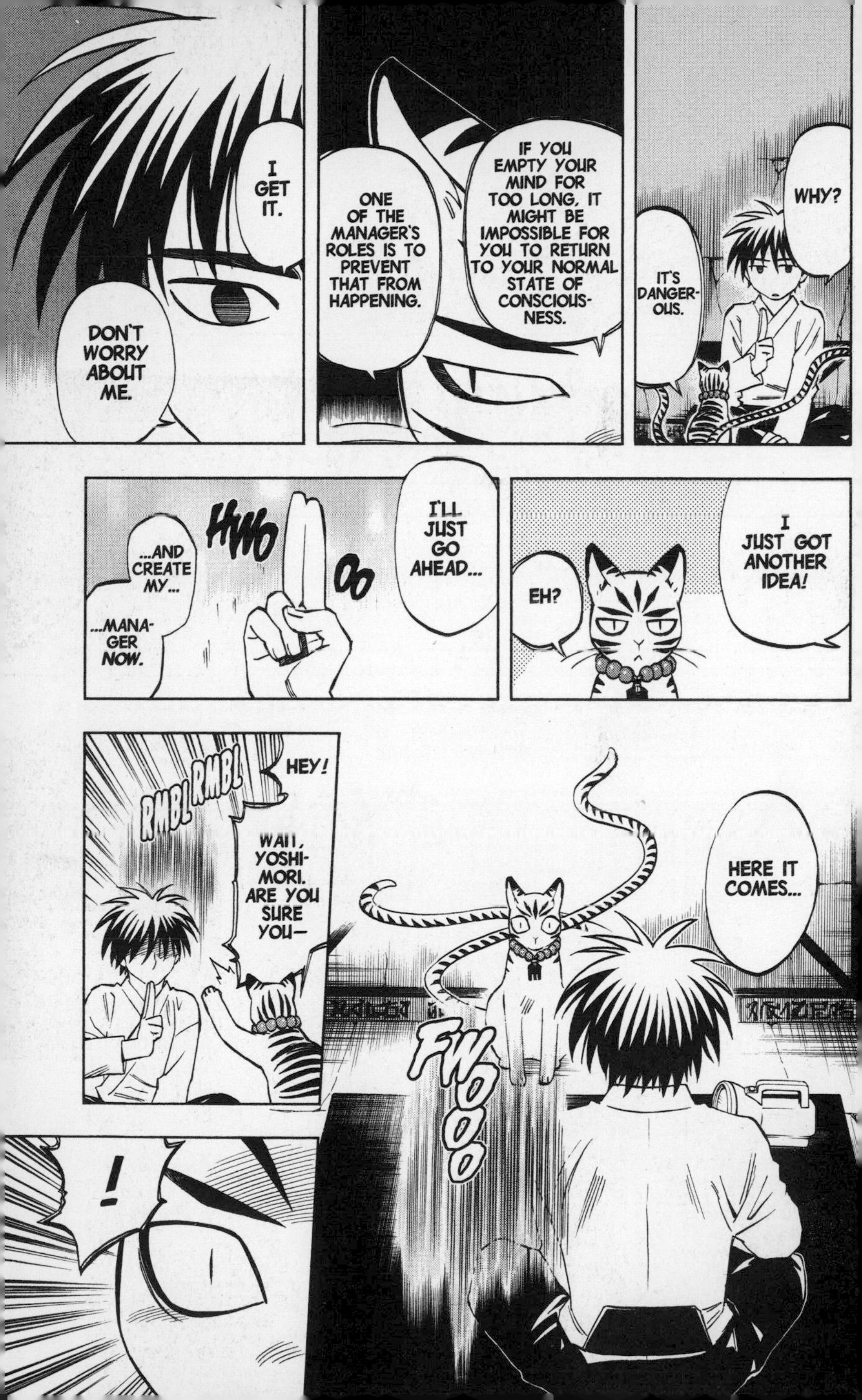
WHY?
IT'S DANGER-OUS.
IF YOU EMPTY YOUR MIND FOR TOO LONG, IT MIGHT BE IMPOSSIBLE FOR YOU TO RETURN TO YOUR NORMAL STATE OF CONSCIOUS-NESS.
ONE OF THE MANAGER'S ROLES IS TO PREVENT THAT FROM HAPPENING.
I GET IT.
DON'T WORRY ABOUT ME.
I JUST GOT ANOTHER IDEA!
EH?
I'LL JUST GO AHEAD...
HWOO
...AND CREATE MY...
...MANA-GER NOW.
HERE IT COMES...
FWOOOO
HEY!
RMBL RMBL
WAIT, YOSHI-MORI. ARE YOU SURE YOU—
!

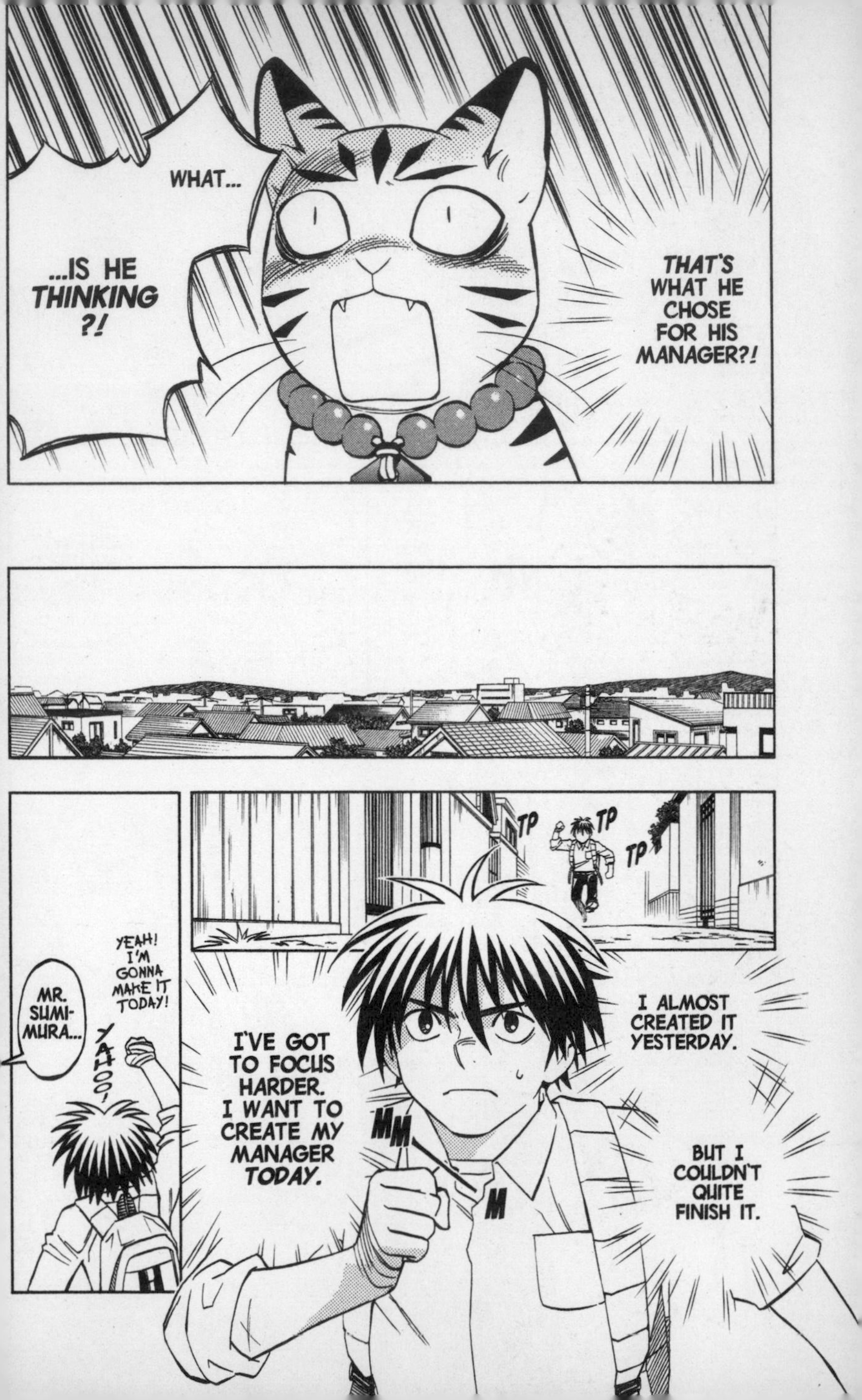
THAT'S WHAT HE CHOSE FOR HIS MANAGER?!
WHAT...
...IS HE THINKING ?!
TP
TP
TP
I ALMOST CREATED IT YESTERDAY.
BUT I COULDN'T QUITE FINISH IT.
MM
M
I'VE GOT TO FOCUS HARDER. I WANT TO CREATE MY MANAGER TODAY.
YEAH! I'M GONNA MAKE IT TODAY!
YAHOO!
MR. SUMI-MURA...

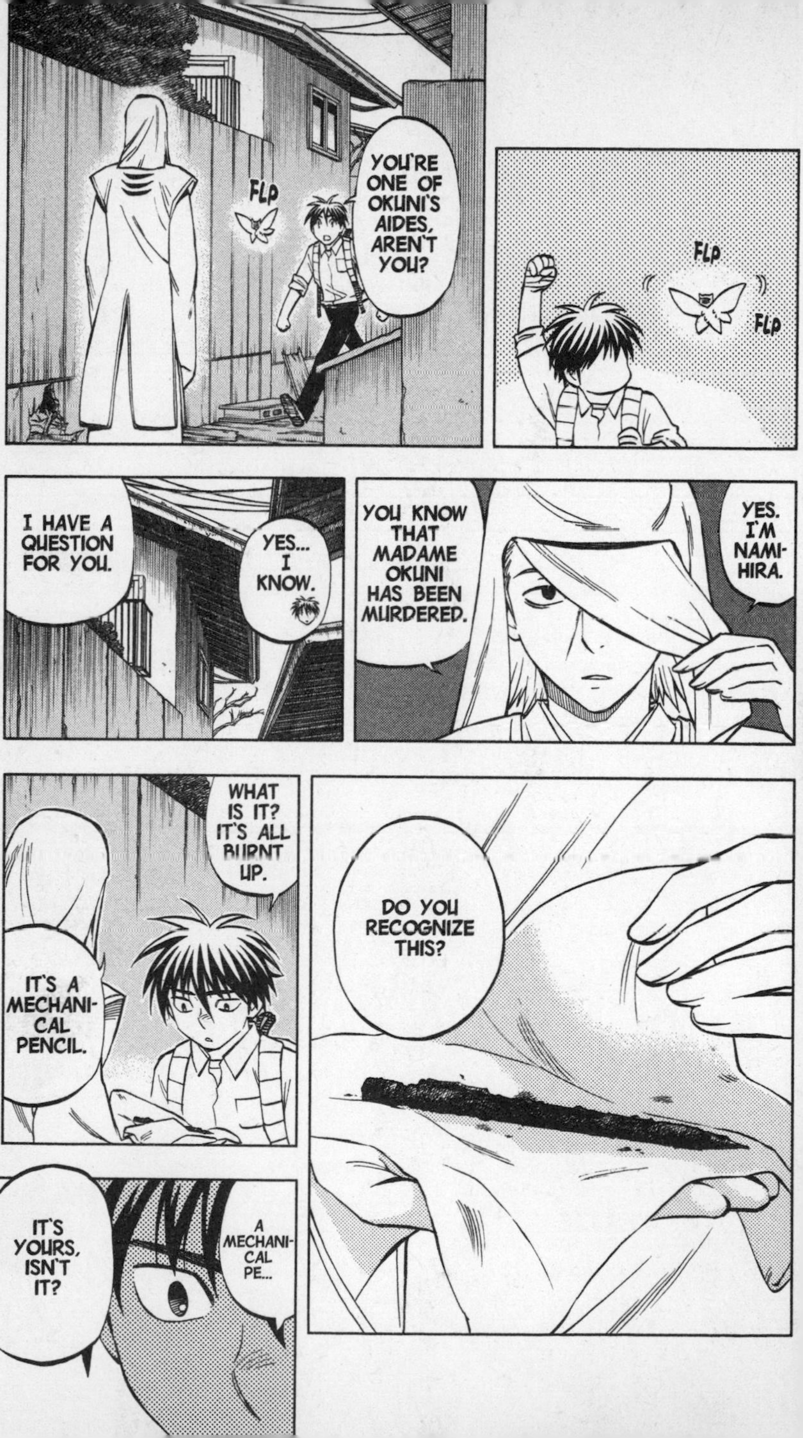
FLP
FLP
FLP
YOU'RE ONE OF OKUNI'S AIDES, AREN'T YOU?
YES. I'M NAMI-HIRA.
YOU KNOW THAT MADAME OKUNI HAS BEEN MURDERED.
YES... I KNOW.
I HAVE A QUESTION FOR YOU.
DO YOU RECOGNIZE THIS?
WHAT IS IT? IT'S ALL BURNT UP.
IT'S A MECHANI-CAL PENCIL.
A MECHANI-CAL PE...
IT'S YOURS, ISN'T IT?

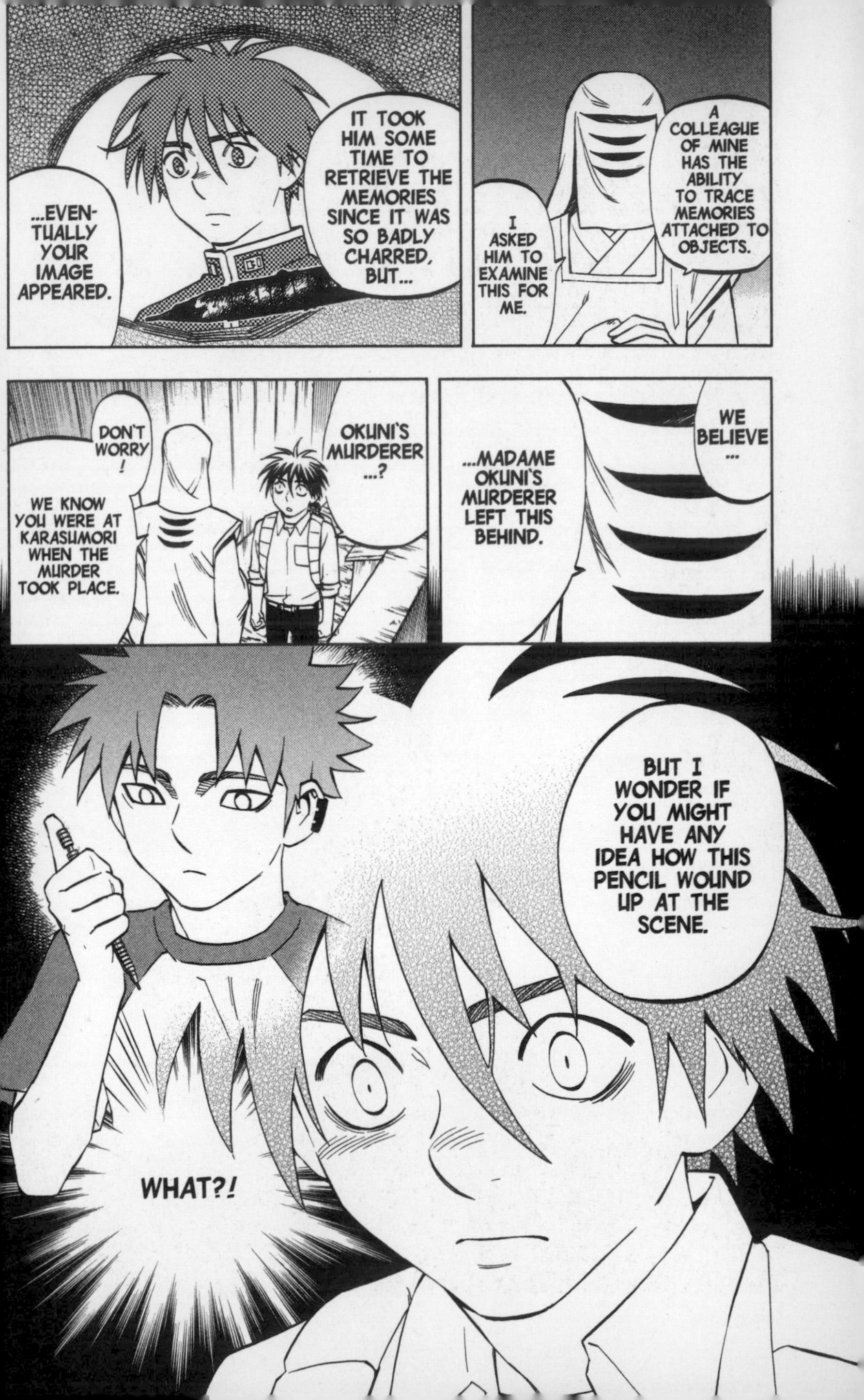

A COLLEAGUE OF MINE HAS THE ABILITY TO TRACE MEMORIES ATTACHED TO OBJECTS.
I ASKED HIM TO EXAMINE THIS FOR ME.
IT TOOK HIM SOME TIME TO RETRIEVE THE MEMORIES SINCE IT WAS SO BADLY CHARRED, BUT...
...EVEN-TUALLY YOUR IMAGE APPEARED.
WE BELIEVE...
...MADAME OKUNI'S MURDERER LEFT THIS BEHIND.
OKUNI'S MURDERER...?
DON'T WORRY!
WE KNOW YOU WERE AT KARASUMORI WHEN THE MURDER TOOK PLACE.
BUT I WONDER IF YOU MIGHT HAVE ANY IDEA HOW THIS PENCIL WOUND UP AT THE SCENE.
WHAT?!

Chapter 253: Assignment & Promise

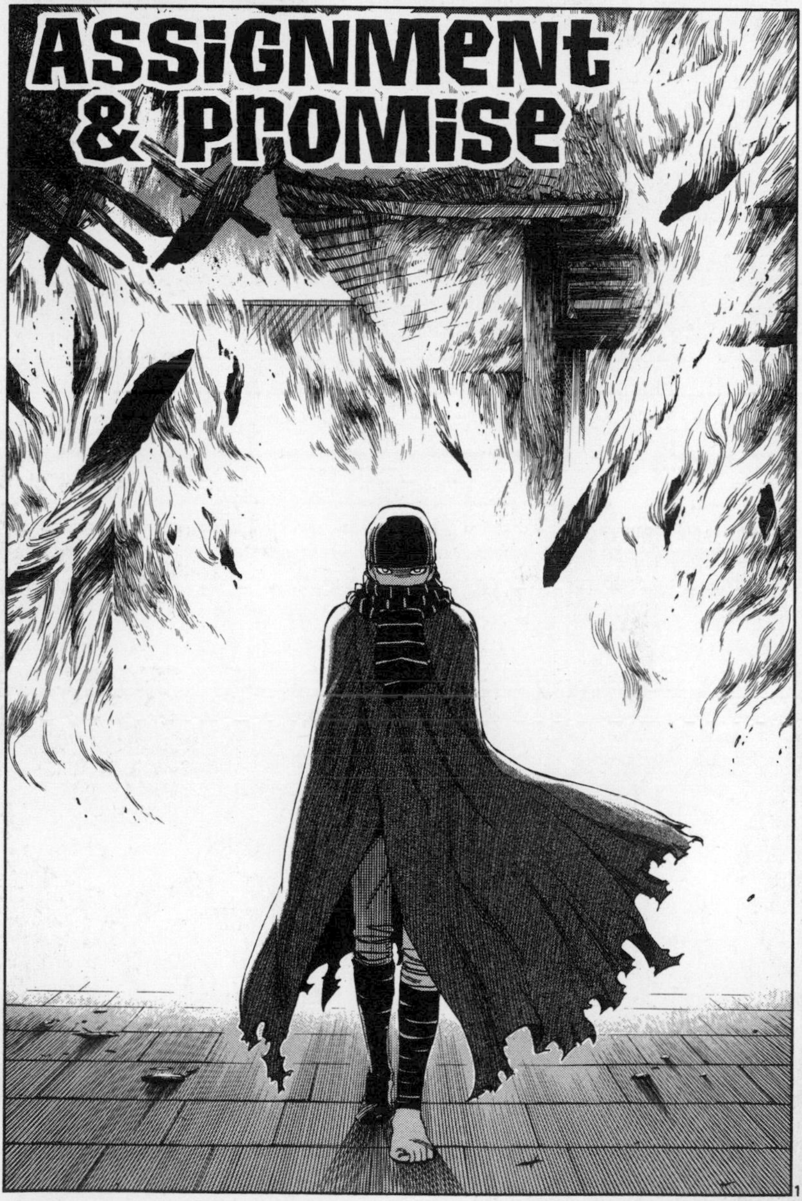

1

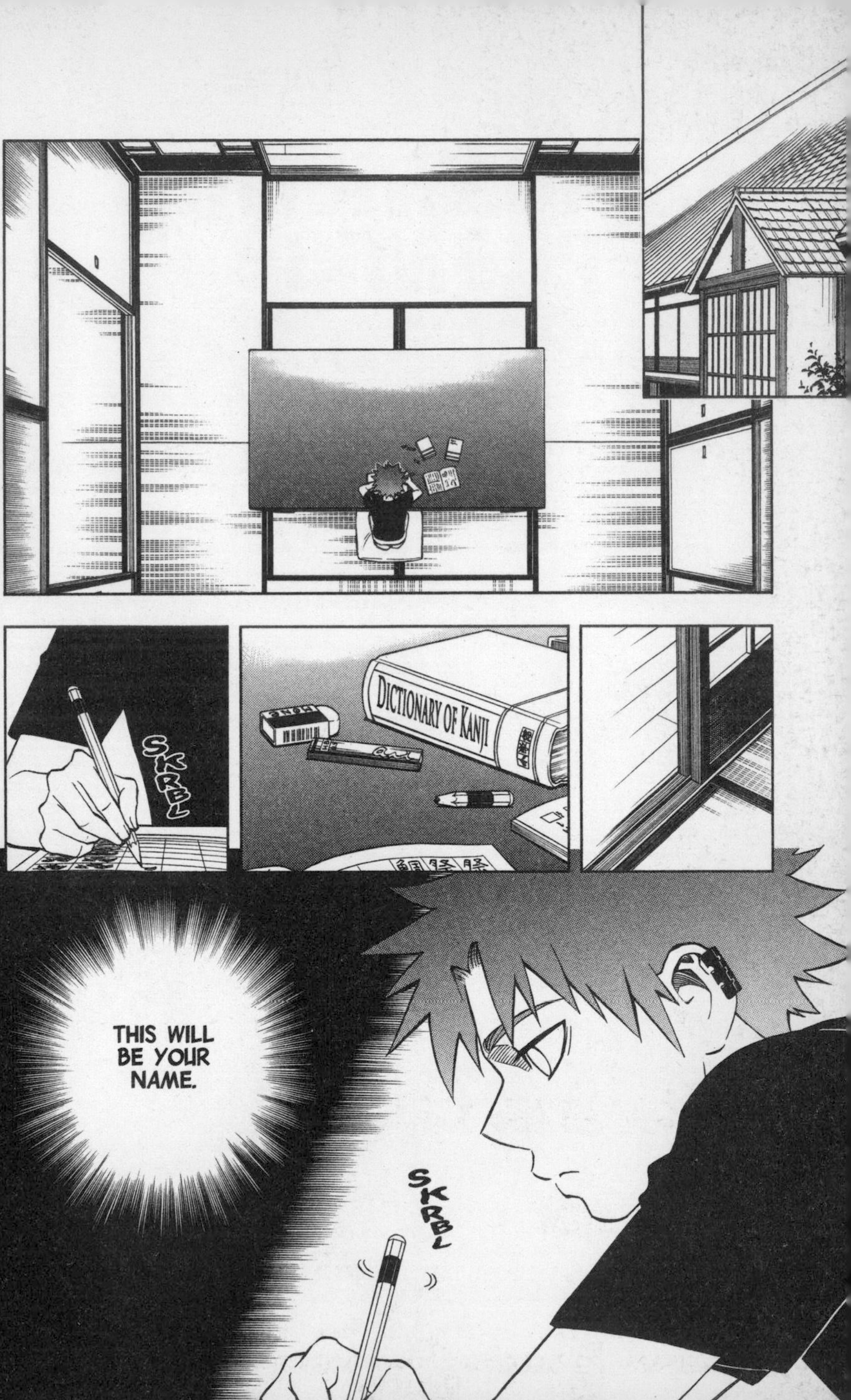
DICTIONARY OF KANJI
SKRBL
THIS WILL BE YOUR NAME.
SKRBL

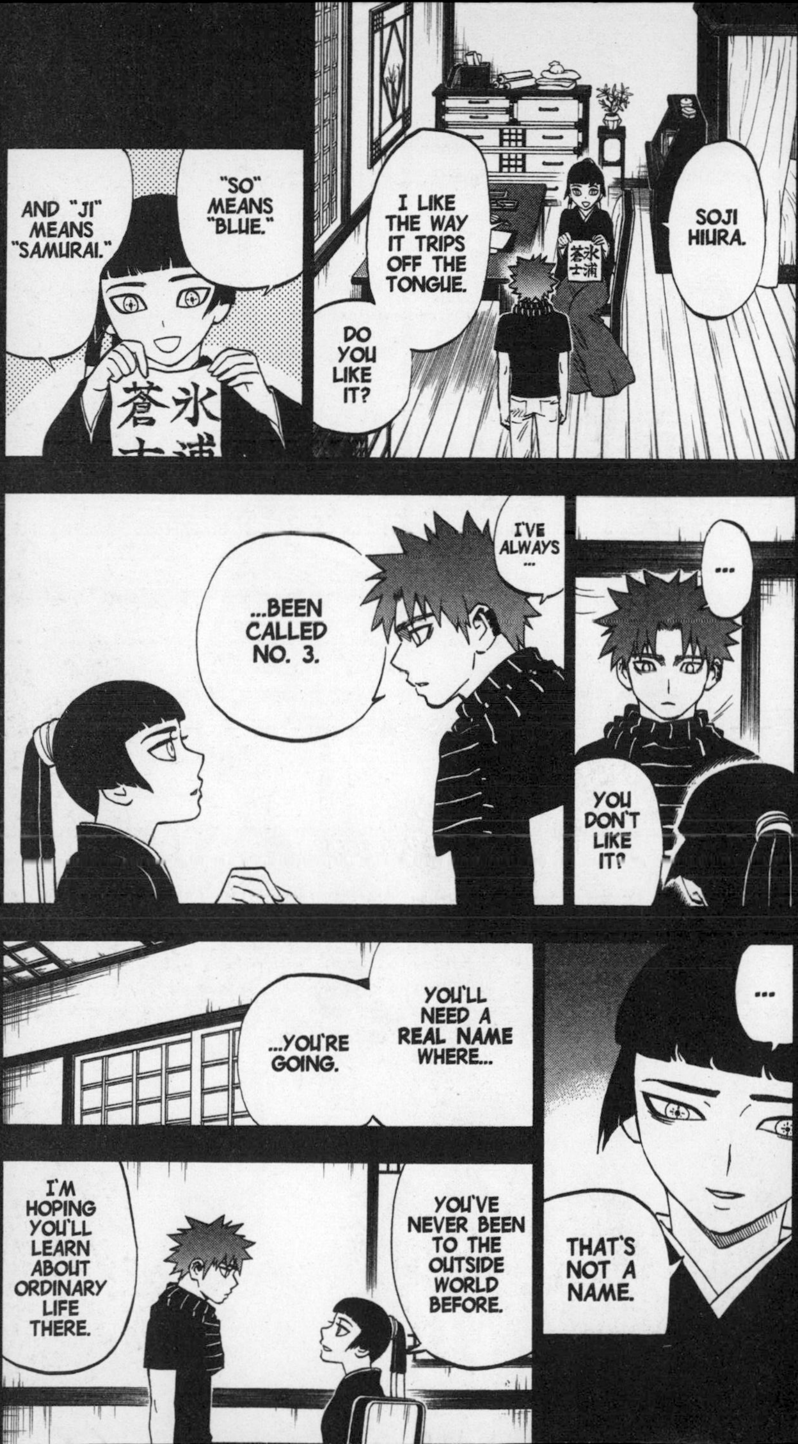

SOJI HIURA.
氷浦蒼士
I LIKE THE WAY IT TRIPS OFF THE TONGUE.
DO YOU LIKE IT?
"SO" MEANS "BLUE."
AND "JI" MEANS "SAMURAI."
...
YOU DON'T LIKE IT?
I'VE ALWAYS ...
...BEEN CALLED NO. 3.
...
THAT'S NOT A NAME.
YOU'LL NEED A REAL NAME WHERE...
...YOU'RE GOING.
YOU'VE NEVER BEEN TO THE OUTSIDE WORLD BEFORE.
I'M HOPING YOU'LL LEARN ABOUT ORDINARY LIFE THERE.

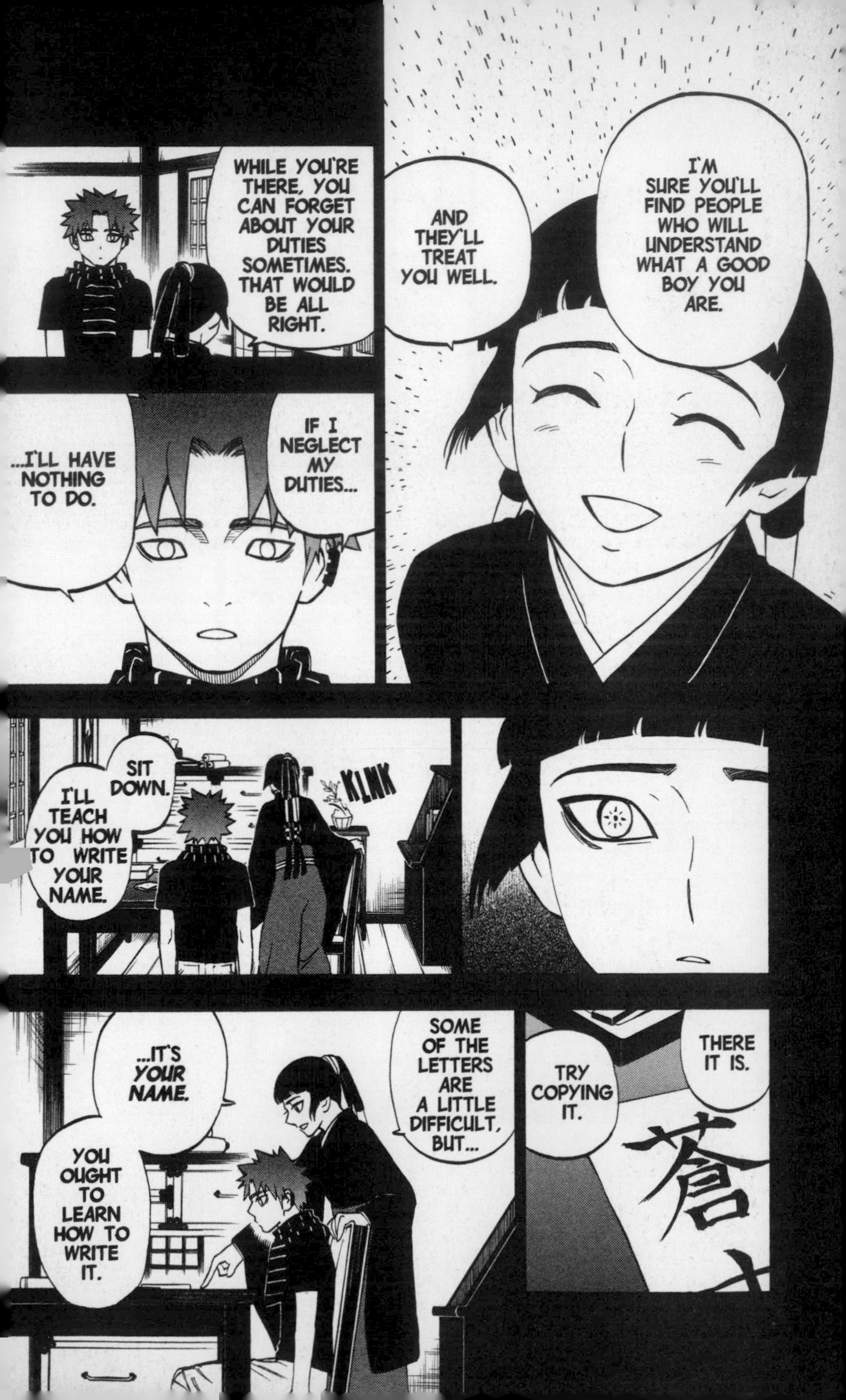
I'M SURE YOU'LL FIND PEOPLE WHO WILL UNDERSTAND WHAT A GOOD BOY YOU ARE.
AND THEY'LL TREAT YOU WELL.
WHILE YOU'RE THERE, YOU CAN FORGET ABOUT YOUR DUTIES SOMETIMES. THAT WOULD BE ALL RIGHT.
IF I NEGLECT MY DUTIES...
...I'LL HAVE NOTHING TO DO.
SIT DOWN.
I'LL TEACH YOU HOW TO WRITE YOUR NAME.
KLNK
THERE IT IS.
TRY COPYING IT.
蒼
SOME OF THE LETTERS ARE A LITTLE DIFFICULT, BUT...
...IT'S *YOUR NAME.*
YOU OUGHT TO LEARN HOW TO WRITE IT.

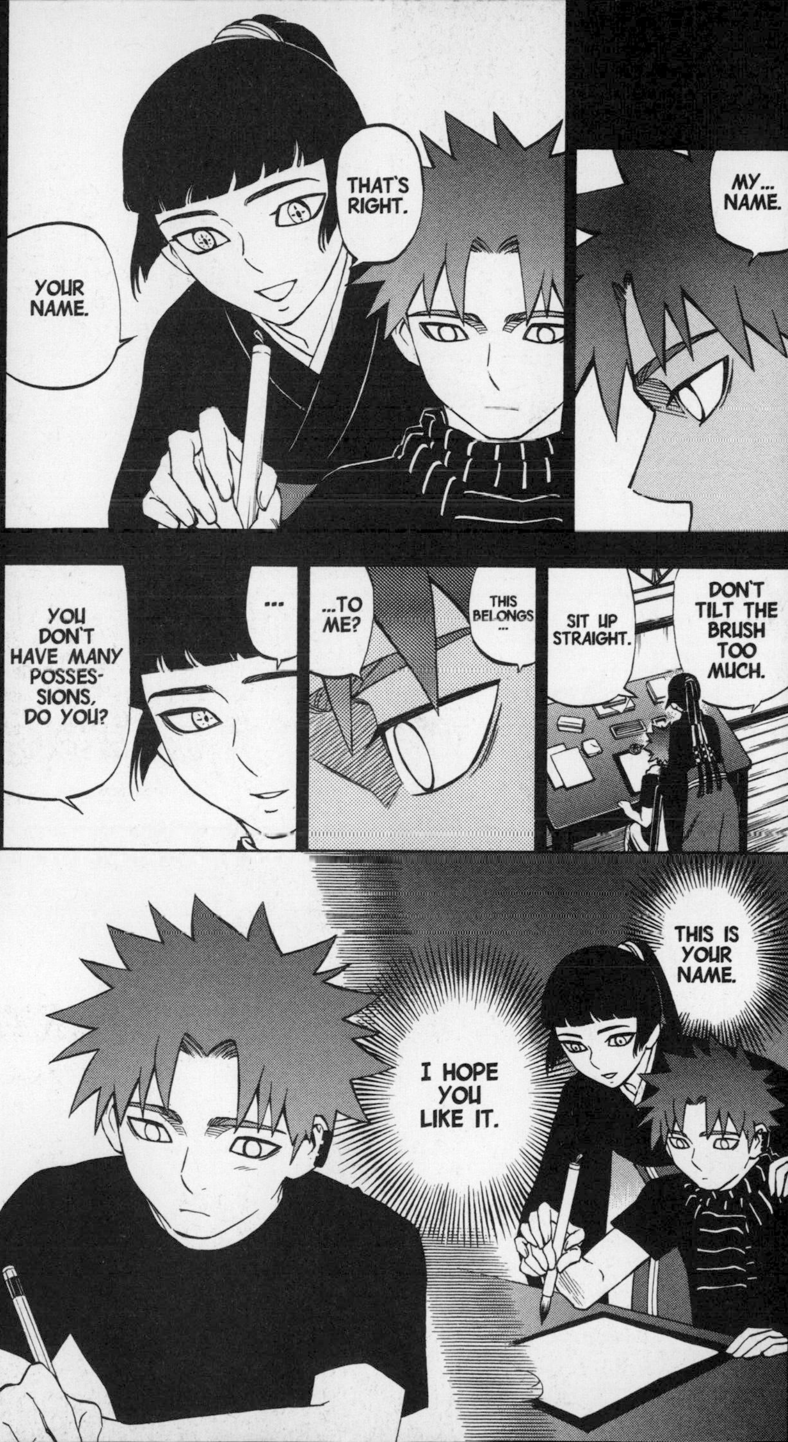
MY... NAME.
THAT'S RIGHT.
YOUR NAME.
DON'T TILT THE BRUSH TOO MUCH.
SIT UP STRAIGHT.
THIS BELONGS ...
...TO ME?
...
YOU DON'T HAVE MANY POSSES-SIONS, DO YOU?
THIS IS YOUR NAME.
I HOPE YOU LIKE IT.

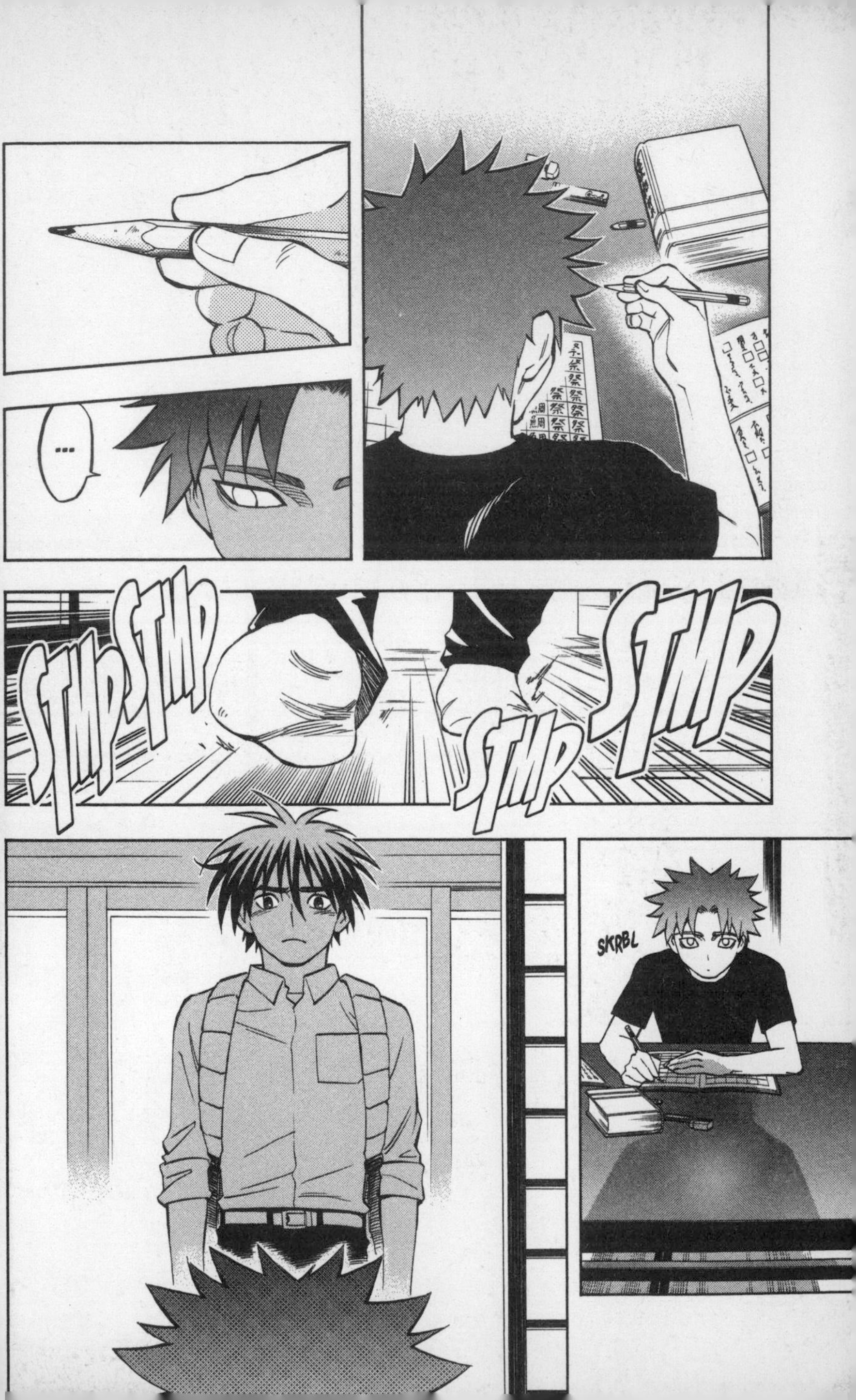
...
STMP
STMP
STMP
STMP
SKRBL

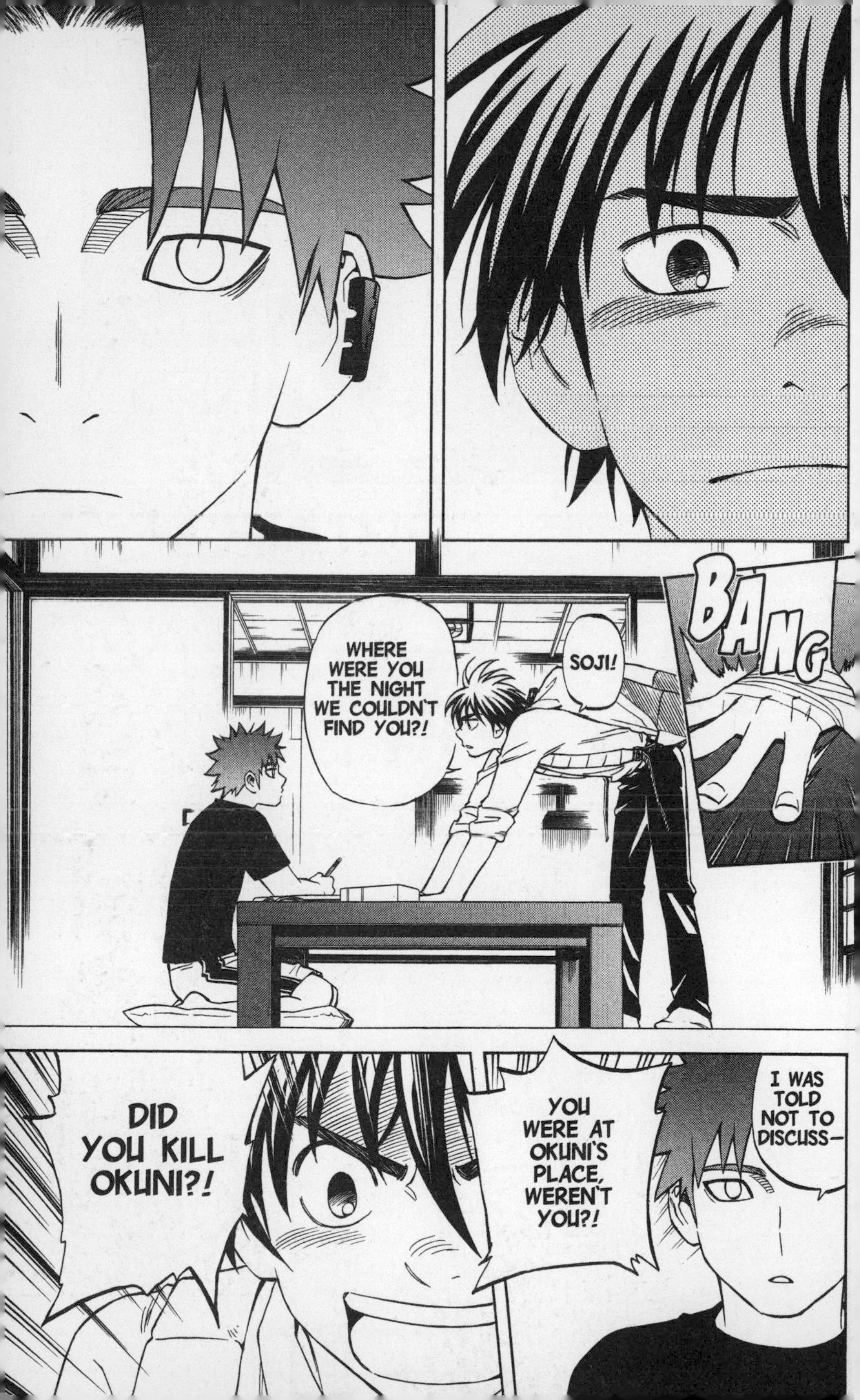
BANG
SOJI!
WHERE WERE YOU THE NIGHT WE COULDN'T FIND YOU?!
I WAS TOLD NOT TO DISCUSS—
YOU WERE AT OKUNI'S PLACE, WEREN'T YOU?!
DID YOU KILL OKUNI?!

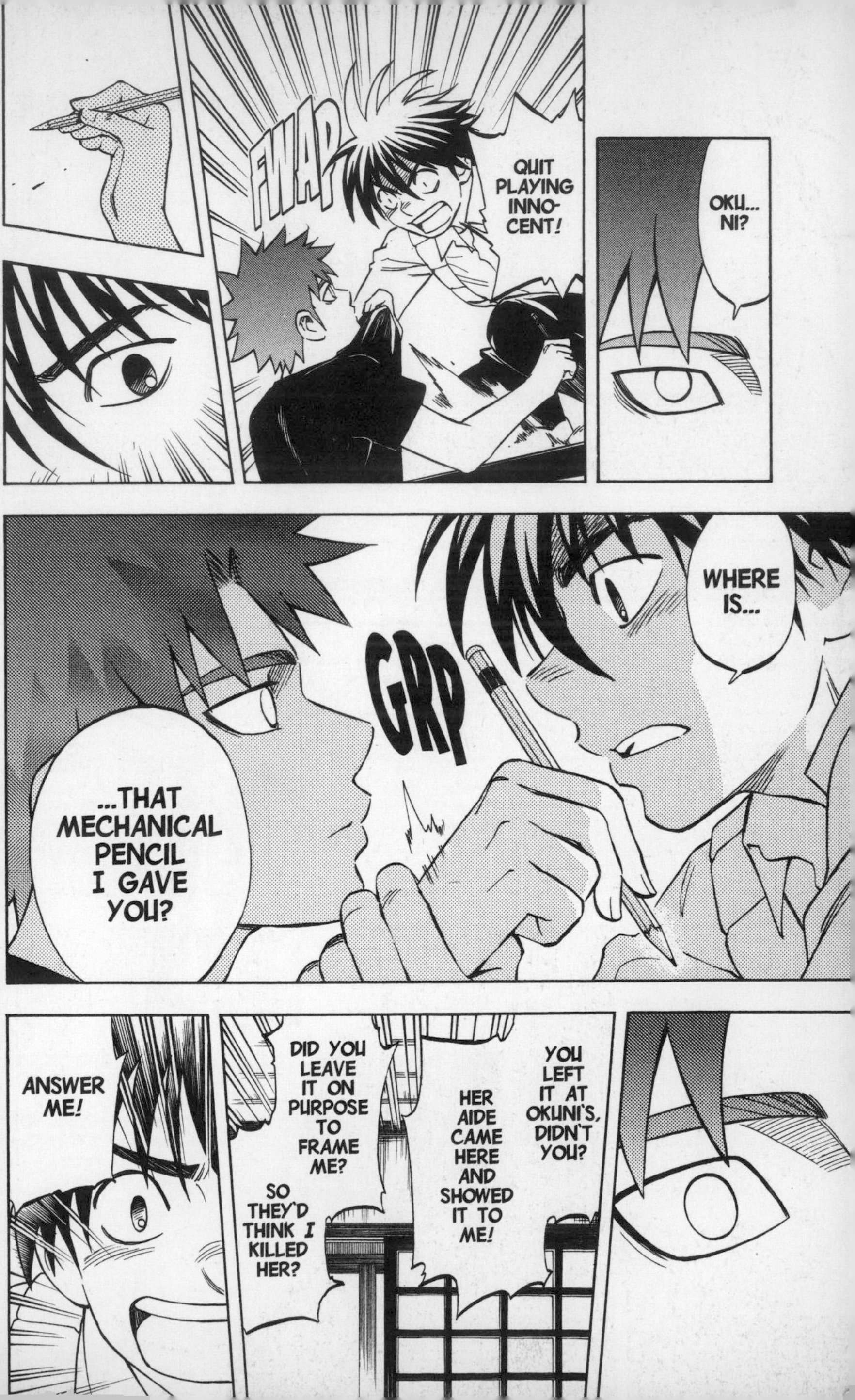
OKU... NI?
FWAP
QUIT PLAYING INNO-CENT!
WHERE IS...
GRP
...THAT MECHANICAL PENCIL I GAVE YOU?
YOU LEFT IT AT OKUNI'S, DIDN'T YOU?
HER AIDE CAME HERE AND SHOWED IT TO ME!
DID YOU LEAVE IT ON PURPOSE TO FRAME ME?
SO THEY'D THINK I KILLED HER?
ANSWER ME!

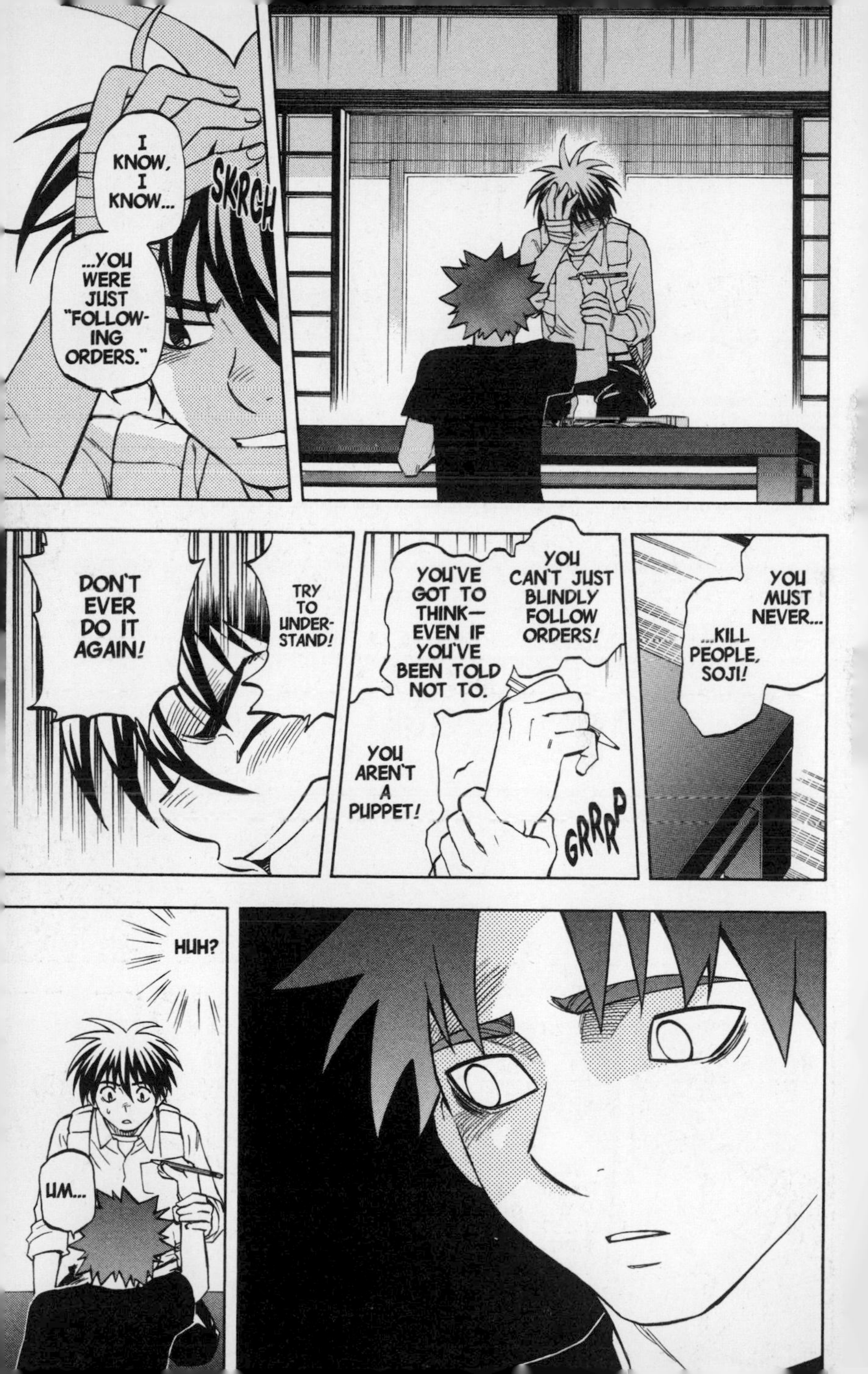
I KNOW, I KNOW...
SKRCH
...YOU WERE JUST "FOLLOWING ORDERS."
YOU MUST NEVER...
...KILL PEOPLE, SOJI!
YOU CAN'T JUST BLINDLY FOLLOW ORDERS!
YOU'VE GOT TO THINK— EVEN IF YOU'VE BEEN TOLD NOT TO.
YOU AREN'T A PUPPET!
GRRRP
TRY TO UNDER-STAND!
DON'T EVER DO IT AGAIN!
HUH?
UM...

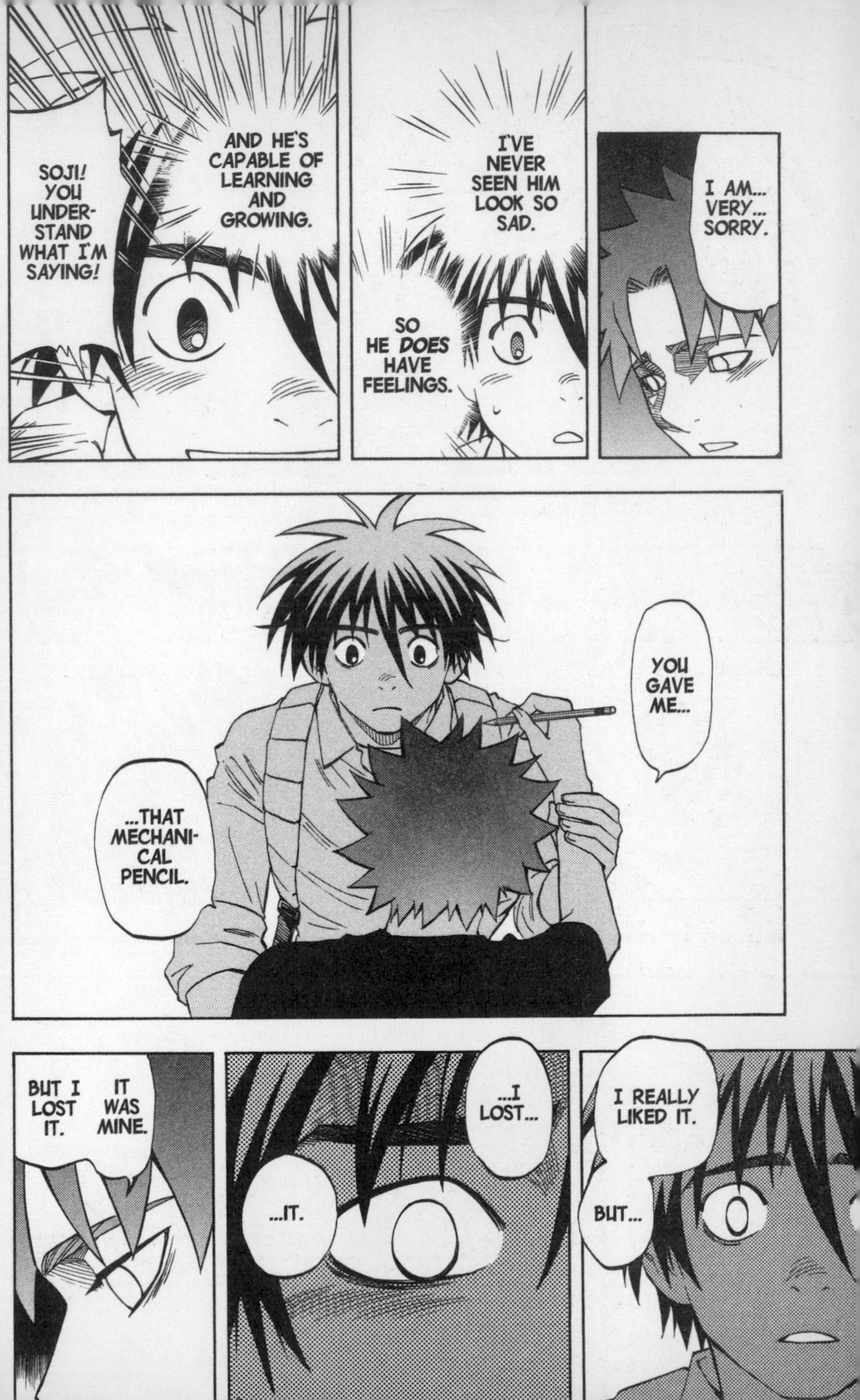
I AM... VERY... SORRY.
I'VE NEVER SEEN HIM LOOK SO SAD.
SO HE *DOES* HAVE FEELINGS.
AND HE'S CAPABLE OF LEARNING AND GROWING.
SOJI! YOU UNDER-STAND WHAT I'M SAYING!
YOU GAVE ME...
...THAT MECHANI-CAL PENCIL.
I REALLY LIKED IT.
BUT...
...I LOST...
...IT.
IT WAS MINE.
BUT I LOST IT.

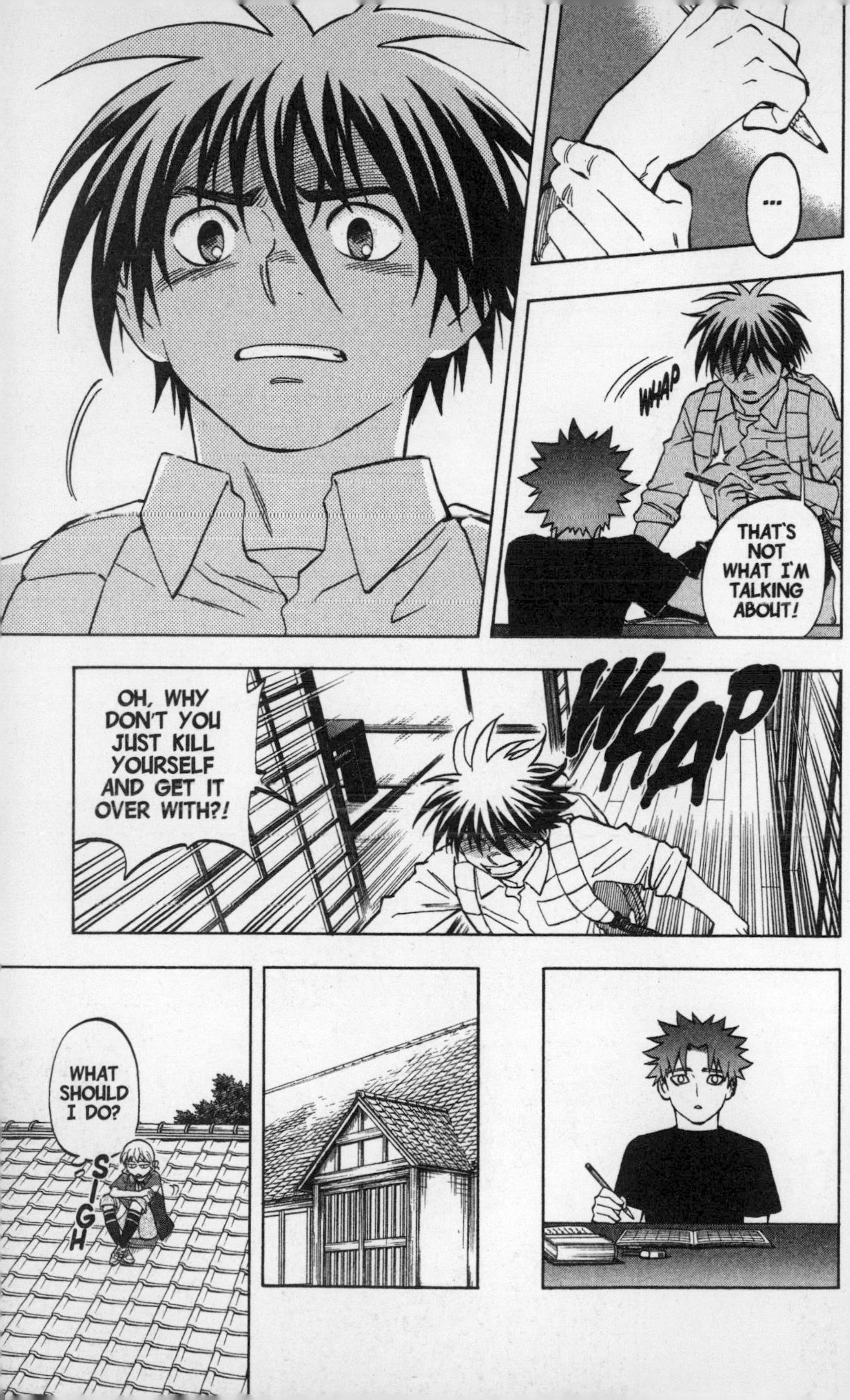
...
WHAP
THAT'S NOT WHAT I'M TALKING ABOUT!
WHAP
OH, WHY DON'T YOU JUST KILL YOURSELF AND GET IT OVER WITH?!
WHAT SHOULD I DO?
SIGH

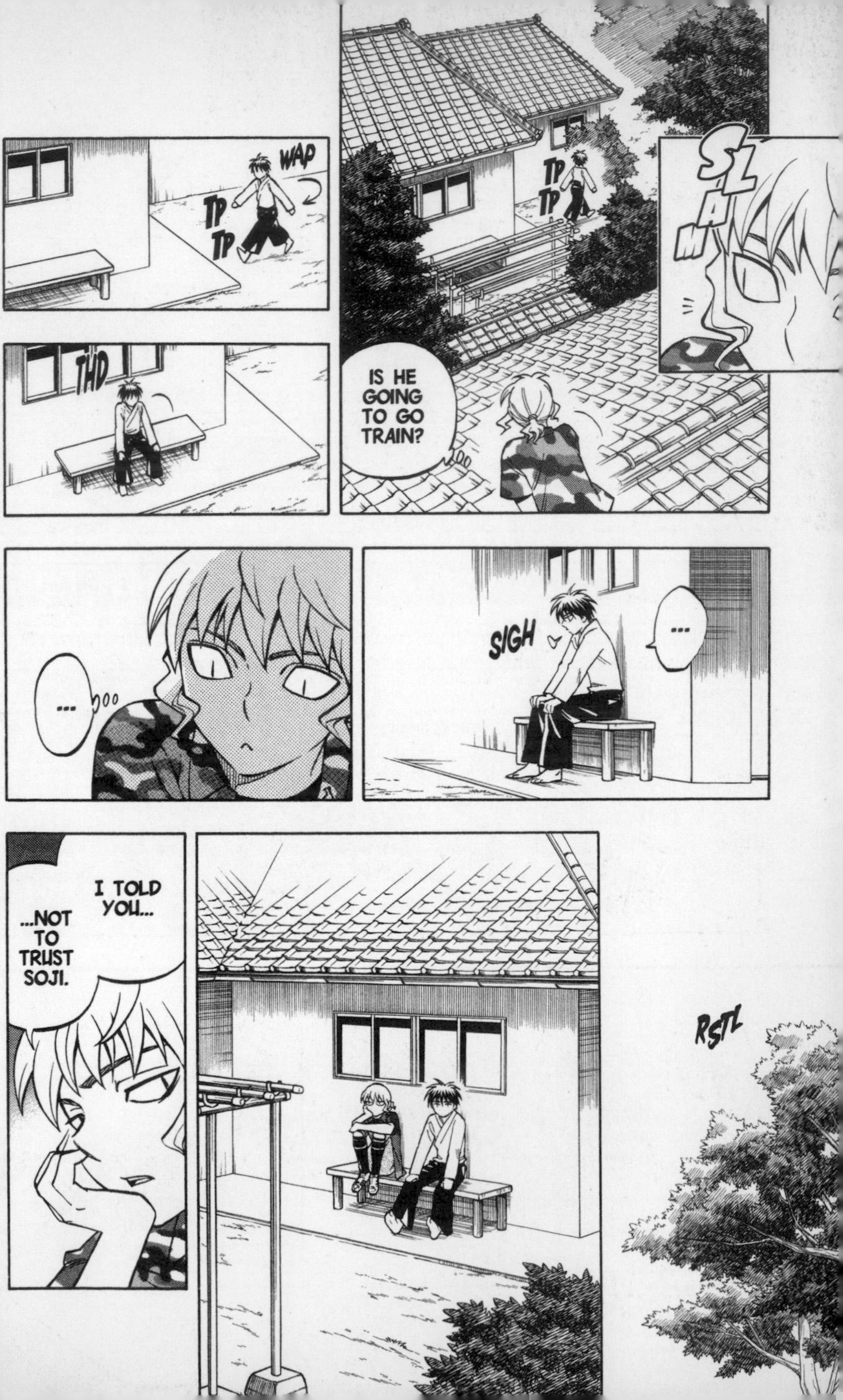
SLAM
TP TP
IS HE GOING TO GO TRAIN?
WAP
TP TP
THD
SIGH
...
...
RSTL
I TOLD YOU...
...NOT TO TRUST SOJI.

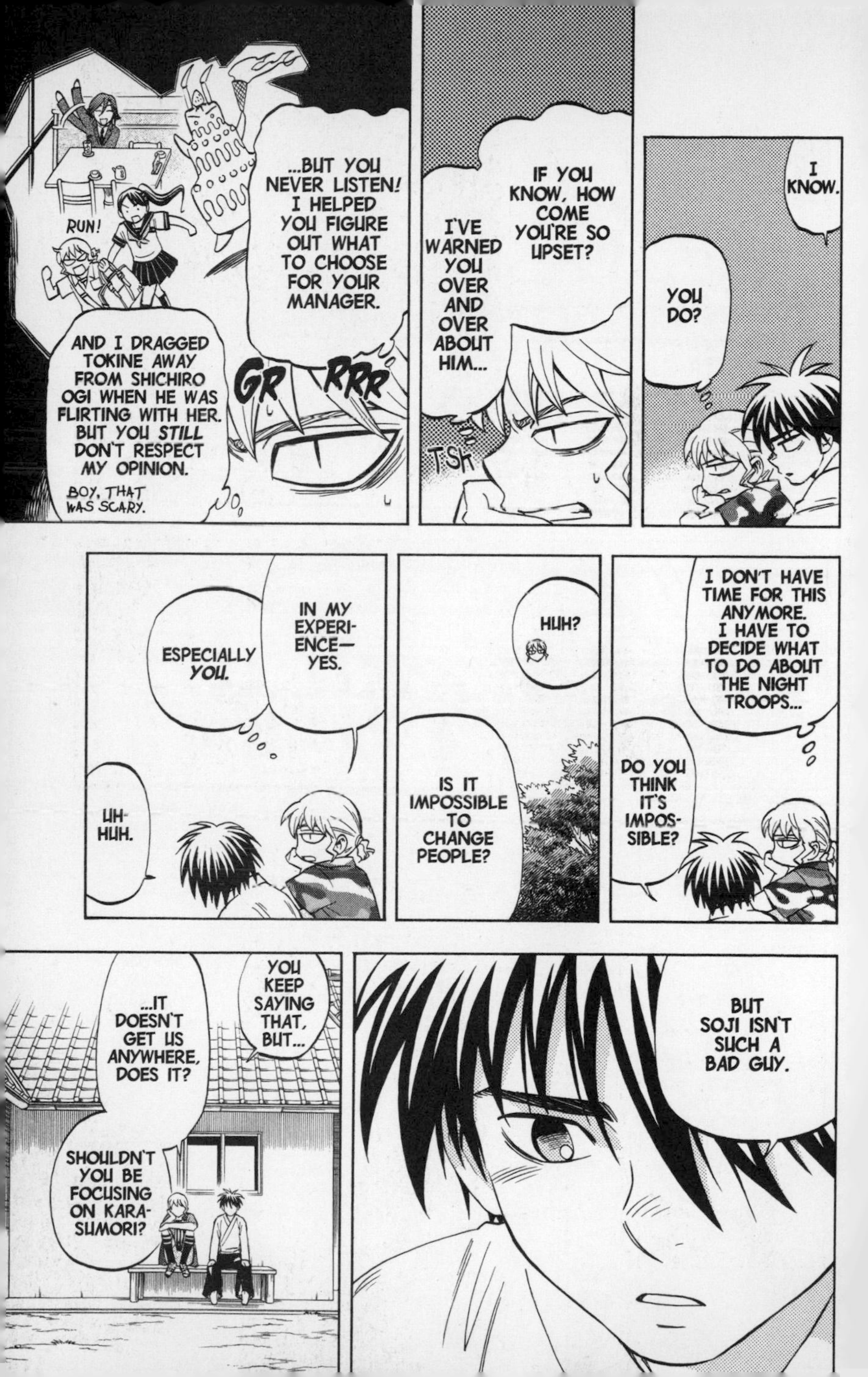
I KNOW.
YOU DO?
IF YOU KNOW, HOW COME YOU'RE SO UPSET?
I'VE WARNED YOU OVER AND OVER ABOUT HIM...
TSK
...BUT YOU NEVER LISTEN! I HELPED YOU FIGURE OUT WHAT TO CHOOSE FOR YOUR MANAGER.
GR RRR
RUN!
AND I DRAGGED TOKINE AWAY FROM SHICHIRO OGI WHEN HE WAS FLIRTING WITH HER. BUT YOU *STILL* DON'T RESPECT MY OPINION.
BOY, THAT WAS SCARY.
I DON'T HAVE TIME FOR THIS ANYMORE. I HAVE TO DECIDE WHAT TO DO ABOUT THE NIGHT TROOPS...
DO YOU THINK IT'S IMPOSSIBLE?
HUH?
IS IT IMPOSSIBLE TO CHANGE PEOPLE?
IN MY EXPERIENCE—YES.
ESPECIALLY *YOU.*
UH-HUH.
BUT SOJI ISN'T SUCH A BAD GUY.
YOU KEEP SAYING THAT, BUT...
...IT DOESN'T GET US ANYWHERE, DOES IT?
SHOULDN'T YOU BE FOCUSING ON KARASUMORI?

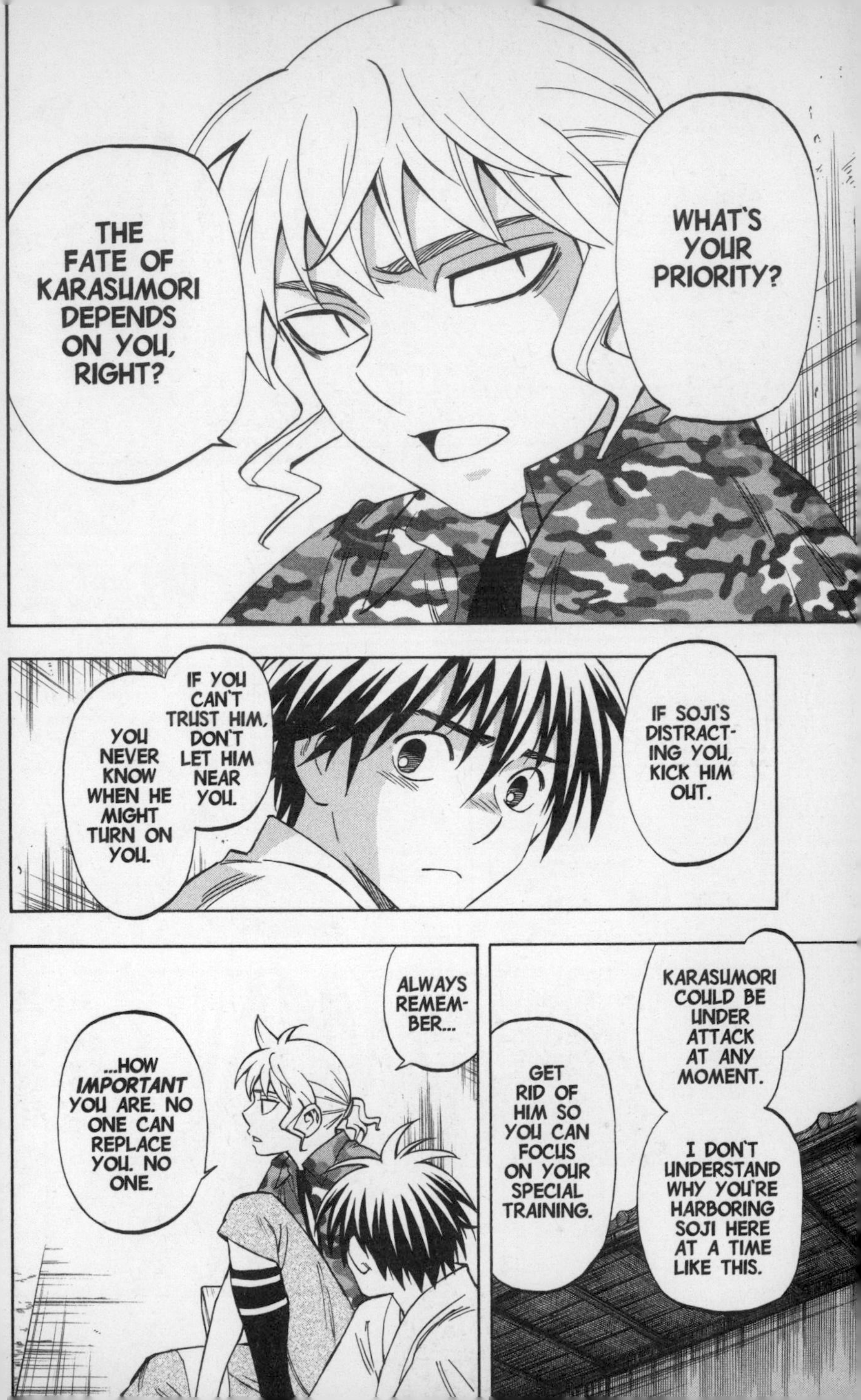
WHAT'S YOUR PRIORITY?
THE FATE OF KARASUMORI DEPENDS ON YOU, RIGHT?
IF SOJI'S DISTRACTING YOU, KICK HIM OUT.
IF YOU CAN'T TRUST HIM, DON'T LET HIM NEAR YOU.
YOU NEVER KNOW WHEN HE MIGHT TURN ON YOU.
KARASUMORI COULD BE UNDER ATTACK AT ANY MOMENT.
I DON'T UNDERSTAND WHY YOU'RE HARBORING SOJI HERE AT A TIME LIKE THIS.
GET RID OF HIM SO YOU CAN FOCUS ON YOUR SPECIAL TRAINING.
ALWAYS REMEMBER...
...HOW *IMPORTANT* YOU ARE. NO ONE CAN REPLACE YOU. NO ONE.

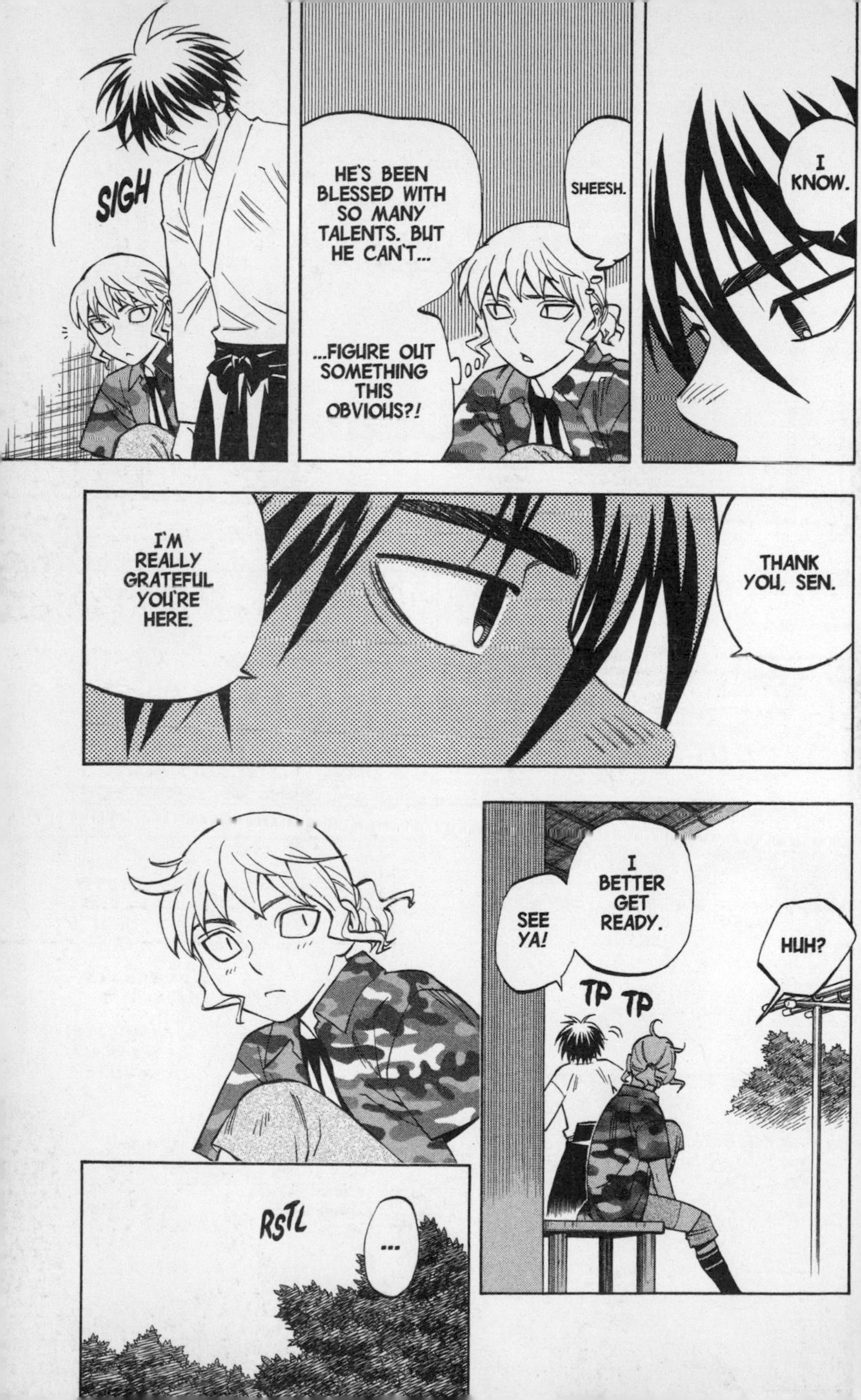
I KNOW.
SHEESH.
HE'S BEEN BLESSED WITH SO MANY TALENTS. BUT HE CAN'T...
...FIGURE OUT SOMETHING THIS OBVIOUS?!
SIGH
THANK YOU, SEN.
I'M REALLY GRATEFUL YOU'RE HERE.
HUH?
I BETTER GET READY.
SEE YA!
TP TP
...
RSTL

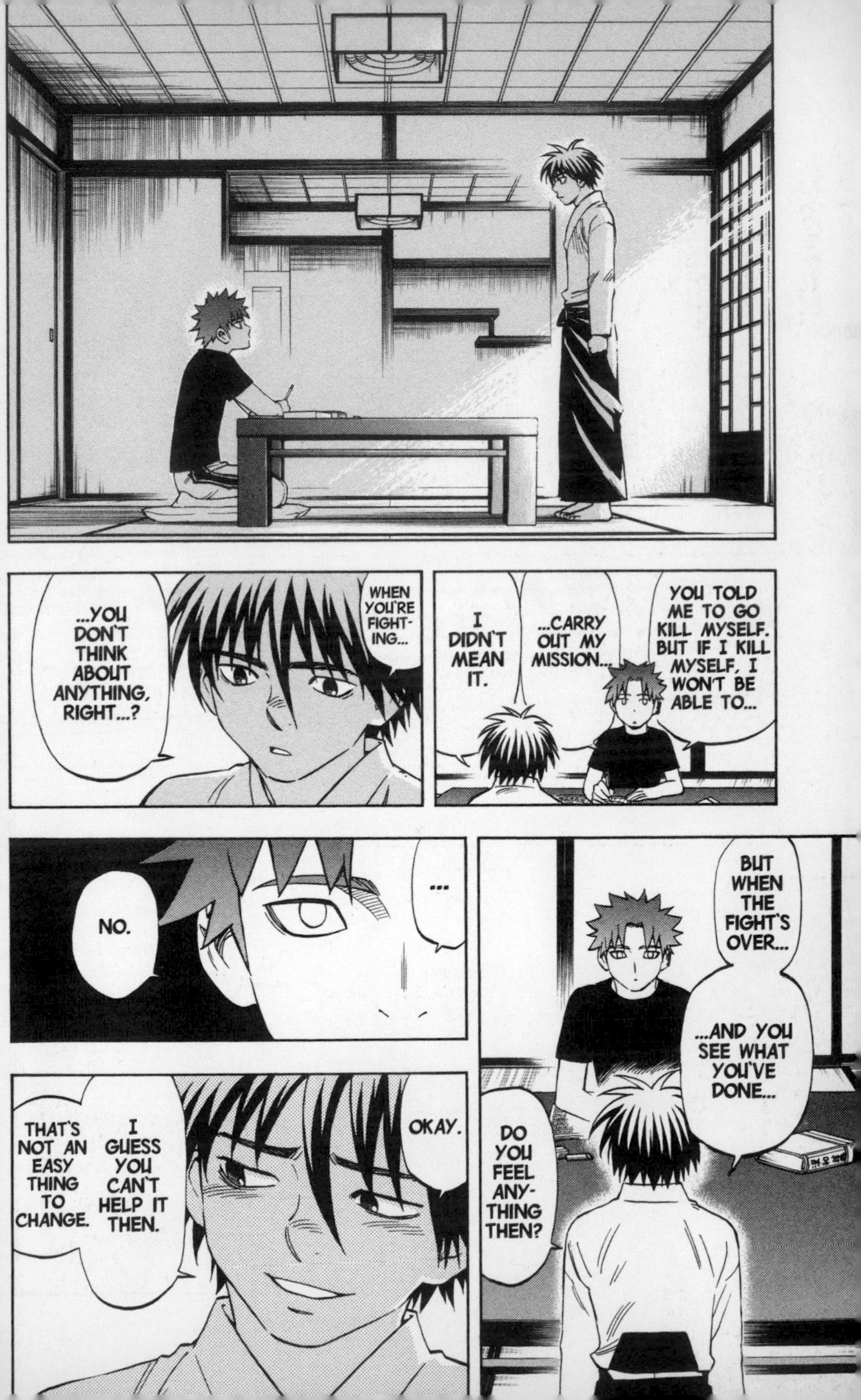
YOU TOLD ME TO GO KILL MYSELF. BUT IF I KILL MYSELF, I WON'T BE ABLE TO...
...CARRY OUT MY MISSION...
I DIDN'T MEAN IT.
WHEN YOU'RE FIGHT-ING...
...YOU DON'T THINK ABOUT ANYTHING, RIGHT...?
BUT WHEN THE FIGHT'S OVER...
...AND YOU SEE WHAT YOU'VE DONE...
DO YOU FEEL ANY-THING THEN?
...
NO.
OKAY.
I GUESS YOU CAN'T HELP IT THEN.
THAT'S NOT AN EASY THING TO CHANGE.

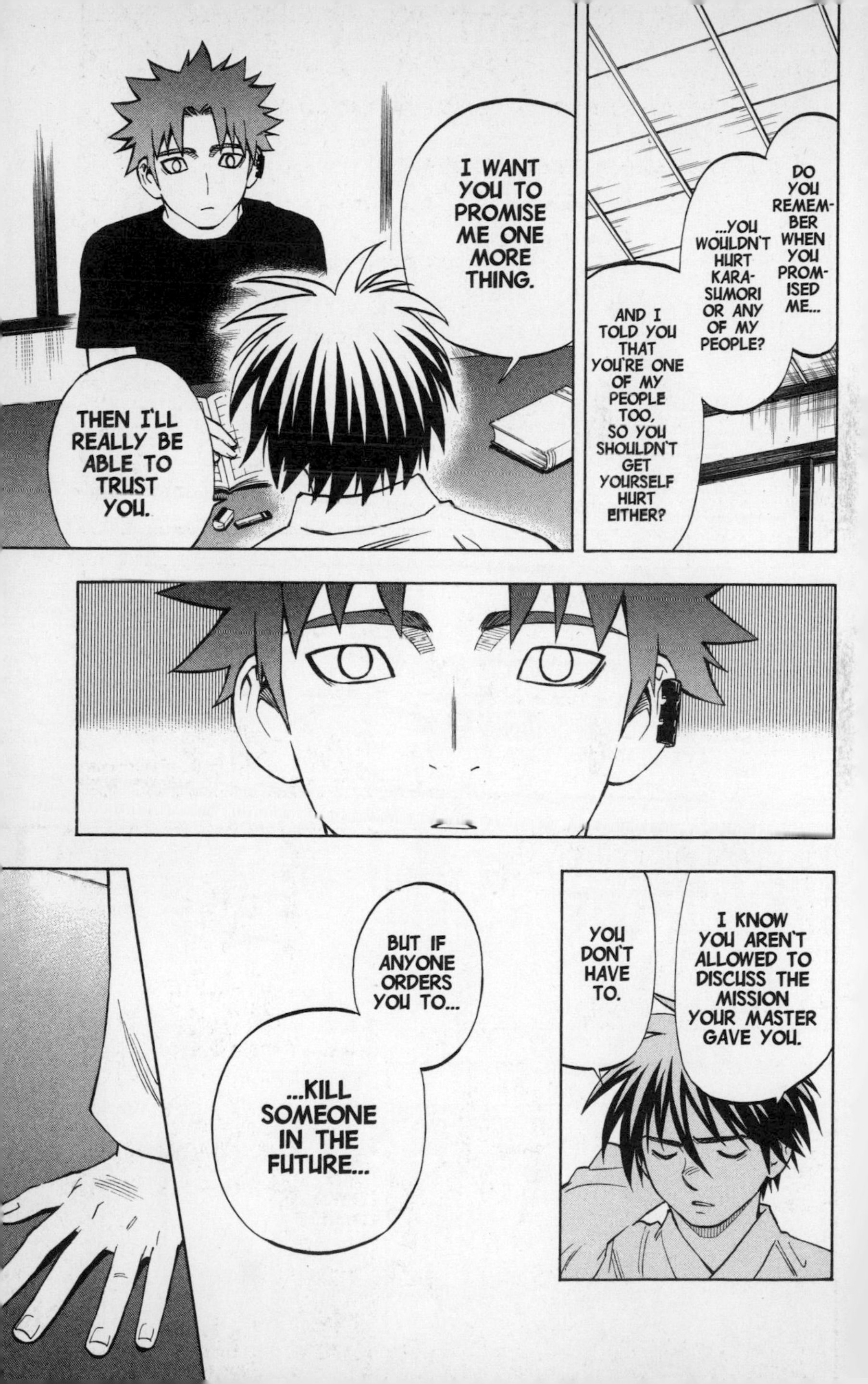
DO YOU REMEMBER WHEN YOU PROMISED ME...
...YOU WOULDN'T HURT KARASUMORI OR ANY OF MY PEOPLE?
AND I TOLD YOU THAT YOU'RE ONE OF MY PEOPLE TOO, SO YOU SHOULDN'T GET YOURSELF HURT EITHER?
I WANT YOU TO PROMISE ME ONE MORE THING.
THEN I'LL REALLY BE ABLE TO TRUST YOU.
I KNOW YOU AREN'T ALLOWED TO DISCUSS THE MISSION YOUR MASTER GAVE YOU.
YOU DON'T HAVE TO.
BUT IF ANYONE ORDERS YOU TO...
...KILL SOMEONE IN THE FUTURE...

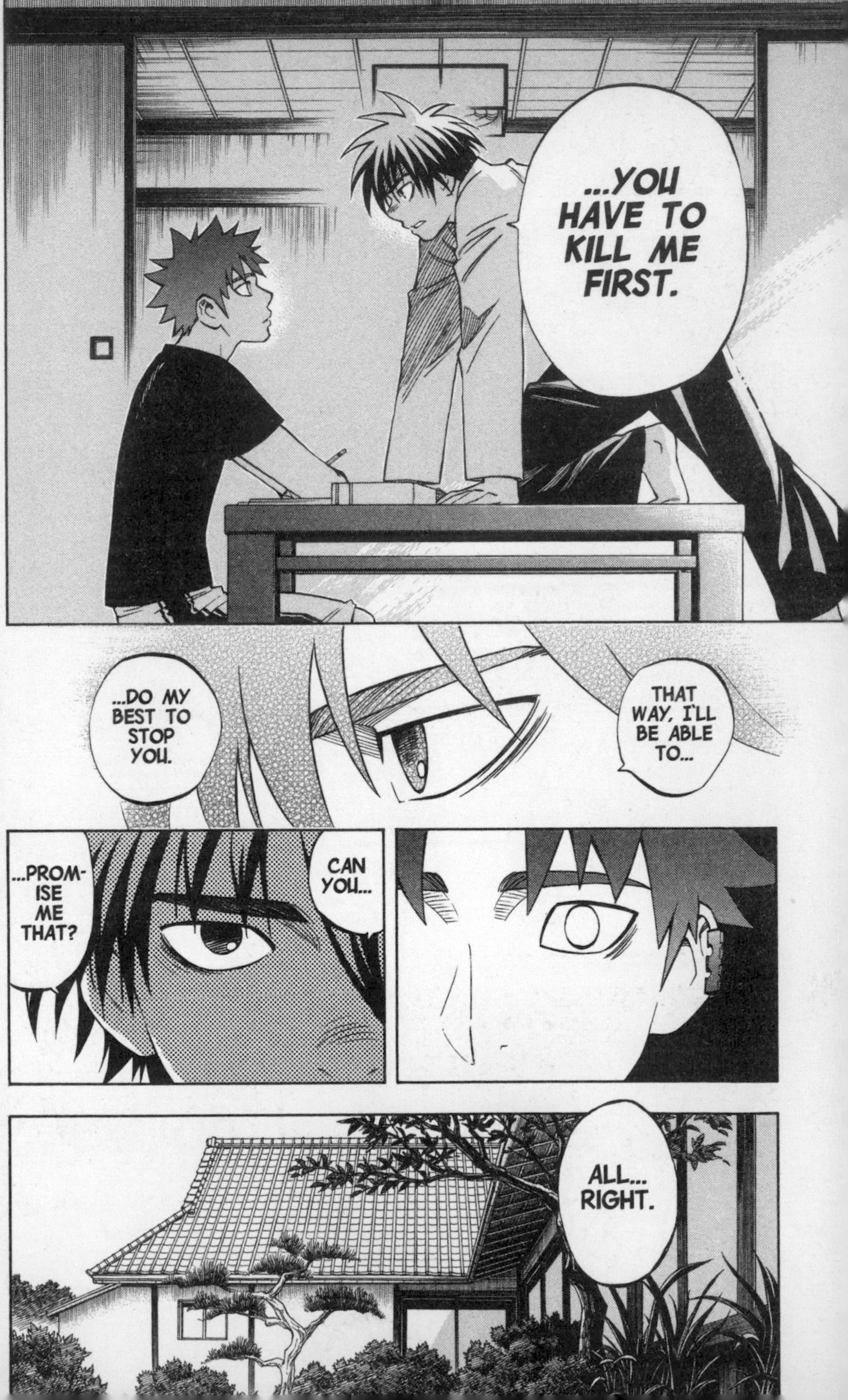
...YOU HAVE TO KILL ME FIRST.
THAT WAY, I'LL BE ABLE TO...
...DO MY BEST TO STOP YOU.
CAN YOU...
...PROMISE ME THAT?
ALL... RIGHT.

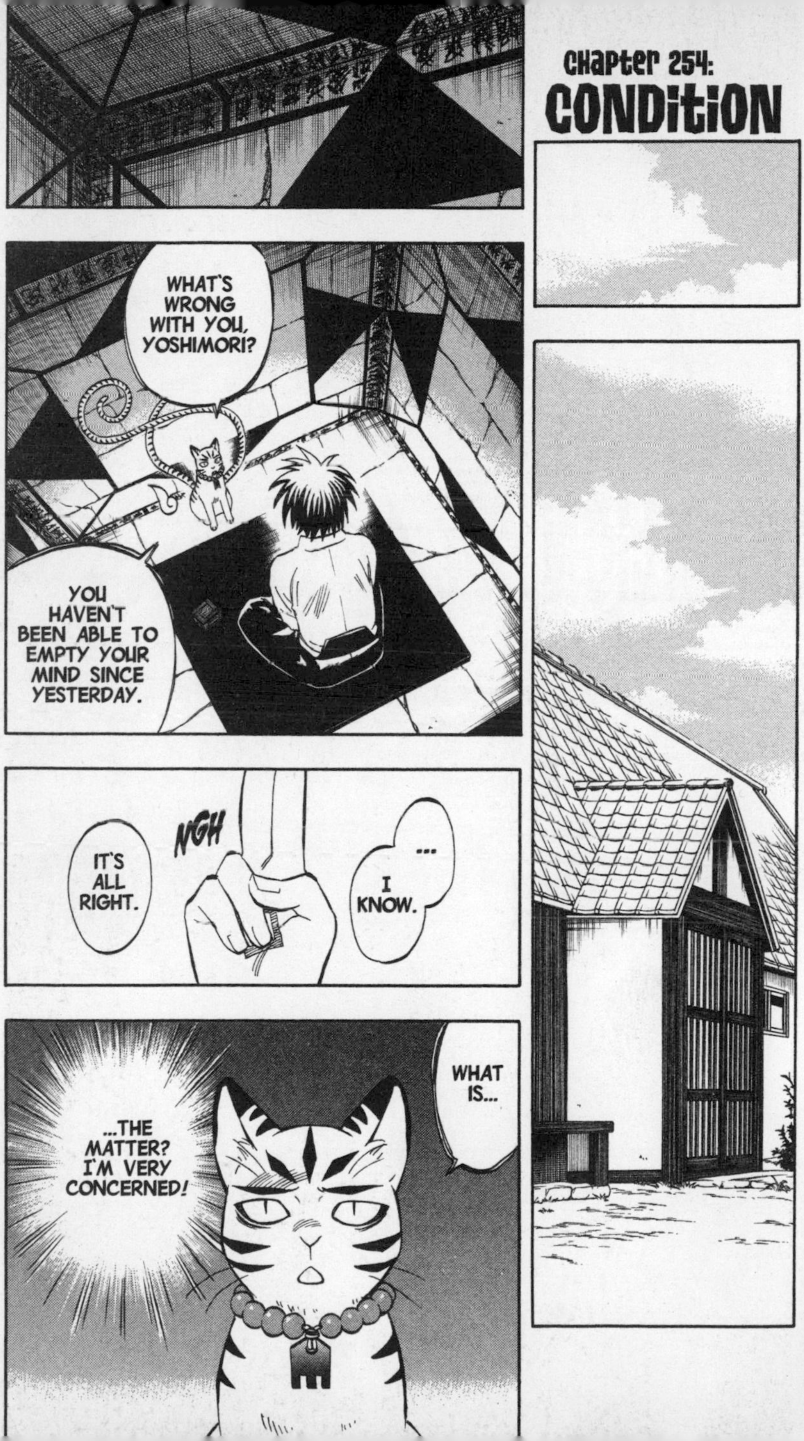
Chapter 254:
CONDITION
WHAT'S WRONG WITH YOU, YOSHIMORI?
YOU HAVEN'T BEEN ABLE TO EMPTY YOUR MIND SINCE YESTERDAY.
... I KNOW.
NGH
IT'S ALL RIGHT.
WHAT IS...
...THE MATTER? I'M VERY CONCERNED!

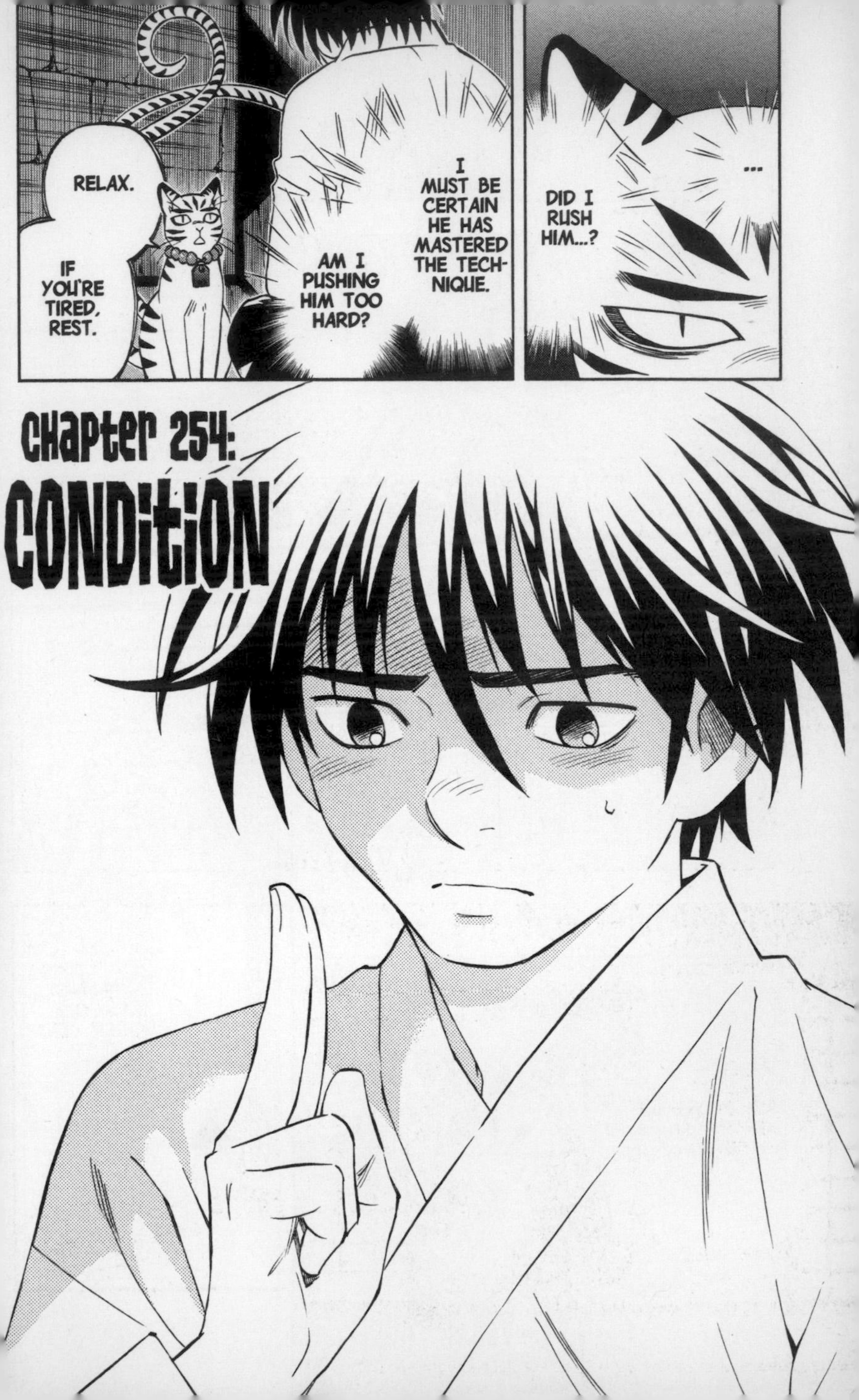
...
DID I RUSH HIM...?
I MUST BE CERTAIN HE HAS MASTERED THE TECHNIQUE.
AM I PUSHING HIM TOO HARD?
RELAX.
IF YOU'RE TIRED, REST.
Chapter 254:
CONDITION

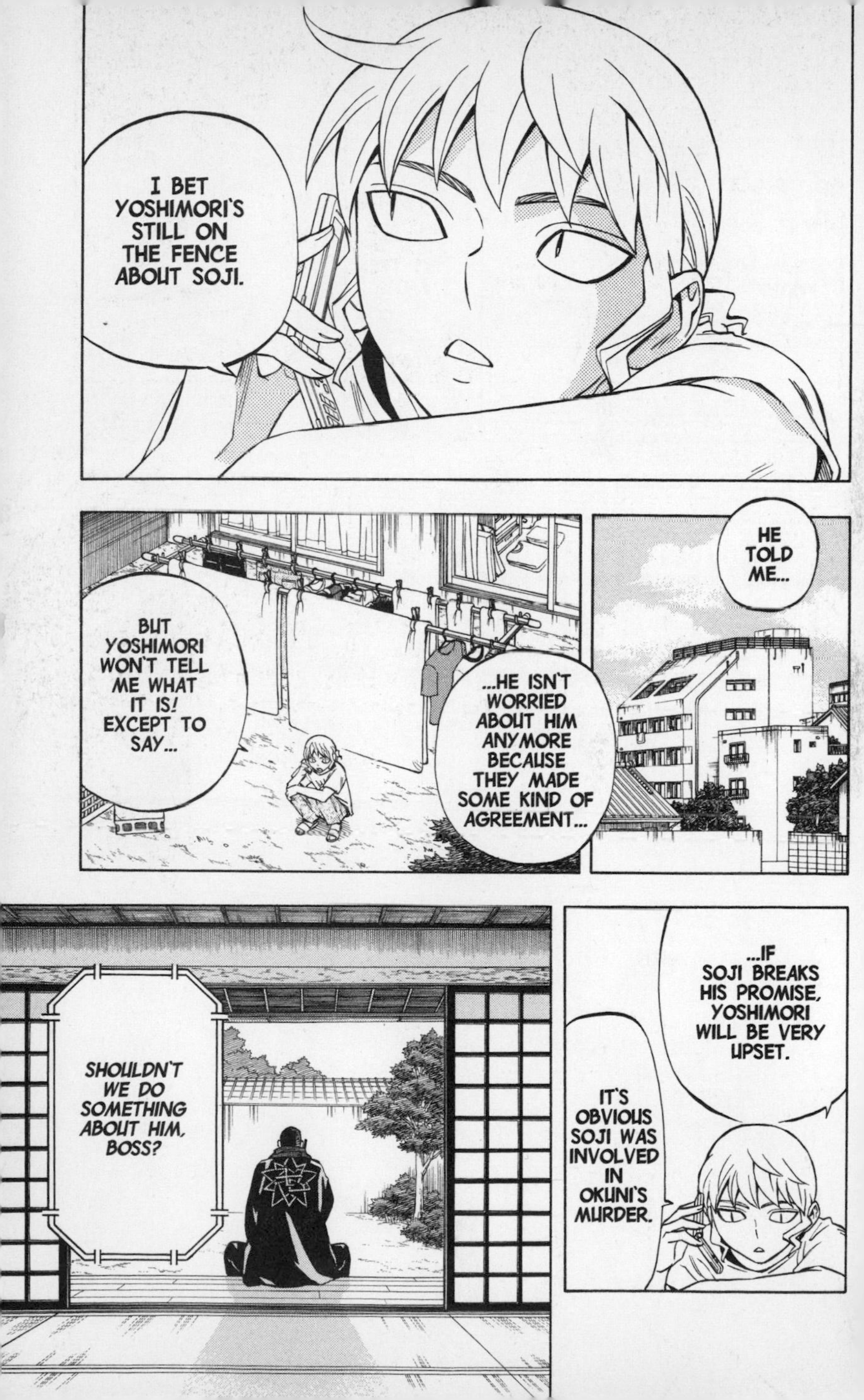
I BET YOSHIMORI'S STILL ON THE FENCE ABOUT SOJI.
HE TOLD ME...
...HE ISN'T WORRIED ABOUT HIM ANYMORE BECAUSE THEY MADE SOME KIND OF AGREEMENT...
BUT YOSHIMORI WON'T TELL ME WHAT IT IS! EXCEPT TO SAY...
...IF SOJI BREAKS HIS PROMISE, YOSHIMORI WILL BE VERY UPSET.
IT'S OBVIOUS SOJI WAS INVOLVED IN OKUNI'S MURDER.
SHOULDN'T WE DO SOMETHING ABOUT HIM, BOSS?

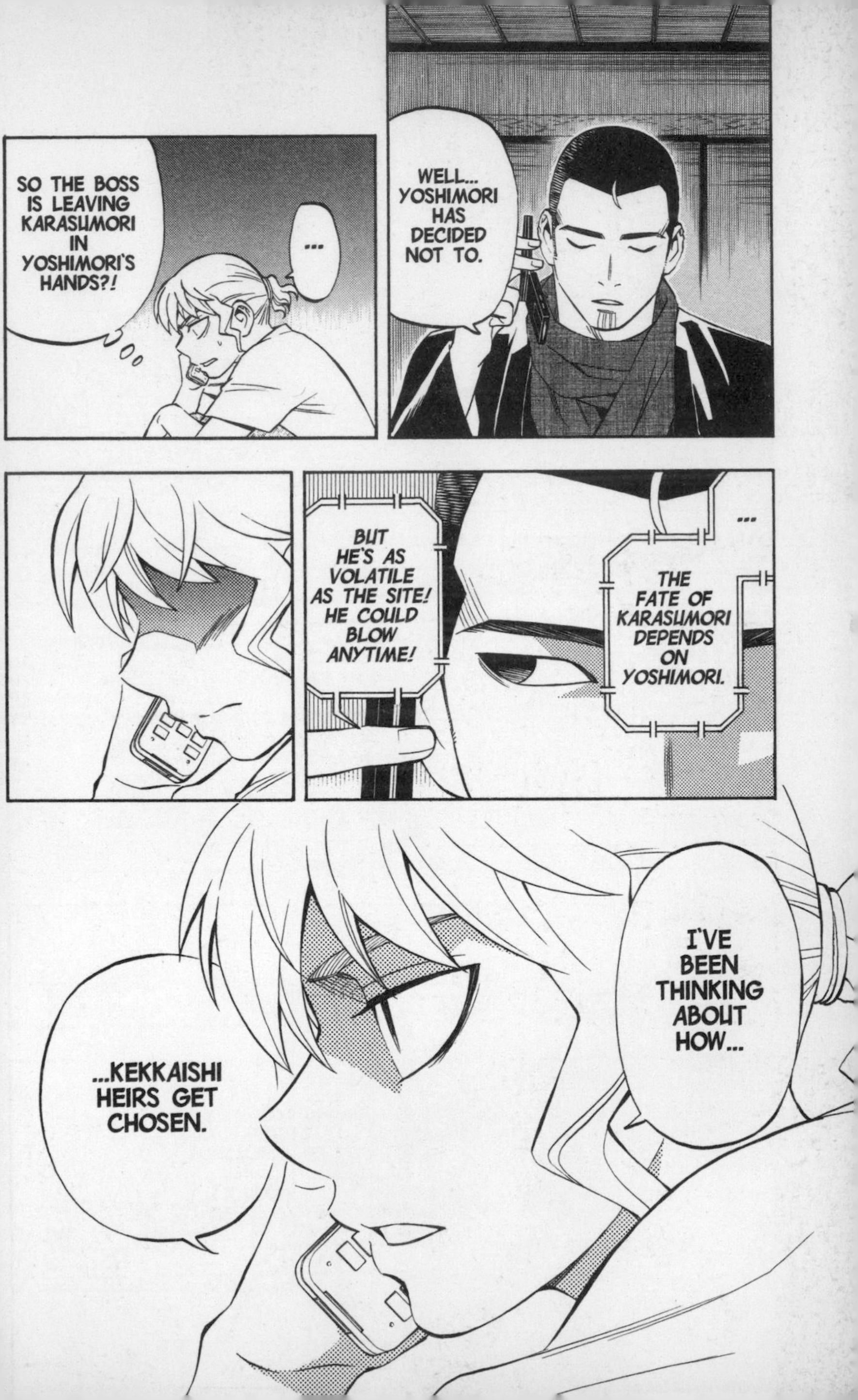
WELL... YOSHIMORI HAS DECIDED NOT TO.
...
SO THE BOSS IS LEAVING KARASUMORI IN YOSHIMORI'S HANDS?!
...
THE FATE OF KARASUMORI DEPENDS ON YOSHIMORI.
BUT HE'S AS VOLATILE AS THE SITE! HE COULD BLOW ANYTIME!
I'VE BEEN THINKING ABOUT HOW...
...KEKKAISHI HEIRS GET CHOSEN.

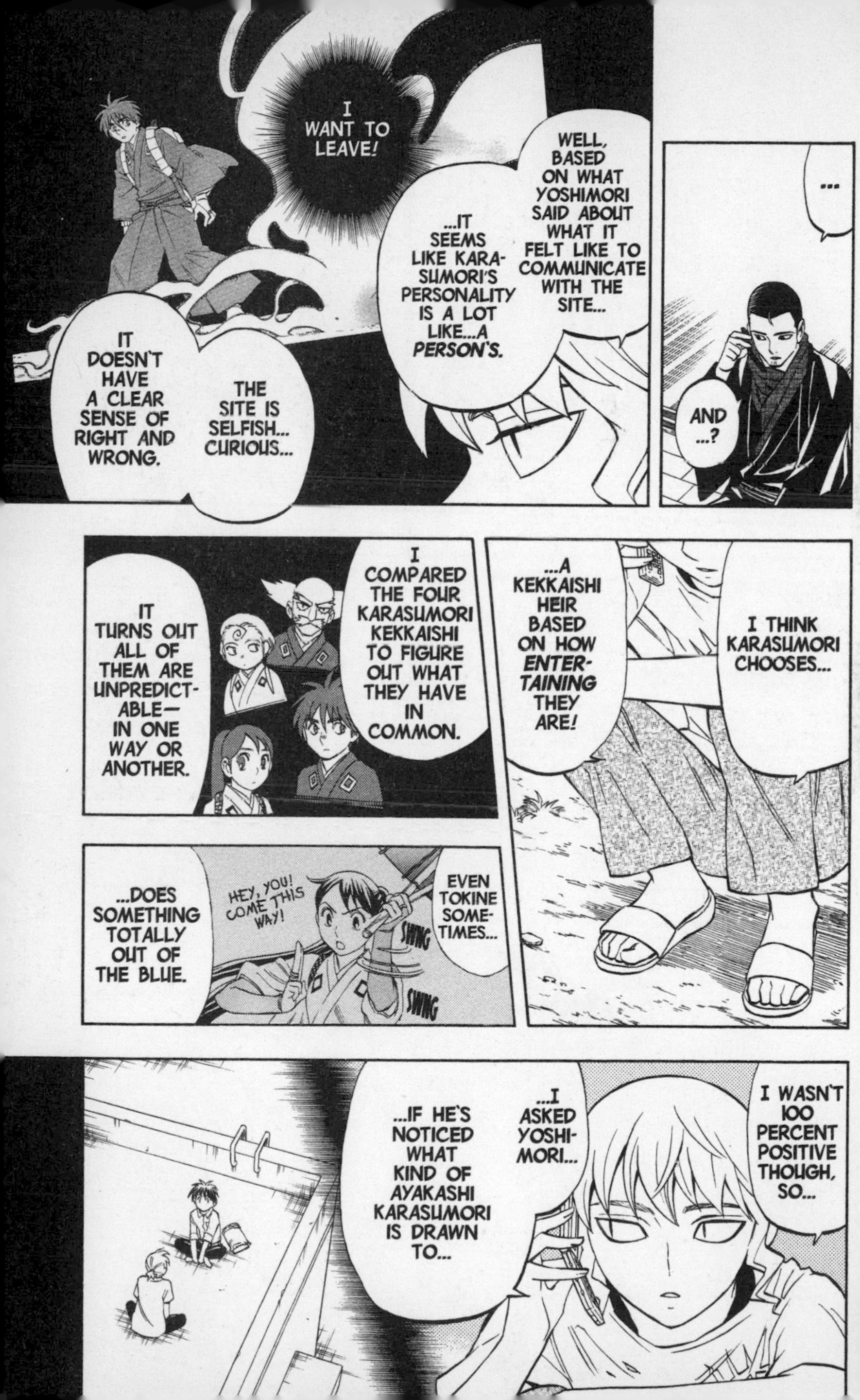
...
AND ...?
WELL, BASED ON WHAT YOSHIMORI SAID ABOUT WHAT IT FELT LIKE TO COMMUNICATE WITH THE SITE...
...IT SEEMS LIKE KARASUMORI'S PERSONALITY IS A LOT LIKE...A *PERSON'S.*
I WANT TO LEAVE!
THE SITE IS SELFISH... CURIOUS...
IT DOESN'T HAVE A CLEAR SENSE OF RIGHT AND WRONG.
I THINK KARASUMORI CHOOSES...
...A KEKKAISHI HEIR BASED ON HOW *ENTERTAINING* THEY ARE!
I COMPARED THE FOUR KARASUMORI KEKKAISHI TO FIGURE OUT WHAT THEY HAVE IN COMMON.
IT TURNS OUT ALL OF THEM ARE UNPREDICTABLE—IN ONE WAY OR ANOTHER.
EVEN TOKINE SOMETIMES...
HEY, YOU! COME THIS WAY!
SWING
SWING
...DOES SOMETHING TOTALLY OUT OF THE BLUE.
I WASN'T 100 PERCENT POSITIVE THOUGH, SO...
...I ASKED YOSHIMORI...
...IF HE'S NOTICED WHAT KIND OF AYAKASHI KARASUMORI IS DRAWN TO...

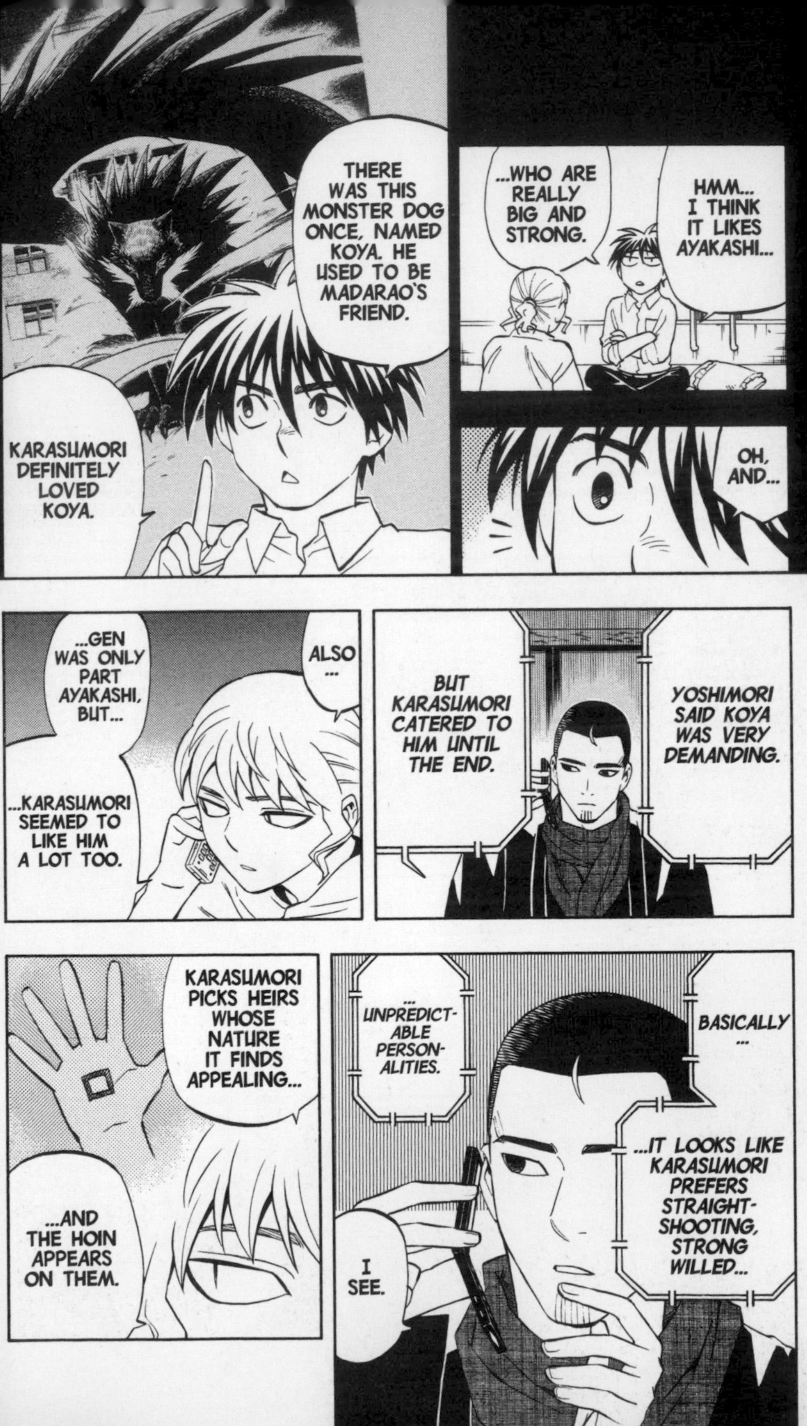
HMM... I THINK IT LIKES AYAKASHI...
...WHO ARE REALLY BIG AND STRONG.
OH, AND...
THERE WAS THIS MONSTER DOG ONCE, NAMED KOYA. HE USED TO BE MADARAO'S FRIEND.
KARASUMORI DEFINITELY LOVED KOYA.
YOSHIMORI SAID KOYA WAS VERY DEMANDING.
BUT KARASUMORI CATERED TO HIM UNTIL THE END.
ALSO...
...GEN WAS ONLY PART AYAKASHI, BUT...
...KARASUMORI SEEMED TO LIKE HIM A LOT TOO.
BASICALLY...
...IT LOOKS LIKE KARASUMORI PREFERS STRAIGHT-SHOOTING, STRONG WILLED...
...UNPREDICT-ABLE PERSON-ALITIES.
I SEE.
KARASUMORI PICKS HEIRS WHOSE NATURE IT FINDS APPEALING...
...AND THE HOIN APPEARS ON THEM.

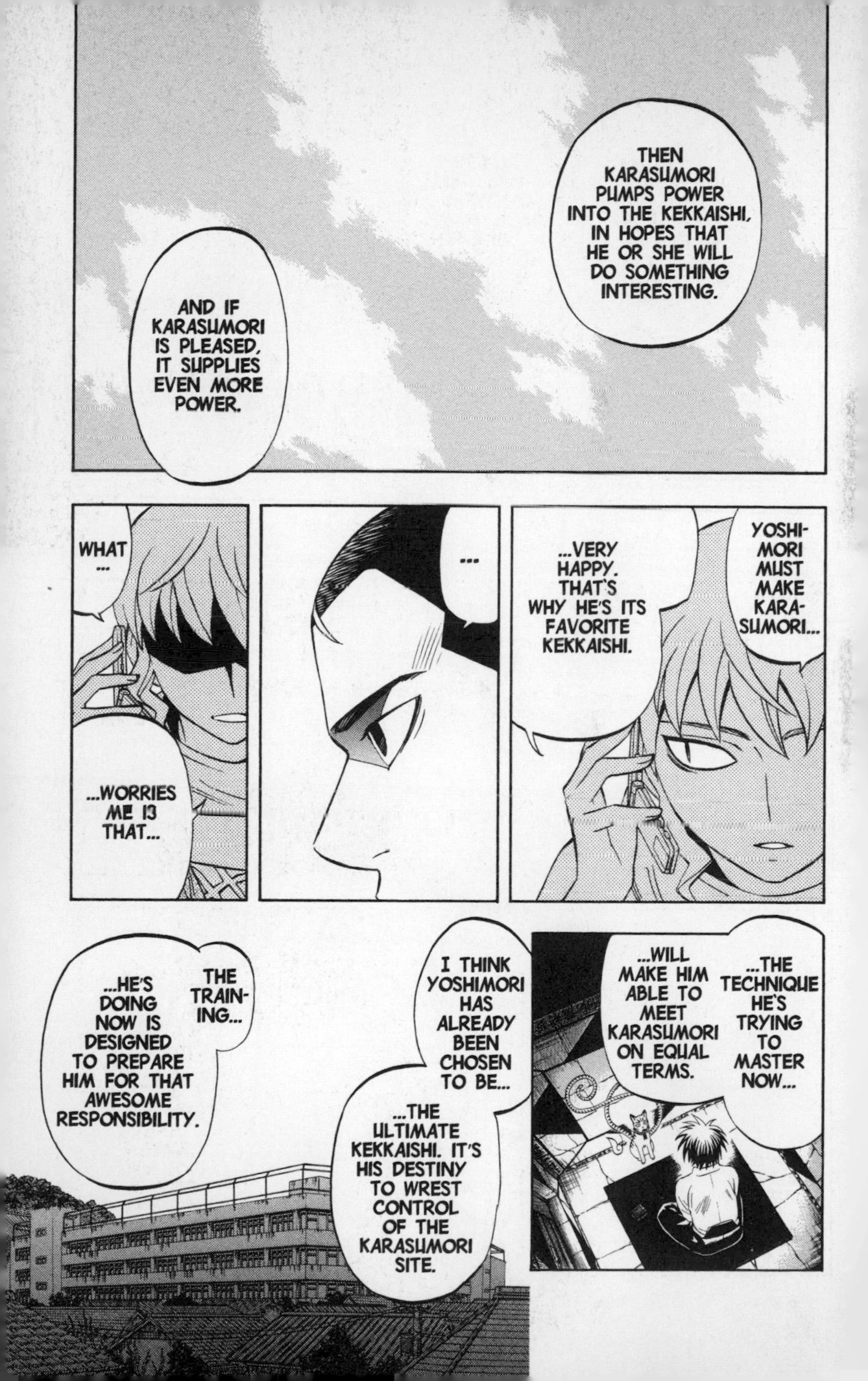
THEN KARASUMORI PUMPS POWER INTO THE KEKKAISHI, IN HOPES THAT HE OR SHE WILL DO SOMETHING INTERESTING.
AND IF KARASUMORI IS PLEASED, IT SUPPLIES EVEN MORE POWER.
YOSHIMORI MUST MAKE KARASUMORI...
...VERY HAPPY. THAT'S WHY HE'S ITS FAVORITE KEKKAISHI.
...
WHAT ...
...WORRIES ME IS THAT...
...THE TECHNIQUE HE'S TRYING TO MASTER NOW...
...WILL MAKE HIM ABLE TO MEET KARASUMORI ON EQUAL TERMS.
I THINK YOSHIMORI HAS ALREADY BEEN CHOSEN TO BE...
...THE ULTIMATE KEKKAISHI. IT'S HIS DESTINY TO WREST CONTROL OF THE KARASUMORI SITE.
THE TRAINING...
...HE'S DOING NOW IS DESIGNED TO PREPARE HIM FOR THAT AWESOME RESPONSIBILITY.

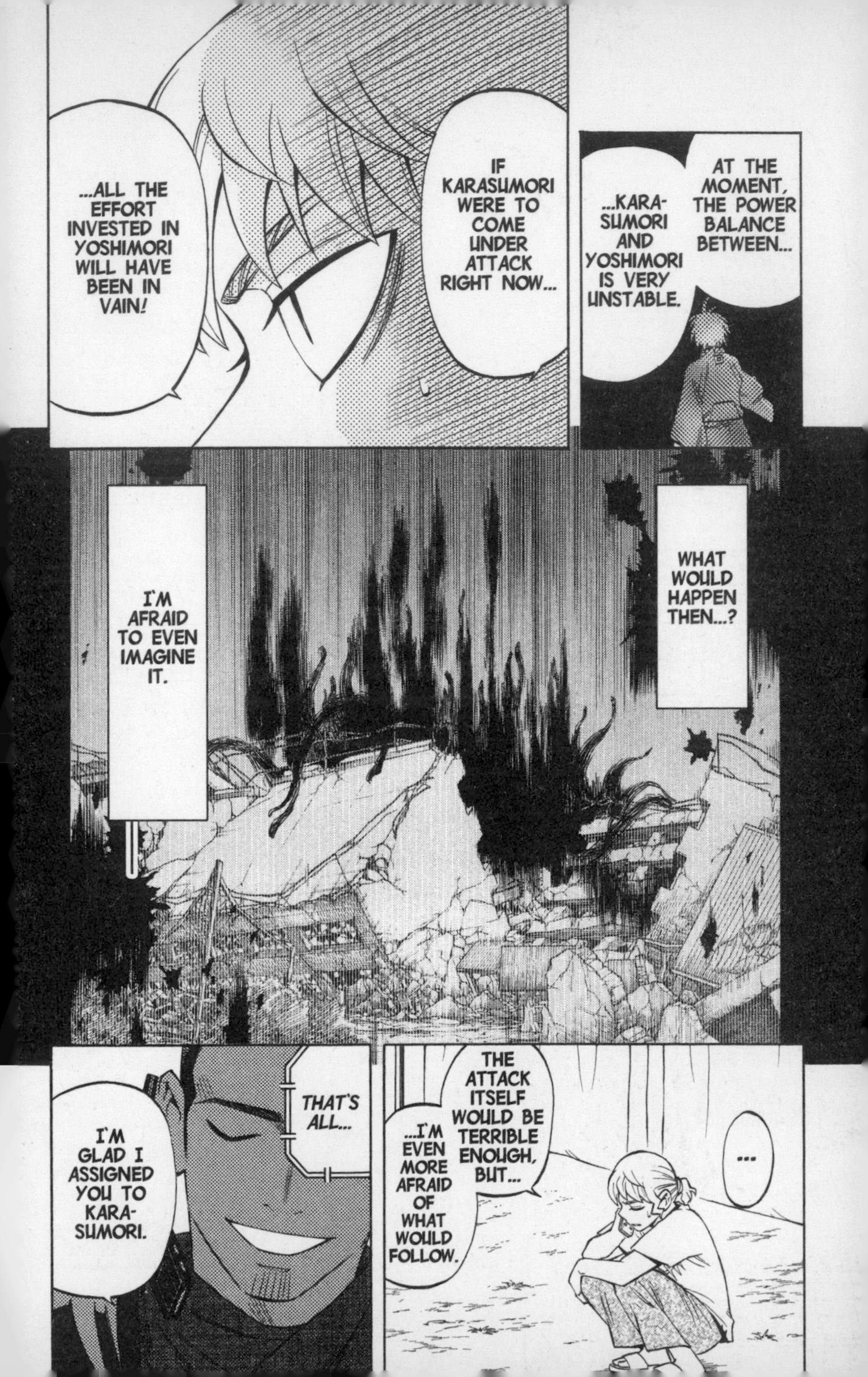
AT THE MOMENT, THE POWER BALANCE BETWEEN...
...KARA-SUMORI AND YOSHIMORI IS VERY UNSTABLE.
IF KARASUMORI WERE TO COME UNDER ATTACK RIGHT NOW...
...ALL THE EFFORT INVESTED IN YOSHIMORI WILL HAVE BEEN IN VAIN!
WHAT WOULD HAPPEN THEN...?
I'M AFRAID TO EVEN IMAGINE IT.
...
THE ATTACK ITSELF WOULD BE TERRIBLE ENOUGH, BUT...
...I'M EVEN MORE AFRAID OF WHAT WOULD FOLLOW.
THAT'S ALL...
I'M GLAD I ASSIGNED YOU TO KARA-SUMORI.

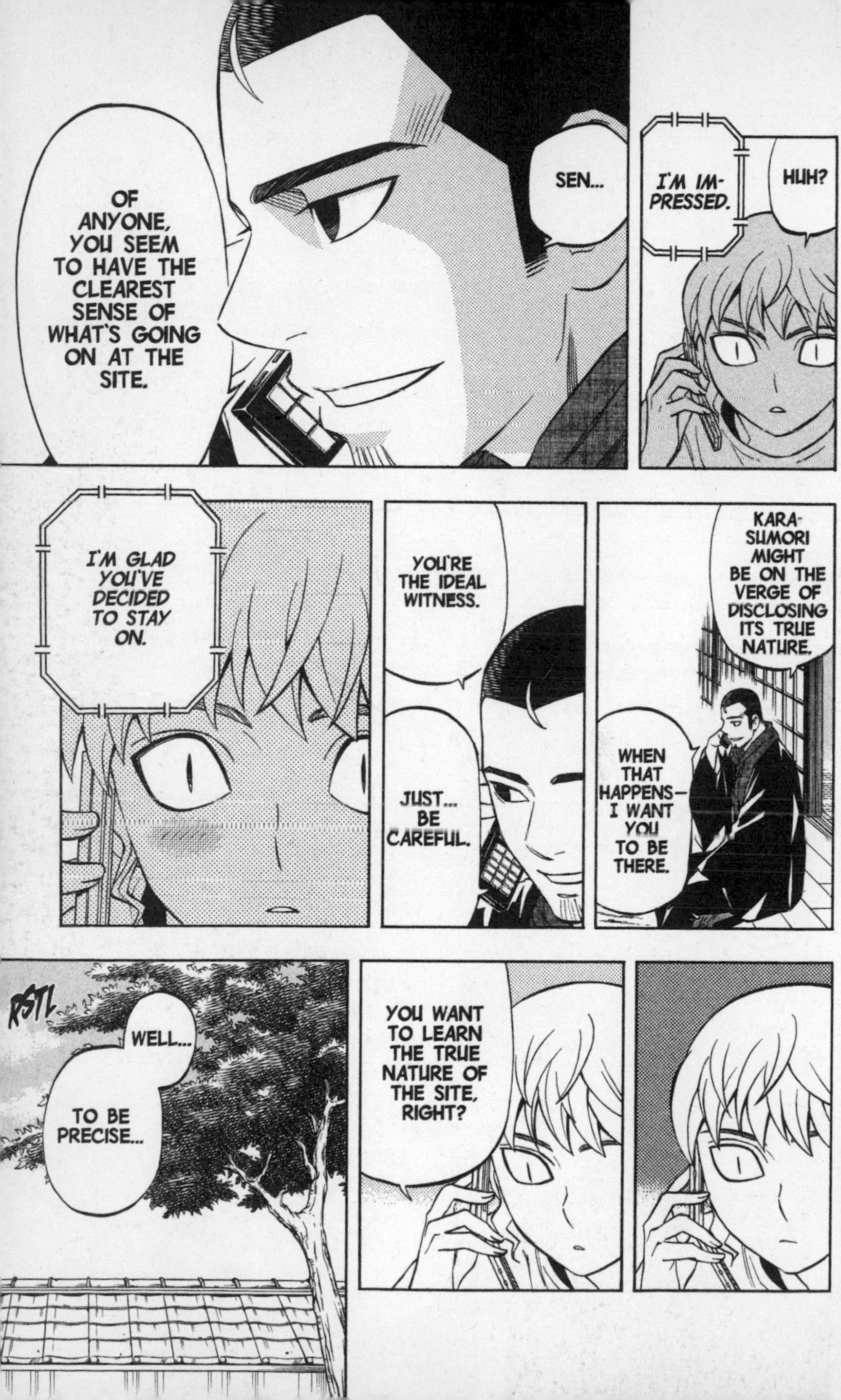
HUH?
I'M IMPRESSED.
SEN...
OF ANYONE, YOU SEEM TO HAVE THE CLEAREST SENSE OF WHAT'S GOING ON AT THE SITE.
KARASUMORI MIGHT BE ON THE VERGE OF DISCLOSING ITS TRUE NATURE.
WHEN THAT HAPPENS— I WANT YOU TO BE THERE.
YOU'RE THE IDEAL WITNESS.
JUST... BE CAREFUL.
I'M GLAD YOU'VE DECIDED TO STAY ON.
YOU WANT TO LEARN THE TRUE NATURE OF THE SITE, RIGHT?
RSTL
WELL...
TO BE PRECISE...

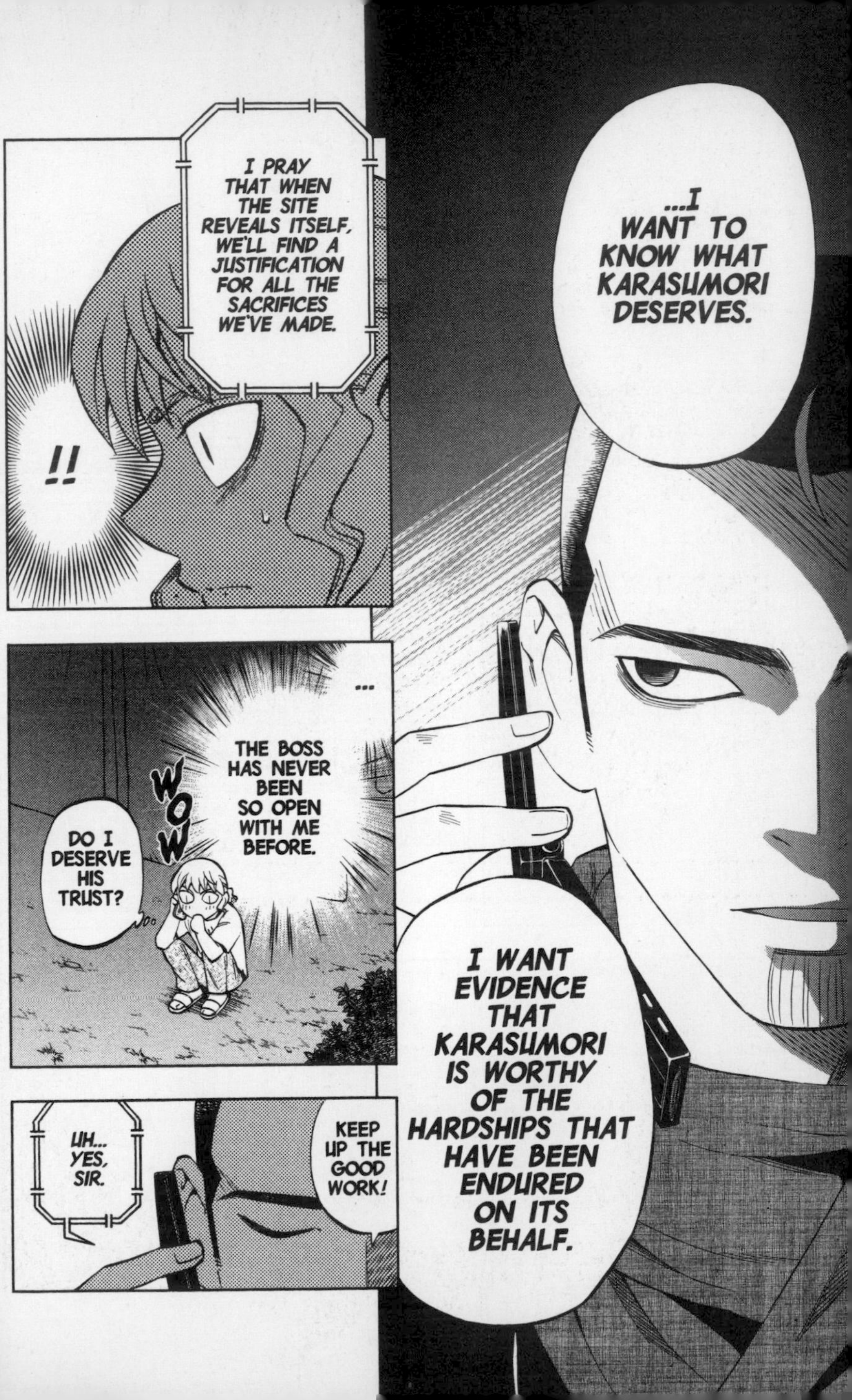
...I WANT TO KNOW WHAT KARASUMORI DESERVES.
I WANT EVIDENCE THAT KARASUMORI IS WORTHY OF THE HARDSHIPS THAT HAVE BEEN ENDURED ON ITS BEHALF.
I PRAY THAT WHEN THE SITE REVEALS ITSELF, WE'LL FIND A JUSTIFICATION FOR ALL THE SACRIFICES WE'VE MADE.
!!
...
THE BOSS HAS NEVER BEEN SO OPEN WITH ME BEFORE.
WOW
DO I DESERVE HIS TRUST?
KEEP UP THE GOOD WORK!
UH... YES, SIR.

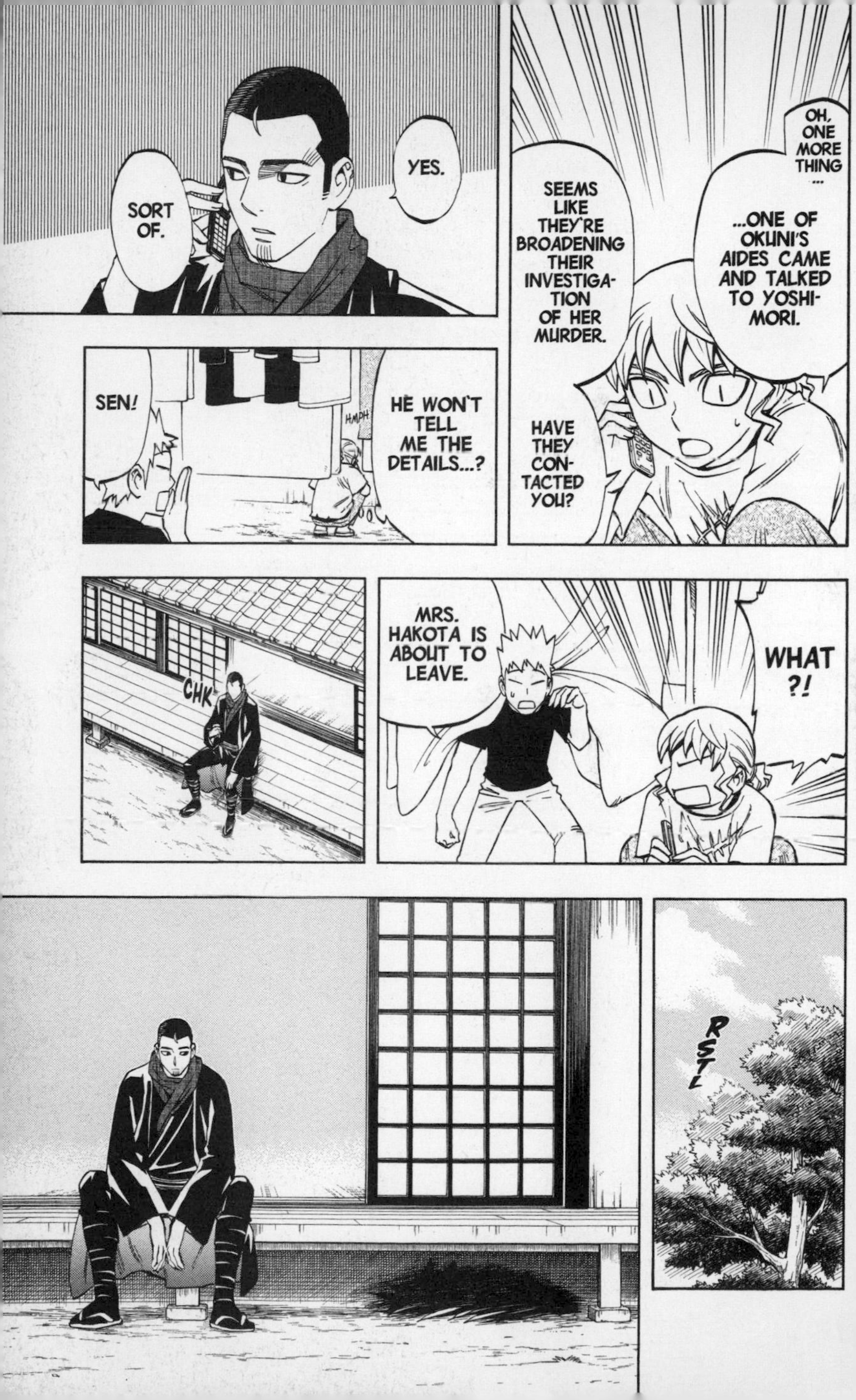
OH, ONE MORE THING ...
...ONE OF OKUNI'S AIDES CAME AND TALKED TO YOSHI-MORI.
SEEMS LIKE THEY'RE BROADENING THEIR INVESTIGA-TION OF HER MURDER.
HAVE THEY CON-TACTED YOU?
YES.
SORT OF.
HE WON'T TELL ME THE DETAILS...?
HMPH
SEN!
WHAT?!
MRS. HAKOTA IS ABOUT TO LEAVE.
CHK
RSTL

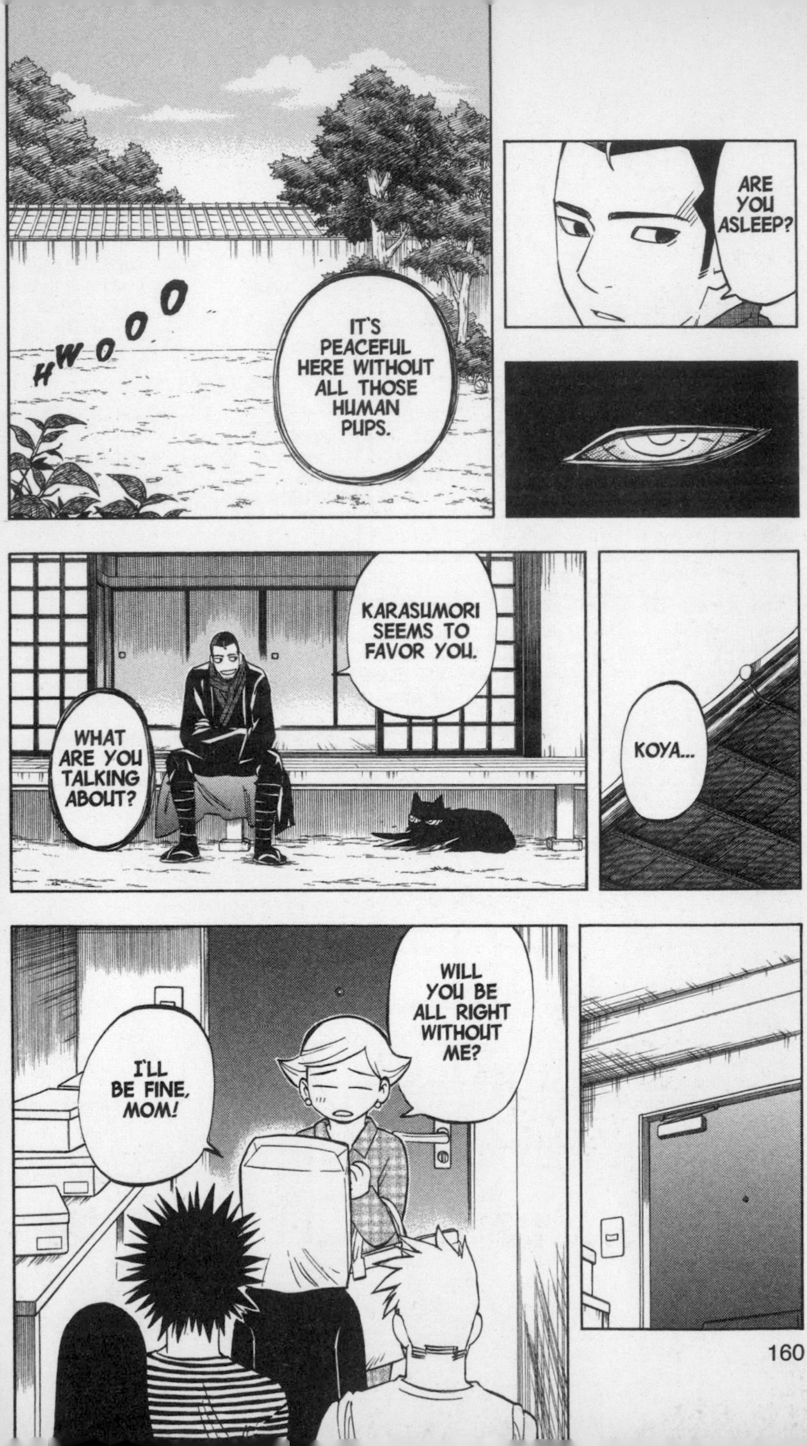
ARE YOU ASLEEP?
HWOOO
IT'S PEACEFUL HERE WITHOUT ALL THOSE HUMAN PUPS.
KOYA...
KARASUMORI SEEMS TO FAVOR YOU.
WHAT ARE YOU TALKING ABOUT?
WILL YOU BE ALL RIGHT WITHOUT ME?
I'LL BE FINE, MOM!

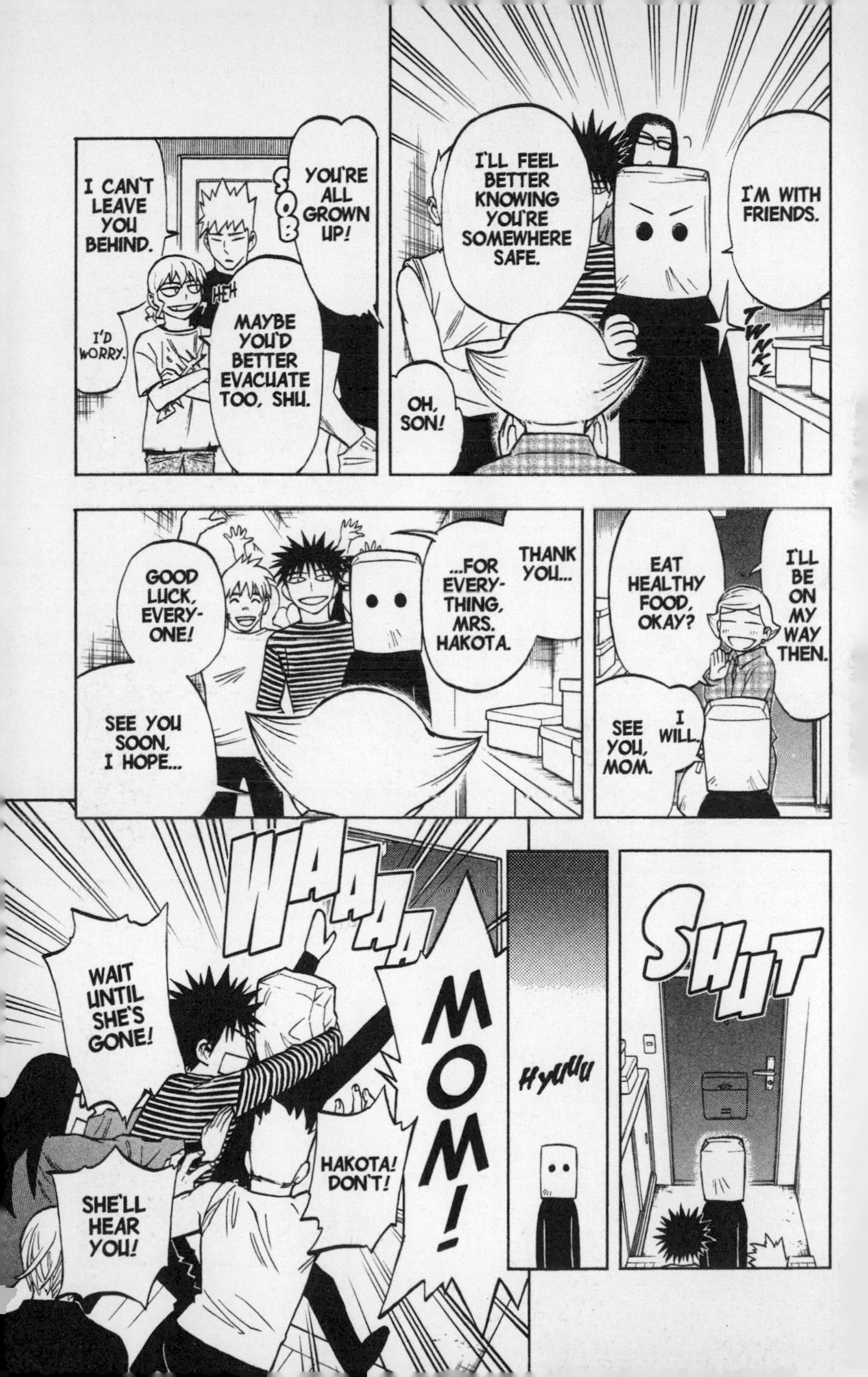
I'M WITH FRIENDS.
TWNKL
I'LL FEEL BETTER KNOWING YOU'RE SOMEWHERE SAFE.
OH, SON!
YOU'RE ALL GROWN UP!
SOB
I CAN'T LEAVE YOU BEHIND.
HEH
MAYBE YOU'D BETTER EVACUATE TOO, SHU.
I'D WORRY.
I'LL BE ON MY WAY THEN.
EAT HEALTHY FOOD, OKAY?
I WILL.
SEE YOU, MOM.
THANK YOU...
...FOR EVERY-THING, MRS. HAKOTA.
GOOD LUCK, EVERY-ONE!
SEE YOU SOON, I HOPE...
SHUT
HYUUU
WAAAAA
MOM!
WAIT UNTIL SHE'S GONE!
HAKOTA! DON'T!
SHE'LL HEAR YOU!

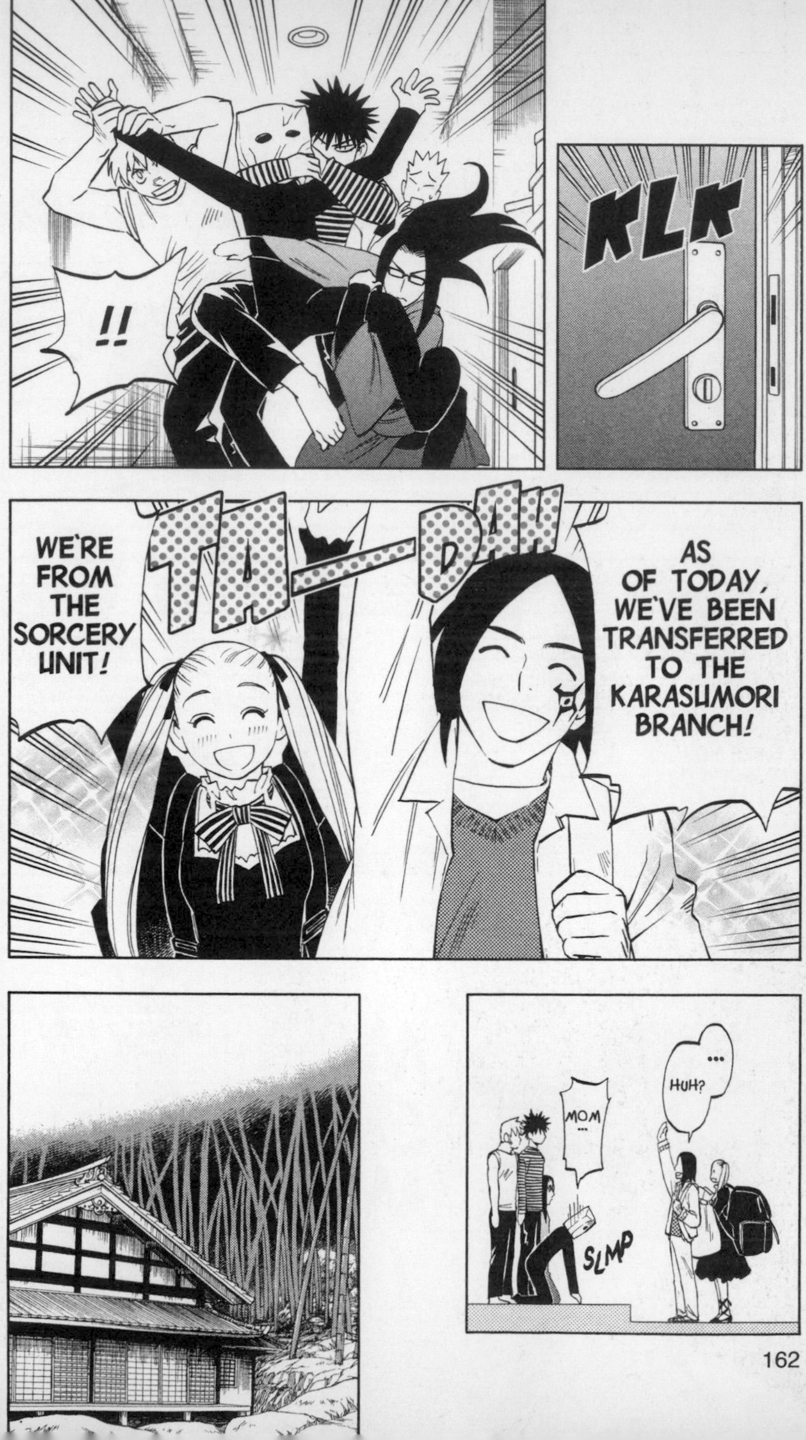
KLK
!!
AS OF TODAY, WE'VE BEEN TRANSFERRED TO THE KARASUMORI BRANCH!
TA-DAH
WE'RE FROM THE SORCERY UNIT!
...
HUH?
MOM...
SLMP

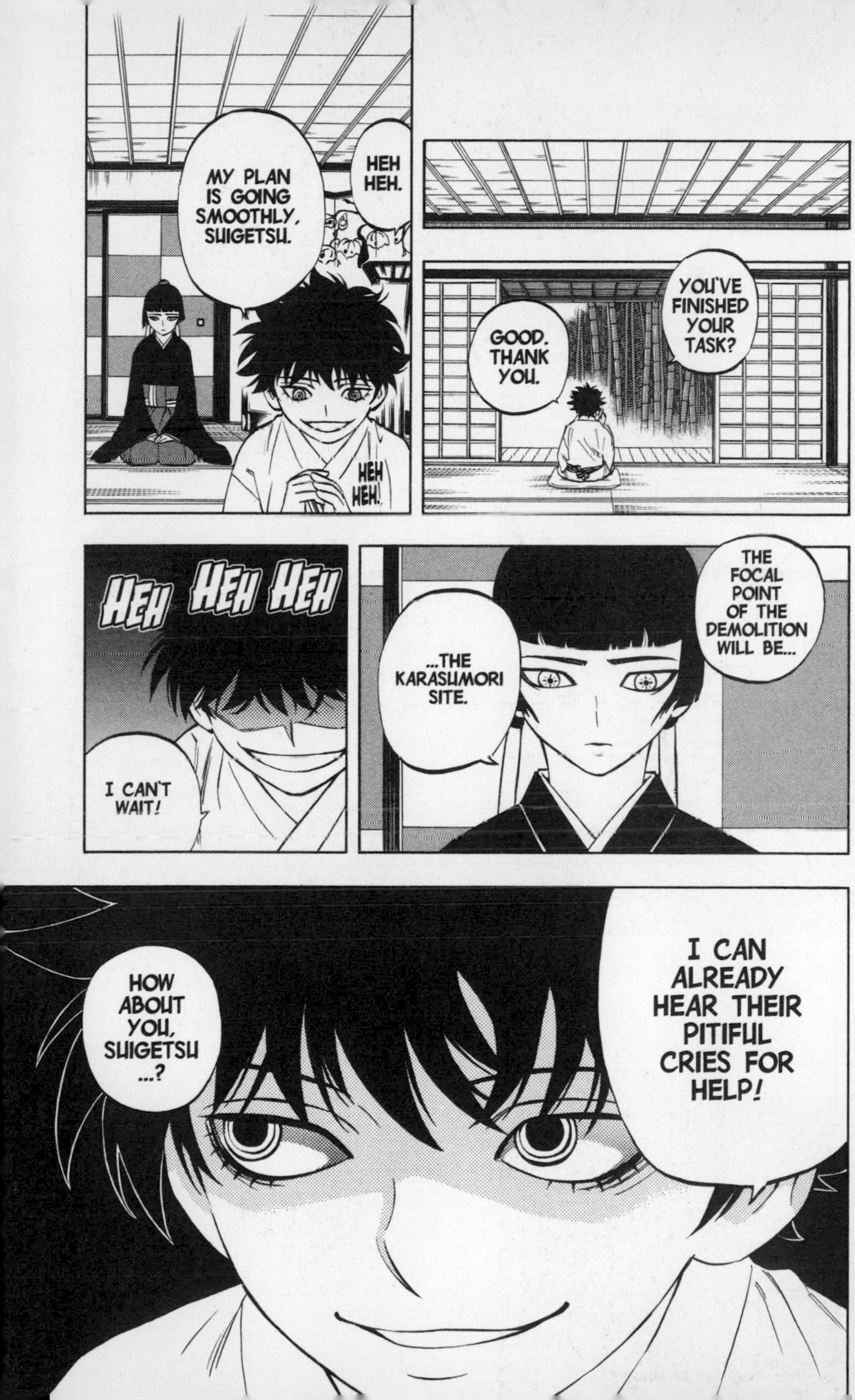
YOU'VE FINISHED YOUR TASK?
GOOD. THANK YOU.
HEH HEH.
MY PLAN IS GOING SMOOTHLY, SUIGETSU.
HEH HEH.
THE FOCAL POINT OF THE DEMOLITION WILL BE...
...THE KARASUMORI SITE.
HEH HEH HEH
I CAN'T WAIT!
I CAN ALREADY HEAR THEIR PITIFUL CRIES FOR HELP!
HOW ABOUT YOU, SUIGETSU ...?

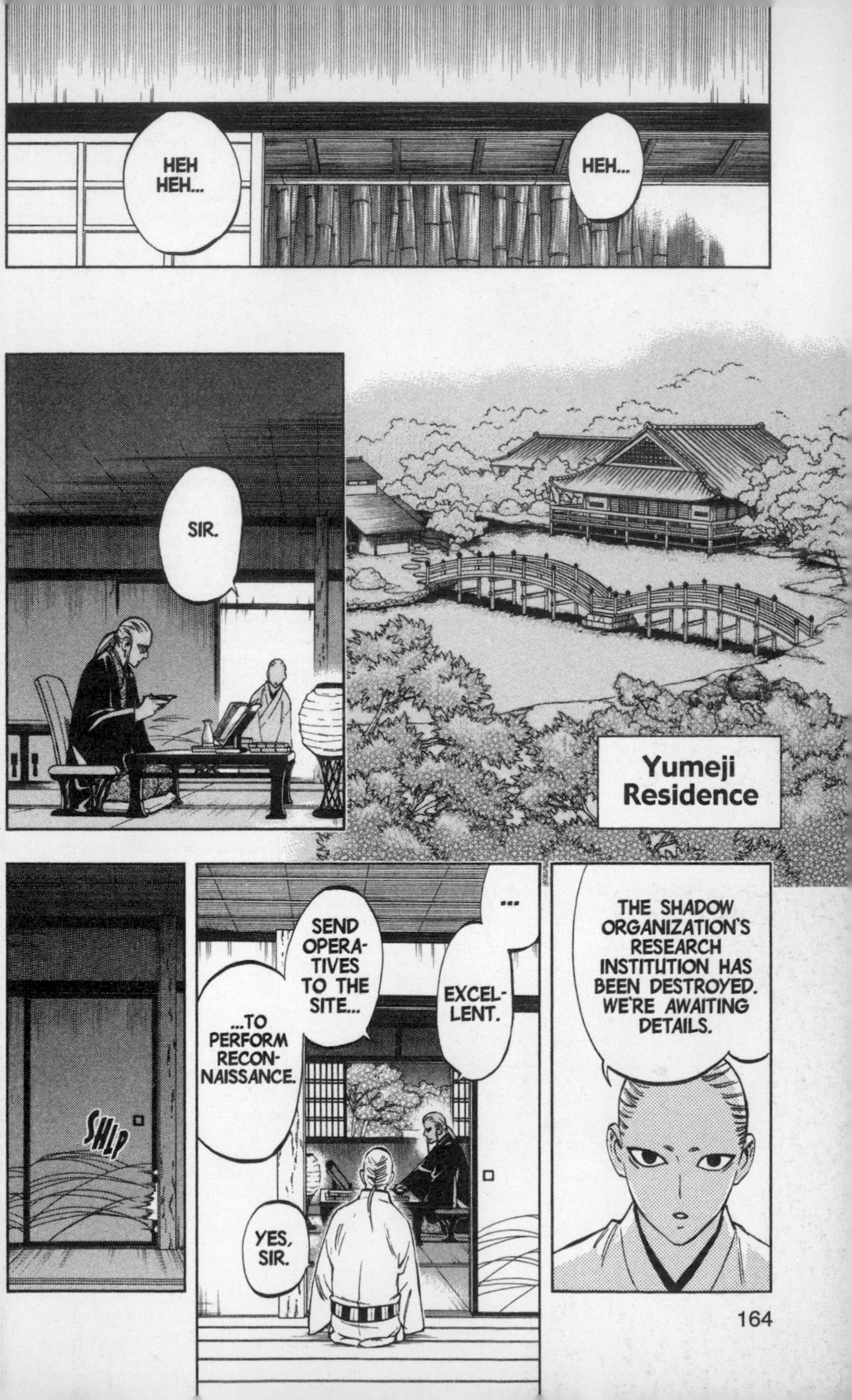
HEH...
HEH HEH...
Yumeji Residence
SIR.
THE SHADOW ORGANIZATION'S RESEARCH INSTITUTION HAS BEEN DESTROYED. WE'RE AWAITING DETAILS.
...
EXCEL-LENT.
SEND OPERA-TIVES TO THE SITE...
...TO PERFORM RECON-NAISSANCE.
YES, SIR.
SHLP

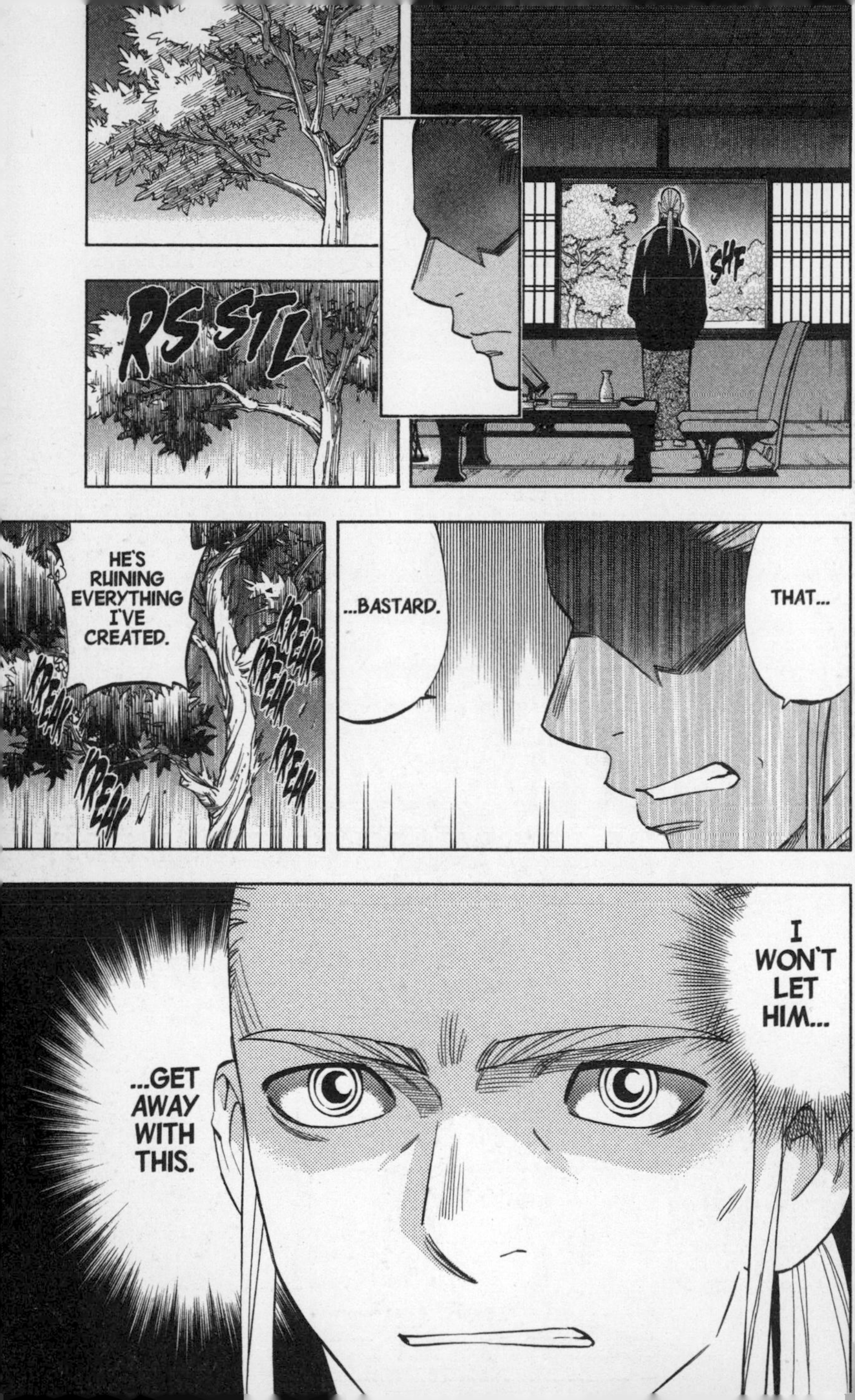
SHF
RS STL
THAT...
...BASTARD.
HE'S RUINING EVERYTHING I'VE CREATED.
KREAK KREAK KREAK KREAK
KREAK KREAK
I WON'T LET HIM...
...GET AWAY WITH THIS.

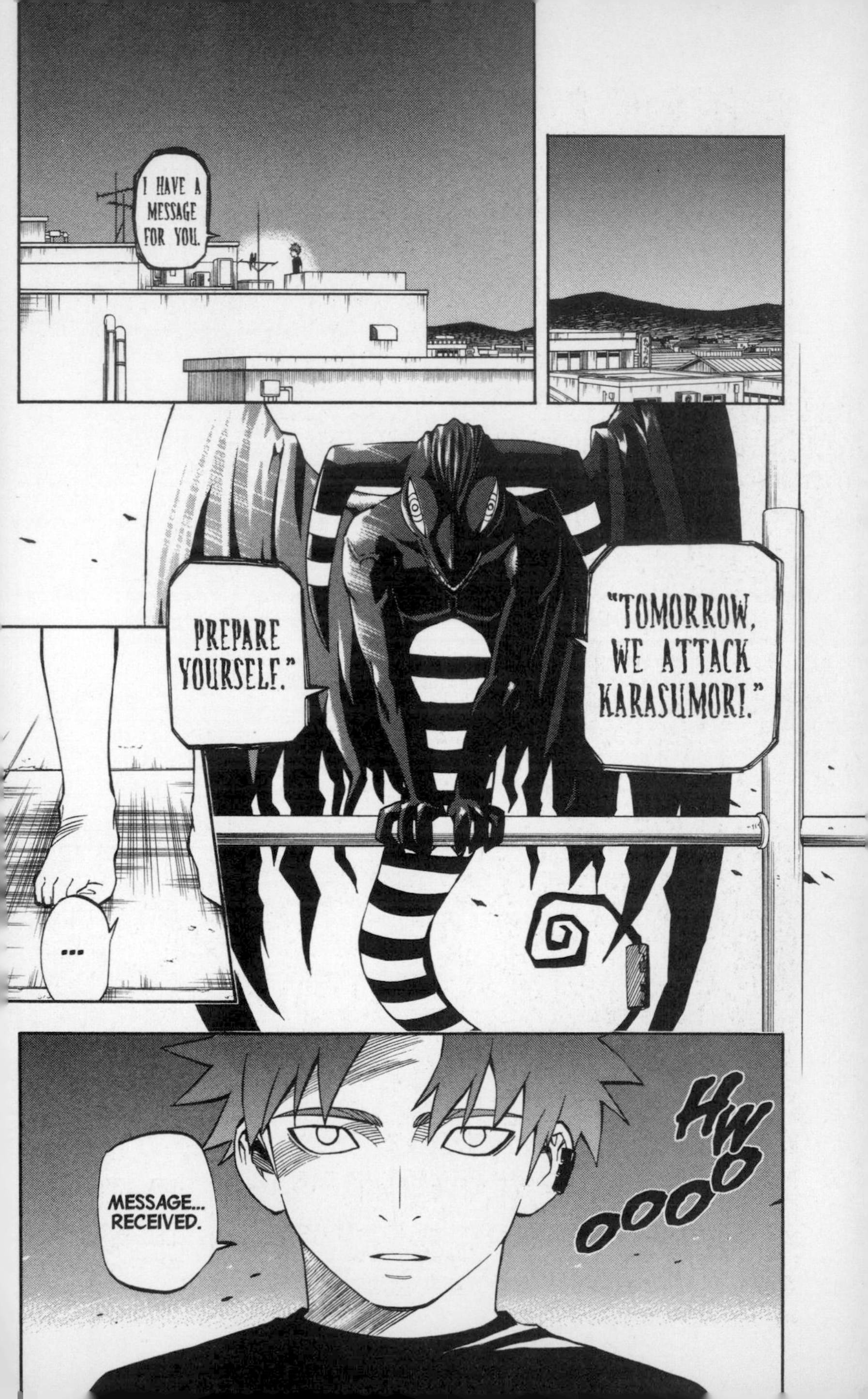
I HAVE A MESSAGE FOR YOU.
"TOMORROW, WE ATTACK KARASUMORI."
PREPARE YOURSELF."
...
HWOOOOO
MESSAGE... RECEIVED.

Chapter 255:

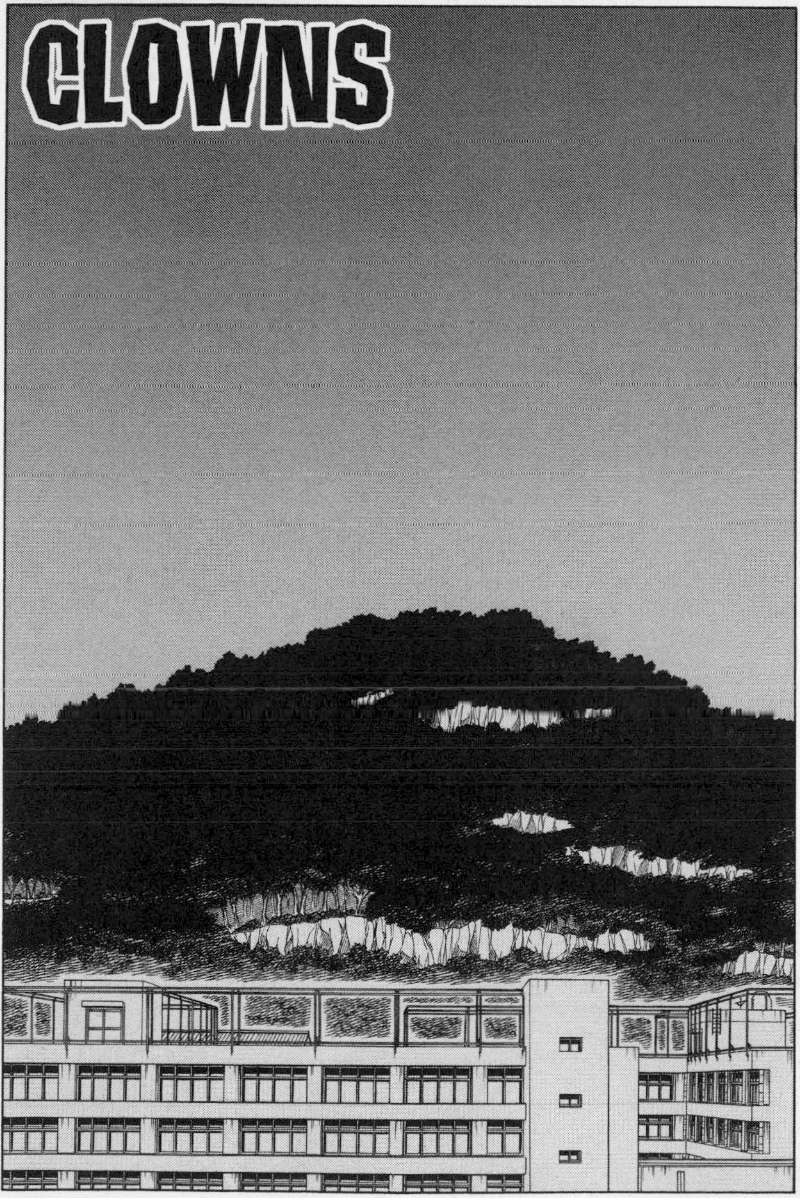
CLOWNS

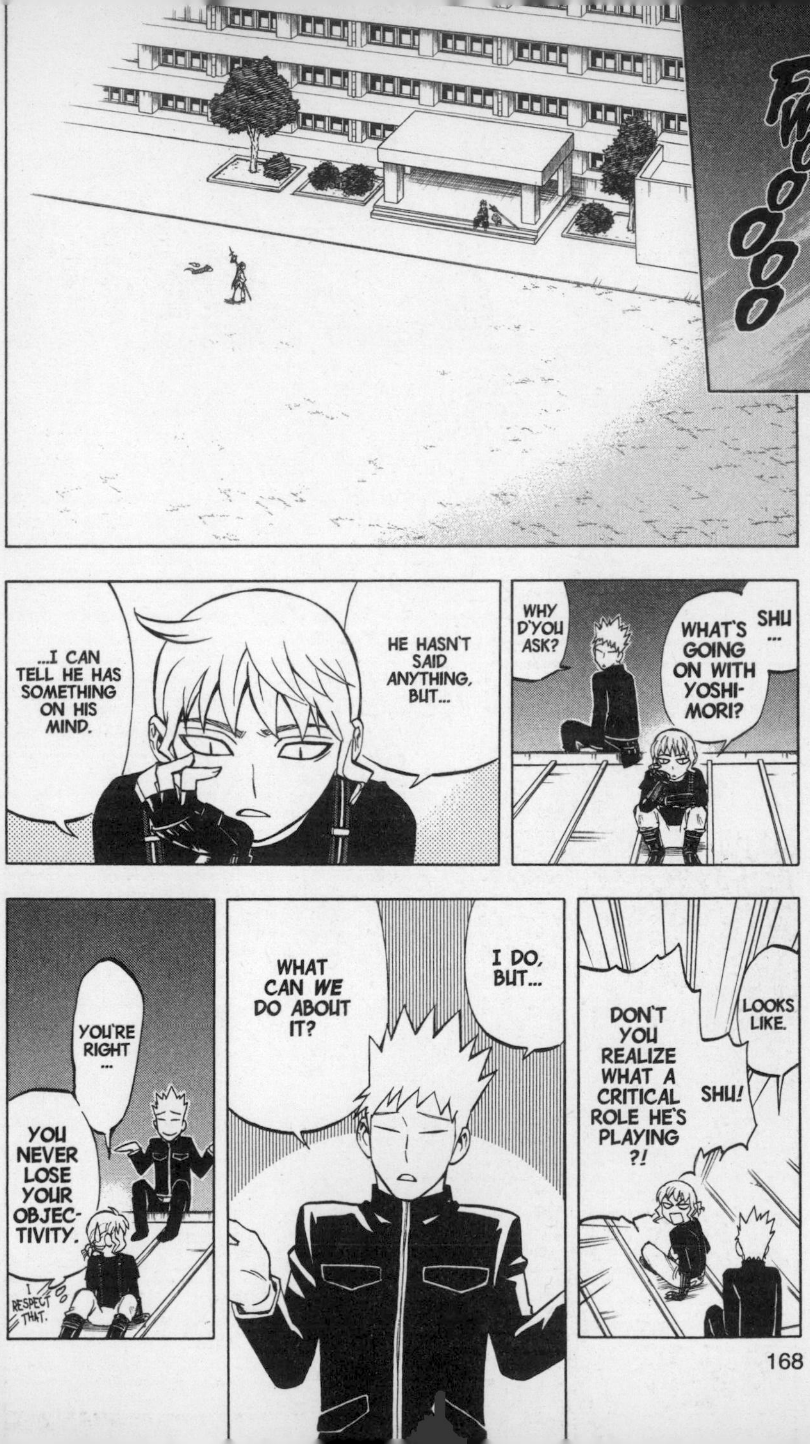
FWOOOOOO
SHU...
WHAT'S GOING ON WITH YOSHIMORI?
WHY D'YOU ASK?
HE HASN'T SAID ANYTHING, BUT...
...I CAN TELL HE HAS SOMETHING ON HIS MIND.
LOOKS LIKE.
SHU!
DON'T YOU REALIZE WHAT A CRITICAL ROLE HE'S PLAYING?!
I DO, BUT...
WHAT CAN *WE* DO ABOUT IT?
YOU'RE RIGHT...
YOU NEVER LOSE YOUR OBJECTIVITY.
I RESPECT THAT.

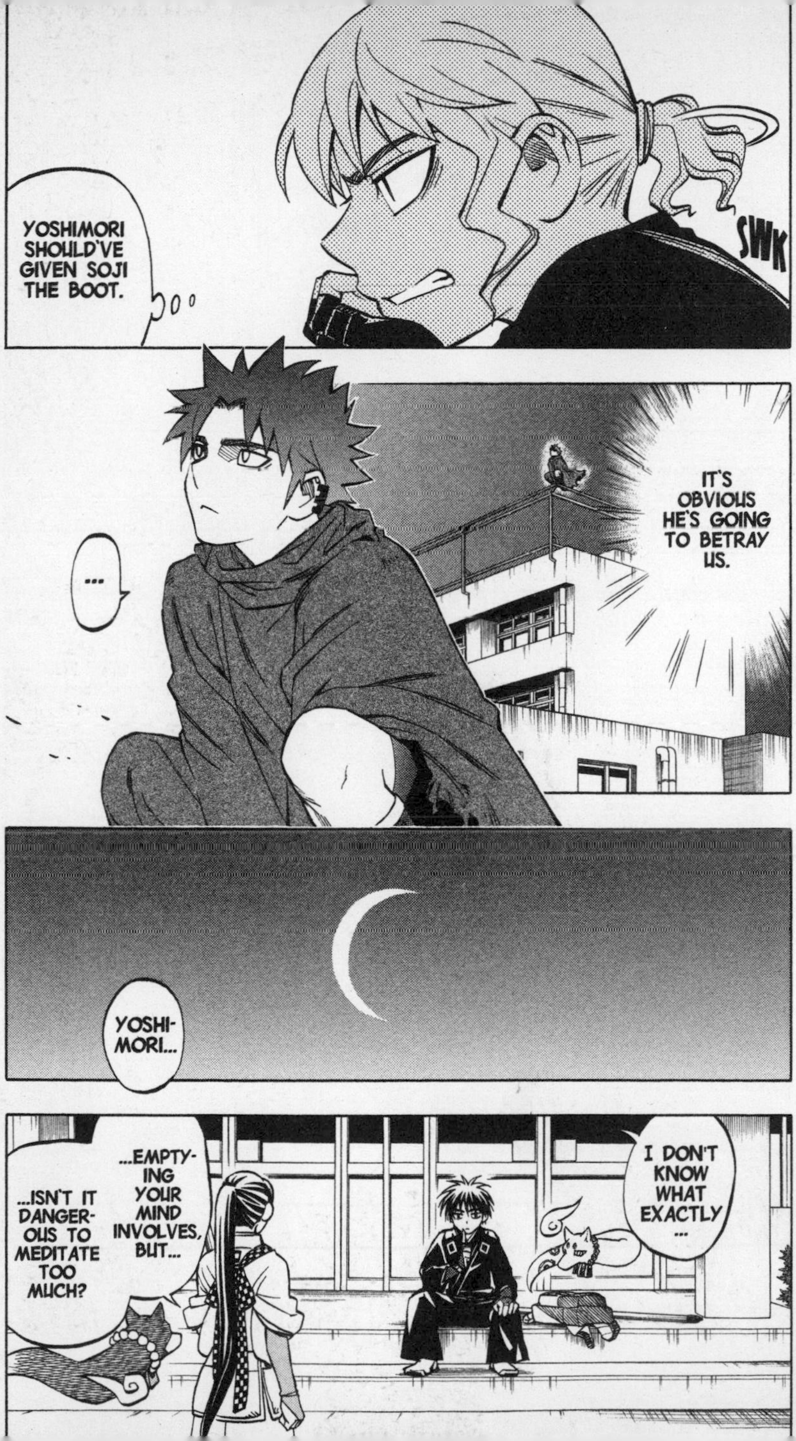
SWK
YOSHIMORI SHOULD'VE GIVEN SOJI THE BOOT.
IT'S OBVIOUS HE'S GOING TO BETRAY US.
...
YOSHI-MORI...
I DON'T KNOW WHAT EXACTLY ...
...EMPTY-ING YOUR MIND INVOLVES, BUT...
...ISN'T IT DANGER-OUS TO MEDITATE TOO MUCH?

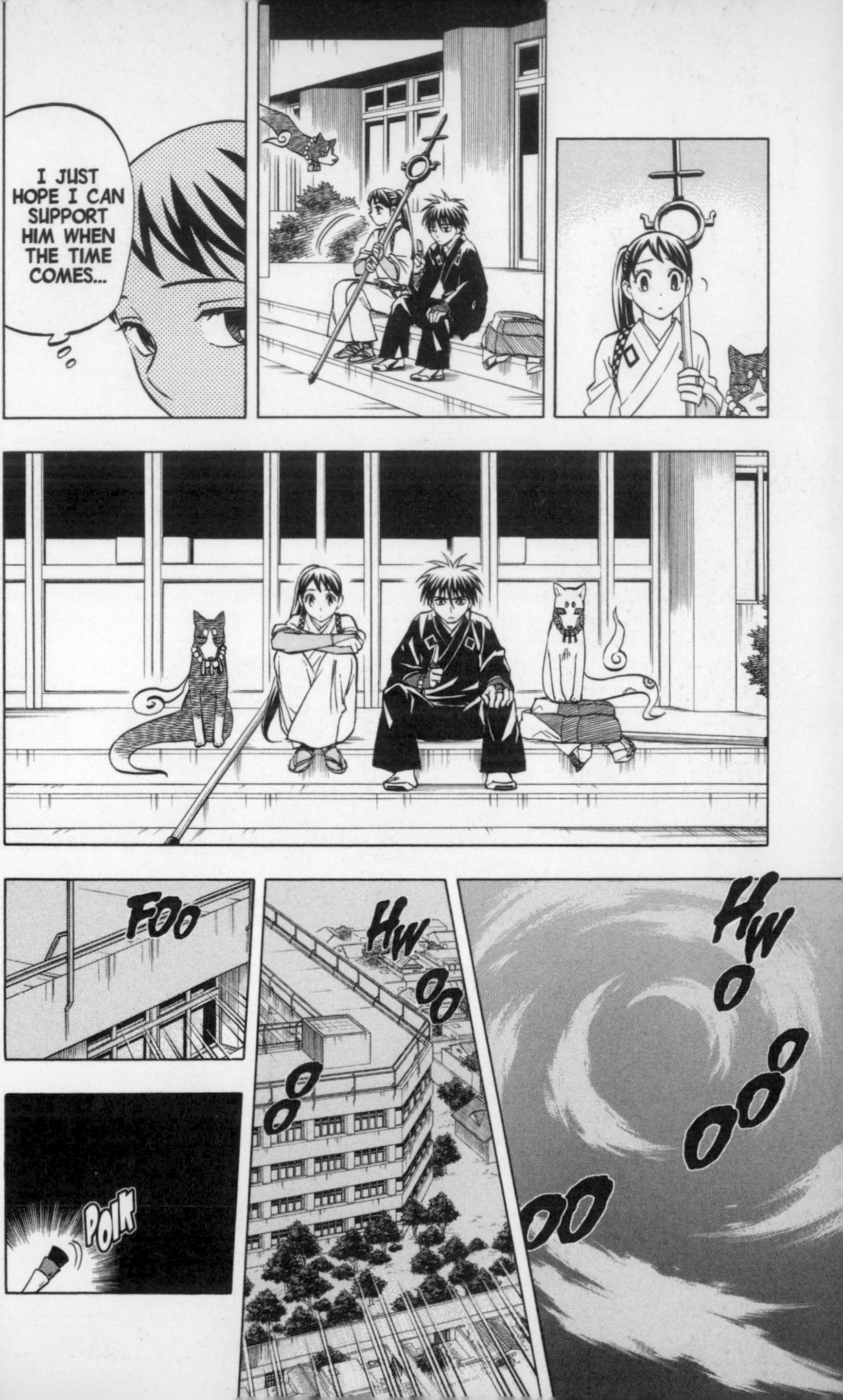
I JUST HOPE I CAN SUPPORT HIM WHEN THE TIME COMES...
HWOOOOOOO
HWOOOO
FOO
POIK

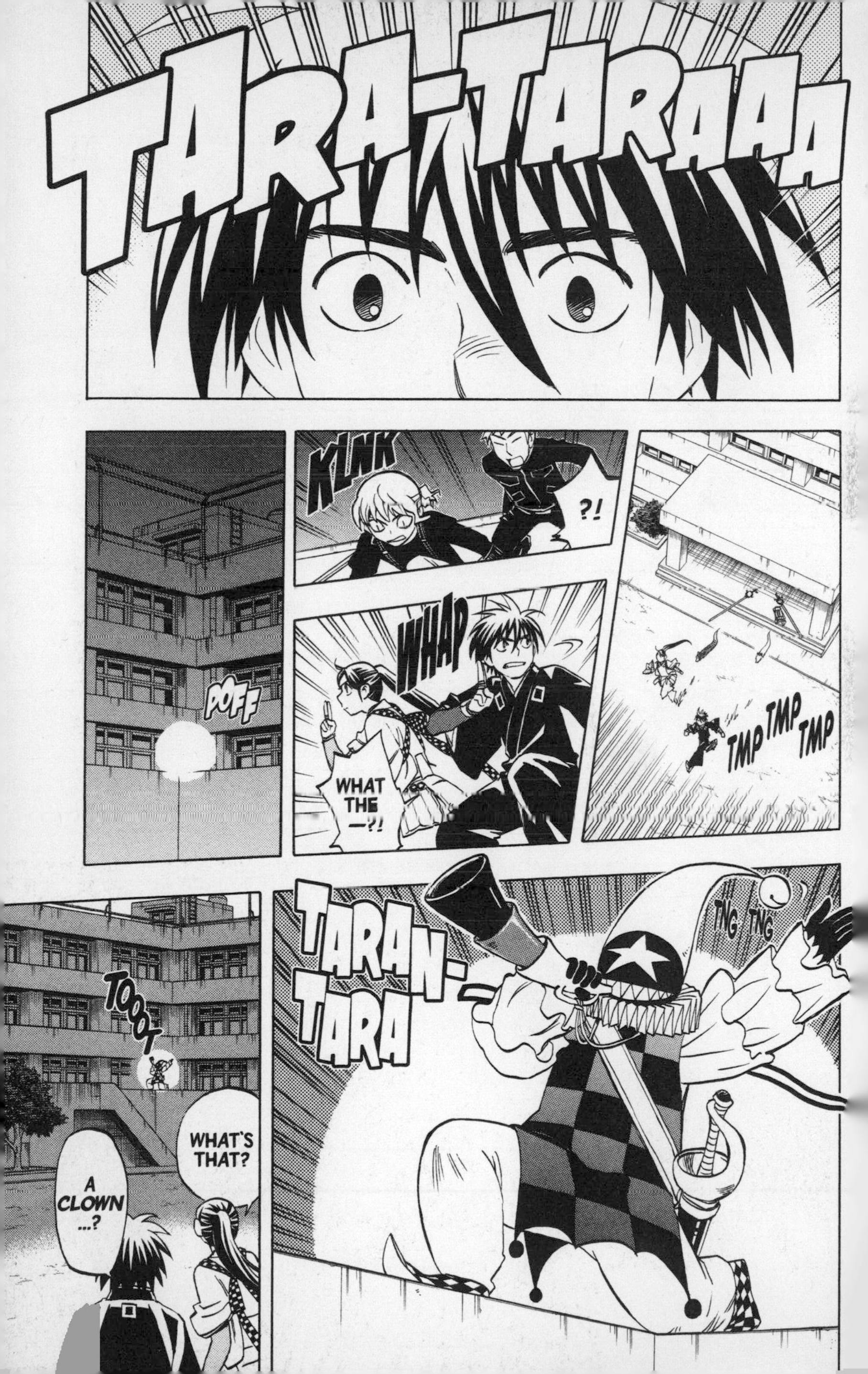
TARA-N-TARAAA
TMP TMP TMP
KLNK
?!
WHAP
WHAT THE—?!
POFF
TARAN-TARA
TNG TNG
TOOOT
WHAT'S THAT?
A CLOWN ...?

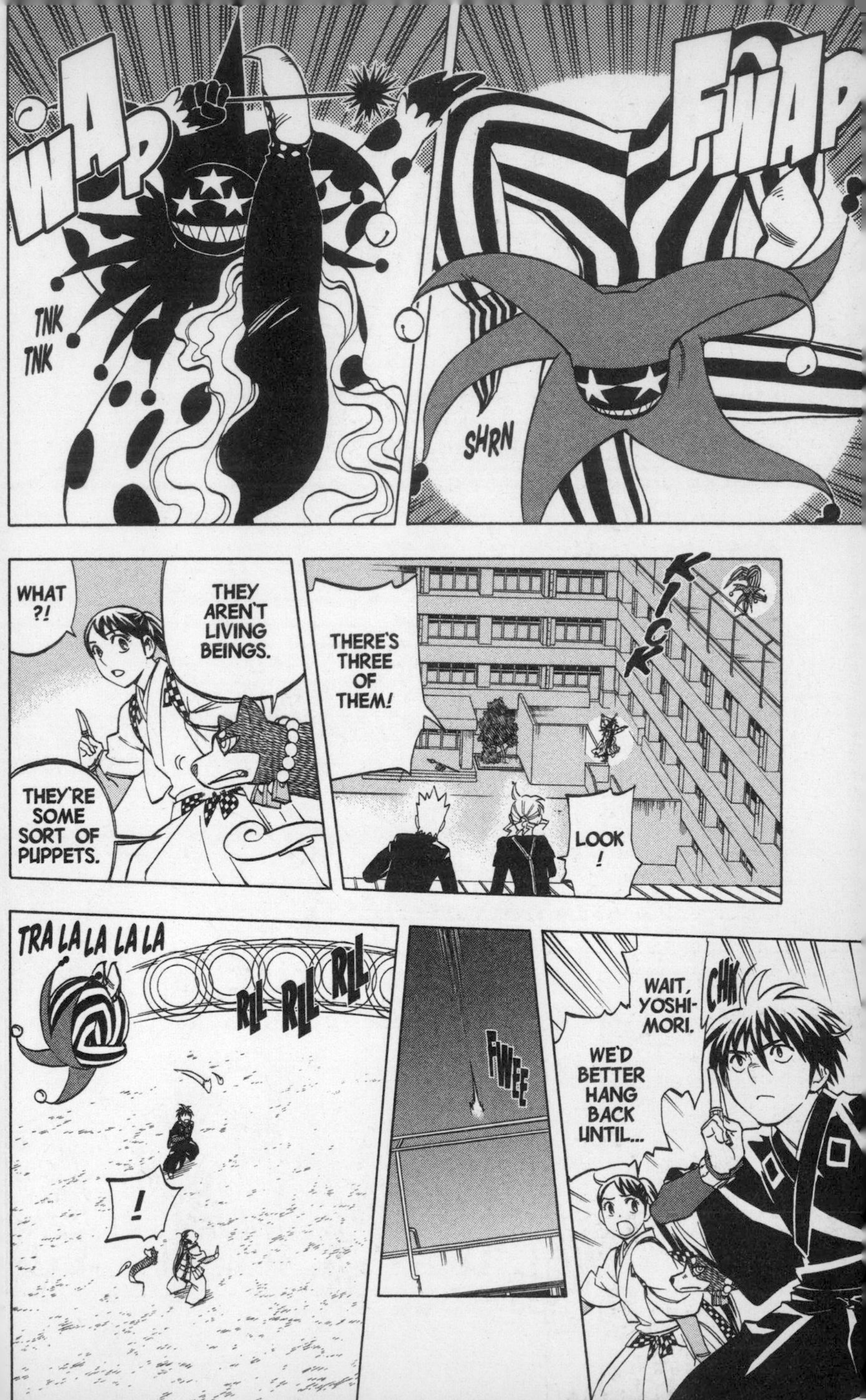
FWAP
SHRN
WHAP
TNK TNK
KICK
THERE'S THREE OF THEM!
LOOK!
THEY AREN'T LIVING BEINGS.
WHAT?!
THEY'RE SOME SORT OF PUPPETS.
CHK
WAIT, YOSHIMORI.
WE'D BETTER HANG BACK UNTIL...
FWEE
TRA LA LA LA LA
RLL RLL RLL
!

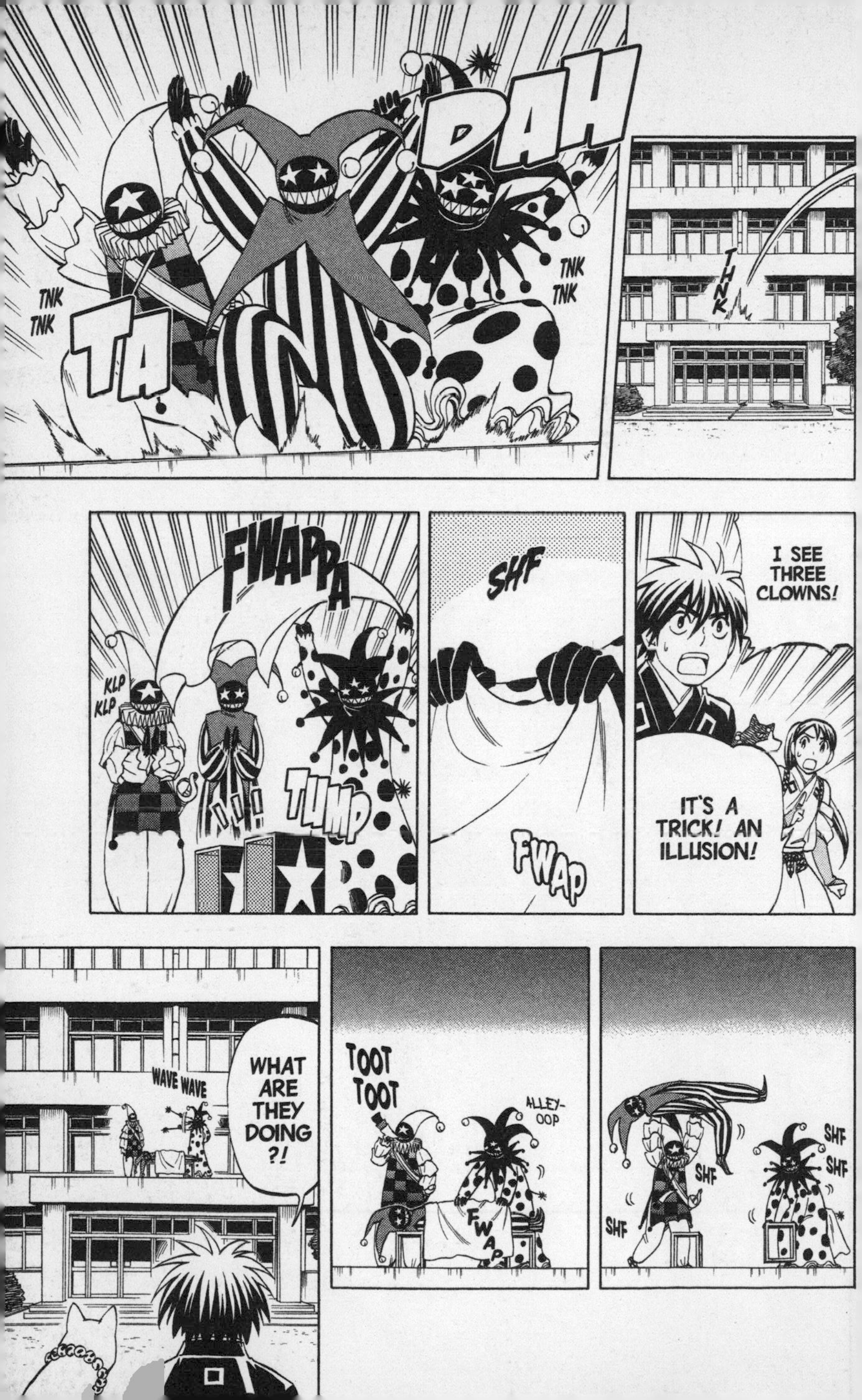
THNK
DAH
TNK TNK
TNK TNK
TA
I SEE THREE CLOWNS!
IT'S A TRICK! AN ILLUSION!
SHF
FWAP
FWAPPA
KLP KLP
TUMP
SHF SHF
SHF
SHF
ALLEY-OOP
TOOT TOOT
FWAP
WHAT ARE THEY DOING?!
WAVE WAVE

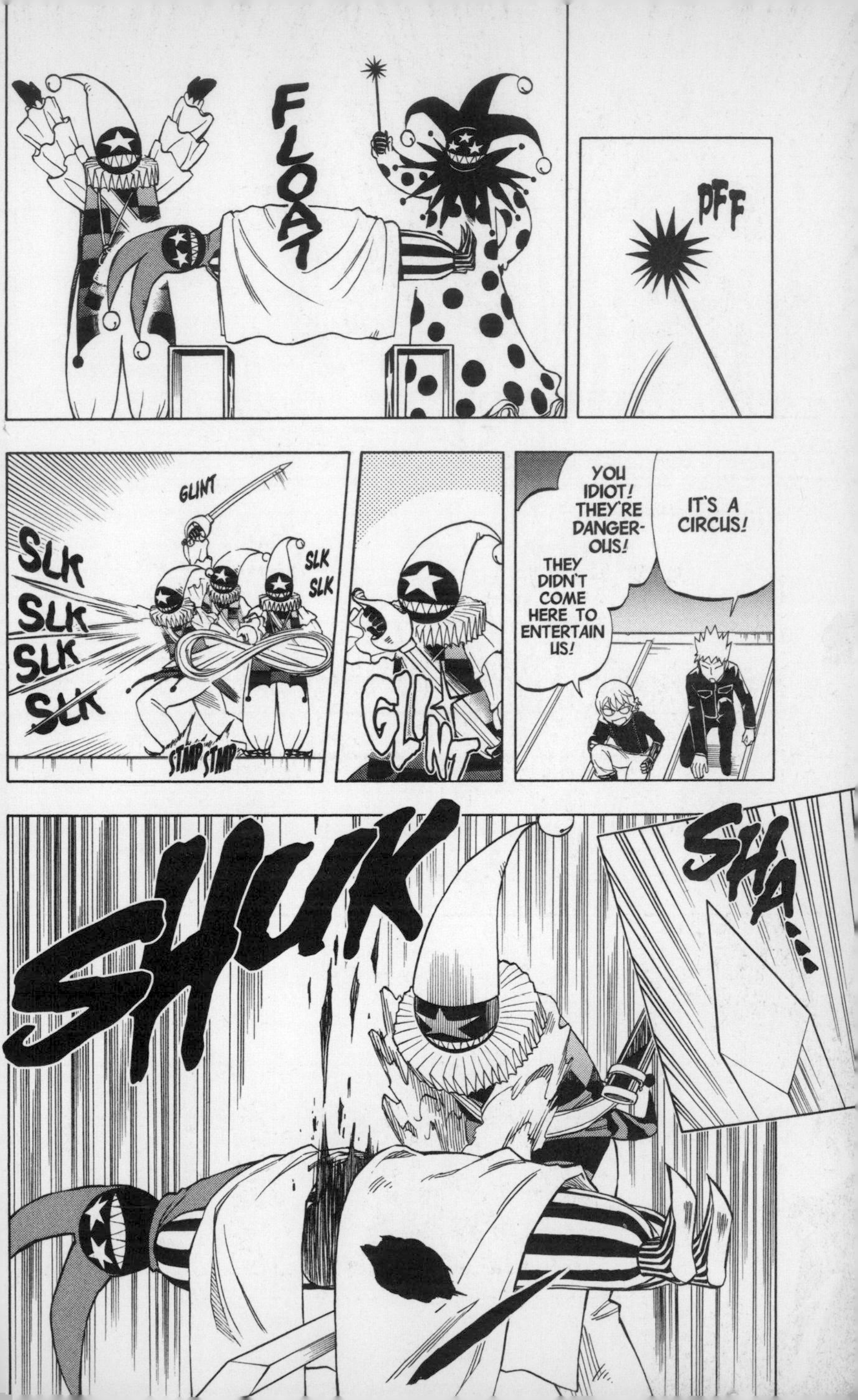
PFF
FLOAT
IT'S A CIRCUS!
YOU IDIOT! THEY'RE DANGEROUS!
THEY DIDN'T COME HERE TO ENTERTAIN US!
GLINT
GLINT
SLK SLK
SLK
SLK
SLK
SLK
STMP STMP
SHA...
SHUK

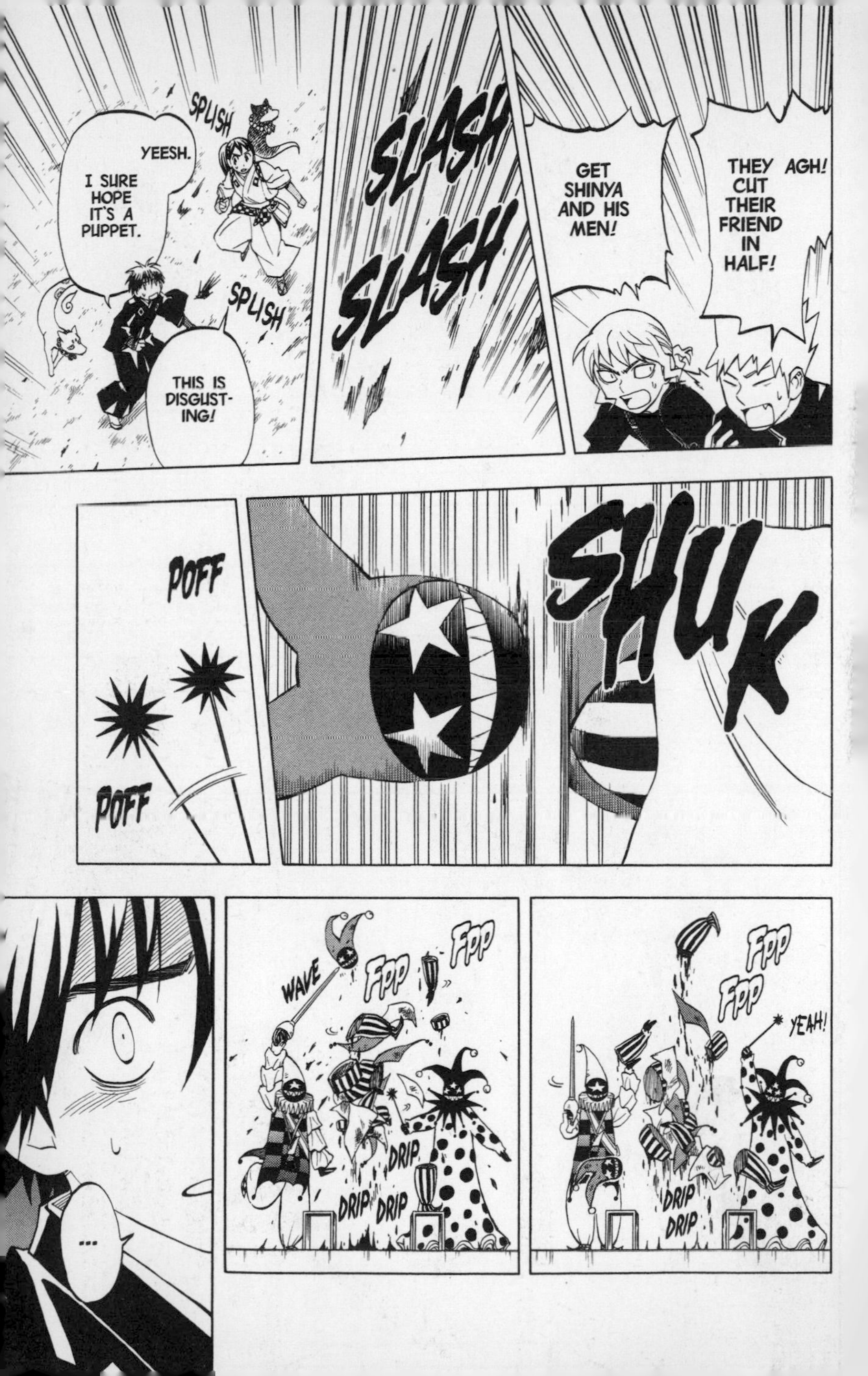
AGH!
THEY CUT THEIR FRIEND IN HALF!
GET SHINYA AND HIS MEN!
SLASH
SLASH
SPLISH
YEESH.
I SURE HOPE IT'S A PUPPET.
SPLISH
THIS IS DISGUSTING!
SHUK
POFF
POFF
Fpp
Fpp
YEAH!
DRIP
DRIP
Fpp
WAVE
Fpp
DRIP
DRIP
DRIP
...

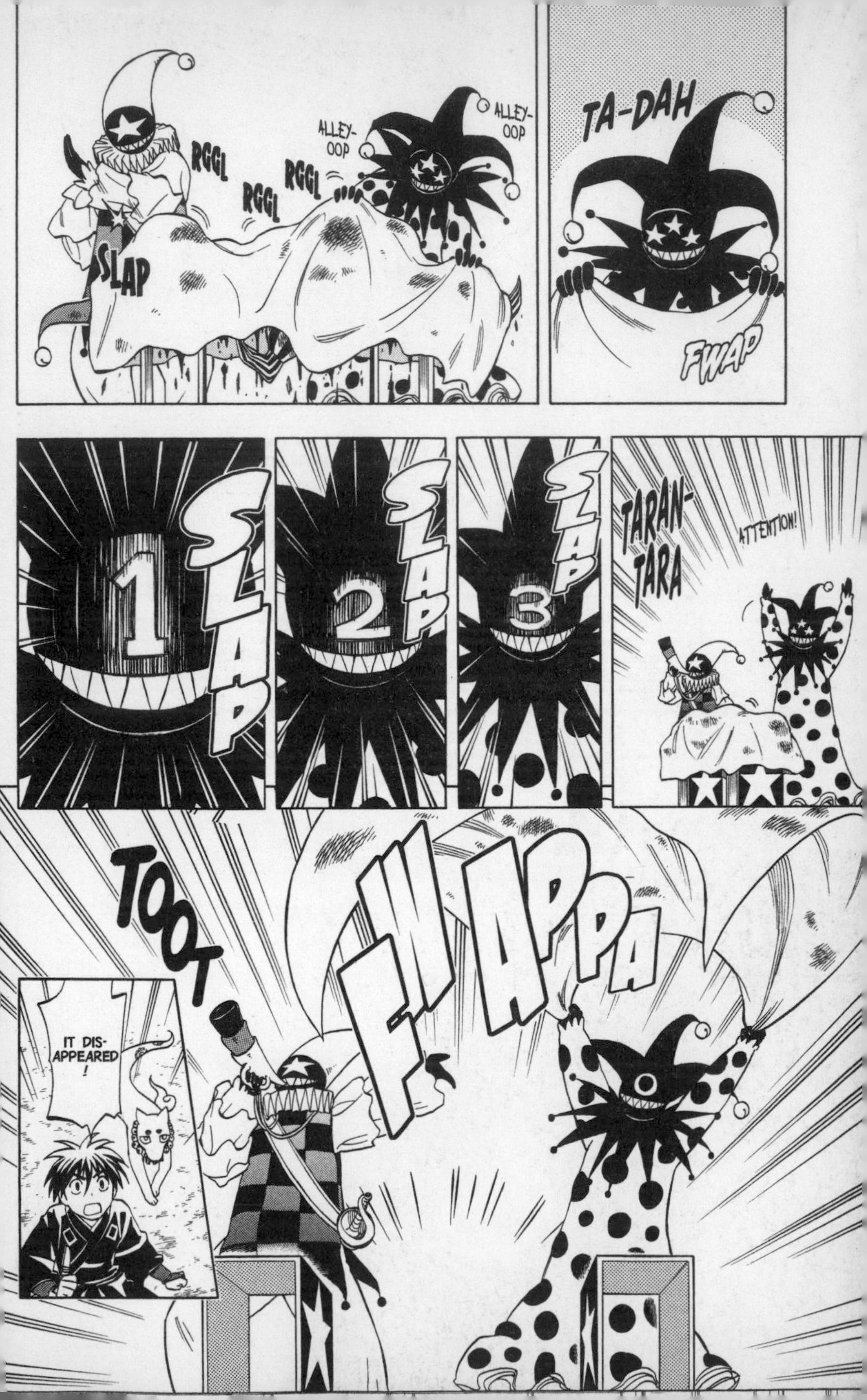
TA-DAH
FWAP
ALLEY-OOP
ALLEY-OOP
RGGL
RGGL
RGGL
SLAP
ATTENTION!
TARAN-TARA
3
SLAP
2
SLAP
1
SLAP
FWAPPA
TOOT
IT DIS-APPEARED!

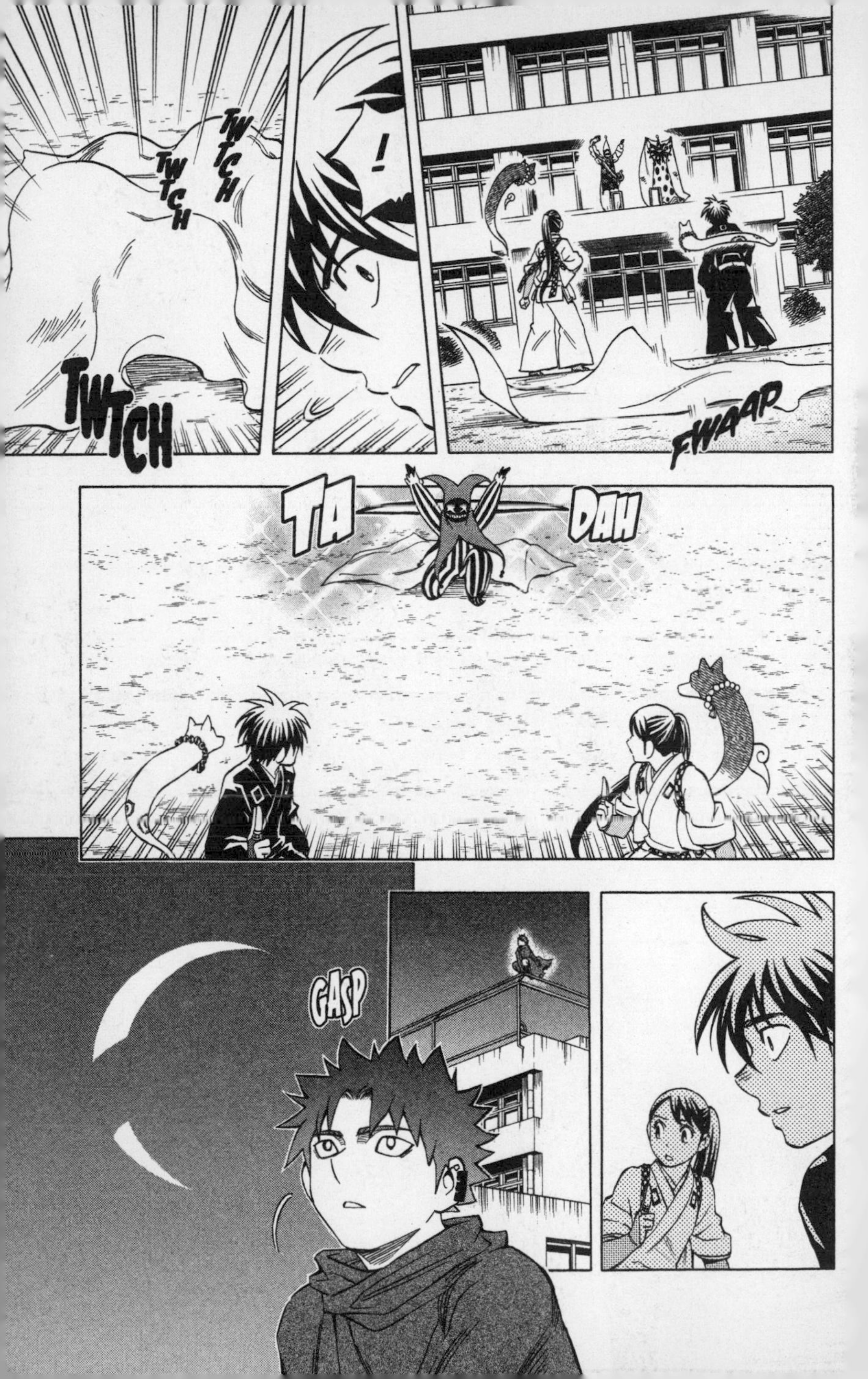

FWAAP
!
TWITCH
TWITCH
TWITCH
TA
DAH
GASP

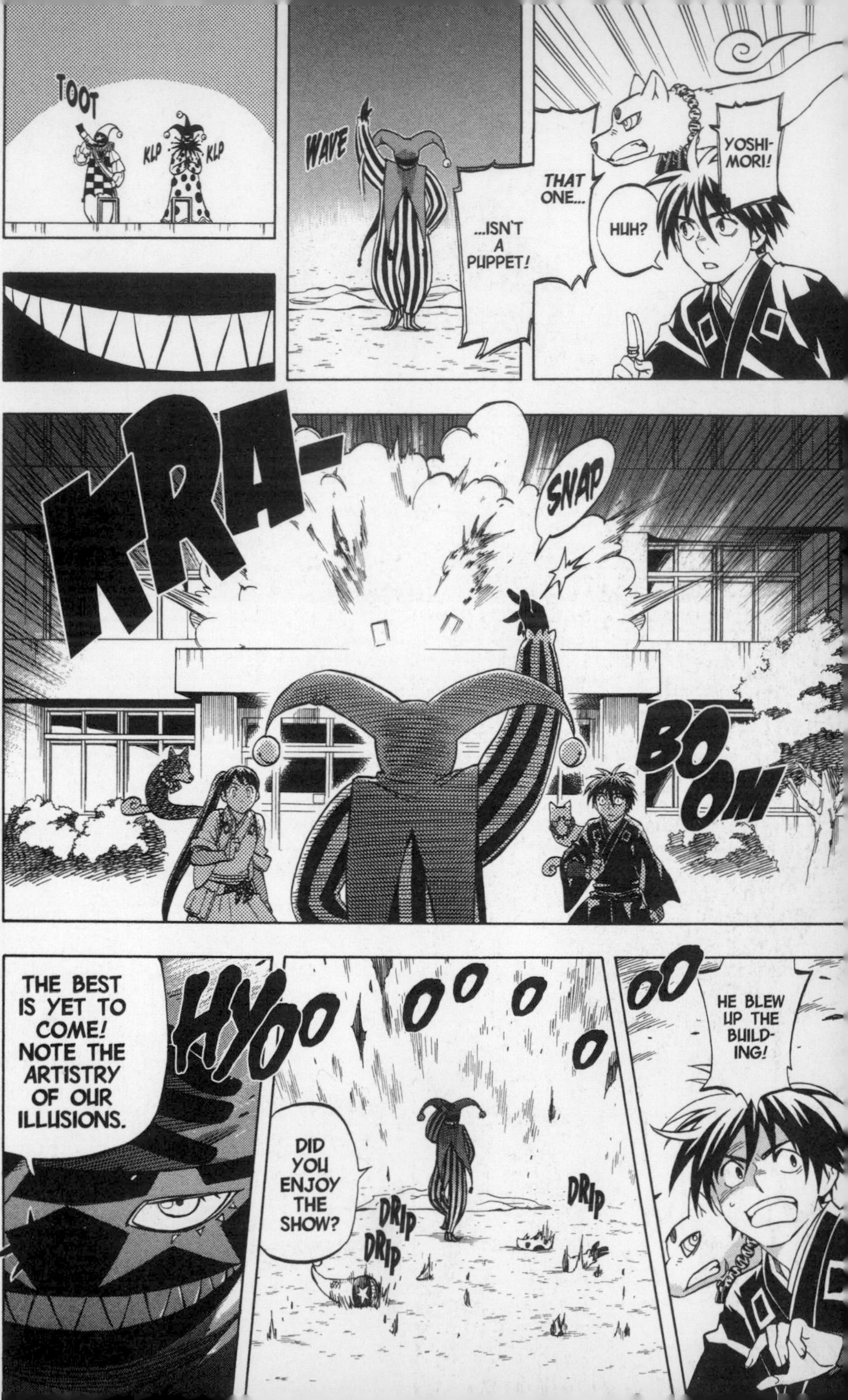
YOSHI-MORI!
THAT ONE...
HUH?
...ISN'T A PUPPET!
WAVE
TOOT
KLP KLP
SNAP
KRA-
BOOM
HE BLEW UP THE BUILD-ING!
HYOOOOOOOO
DID YOU ENJOY THE SHOW?
DRIP
DRIP
DRIP
THE BEST IS YET TO COME! NOTE THE ARTISTRY OF OUR ILLUSIONS.

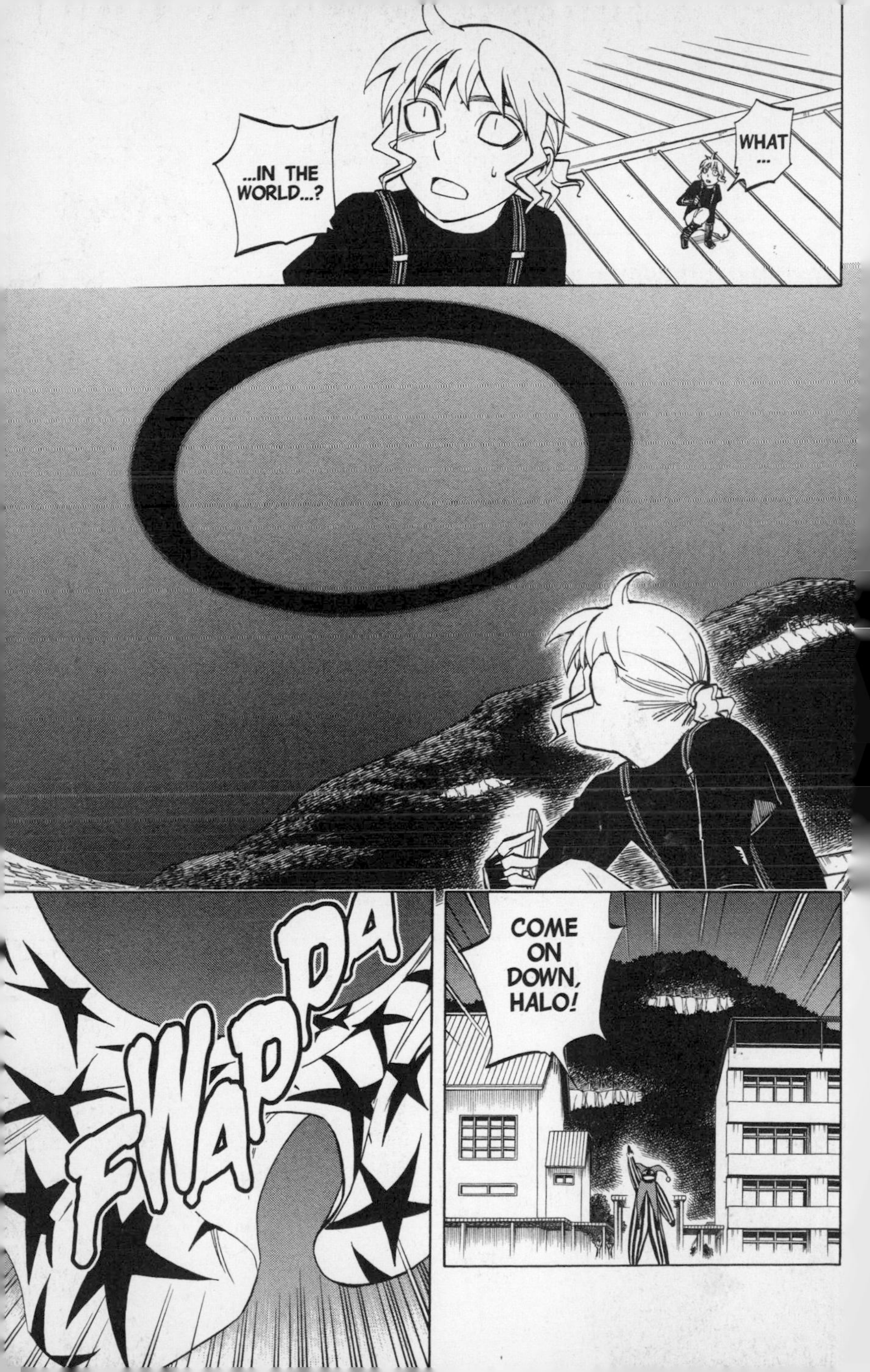
WHAT ...
...IN THE WORLD...?
COME ON DOWN, HALO!
FWAPPA

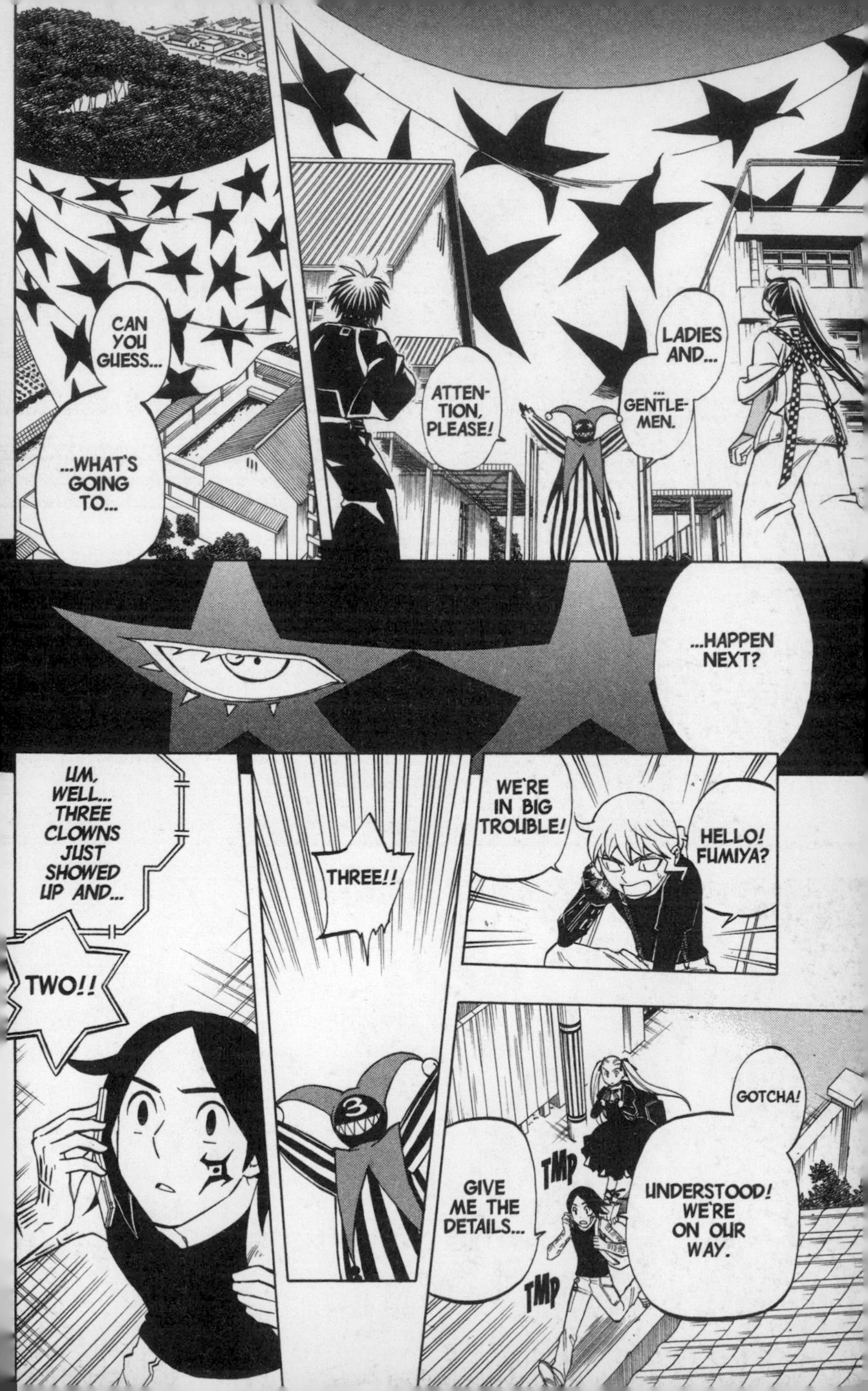
LADIES AND...
...GENTLE-MEN.
ATTEN-TION, PLEASE!
CAN YOU GUESS...
...WHAT'S GOING TO...
...HAPPEN NEXT?
HELLO! FUMIYA?
WE'RE IN BIG TROUBLE!
GOTCHA!
UNDERSTOOD! WE'RE ON OUR WAY.
GIVE ME THE DETAILS...
TMP
TMP
THREE!!
UM, WELL... THREE CLOWNS JUST SHOWED UP AND...
TWO!!

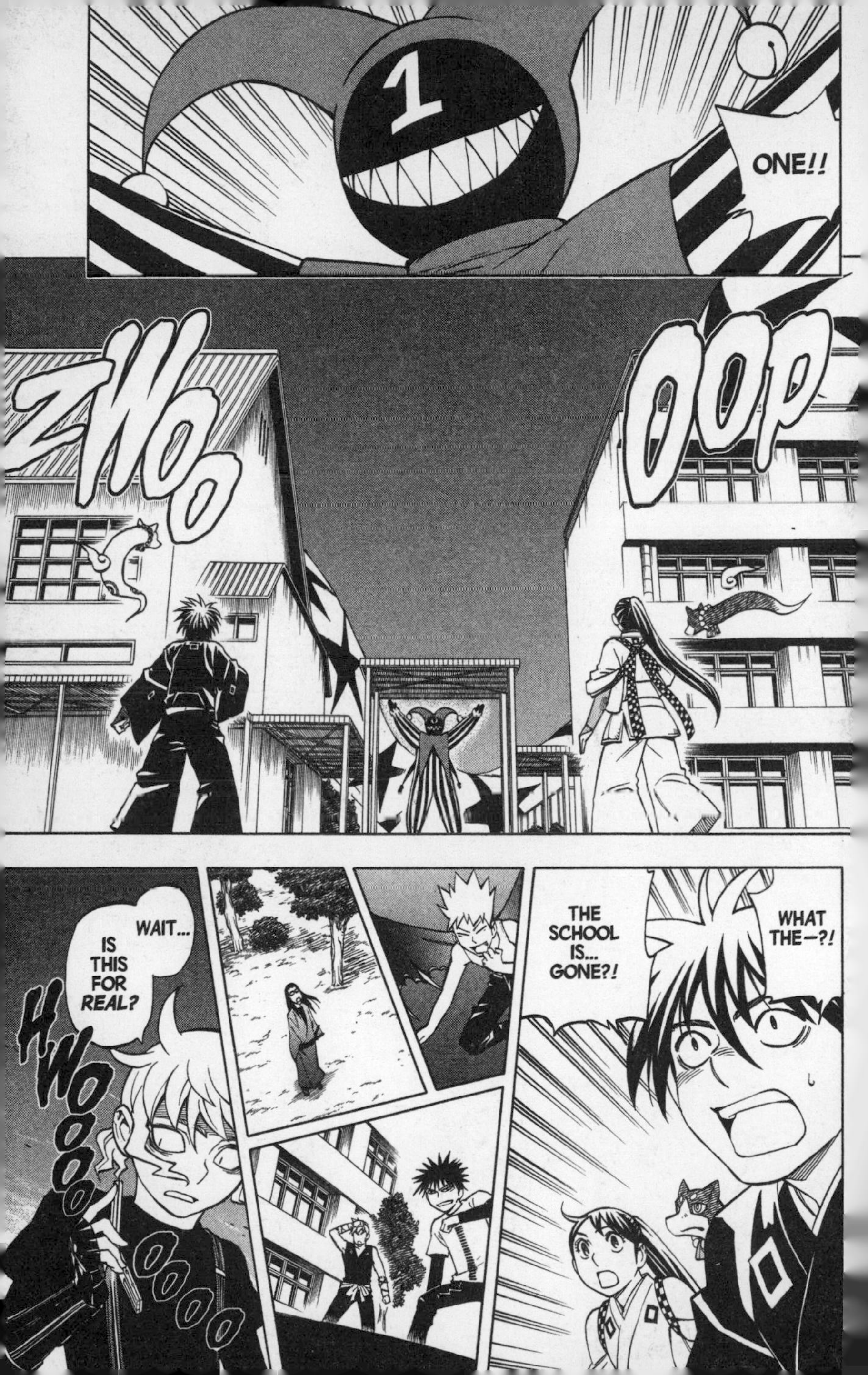
ONE!!
ZWOO
OOP
WHAT THE—?!
THE SCHOOL IS... GONE?!
WAIT... IS THIS FOR *REAL?*
HWOOOOOOOOOO

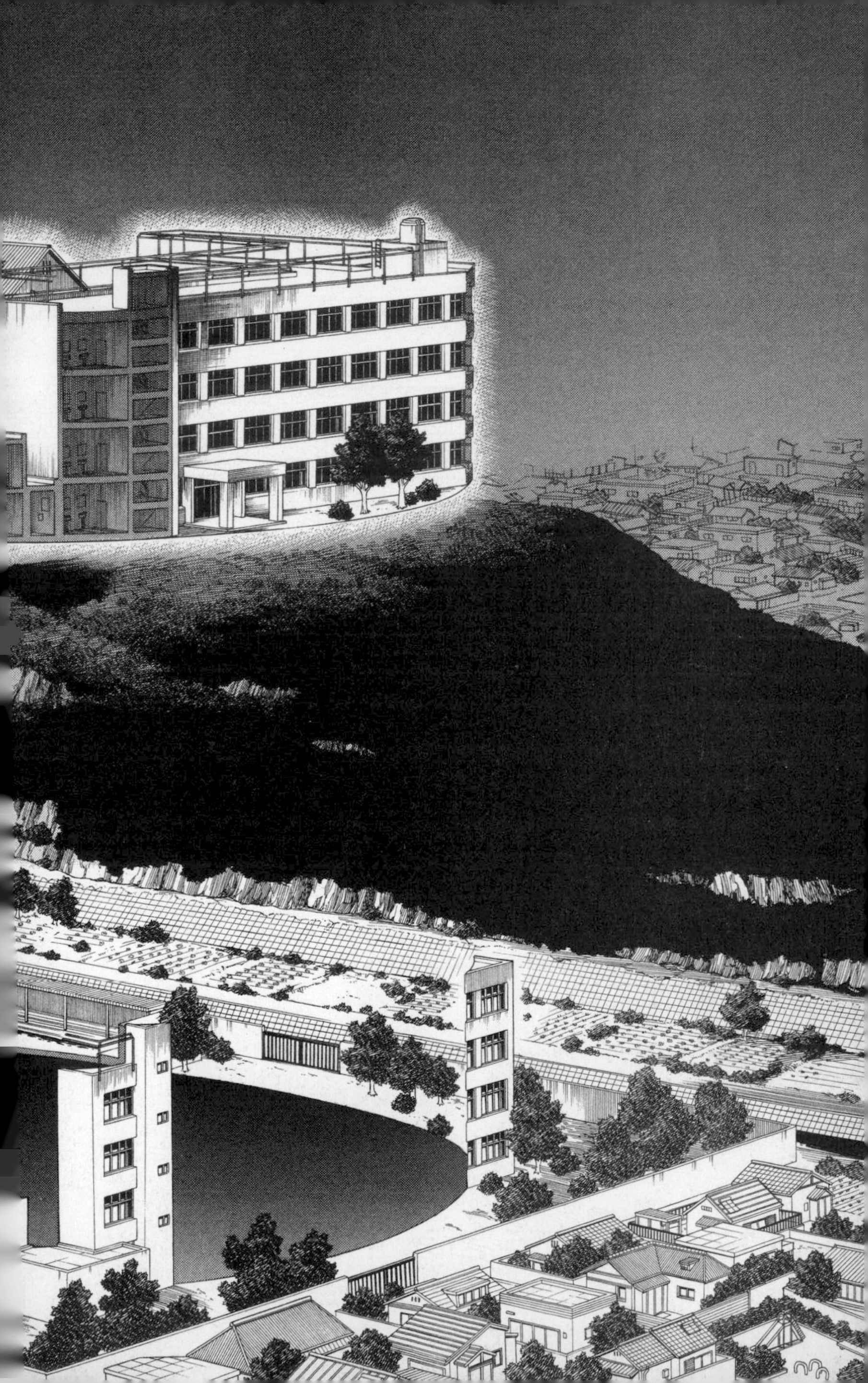

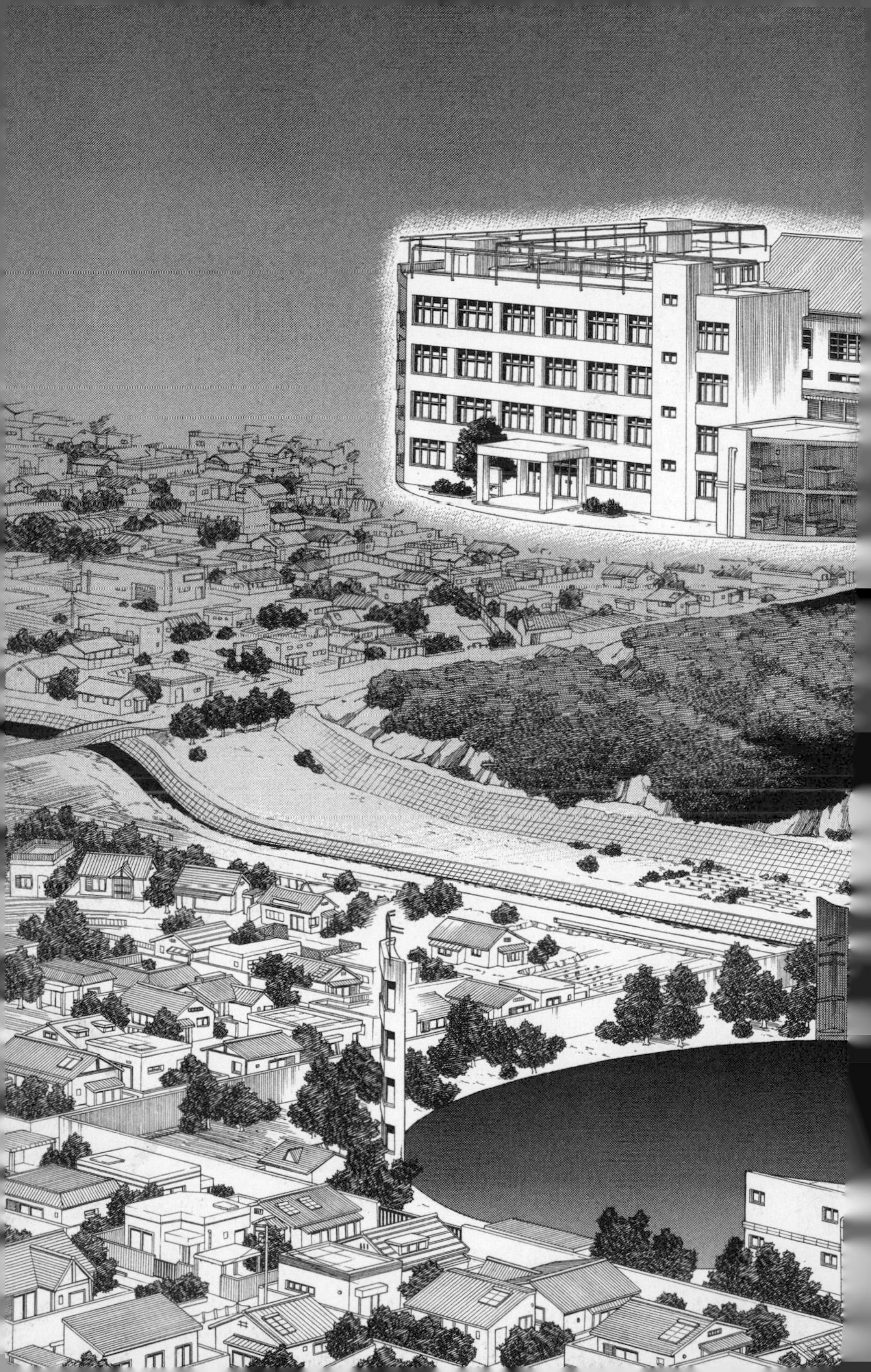

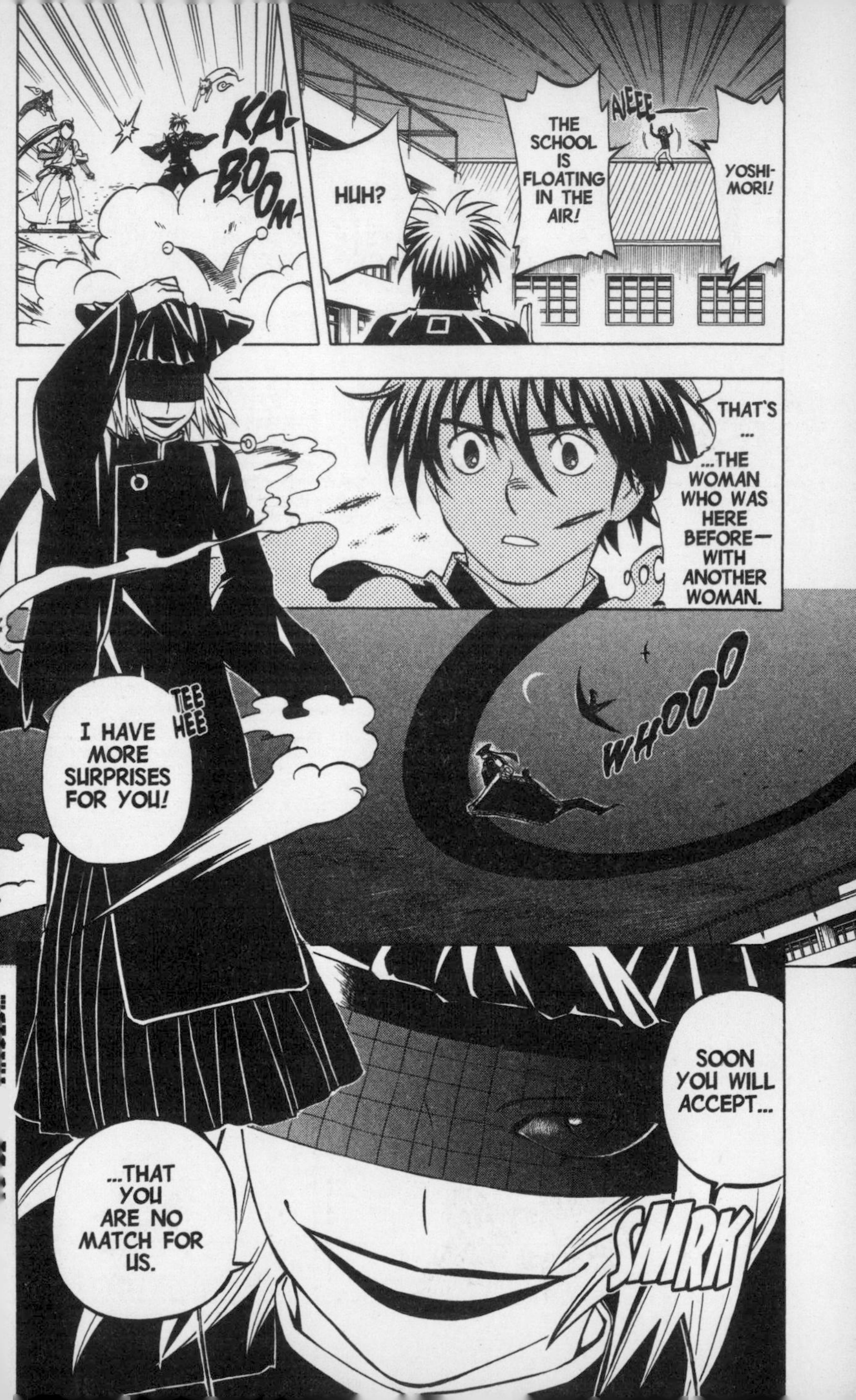
YOSHI-MORI!
AIEEE
THE SCHOOL IS FLOATING IN THE AIR!
HUH?
KA-BOOM
THAT'S ...
...THE WOMAN WHO WAS HERE BEFORE—WITH ANOTHER WOMAN.
WHOOOO
TEE HEE
I HAVE MORE SURPRISES FOR YOU!
SOON YOU WILL ACCEPT...
SMRK
...THAT YOU ARE NO MATCH FOR US.

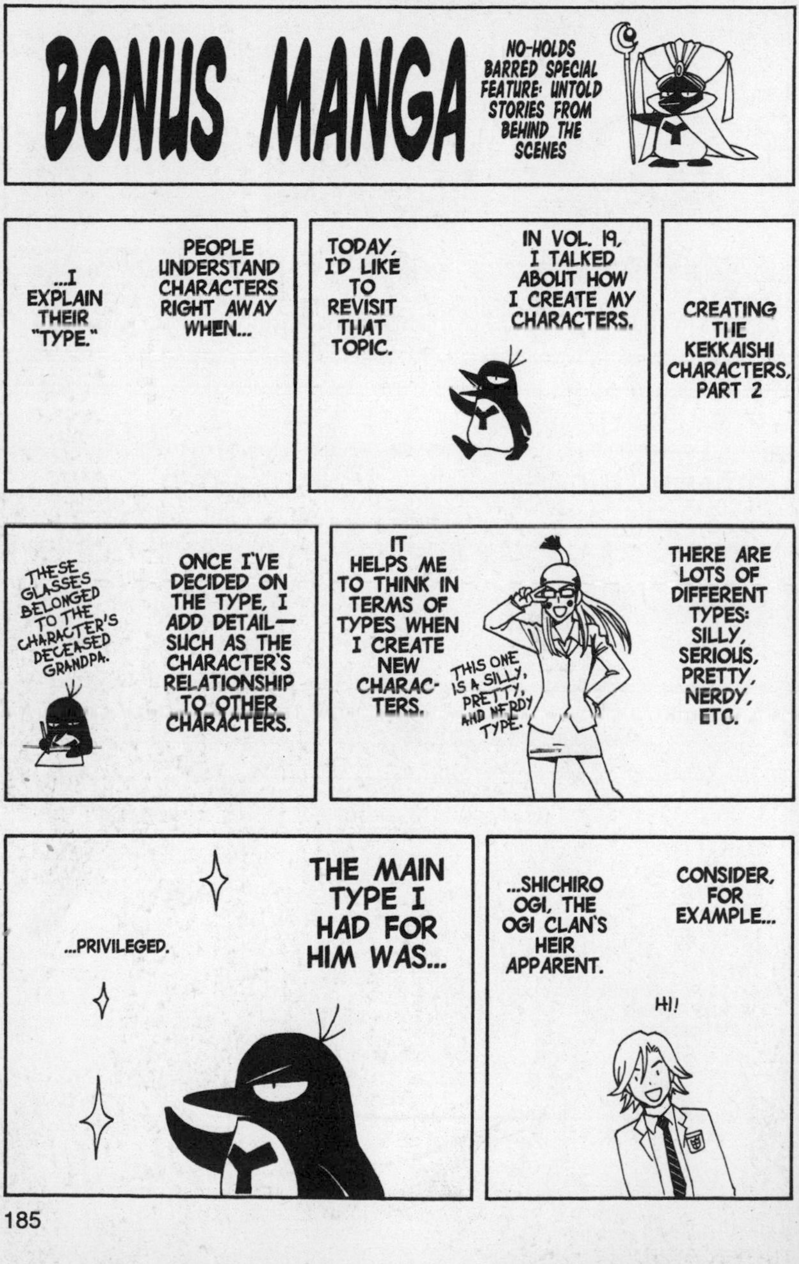
BONUS MANGA
NO-HOLDS BARRED SPECIAL FEATURE: UNTOLD STORIES FROM BEHIND THE SCENES
CREATING THE KEKKAISHI CHARACTERS, PART 2
IN VOL. 19, I TALKED ABOUT HOW I CREATE MY CHARACTERS.
TODAY, I'D LIKE TO REVISIT THAT TOPIC.
PEOPLE UNDERSTAND CHARACTERS RIGHT AWAY WHEN...
...I EXPLAIN THEIR "TYPE."
THERE ARE LOTS OF DIFFERENT TYPES: SILLY, SERIOUS, PRETTY, NERDY, ETC.
THIS ONE IS A SILLY, PRETTY, AND NERDY TYPE.
IT HELPS ME TO THINK IN TERMS OF TYPES WHEN I CREATE NEW CHARAC-TERS.
ONCE I'VE DECIDED ON THE TYPE, I ADD DETAIL—SUCH AS THE CHARACTER'S RELATIONSHIP TO OTHER CHARACTERS.
THESE GLASSES BELONGED TO THE CHARACTER'S DECEASED GRANDPA.
CONSIDER, FOR EXAMPLE...
...SHICHIRO OGI, THE OGI CLAN'S HEIR APPARENT.
HI!
THE MAIN TYPE I HAD FOR HIM WAS...
...PRIVILEGED.

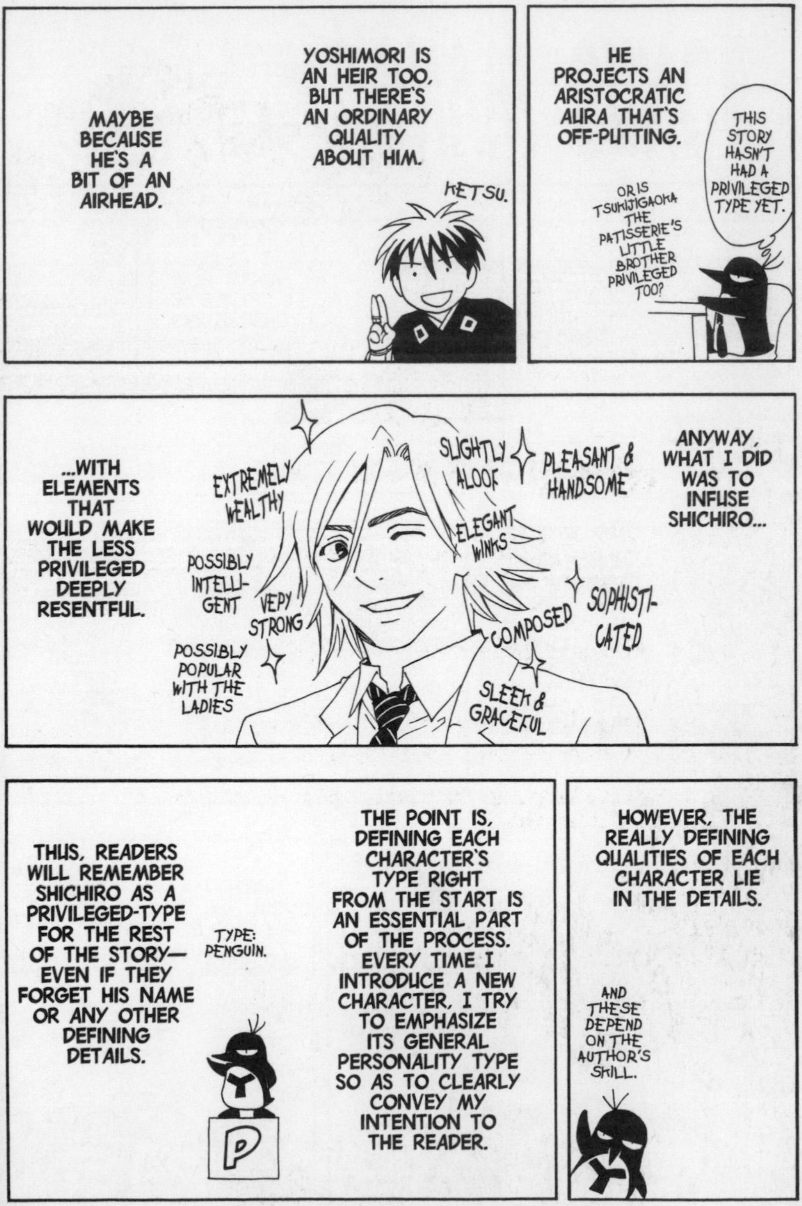
HE PROJECTS AN ARISTOCRATIC AURA THAT'S OFF-PUTTING.
THIS STORY HASN'T HAD A PRIVILEGED TYPE YET.
OR IS TSUKIJIGAOKA THE PATISSERIE'S LITTLE BROTHER PRIVILEGED TOO?
YOSHIMORI IS AN HEIR TOO, BUT THERE'S AN ORDINARY QUALITY ABOUT HIM.
KETSU.
MAYBE BECAUSE HE'S A BIT OF AN AIRHEAD.
ANYWAY, WHAT I DID WAS TO INFUSE SHICHIRO...
PLEASANT & HANDSOME
SLIGHTLY ALOOF
ELEGANT WINKS
SOPHISTICATED
COMPOSED
SLEEK & GRACEFUL
EXTREMELY WEALTHY
POSSIBLY INTELLIGENT
VERY STRONG
POSSIBLY POPULAR WITH THE LADIES
...WITH ELEMENTS THAT WOULD MAKE THE LESS PRIVILEGED DEEPLY RESENTFUL.
HOWEVER, THE REALLY DEFINING QUALITIES OF EACH CHARACTER LIE IN THE DETAILS.
AND THESE DEPEND ON THE AUTHOR'S SKILL.
THE POINT IS, DEFINING EACH CHARACTER'S TYPE RIGHT FROM THE START IS AN ESSENTIAL PART OF THE PROCESS. EVERY TIME I INTRODUCE A NEW CHARACTER, I TRY TO EMPHASIZE ITS GENERAL PERSONALITY TYPE SO AS TO CLEARLY CONVEY MY INTENTION TO THE READER.
TYPE: PENGUIN.
P
THUS, READERS WILL REMEMBER SHICHIRO AS A PRIVILEGED-TYPE FOR THE REST OF THE STORY—EVEN IF THEY FORGET HIS NAME OR ANY OTHER DEFINING DETAILS.

YUM...

MESSAGE FROM YELLOW TANABE

I always keep snacks by my desk when I work on my manga. At the moment, I'm hooked on rice crackers. I find myself munching on the big ones all the time.

Then suddenly I'll notice that I'm covered with crumbs!

When I'm wearing a black T-shirt, the crumbs really stand out. It's a shocking sight!

Still, I keep munching away. Those rice crackers are irresistible!

KEKKAISHI

VOLUME 26
SHONEN SUNDAY EDITION

STORY AND ART BY YELLOW TANABE

© 2004 Yellow TANABE/Shogakukan
All rights reserved.
Original Japanese edition "KEKKAISHI" published by SHOGAKUKAN Inc.

Translation/Yuko Sawada
Touch-up Art & Lettering/Stephen Dutro
Cover Design & Graphic Layout/Julie Behn, Ronnie Casson
Editor/Annette Roman

Printed in the U.S.A.

Published by VIZ Media, LLC
P.O. Box 77010
San Francisco, CA 94107

10 9 8 7 6 5 4 3 2 1
First printing, June 2011

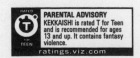

PARENTAL ADVISORY
KEKKAISHI is rated T for Teen
and is recommended for ages
13 and up. It contains fantasy
violence.
ratings.viz.com

www.viz.com

WWW.SHONENSUNDAY.COM

TV SERIES & MOVIES ON DVD!

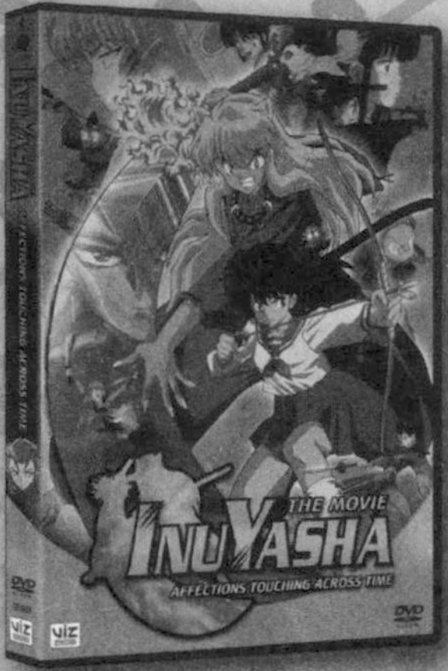
THE MOVIE
INUYASHA
AFFECTIONS TOUCHING ACROSS TIME

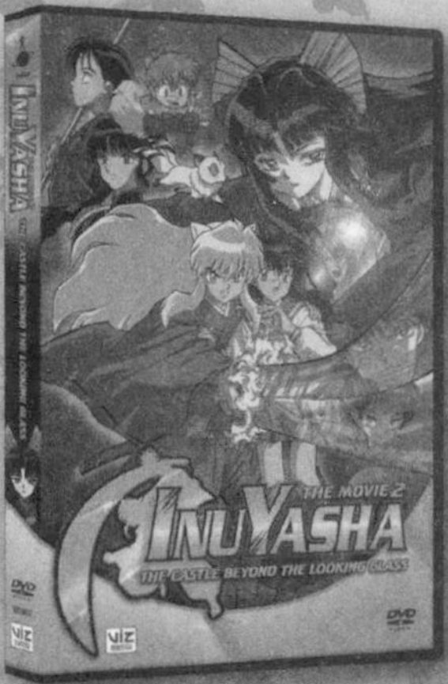
THE MOVIE 2
INUYASHA
THE CASTLE BEYOND THE LOOKING GLASS

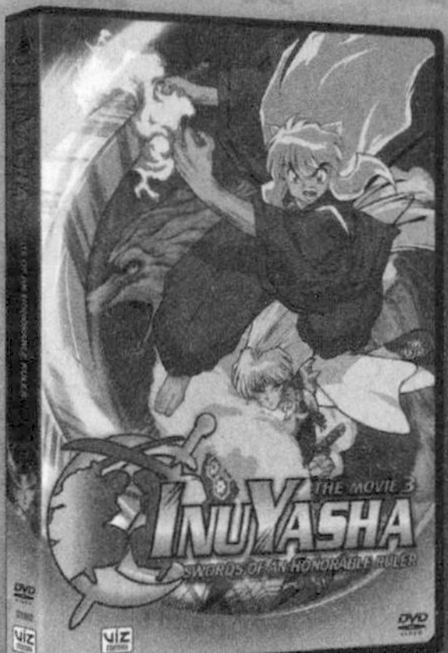
THE MOVIE 3
INUYASHA
SWORDS OF AN HONORABLE RULER

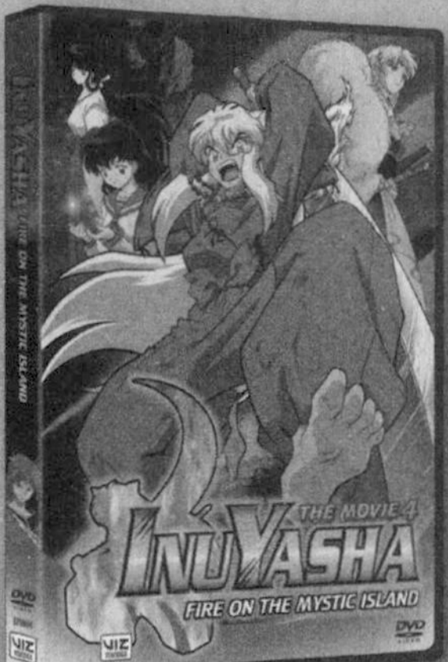
THE MOVIE 4
INUYASHA
FIRE ON THE MYSTIC ISLAND

See more of the action in *Inuyasha* full-length movies

RATED T FOR TEEN
ratings.viz.com

www.viz.com
inuyasha.viz.com

The popular anime series now on DVD—each season available in a collectible box set

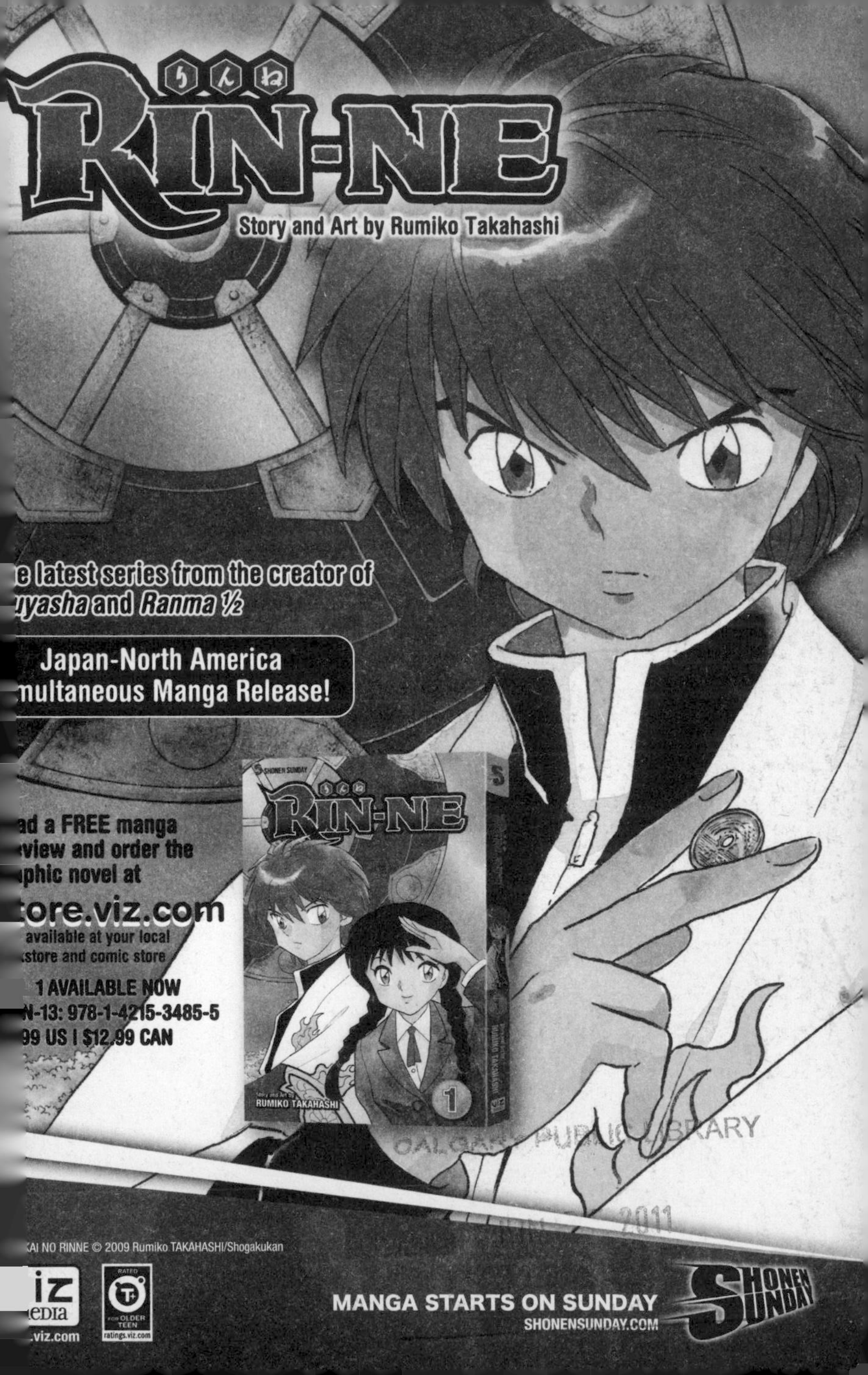

りんね
RIN-NE
Story and Art by Rumiko Takahashi
e latest series from the creator of
uyasha and Ranma ½
Japan-North America
multaneous Manga Release!
ad a FREE manga
view and order the
phic novel at
tore.viz.com
available at your local
store and comic store
1 AVAILABLE NOW
N-13: 978-1-4215-3485-5
99 US | $12.99 CAN
SHONEN SUNDAY
RIN-NE
Story and Art by
RUMIKO TAKAHASHI
1
AI NO RINNE © 2009 Rumiko TAKAHASHI/Shogakukan
iz
EDIA
.viz.com
RATED
T+
FOR OLDER TEEN
ratings.viz.com
MANGA STARTS ON SUNDAY
SHONENSUNDAY.COM
SHONEN SUNDAY